SO NEAR yet so FAR

SO NEAR
yet so FAR

THE PUBLIC AND HIDDEN WORLDS
OF CANADA–US RELATIONS

Geoffrey Hale

UBCPress · Vancouver · Toronto

21 20 19 18 17 16 15 14 13 12   5 4 3 2 1

Printed in Canada on FSC-certified ancient-forest-free paper (100% post-consumer recycled) that is processed chlorine- and acid-free.

Library and Archives Canada Cataloguing in Publication

Hale, Geoffrey
    So near yet so far: the public and hidden worlds of Canada–US relations / Geoffrey Hale.

Includes bibliographical references and index.
Issued also in electronic formats.
ISBN 978-0-7748-2041-7 (bound). – ISBN 978-0-7748-2042-4

    1. Canada – Foreign relations – United States. 2. United States – Foreign relations – Canada. 3. Canada – Foreign relations – 1945-. 4. United States – Foreign relations – 2001-. I. Title.

| FC249.H359 2012 | 327.7107309'051 | C2012-901876-7 |

Canadä

UBC Press gratefully acknowledges the financial support for our publishing program of the Government of Canada (through the Canada Book Fund), the Canada Council for the Arts, and the British Columbia Arts Council.

This book has been published with the help of a grant from the Canadian Federation for the Humanities and Social Sciences, through the Aid to Scholarly Publications Program, using funds provided by the Social Sciences and Humanities Research Council of Canada.

UBC Press
The University of British Columbia
2029 West Mall
Vancouver, BC V6T 1Z2
www.ubcpress.ca

Contents

Tables and Figures

Tables

Figures

Acknowledgments

No project of this scale could be completed without the insights, support, and assistance of others. I gratefully acknowledge the 170 government officials, interest group representatives, policy experts, and journalists who shared their time and insights with me at different times between 2005 and 2010 in almost 200 interviews, mostly on a not-for-attribution basis. Their varied perspectives and on-the-ground experience provided an indispensable foundation and reality check for my research.

The University of Lethbridge, the Canada–US Fulbright program, and the Canadian International Council graciously provided financial support at different stages of my research. I appreciate the hospitality of the School of Public Policy and Administration at Carleton University and the Center for Canadian Studies at Duke University, which graciously hosted me during my research leave in 2005-6. The Border Policy Research Institute at Western Washington University has provided frequent opportunities to test my research and engage different elements of the cross-border policy community. Jamie Huckabay and Christina Marcotte provided valuable research assistance and insights that contributed to the development of different sections of the book.

I also acknowledge the intellectual and practical contributions of academics and practitioners engaged with different aspects of Canada–US relations – including Don Alper, Stephen Blank, Emmanuel Brunet-Jailly, David Davidson, Charles Doran, Paul Frazer, Monica Gattinger, Scotty

Greenwood, Michael Kergin, Christopher Sands, and the many federal, provincial, and US government officials who generously provided their time and insights – as well as the helpful comments of anonymous reviewers for UBC Press.

Emily Andrew and Holly Keller at UBC Press patiently and graciously shepherded me through the publishing process. Completing this project would have been impossible without the patient support and encouragement of my wife, Susan.

SO NEAR yet so FAR

1 INTRODUCTION

The Elephant and the Beaver

Proximity and Distance in Perspective

Pierre Trudeau once famously likened the Canada–US relationship to that of a mouse and an elephant.[1] Although this analogy suggests that the former's world shakes every time the latter rolls over, it also speaks to traditional Canadian outlooks on the two countries' respective national characters. An elephant is very large and quite capable of dominating its environment without much attention to the preoccupations of smaller animals. The mouse, on the other hand, seems to have a distinct problem with its self-image. It is small, agile, able to fit through places the elephant would never think of travelling, but potentially vulnerable to the lurching around of its much larger neighbour and apparently rather insecure about the whole business.

This image of the Canada–US relationship is captured in the titles of a series of books written over several decades: *Neighbours Taken for Granted, Forgotten Partnership,* and, more recently, *Invisible and Inaudible in Washington.*[2] So, in a way, does the title of this book, *So Near Yet So Far.* This phrase, derived from the late-nineteenth-century Mexican strongman Porfirio Diaz's exclamation "Poor Mexico: so far from God, so near to the United States," can be taken as a lament or as a hard-headed recognition of reality.

Certainly, from the perspective of the animal kingdom, the elephant analogy works well. The United States is large, with interests that stretch as far as the eye can see (or farther). At the same time, like most large animals, its size enables it to dominate its immediate surroundings and ignore all but the largest predators when it so chooses. When alarmed or taken by surprise, it can stampede in any direction, trampling other animals heedless enough to get in its way. However, when one looks around an unstable and often violent world, one finds many countries that, given the chance, would happily exchange their large, ambitious neighbours for Canada's border of 8,893 kilometres with the United States.

Canadians can identify, if they wish, with the small, cute, and slightly neurotic mouse of Trudeau's analogy, but they have other national symbols, such as the beaver. Small, amphibious, industrious, resilient, the beaver is a reasonable symbol, with deep historical roots, for a certain kind of Canadian who bridges traditional linguistic and cultural solitudes. Despite its size, the beaver finds ways to function within a much bigger natural environment and to shape parts of that environment for its own security and comfort.

Certainly, there are limits to this analogy as applied to Canada–US relations. Elephants and beavers generally do not share the same ecosystem. Were they to do so, chances are that the denizens of the beaver colony would be far more conscious of the local elephant herd on its way to the watering hole than the other way around. Yet Canadians and Americans do share a continent (as do Mexicans, if largely beyond the political horizons of the former).

This book explores the evolving context of the Canada–US relationship and the ways in which the smaller country attempts to manage that relationship at different levels. On the one hand, Canadians want to make the most of the opportunities provided by their proximity to the world's largest economy and its dynamic society, whatever its economic challenges of recent years. On the other, most Canadians place a high value on preserving and, where possible, expanding opportunities for choice – or "exercising policy discretion" – in their domestic and foreign policies. Rather than the historical lament of Mexican political life and culture, *So Near Yet So Far* expresses the continuing paradox[3] evoked by the relationship from the multiple perspectives of both Canadians and Americans.

Canada's physical and cultural proximity to the United States leads many Americans and other observers to overlook differences between the two countries – not least many Canadians' heartfelt desires to be different and to have Americans (and others) notice the differences. It is no accident, as discussed at greater length in Chapter 4, that these Canadians' assertions of their differences from the United States or from Americans – two notably different concepts – are most intense when the government of their southern neighbour is most assertive in exercising its claims to global political or economic leadership. Nor is it an accident that Americans are confused when such cultural and political differences are framed as questions of Canadian "identity" – given the tendency of politicians on both sides of the border to speak of the two countries as "friends" and "family," not just neighbours, when trying to cultivate mutually beneficial relations.[4]

Canada is "so near" to the United States in terms of economic interdependence and integration. Shifts in US economic policies or the domestic political environment often affect Canadian interests directly. This impact is usually most significant on the economic security and opportunities – major preoccupations of any Canadian government – that arise from the two countries' economic and sometimes social interdependence. This interdependence, driven by a combination of physical proximity, market forces (i.e., the actions and preferences of businesses, consumers, and investors on both sides of the border), and government policies that accommodate and reinforce these realities, often blurs distinctions between domestic and international policies in both countries.

Social interdependence can reflect the accustomed interactions of citizens in border regions, the actual or threatened spillover of environmental problems, food safety scares, outbreaks of disease from one country to the other, or the efforts of individual citizens or organized groups to take advantage of policy differences between the two countries. For the beaver to maintain its capacity to choose economic policies that serve its priorities and interests, it must pay careful attention to the habits and actions of the elephant whether or not the latter returns the compliment. At the same time, as noted by American political scientist Helen Milner, "cooperation among nations is affected less by fears of other countries' [actions] ... than it is by the domestic distributional consequences of cooperative endeavours."[5]

Another reality of this interdependence – particularly when combined with the global scope of US foreign, security, and international economic policies and the structure of the American political system – is that most issues of bilateral economic interdependence are dealt with in the context of US *domestic* policy processes and, often, US *domestic* politics. From the perspective of American foreign policy, Canada's political and economic interests are important only to the extent that they reinforce, complement, or impede broader US strategic objectives and the policies chosen to achieve them. US domestic policies tend to engage Canadian interests and objectives only to the extent that they affect politically important domestic interests in the United States. At such times, the political priorities of interests based in Ottawa, Toronto, Montreal, Calgary, or Vancouver can be "so far" from the consciousness or priorities of American politicians or journalists that navigating the cross-currents of American bureaucratic or congressional politics requires skilful and creative management by Canadian diplomats and interest groups.

These realities highlight the disparity between the importance of American political and economic processes (whether as sources of opportunities or risks) to Canadians and the latter's limited relevance, importance, or visibility to Americans, except in the very selective contexts of particular interest groups.[6] Indeed, growing numbers of Americans are likely to think of Mexico rather than Canada when they think of cross-border issues in North America given the progressive shifts of population, wealth, and power toward the American south and west and the rising influence of rapidly growing Mexican–American (and other Hispanic) communities across the United States.[7]

The paradox of *So Near Yet So Far* applies to Americans as much as it does to Canadians or Mexicans. Americans are more likely to understand the realities and complexities of interdependence with their northern and southern neighbours if they live in border regions or have close economic, cultural, or family ties across the border. However, the normal human tendency toward self-absorption often leads individuals and social groups to project their own realities, desires, and expectations onto those "others" outside their immediate circles. This projection can easily lead to disappointments and misunderstandings when, guided by their own perspectives and priorities, "they" do not live up to "our" expectations. Americans are not much different from Mexicans or Canadians in this respect, except that their country's relative size, power, and self-confidence limit their felt need to know or engage their neighbours, particularly the more distant ones. However, the spread of North American integration increases the challenges of what political scientists describe as "intermesticity"[8] – the blurring of traditional distinctions between international and domestic policies and politics.

These challenges are visible in recent American debates over issues ranging from the use of federal stimulus policies to promote local industries, to border security, and to immigration policies. They are inherent in ongoing debates over the relationship between America's sovereignty and capacity for self-government and international institutions whose effectiveness depends to some extent on American participation and leadership. These debates take place in Canada (and Mexico) as well, though often in different contexts. The ways in which Americans treat their neighbours are likely to condition the ways in which the governments and peoples of other countries respond to American interests, policies, and efforts to provide leadership around the world. American leadership on regional and global issues is far more likely to be effective when approached as a process of building alliances based on complementary and overlapping interests, objectives, and values while recognizing the sometimes competing interests of other nations, than when treated as a simple exercise in power politics.[9]

Similarly, the ways in which Canadians (and Mexicans) seek to protect and advance their own interests when engaging American governments and the broader American political system can contribute to greater American understanding of how their respective national interests can complement one another while also differing in many ways. Alternatively, they can reinforce the mutual incomprehension and opportunities for political and economic conflict that are never far from the surface given persistent differences in size and power and the tendency of some groups to exploit memories of historical grievances to serve their own agendas.

This is a book for people who wish to approach these issues with open minds rather than preconceived political or ideological agendas or a misplaced sense of moral (or cultural) superiority – phenomena that can occur in any cultural setting and across the ideological spectrum. It is intended as a journey of exploration, not as a definitive set of answers to the questions of a relationship whose scale, scope, complexity, and continuing evolution defy pat answers.

The book explores the fundamental challenges of the Canada–US relationship and the ways in which they shape both US policies toward Canada and Canadian efforts to engage and influence those policies. It examines the different levels and aspects of US policy making toward Canada – and the different institutional settings in which they take place. It engages US policies since the 1990s in three broad policy clusters: "homeland security" policies and how they affect economic integration and interdependence, the management of trade disputes arising from policy differences and interest group competition, and the evolution and partial integration of energy policies in each country, including the related influence of environmental issues. Finally, *So Near Yet So Far* suggests some tentative lessons to be drawn from this exploration, their implications for Canada's international economic policies, and their more sector-specific implications for bilateral and trilateral relations in North America.

Key Features of the Canada–US Relationship

The relationship between the United States and Canada, though unique in some ways, epitomizes the relations between major powers and smaller neighbours with which they share cultural similarities and a degree of interdependence but also have fundamental differences in size, power, and the relative importance of the relationship to each country.

The Canada–US relationship has been the subject of a number of studies in recent years. Hoberg, followed more recently by Bow and Lennox, have explored Canada's capacity for policy autonomy or policy choice in a wide range of settings. Clarkson has analyzed Canada's policy relations, both strategic and sectoral, within the broader context of governance within North America.[10] Dyment has explored the ideological polarization of Canadian domestic debates on bilateral relations and argued for a new "interest-based" paradigm that acknowledges interdependence as an "enduring situation to be managed," not a problem requiring a solution.[11] Heynen and Higginbotham and Mouafo and colleagues have documented the mechanics of "advancing Canada's interests within the United States" and the detailed interactions of transgovernmental relations at the departmental and agency levels. Gattinger and Hale and, more recently, Anderson and Sands have sought to map the contours of cross-border sectoral and subsectoral relations as part of a broader study of factors structuring policy relations.[12]

Gattinger and Hale note five major and enduring structural features of the Canada–US policy relationship: asymmetries on multiple levels; the primacy of economic factors, especially for Canada, in shaping the two countries' growing interdependence; the lack of formal political integration (bilateral or trilateral) or the institutions necessary to facilitate it, which has reinforced what they characterize as the shift from government to governance; the extent of policy decentralization in both countries – characterized as "the staggering ... breadth, depth and complexity of ... administrative relations"; and "continuing policy differentiation amid economic and policy integration."[13]

A sixth important feature noted by Clarkson is the integration of decentralized North American governance within comparable global systems so that "North America is not a self-contained region *of* the world. It is one region *in* the world."[14] The continued decentralization of governance sys-.tems enables both US and Canadian governments to tailor their participation to the requirements of domestic political institutions and distinct coalitions of domestic interests to secure greater political legitimacy for their actions.[15]

These findings overlap with several persistent features of the Canada–US relationship noted by Charles Doran in his 1984 study *Forgotten Partnership* – if from the perspective of "intermestic" relations rather than the international relations emphasis of the earlier work. Doran suggests that, in addition to the features noted above, key elements of the relationship include a "tradition of prudence in foreign policy conduct" by both countries; Canadian bargaining strengths that offset the inherent asymmetries of the relationship; ambiguity of foreign policy interests, especially in Canada; and intervulnerability, "the cost to one's neighbours of one's own domestic policy choices," so that "neither polity can avoid the external impacts of its neighbour's policies, enjoying only the benefits of its own domestic politics."[16] Whatever the changes in the bilateral relationship since the 1980s, these central features have persisted.

The institutional contexts (and contexts for interest group competition) in each country, and the different ways in which national, North American, and international governance structures interact from one policy field (and often subfield) to another, give rise to several American policy styles toward Canada that will be discussed at the end of this section.

Asymmetries
Bilateral Canada–US relations are characterized by a high degree of asymmetry: of relative size and power within the international system, of security commitments and capacities, and of the relative importance attributed to and the attention paid to the relationship by each national government – whatever its partisan or ideological orientation. Understanding these asymmetries, both as relevant facts and as underlying political realities, is vital to understanding the nature and dynamics of the bilateral relationship.

As one American diplomat noted in a conversation with me several years ago, "every relationship the US has in the world right now is asymmetrical."[17] Despite mounting challenges, the United States remains the world's pre-eminent political and military power. This reality is significant for the geopolitical considerations of every major international power (and most smaller ones), whether as a potential ally, a rival, or simply a strategic fact of life. Although Canada's position in the international order is often debated, not least by Canadians themselves, a leading former diplomat describes it as a "regional power without its own region,"[18] striving to manage its dependence on the United States through active engagement in international institutions and the selective pursuit of independent policy positions across a wide range of policy fields. Respective Canadian and American views of the relationship are explored further in Chapter 2.

A central reality of North American economic integration is the substantial interdependence between the United States and its Canadian and Mexican neighbours as its largest and third largest trading partners, respectively. The concept of interdependence is relatively simple: the actions of political and economic actors in each country are conditioned, directly or indirectly, by the actions or anticipated responses of the other – or of overlapping interests.

However, the interdependence of the United States with both of its neighbours is heavily asymmetrical. The United States is a central preoccupation of Canadian foreign and international economic policies, whereas American foreign policies are focused primarily on managing political, security, and economic alliances and relationships in a global context. Although this distinction gives Canada a modest advantage by enabling its senior policy makers to devote relatively more time and greater resources to the relationship, it might relegate Washington's consideration of Canadian concerns to categories described by different secretaries of state as "weeding the garden" or "condominium association issues." Except when critical US security priorities are at stake, as with the dual imperatives of securing US airspace and US borders in the months and years after 9/11, American policies toward Canada have been driven more by competing and overlapping constellations of bureaucratic, societal, and related congressional interests than by broader foreign policy considerations.[19]

Both Canada and Mexico depend far more on US markets for their trade and prosperity than the United States typically does on them or, indeed, any foreign country. Table 1.1 summarizes key differences in the economic dimensions of interdependence, including relative economic size, average incomes, openness, dependence on one another's markets, and foreign investment.

The asymmetries of economic (and, to some extent, political) interdependence have been reinforced since the 1980s in at least four major ways. First, Canada's (and Mexico's) greater openness and trade dependence reinforce historical asymmetries of market openness and interdependence

TABLE 1.1
North American economic symmetries and asymmetries

Relative economic size and prosperity in terms of GDP (2010)

	GDP ($millions)	Rank	Per capita ($)	Rank
US	14,660	2	47,200	2
Canada	1,330	15	39,400	22
Mexico	1,567	12	13,900	85

Merchandise trade as share of GDP (2010)

	Exports (%)	To US (%)	Imports (%)	From US (%)
US	8.8	*19.4**	13.2	*14.2†*
Canada	25.0	74.9	25.5	50.4
Mexico	28.7	73.5	29.0	60.6

Foreign investment as share of GDP (2010)

	Inward (%)	Outward (%)	Ratio
US	18.2	26.0	0.685
Canada	35.6	39.1	0.910
Mexico	31.3	7.5	4.173

NOTE: GDP figures are based on $US at purchasing power parity.
* Exports from US to Canada.
† Imports to US from Canada.
SOURCES: CIA, *The World Factbook* (Washington, DC: CIA, 2011), https://www.cia.gov/.

with the United States (see Table 1.1). Second, these factors contribute to asymmetries of vulnerability, including those arising from security sensitivities and foreign trade "threats," especially since 2001. Third, the relatively centralized US (and Mexican) federal systems, with their extensive checks and balances between the federal executive and Congress, and the much more decentralized Canadian model create important institutional asymmetries. Fourth, these differences are reinforced by asymmetries of policy processes, especially in legal requirements for the timing and nature of public consultation on regulatory measures in the United States compared with Canada, processes that have become central to managing bilateral policy relations.[20]

Primacy of Economic Factors

Both Canada's economic strategy and its broader interactions with US policies since the 1980s have been driven by the logic of Canada–US free trade and the restructuring of many Canadian industries within North

American markets. Clarkson characterizes this process as one of "market reconfiguration on a continental level."[21] As a result, trade policy imperatives, particularly securing access to US markets and strengthening bilateral economic relations, have become Canadian foreign policy priorities – whatever the Harper government's efforts to negotiate a broader range of trade agreements since 2006. In contrast, the cross-border effects of domestic policies are largely an afterthought for US policy makers, viewed primarily through the prism of their effects on domestic interests – even if Canada remains the largest market for American exports.

Even so, the web of economic, cultural, and social relationships between the United States and Canada is so extensive that intergovernmental cooperation is a matter of "structural necessity rather than conscious choice"[22] in facilitating and managing these relationships. Doran describes this reality as "intervulnerability," defined above.

However, this cooperation is mediated by three other major factors: resistance to the creation of binational or continental institutions involving substantial transfers (as opposed to the limited delegation) of sovereignty, the decentralization of policy processes in both countries, and the latter's expression in different approaches to reconciling regional interests within national politics. This regional dimension is more visible in Canada, where it is expressed through powerful provincial governments' control over many aspects of economic policy. But it is also deeply embedded in the structures of US congressional and special interest politics.

Lack of Formal Political Integration/Weakness of Shared Institutions
A fundamental contrast between North America and the European Union in recent decades has been the deliberate choice of national governments *not* to use NAFTA to create shared political institutions on either a bilateral or a trilateral basis, as opposed to the European Union's longer-term trend toward greater political integration. These choices have reflected the clear and persistent attitudes of policy makers and publics in both the United States and Canada – despite the persistent willingness of Mexican elites to pursue more extensive integration.[23]

Processes for bilateral and trilateral policy coordination under the Security and Prosperity Partnership of North America (2005-8), while serving as a lightning rod for nationalist elements in all three countries, lacked any mandate to pursue legislative changes. Instead, they were explicitly designed to address only those administrative measures on which bilateral or trilateral consensus could be achieved.[24] Similar concerns have been expressed over bureaucratic processes to strengthen cooperation on border security and regulatory issues announced in the Washington Declaration of February 2011.[25]

Policy Decentralization

Another major result of this extensive interdependence is that Canada–US relations are highly decentralized, unlike each country's relationship with virtually any other country. Neither country is a unitary actor in its bilateral or North American relationship. As with broader trade policies, Milner notes that "no single group sits at the top: power or authority over decision-making is shared, often unequally. Relations among groups ... entail reciprocal influence and/or the parceling out of distinct powers among groups."[26] Rather than being focused on relations between heads of state and their respective foreign ministers, most intergovernmental relations, from important sectoral policy issues to day-to-day contacts, are carried out through transgovernmental relations: extensive networks of personal and institutional contacts among officials of each country's executive departments and regulatory agencies.[27] Although power politics are not absent from either the domestic or the cross-border dimensions of these relations, the overlap and interpenetration of economic and social interests between the two countries generally limit the extent to which political action on one set of issues is explicitly linked to corresponding action on other sets of issues.[28]

The extent of intergovernmental, economic, and societal relationships also brings into focus important differences between the two countries' political systems. The breadth and depth of Canada–US economic, societal, political, and administrative relations have resulted in the widespread distribution of responsibility for different elements of the relationship across dozens of executive departments and agencies in both governments. This reality is reinforced by the decentralized character of congressional policy making, the US executive branch's frequent deference to Congress on domestic and North American policy issues, and in recent years the steady growth of cross-border relations among subnational governments.[29] Some observers have described this process as the politics of "fragmegration": the interaction of integrating and fragmenting tendencies at multiple levels of analysis.[30] As a result, Canadian governments that pursue favourable policy outcomes – or seek to avoid unfavourable policy outcomes – in Washington must engage not one but two American governments: the current administration and Congress.[31]

Conversely, the processes of federalism and intergovernmental relations serve many of the same functions for Canadian politicians and civil servants as the interactions of the executive and Congress do in Washington. Provincial governments typically enjoy far greater political, regulatory, and budgetary power relative to their federal counterpart than do American states, whose legislative authority can often be neutralized through the unilateral application of federal authority. As a result, the capacity of Canadian government officials to deliver policy outcomes desired in Washington is often constrained by the prospect of having to secure provincial acquiescence or consent to federal actions whose implementation might require provincial cooperation.

As a result, the resolution of competing interests and policy conflicts, or the introduction of new policy and institutional arrangements, often resembles a "two-level" or "multilevel" game in which officials of each government (and sometimes outside policy entrepreneurs) attempt to assemble compatible coalitions of interests in each country and often in other international settings.[32] Such "gamesmanship" is necessary to legitimate proposed changes and secure the necessary support to navigate them through each country's very different policy processes.

National and North American Governance in a Broader Global Context
The decentralization of governance within North America tends to parallel the decentralization of global governance and for many of the same reasons. Technical issues of financial sector regulation, competition law, intellectual property law, and many others are embedded within specific national legal and institutional contexts. Reconciling these national differences (or supraregional ones, as with the European Union) can be accomplished more easily in sector-specific forums that can be used to structure shared principles to enable mutual recognition of national or regional standards oriented toward similar policy objectives. Such arrangements are often reinforced by extending "national treatment" to participating countries' citizens and businesses.[33]

Continuing Policy Differentiation amid Economic and Policy Integration
The result is a varied mix of cross-border policy styles outlined in Figure 1.1, ranging from *independence,* in which the two countries make and implement policies in selected areas largely without reference to each

FIGURE 1.1
The continuum of Canada–US policy relations

Conflict - - - - - - - Independence- - - - - - - - - - - - - - - - - -Harmonization

|-Parallelism-|-Coordination-|-Collaboration-|

SOURCE: Gattinger and Hale, *Borders and Bridges*, 13.

other; to *parallelism,* in which one government might unilaterally adopt goals comparable to those of the neighbouring country but use different mixes of policy instruments and settings in recognition of different domestic institutions and conditions; to *coordination,* involving mutual adaptation by governments in the pursuit of common policy goals; to *collaboration,* involving the exchange of data, expertise, and knowledge in pursuit of common objectives; and to *harmonization,* referring to the development of common policy frameworks characterized by similar and often common policy instruments.[34]

As noted by Hale and Gattinger, this continuum is at least two-dimensional in nature since transgovernmental relations in specific policy fields are shaped by the relative centralization and decentralization of policy processes in each sector (and often their different subsectors) and by the number and diversity of domestic interests implicated in relevant national and cross-border policy communities.[35]

Thus, as the processes of "intermesticity" progressively blur traditional distinctions between domestic and foreign policies, the effectiveness of Canadian policies in both spheres often depends on engaging American domestic policy actors and processes whose effects frequently transcend national boundaries or, more simply, influencing American policies toward Canada.

Conceptualizing American Policies toward Canada

> *The United States doesn't have a Canada policy. It has Canada policies.*
>
> – *Confidential interview, US Department of State, 2006*

The decentralization of the American political system, the exceptional breadth and depth of the bilateral relationship, the challenges of effective policy coordination within both governments, and Canada's relatively low political profile in the United States combine to ensure that "there is no single American policy towards Canada, but rather a number of policies applied at different times."[36] The diversity and decentralization of political, economic, and societal relationships inherent to bilateral relations are shaped, in turn, by different mixes of domestic political considerations, bureaucratic politics reflecting competing institutional interests *within* each government, and the personal agendas of senior policy makers.[37]

Canadian historians Edelgard Mahant and Graham Mount suggest that US policies toward Canada tend to fit into five broad categories: "exceptionalism," "exemptionalism," alliance related, unilateral and deliberate assertions of American power, and inadvertent effects arising from domestic policy processes.[38] In reality, particular policies can combine elements of more than one of these categories.

The first category, exceptionalism, suggests that American policies toward Canada are distinctive. Such policies can reflect either US recognition of Canada's distinct interests as an independent ally or its capacity to make a distinctive contribution to US interests. The idea of exceptionalism is sometimes described as "the special relationship"[39] – a phrase also used to describe the periodic pursuit of political and military partnerships as a major element of Canadian and British foreign policies since the Second World War. However, the erosion of Canada's relative economic and military position in the industrial world since the 1950s, the retirement of senior officials who worked together to build the post–Second World War international order, and past efforts to assert greater distance from Washington in international relations have largely eroded Canada's claims to any such relationship in Washington.[40] So have the decline of the "imperial presidency," the reassertion of congressional power over economic, trade, and, to a lesser extent, foreign policies, and the substantial decentralization of power in Congress between the 1970s and the 1990s.[41]

Examples of exceptionalism in American policies toward Canada tend to be heavily weighted toward the "political–strategic" dimension of the relationship, discussed further in Chapter 2, or toward security issues directly related to Canada's geographic location – sprawled across the "top" of the North American continent. These factors contributed to the creation of NORAD, the North American Aerospace Defence Agreement, the Defence Production Sharing Agreement of 1958, which formalized the effective integration of the two countries' defence industries, and broader issues of defence cooperation.[42]

President Gerald Ford's inclusion of Canada in the G-7 (now G-8) summits during the 1970s was a way of balancing the preponderance of European nations whose interests often diverged significantly from those of the United States.[43] When bilateral tensions over the nationalist policies of the Trudeau government threatened to get out of control in the early 1980s, Secretary of State George Shultz initiated quarterly meetings with his Canadian counterpart, Allan MacEachen, as a way of facilitating the timely sharing of information, lowering tensions, and ensuring high-level attention to ongoing issues.[44]

More recently, heightened security concerns after 9/11 resulted in the negotiation of the Smart Border Accord, a comprehensive agreement formalizing extensive cooperation on security issues along the two countries' shared border. This process, which became the model for a similar agreement between the United States and Mexico, contributed to the creation of the Security and Prosperity Partnership (SPP) announced in 2005 to coordinate assorted security, regulatory, and microeconomic policy arrangements among the three countries. However, as with the SPP, quietly abandoned by the Obama administration shortly after taking office, most such arrangements require ongoing political support and bureaucratic commitment to survive the cross-currents and shifting priorities of domestic politics in each country. Elements of the border action plan released in December 2011, which aimed to formalize a bilateral security perimeter, suggest that the White House remains open to "exceptionalist" policies with Canada to the extent that they complement broader US policy goals.

The second category, exemptionalism, has a long history resulting from the two countries' economic interdependence. Canada has repeatedly sought and often received exemptions from US policies intended to regulate international capital flows, in recognition of the historical dependence of Canadian firms (and some Canadian governments) on US capital markets to finance their expansion and operation. Canadian citizens traditionally were exempted from having to show a passport when entering the United States, a reciprocal privilege based on the close social and economic ties linking communities in both countries. Although this exemption has been removed for both Americans and Canadians entering the United States, domestic political pressures led it to be replaced by provisions for enhanced drivers' licences issued by state and provincial governments based on common standards – suggesting a partial shift from exemptionalism to exceptionalism.[45] The politics of exemptionalism are most visible in the fine-tuning of microeconomic or regulatory initiatives in the day-to-day activities of diplomats, interest groups, and policy makers on each side of the border.

A third category, policies toward allies, is visible both in traditional US diplomacy and in the growth of specialized international networks to co-ordinate or negotiate technical policy and administrative arrangements between the United States and other nations. Such agencies can provide a forum to negotiate policy differences or develop broad principles and guide-lines for policy coordination, particularly among industrial countries. They can also be used to project US policy goals or arrangements in particular policy fields.[46] Regional trade agreements such as CUFTA and NAFTA have clearly been used as vehicles to advance each country's trade policy agenda within GATT (and subsequently WTO) negotiations. Other policies, such as the post-9/11 Container Security Initiative, began as bilateral projects that were subsequently extended internationally through the World Customs Organization. Pressures applied to NATO allies, including Canada, to increase their defence spending by the Clinton and Bush administrations both before and after 9/11 would also fall into this category.

A fourth set of policies – ones that treat Canada as a "dependent" or "satellite" nation – is more likely to arouse tensions. Such policies often involve efforts to project American power through the extraterritorial ap-plication of American laws (though such arrangements rarely single out Canada for "special treatment") or the systematic use of regulatory pres-sures or private litigation to secure political and economic concessions in bilateral disputes. Although it is tempting for some observers to dismiss the use of terms such as "dependent" or "satellite" as emotive or ideologic-ally driven terms inconsistent with serious policy analysis, references to Canada in the mainstream US foreign policy literature often comment on its economic and/or military dependence on the United States as a signifi-cant, if not defining, characteristic of Canada's position in regional and global politics.[47]

This category, open to both subjective interpretations and ideologically driven disputes, is both the most contentious and the most difficult to de-fine with precision – particularly since it is often asserted in connection with national security–related policies that highlight differences of sub-stance or emphasis between US and Canadian foreign policies. Long-standing debates over measures such as the Trading with the Enemy Act, the Helms-Burton Act of the early 1990s, the US Department of State's

International Trade in Arms Regulations (ITAR), or more recent restrictions on international banking activities point to the fine line between interdependence and "intervulnerability." Some American observers argue that such policies are merely variations of American policies toward allies that define the limits of behaviour considered acceptable for "allies" or their citizens seeking economic benefits from doing business with US firms or strategic industries.

Equally contentious, especially for Canadians, are measures that provide for the extraterritorial application of economic policies by private interests – notably the use of US trade remedy laws to enforce the policy preferences of American interest groups in areas historically reserved for other countries' domestic policy spheres. The repeated disputes over Canadian softwood lumber exports to the United States, culminating in the managed trade agreement of 2006, are probably the outstanding example of this category in recent years.[48]

Not included in this category are US government objections to Canadian policies that might affect American domestic interests adversely; these objections mirror Canadian objections to US domestic policies that ignore or adversely affect Canadian interests. Such disputes often overlap with partisan and interest group contests *within* Canada, such as debates over the National Energy Program of the early 1980s, the intensification or liberalization of foreign investment restrictions, or the demonstration effects of changes to sectoral economic regulations in fields such as transportation, financial services, and telecommunications.

Finally, the realities of economic integration between the two countries often result in measures that appear to fall into the fifth category: policies that often "forget or ignore" Canada unless or until technical adaptations can be made to US legislation to accommodate Canadian interests, circumstances, or sovereign rights. Such measures are often sectoral or micropolicy initiatives designed to apply in a US domestic policy context, whether by the executive branch or, more often, Congress. They create much of the day-to-day workload of Canadian diplomats in the United States – both in monitoring proposed legislative and regulatory measures for their prospective impacts on Canada and in attempting to influence, adapt, or counter measures that might be seriously detrimental to Canadian governmental or societal interests.

As noted above, the result of "dispersed relations"[49] on political, security, and related economic issues is that bilateral relations are often the product of a series of two- (or multi) level games with differing patterns of cooperation, "satisficing," or conflict in which the behaviour of each party is contingent on the other's expected response. Milner suggests that "cooperation may be tacit, in which parties retain considerable freedom of action, negotiated or coercive – involving the actual or threatened use of unilateral action."[50]

Coordination, whether formal or informal, can involve "mutual enlightenment" on participants' policy goals and intentions; "mutual reinforcement" of policy goals to overcome domestic or foreign opposition; "mutual adjustment" involving adaptations of national policies to reduce conflicts; or "mutual concessions" in which policy adjustments by one state are conditional on reciprocal adjustments by another.[51] One key element in this process is the building of supportive (and sometimes oppositional) coalitions of domestic interests in each country that anticipate benefits (or potential losses) from the details of such agreements. It can also involve efforts to defuse domestic opposition from groups with competing interests and policy objectives.

The concept of political actors "gaming" the system results from competition among overlapping and competing political, bureaucratic (or institutional), economic, and societal interests that attempt to project their *particular* policy goals onto relevant policy processes – whether legislative, regulatory, or diplomatic. In contrast to the traditional "high politics" of international relations among authoritative state actors, these processes are heavily influenced by "low politics" in which governments do not consistently function as unitary actors. Both the institutional interests of political and bureaucratic actors and the economic and other policy goals of societal actors often encourage the decentralization of policy processes noted above. These factors can contribute to cross-border or broader international cooperation by limiting the range of actors to be consulted or accommodated on any issue or set of related issues or by cultivating cross-border policy communities that develop a shared outlook on specific policy issues.[52]

However, as noted by Hale and Gattinger, the challenges of mobilizing political, bureaucratic, and interest group support to manage and reconcile cross-cutting interests and policy objectives increase in proportion to the number and range of interests in each country implicated in such policy communities. As a result, two-level games that attempt to balance international cooperation with domestic legitimacy can evolve into complex multilevel games that constrain national governments from serving as unitary, let alone autonomous, actors. These realities are visible within individual governments (as with interdepartmental or interagency competition in setting priorities or competing for scarce resources), between different governments (as in Canada's relatively decentralized federal system), or between independent branches of government (as in relations between the US executive branch and Congress and between the two houses of Congress).[53]

Any study of American policies toward Canada – or of the interaction of primarily domestic policy processes in each country – must thus come to grips with three basic realities that increase the challenges of being able to relate particular elements of the bilateral relationship to a coherent picture of the whole.

First, neither the United States nor Canada is a unitary actor politically or economically. There are too many competing political, institutional, economic, and social interests at play for either country to speak consistently with one voice – except when faced with serious crises that transcend major partisan and ideological differences.

This assessment of the Canada–US relationship fundamentally challenges the central assumption of traditional international relations built on dealings among sovereign national states serving as authoritative representatives of their countries' interests and citizens. This challenge can be threatening for both Americans and Canadians alike. For many Canadians, it suggests that the federal state's capacity to assert or defend their interests in dealings with the United States is contingent on the ability of its leaders or diplomats to secure the support of foreign political leaders or domestic political interests in a foreign country. For many Americans, it suggests either that foreign governments are "interfering" in what they view as primarily domestic policy processes or that particular "special" interests are cooperating with foreign powers in ways calculated to subordinate "American" interests and values to those of other countries.

Second, bilateral policies are heavily influenced by the institutions and processes of particular policy sectors: their relative openness, the number and relative cohesion or diversity of institutions and interests associated with particular policy systems or subsystems, and the relative interdependence of domestic interests in each country.

Policy processes and market activity can be studied at several different "levels of analysis" that interact with one another but that also require a degree of focus by policy makers and related economic and societal actors who might not be able to influence the broader policy environment but must learn how to function effectively within it. At the level of particular policies, such conditions often lend themselves to the politics of "satisficing" and of working through informal channels to resolve potential conflicts or work out arrangements that are "functional" for both governmental and societal interests without attracting much public attention.

This approach, sometimes described as "quiet diplomacy," is often criticized on both sides of the border, particularly by groups that perceive their interests to be threatened by the quiet arrangements of diplomatic or economic elites.[54] However, for many issues, it is an indispensable element in lubricating a relationship that has too many moving parts to be controlled by any single set of political or bureaucratic actors.

In this study, I explore four particular dimensions of the broader Canada–US relationship – political–strategic, trade–commercial, cultural –psychological, and institutional–procedural – building on concepts introduced a generation ago by American political scientist Charles Doran. Writing in 1984, Doran points to a third critical reality: *"the primary theoretical consideration in the U.S.-Canada relationship is that each government starts from different assumptions about international politics, and these assumptions in turn affect the weighting of the bargaining dimensions themselves."*[55]

Doran divides the study of US–Canada relations into three broad dimensions. The first, the political–strategic dimension, addresses broad issues of foreign policy, national security, and international relations, including formal and informal systems of alliances and the role of international institutions in ordering relations between and among states. The second, the trade–commercial dimension, focuses on the economic dimensions of international relations and more recently the blurring of distinctions between domestic and international economic policies in response to the forces of economic globalization and North American integration. The third, the psychological–cultural dimension, explores the impact of domestic political cultures, competition, and concerns on the "democratic" context for policy making in other areas. Depending on trends in bilateral relations and the political evolution of each country, environmental policies could eventually become a fourth dimension, capable of shaping or constraining policy developments in other fields. Each dimension involves a variety of institutions and processes that help to structure bilateral relations – whether in the context of domestic, "intermestic," or broader international relations.

I will then apply these concepts to three broad sets of policy issues: post-9/11 efforts to combine the enhancement of security measures with trade facilitation along the Canada–US border, energy and related policies, and the management of trade-related disputes that arise from continuing differences in the economic and regulatory structures of the two countries.

A Note on Methodology

Of necessity, any topic as broad as Canada–US relations engages a rich variety of literature on both bilateral policy issues and their interactions with the domestic and foreign policies of each country. Not surprisingly, perspectives on these issues – and their locations within the broader literature – vary substantially between the United States and Canada. The conceptual framework of this book lends itself to a comparative approach – examining the institutions, interests, and perceptions of academics and practitioners in each country and the ways in which they influence both the actions and the perspectives of policy actors in each country.

I have evaluated and refined this theoretical background through extensive interviews with policy makers and analysts in each country – primarily with senior officials, policy practitioners, and government relations specialists in Canada, their counterparts in the United States, Canadian diplomatic representatives in the United States, US Embassy officials in Canada, selected provincial governments, business and other interest group representatives, and Canadian media representatives in Washington. I conducted more than 170 semi-structured interviews between late 2005 and early 2010, most on a "not-for-attribution" basis to allow policy makers, government officials at varying levels of responsibility, and other participants in the policy process to speak freely about their activities and engagements with various aspects of bilateral relations.

A significant dimension of Canadian efforts to influence American policies toward Canada also involves the processes of public diplomacy: the efforts of governments to influence broader patterns of public opinion both within their "host" country and in leading or responding to domestic public opinion. Here I assess the continuing efforts of Canadian government officials to engage public and interest group opinion in the United States at several levels, using both the public statements of government officials, analyses of media coverage in Washington, DC, and major regional centres, and published polling data in each country. I also note the perennial "two-audience" problem of Canadian diplomacy in the United States: the far higher profile of bilateral issues in Canadian media outlets compared with American ones and the tendency of Canadian politicians to exploit this reality for domestic political purposes.

PART 1

Three Dimensions of Canada–US Relations

2

Guns, Globes, and Gardening
The Political–Strategic Dimension

Foreign policy and security relations are fundamental to questions of national interest, national sovereignty, and the capacity of national governments to speak for their citizens as a whole in dealings with other countries – whatever the domestic debates that inform these positions.

The role of the United States as the leading global power – and the ways in which Canadian policies should cultivate, accommodate, or challenge American policies and power in the name of Canada's national interests or "Canadian values" – have long been central to internal debates over Canadian foreign policy. This reality has not changed under the Obama administration, although President Obama's rhetoric has reduced political conflicts *within* Canada over the possibility and extent of such cooperation.

Canadian policy makers and commentators pay close attention to American policy priorities and decisions, balancing competing political pressures to cooperate with or distance themselves from their giant neighbour. Canadian governments typically view positive, if not necessarily cordial, relations with the United States as consistent with national interests and seek to maintain a more "independent" profile in various international settings. Trade-offs between these approaches can reflect policy makers' sometimes competing views of Canadian interests (or "values"), domestic pressures, and assessments of their capacity to influence American foreign and security policies at the margins.

US political and security relations with Canada are often characterized by a mixture of benign neglect, occasional irritation, and routine cultivation of political and administrative contacts to manage the many bilateral issues that often blur distinctions between foreign and domestic policies. Reagan-era Secretary of State George Schulz described this process as "weeding the garden." More recently, Condoleezza Rice likened it to attending meetings of a condominium association.[1] American officials generally seek close cooperation in the defence of North America while quietly favouring the preservation of Canada's national integrity against challenges from Quebec's separatist movement – though Bill Clinton's outspoken defence of Canadian federalism in 1999 was certainly welcomed in Ottawa.[2]

Christopher Sands suggests that Canadian engagement with "third countries" to position Canada as part of the US core alliance is critical to avoid future downgrading of the Canada–US relationship in ways detrimental to Canadian priorities within North America.[3] Arguably, this principle is even more applicable under the Obama administration, which has often appeared to de-emphasize such alliances as of limited and contingent value to the United States in favour of closer engagement with strategic competitors and major regional powers around the world. It applies not only to "political–strategic" relations based on political and military alliances but also to the subtler uses of Canadian influence and resources, sometimes described as "soft power," and to Canada's international economic engagements.

Security relationships, whether conducted through political or military channels, focus mainly on issues related to the defence of North America, given the huge disparity of resources devoted to defence by the two countries, and more recently on questions of "homeland" and border security.[4]

This chapter examines Canadian efforts to influence American policies toward Canada in the context of bilateral political and security relations. It begins with an overarching summary of theoretical considerations informing the study. It then identifies central areas of complementarity and asymmetry at different levels of analysis – macropolitical, binational, and bilateral institutions and processes within North America and broader sectoral questions central to the relationship in recent years. It concludes that the highly segmented nature of the bilateral political/security relationship currently suits both national governments by enabling "cooperation as necessary" but also, from Canada's perspective, what Stuart describes as a "perpetual courtship designed to avoid the altar."[5]

The Political–Strategic Context in US and Canadian Foreign Policies

Despite a general commitment to principles of liberal internationalism, US and Canadian government approaches to international relations reflect major differences in their countries' respective power and international status. The former, as befitting the world's leading political and military power, are preoccupied mainly with the political–strategic dimension of foreign policy. The priorities of senior US foreign policy decision makers are largely focused on national defence, regional stabilization, and engagement with strategic competitors. Under the Obama administration, the management of global and regional alliances and the promotion of stable democracies have often taken a back seat to these priorities.

As a result, bilateral relations with Canada are secondary if not peripheral to American foreign and security policies. Indeed, a recent comparative study suggested that, during the 1990s, Canada became "almost irrelevant to U.S. foreign policy making."[6] Senior American policy makers generally treat North American issues as subsets of hemispheric diplomatic and security considerations or of relevant domestic policies in setting national priorities and organizing their diplomatic activities.

The Department of State's shift of its Canada desk from the Bureau of European Affairs to Western Hemispheric Affairs during the 1990s symbolized the shift of Canada's diplomatic standing in Washington from that of a generally supportive power within the trans-Atlantic alliance to that of a peripheral actor in US hemispheric diplomacy – though the Harper government's more systematic engagement in both global and hemispheric dimensions of foreign policy has begun to modify this perspective.[7]

A survey of recent academic studies of US foreign and security policies reinforces this outlook. References to Canada are minimal – averaging one or two per book – and utterly peripheral to broader discussions of American policies or priorities. The primacy of political–strategic issues to US policy makers is also reflected in recent editions of the Congressional Research Service's annual survey of US–Canada relations. Almost two-thirds of its initial summary is typically devoted to defence and security issues, with the balance divided between economic and environmental matters.[8]

Conversely, the United States is a principal preoccupation of Canadian foreign policy. Canadian politicians and governments might seek to differentiate themselves from American policy positions in attempting to project an independent foreign policy on the global scene. Alternatively, as under the Harper government, they might attempt to influence or complement American policies on questions of substantial interest to Canada. Canada's capacity to pursue an independent foreign policy – and the range of meanings invested in that concept – largely depends on whether Canada's enduring national interests are seen to require careful and creative engagement of the United States and its policy goals and interests, the pursuit of counterweights to American power and influence, or a combination of them.[9]

This balancing act is complicated by four major factors. First, Canadian governments place a high priority on strengthening bilateral economic relations with the United States; however, securing White House cooperation can become more difficult if American political leaders or senior policy makers view Canada as indifferent or hostile to major US interests. Second, the intertwining of border security and trade issues since September 2001 has "thickened" the border for trade purposes, whatever the efforts made to facilitate low-risk trade and travel. Third, Canadian policy makers must anticipate the Canadian public's responses to perceptions of undue deference to US foreign policy and security priorities. Fourth, policy makers must anticipate the extent to which Canadian foreign and security policy cooperation is likely to influence American policy responses in either dimension of bilateral relations.

The mutual recognition of interdependence is central to the generally cooperative character of Canada–US relations despite periodic cycles of relative closeness or friction.[10] Domestic political cycles can contribute to relative convergence or divergence of political and ideological trends in each country, including the degree to which key policy makers share outlooks on external threats to major domestic interests or national security. These trends can be reinforced by a greater orientation toward multilateralism or unilateralism in American foreign and security policies, which directly affect the domestic political risks for Canadian governments of cooperating with Washington, especially if vulnerable to partisan challenges based on anti-American aspects of Canadian nationalism and its ideological cousin, self-congratulatory moralism.[11]

Canadian senior officials and foreign policy elites often have competing views of national interests and how to secure them against actual and potential threats – including the unilateral exercise of American power. These differences overlap with debates over how to secure a consistent American commitment to liberal internationalist principles of diplomatic, security, and economic cooperation and with domestic political constraints, discussed in Chapter 4, rooted in small country nationalism and its generally adverse view of the exercise of US power in international relations.

Liberal "idealists" such as Lloyd Axworthy and Michael Byers have tended to argue that American power needs to be contained by international institutions and that Canada should seek to exert its international influence to assert the pre-eminence of international institutions and "norms of global citizenship" over the projection of national influence in international relations. These attitudes are reflected in Axworthy's leadership in promoting the 1997 Ottawa Convention on landmines in a form that largely disregarded American interests and concerns.[12]

However, Canadian critics of this approach argue that its systematic efforts to use international institutions to constrain US leadership, whether disregarding or expressing hostility to American interests, are an inadequate, even dysfunctional, basis for Canadian foreign policy or constructive bilateral relations. For example, Derek Burney argues that "the relevance and effectiveness of Canada in global affairs [are] never greater than when its views are trusted and considered by the U.S. government, and when Canada is perceived by the rest of the world as having such a special relationship."[13] Political access, trust, and influence with senior US policy makers are generally restricted to nations viewed as reliable and trusted allies. Other governments might be given selective access to the extent that they support particular US policies or have the capacity to frustrate major American policy objectives.

From this perspective, Canada's foreign policies should be guided by pragmatic views of its national interests, whether in cooperating with Washington, pursuing diverging policies, or seeking to broker differences between the United States and other countries. Canada should approach both multilateralism and bilateral engagement with the United States as "means to an end, and not an end in itself."[14] This outlook views Canada's "North Americanist" and "internationalist" priorities as complementary and interdependent rather than competing elements in a conflicted foreign policy.[15]

This ambivalence among both Canada's foreign policy elites and the Canadian public has had three practical implications. First, the main emphasis of Canada's relations with the United States since the mid-1980s has been to maximize economic advantages to be derived from the trade–commercial dimension. Since 2001, an effective condition of securing these benefits has been to reduce real or perceived risks that political indifference or administrative negligence could allow Canada to become a conduit or staging point for terrorist attacks against the United States – thus strengthening the position of American domestic interests indifferent to the economic costs of "thickening" the border.

Second, with the brief exception of Canada's combat mission in Afghanistan between 2004 and 2011, its broader foreign and defence policy goals have tended to be relatively segmented and poorly coordinated in recent years, often lacking the commitment of fiscal resources necessary to translate intentions into effective actions.[16]

Third, the two countries tend to address bilateral political and security issues on a case-by-case basis, with the nature and extent of cooperation being heavily contingent on the political salience of particular questions – their sustained public visibility and perceived importance – and the perceived balance of political risks and benefits of accommodating US interests in Canada. However, Stuart suggests that political and economic relations between Ottawa and Washington have become sufficiently institutionalized at the level of individual departments and agencies that they are largely immune to these periodic cycles of political friction.[17] His comment was echoed by numerous Canadian officials whom I interviewed whose positions require day-to-day involvement with their American counterparts – though they tended to distinguish between working-level relations and the pursuit of major policy initiatives.

These are all elements of balancing means and ends within a credible foreign policy that combines the pursuit of Canadian interests and "values," however defined, with the recognition of Canada's limited resources and the value of cultivating constructive relations with its American neighbour. The next section explores several different elements of Canada's political–strategic relationship with the United States and their effects on Canadian governments' capacity to influence this dimension of American policies toward Canada.

Unpacking the US–Canada Political–Strategic Relationship

The range and depth of American dealings with Canada in the political–strategic dimension of international relations can be traced to Canada's active but often conflicted engagement in the global commons through a wide range of international organizations, its close hemispheric relationship with the United States on security and defence issues, and the varying levels of cooperation and interoperability between the two countries' armed forces, defence and aerospace industries, and civilian security services.

Historically, both governments have dealt with these issues on a piecemeal and uncoordinated basis to maintain their respective policy discretion, to limit the extent to which power relationships define a fundamentally asymmetrical relationship, and to accommodate varied and cyclical domestic political conditions in each country.[18] This section examines the institutional context of managing bilateral security relations at three levels: macropolitical relations, North American defence relations, and the broadening of security relationships since 9/11.

The Institutional Context

Responsibility for foreign and security policy decision making is broadly distributed among different departments and agencies of each government, with elements of Congress also playing a significant role in the United States, based on their capacity to exercise political leverage through relevant committees of the House or Senate. Several Department of State officials interviewed for this study noted the absence of any formal interagency process in Washington for managing US–Canada relations.[19] Defence policy observers note a similar reality within the sprawling US defence bureaucracy.[20]

In Canada, the management and tone of bilateral relations often reflect the respective priorities of the Prime Minister's Office (PMO), individual foreign ministers (whose term in office rarely extends more than two or three years), and other agencies responsible for policy coordination, particularly the Privy Council Office (PCO) and the Department of Foreign Affairs and International Trade (DFAIT). Former ambassador Allan Gotlieb, who served in Washington under both Trudeau and Mulroney governments during the 1980s, writes that each set of actors was capable of pursuing its own foreign policy reflecting different versions of the national interest: "one to enhance our relations with the United States, the other to distance ourselves whenever we can get the chance."[21]

Interviews that I conducted with officials of these agencies suggest similar patterns of behaviour during the Chrétien-Martin era that reflect this central paradox of Canadian foreign policy. Perhaps in recognition of this reality, most Canadian ambassadors since the early 1980s have either been political appointments or senior foreign service officials enjoying the personal confidence of and direct access to the current prime minister (see Table 2.1). Competing institutional priorities between Foreign Affairs and military officials responsible for cross-border policy coordination are also a recurring theme in the literature – sometimes leading them to function at

TABLE 2.1

Canadian ambassadors to Washington since 1981

1981-89	Allan Gotlieb	Undersecretary of external affairs; career head of Canadian foreign service, 1977-81
1989-93	Derek Burney	Former chief of staff to Prime Minister Brian Mulroney; previously senior official at DFAIT
1993-94	John de Chastelain	Career soldier; former chief of the defence staff
1994-2000	Raymond Chrétien	Career foreign affairs official; nephew of Prime Minister Jean Chrétien
2000-5	Michael Kergin	Career foreign service official; former senior foreign policy adviser to Prime Minister Jean Chrétien
2005-6	Frank McKenna	Former (Liberal) premier of New Brunswick
2006-9	Michael H. Wilson	Former finance minister in cabinet of Prime Minister Brian Mulroney; negotiated final stages of Canada–US Free Trade Agreement; oversaw NAFTA negotiations
2009-	Gary Doer	Former (NDP) premier of Manitoba

cross-purposes in managing security-related aspects of the relationship.[22] However, like most other aspects of Canadian public policy, the higher the political salience of particular questions, the more likely they are to be managed by the prime minister and senior political and bureaucratic advisers.

Since 9/11, Canadian cabinet ministers responsible for foreign and security policies have sought to build close personal relationships with their US counterparts; success has been partial given the turnover in Canadian cabinet ministers and periodic frictions.[23] However, the range of issues at play in the relationship helps to ensure that neither Canada nor the United States has a single overarching policy toward the other in the context of political–strategic relations, as in other aspects of their bilateral relationship.

US diplomatic relations with Canada are managed through the Canada Desk of the Bureau of Western Hemispheric Affairs in the Department of State, ultimately reporting to an assistant secretary of state. However, the Department of State lacks any formal coordinating role in the extensive transgovernmental relations across multiple departments and agencies of both governments. In the absence of a central "interagency" process governing US–Canada relations, this vacuum can be partially filled by the US Embassy in Ottawa, depending on the ambassador's policy interests and access to senior White House and Department of State decision makers.

Since the early 1980s, individual secretaries of state have chosen to meet periodically with their Canadian counterparts in efforts to manage the relationship. The nature, scope, and frequency of those meetings, which often range well beyond traditional diplomatic priorities, depend partly on the approaches of individual cabinet officers and partly on the broader state of political relations.[24] However, the breadth and depth of US–Canada relations generally insulate the management of bilateral issues from cycles of relative political closeness or distance between the foreign policies and personal relationships of particular administrations and governments.[25]

Foreign and Security Policies beyond North America

> *When the US looks at foreign policy and the issues that concern the president on an ongoing basis, we are looking at the big international issues. On some of those issues, Canada is important. Policy towards Canada is almost always a generic US policy in which Canada figures as an ally, a partner, or a country that's not particularly engaged.*
>
> *– Confidential interview, US Department of State, 2006*

The breadth and depth of Canada's political–strategic relationship with the United States, together with the multiple political, military, and bureaucratic actors who manage its many aspects and the different levels of importance given to particular issues by each government, offer numerous points of application for Mahant and Mount's policy typology discussed in Chapter 1.

The US government's historical view of Canada is that of a friendly neighbour oriented toward cooperation in international relations and with many common national interests but with a domestic political need to assert a degree of independence from American policies and priorities. However, as noted in Chapter 1, the special relationship of the immediate postwar era steadily declined in response to the shifting foreign policy priorities of both countries.[26]

As a result, US foreign and security policies relating to Canada often fall into the category of "policies toward allies," particularly in broader international settings. The single biggest priority of broader US foreign and security policies toward Canada since the late 1990s – in common with US attitudes toward other allies – has been consistent pressure to bear a larger share of the burden of collective security while recognizing that Canadian defence priorities and the resources used to meet them are a matter of domestic politics.[27]

During the 1990s, most Western nations reduced their defence spending. Defence spending by larger powers, including the United States, Britain, and France, dropped from between 4 and 6 percent of GDP to between 2.5 and 3.1 percent. Canadian defence spending declined proportionately to 1.2 percent of GDP during the same period, among the lowest of any NATO member country,[28] though these trends did not prevent Canada from supporting NATO interventions in Bosnia and Kosovo. These budget reductions reflected growing fiscal constraints, competing domestic priorities, and perceptions that Canada's defence contribution had become peripheral to American security needs.[29]

Disputes over defence spending trends become more acute during periods of increased international tension, when demands for consultation by prospective US allies are not matched by their actual or potential contributions to collective security. Canadian defence resources were unequal to persistent demands for NATO and other peacekeeping operations during the 1990s, leading to growing American pressures for increased spending, especially after 9/11. Some observers in both countries suggested that Canada was taking a largely free ride on the US security umbrella[30] – at least until rising Canadian combat casualties in Afghanistan after 2004 provided clear evidence to the contrary.

The events of 9/11 triggered a re-evaluation of defence and collective security policies after Washington invoked NATO's collective security clause against Afghanistan's Taliban government. The result was a series of awkward and often equivocating Canadian policies and military commitments. Political conflicts within NATO before the 2003 Iraq War left Canada in a highly ambivalent position. On the one hand, it supported NATO intervention in Afghanistan and collaborated extensively with American officials on numerous security and counterterrorism measures involving police and intelligence cooperation, border security, and the internationalization of new cargo and air travel security standards. On the other, the Chrétien government opposed American intervention in Iraq and the Bush administration's claims to a pre-emptive right of self-defence – a position that evoked considerable resentment in Washington.[31] Some US academics and policy makers even suggested that countries that "shirk their fair burden" in the provision of collective security should face losing "lucrative, American tax-funded defense contracts."[32] During its first term, the Bush administration often distinguished between core and peripheral members of US alliance networks, extending advantages or concessions in unrelated policy fields in recognition of such countries' cooperation with significant US policy objectives.[33]

Stein and Lang have discussed at length the political straddle involved in Canadian command of a multinational naval task force in the Arabian Sea providing cover for Afghan and Iraq missions as well as the continued service of Canadian liaison officers with US forces in the Persian Gulf.[34] Similar calculations contributed to Canada's initial decision to accept command of the ISAF (International Security Assistance Force) Task Force in Kabul, Afghanistan, and later to take on reconstruction functions with a higher risk of combat in the Taliban heartland around Kandahar.[35] Indeed, former Liberal defence and foreign minister Bill Graham asserts that "there was no question; every time we talked about the Afghan mission (in cabinet), it gave us cover for not going into Iraq."[36] As Canada's Kandahar commitment stretched from six months to six years, it forced a complete re-evaluation of Canadian defence and related budget priorities by the Martin and Harper governments.

Arguably, American expectations of support in Afghanistan combined with successive governments' calculations of national interest, the long-deferred replacement of obsolete equipment, senior military leaders open to taking on greater combat roles, and the resulting operational requirements of the Canadian Forces to bring about these policy changes. There is little doubt that Canada's participation in Afghanistan provided significant political benefits in bilateral relations after 2004. Growing American awareness of Canadian engagement – and casualties – in Afghanistan was significant in strengthening American public goodwill toward Canada (see Chapter 4).

Canada's approach to what Christopher Sands calls "third country issues" – foreign and security policy questions beyond North America – reflects both the continuing trade-offs and the cyclical patterns of Canada–US relations. At times, they enable Canadian governments to "demonstrate independence from Washington"; at others, they emphasize Canada's "value as a strategic U.S. ally" – if often in ways not overly visible to Canadians.[37]

The Martin government's International Policy Statement of 2005 highlighted four major sets of international priorities – diplomacy, trade, development, and defence – complementing several American policy goals in Afghanistan, Haiti, Latin America, and other parts of the world, carefully obscured by "Made in Canada" packaging.[38] The Harper government continued this pattern, adopting the rhetoric of liberal internationalism and cooperation through international institutions while pursuing a number of policy initiatives that paralleled US measures.[39] They included taking substantial domestic political risks to extend Canada's combat role in Afghanistan through 2011, the promotion of trade liberalization and democratic stabilization in Latin America, support for NATO expansion to Ukraine and Georgia, and operational support for NATO's intervention in Libya's civil war. Canada's Americas' policy also provided collateral benefits of increased engagement within the hemisphere, a priority welcomed by the Department of State, while maintaining its discretion in the timing and extent of commitments in Mexico and other Latin American countries.

In effect, these initiatives reflect on a much broader scale the goal of Canadian diplomacy in the United States, as described by former ambassador Allan Gotlieb: "the art of penetrating concentric, intersecting circles of influence."[40] Rather than an explicit strategy, they suggest the tactical adaptation of Canadian policies to political circumstances, including the constraints of minority parliaments (2004-11) and the practical need to adapt to changing circumstances – not least the wholesale turnover of policy makers in Washington following the 2008 presidential election. As such, they demonstrate the potential ability of Canadian officials to engage their US counterparts in targeted ways that balance national interests, domestic political considerations, and the pursuit of complementary policy goals and retain a reasonable degree of discretion on specific policy choices and the instruments used to attain them.

However, the continued primacy of domestic political considerations in shaping foreign policy choices can be seen from the Harper government's November 2010 decision to extend Canada's commitment in Afghanistan to 2014. The Obama administration placed heavy pressure on NATO allies to extend even symbolic troop commitments despite growing war weariness among their citizens. The Harper government's decision to accept a less "exposed" commitment to train Afghan soldiers until 2014 depended heavily on the Liberal opposition's earlier decision to support extension of the mission in Afghanistan beyond 2011.[41]

Managing the Security Neighbourhood

The segmentation of US policies toward Canada can clearly be seen in the context of North American policies – whether in the coordination of the political relationship by national leaders and foreign ministers or in the bilateral and binational cooperation on security and defence issues in North America. These two issue sets are complicated by three different sets of asymmetries, each of which has its own institutional architecture: the huge imbalance of power and resources available for national and North American defence; the broader continental and hemispheric security relationships and concerns of each government; and the challenge of engaging the US government independently of the latter's relationship with Mexico.

Moreover, Canada's North American agenda includes numerous trade, sectoral, and regulatory agendas, some of which are heavily enmeshed in interest group politics of the sort that rarely engage senior US foreign policy decision makers. Securing regular access to these decision makers, and organizing the federal government's own policy agenda to make engagement "worthwhile" for its American counterparts, thus become recurring preoccupations of senior Canadian officials and diplomats.

Binationalism and Bilateralism

US–Canada relations are often seen in Washington as an oasis of relative calm amid the broader challenges of trying to "run the world"[42] and the sometimes turbulent waters of hemispheric issues. Canadian leaders and diplomats often find it difficult to secure what they view as adequate attention to their concerns from the White House or the Department of State when the latter must deal with challenges such as protracted conflicts in the Middle East and Latin America, Mexico's narco-insurgency, or Hugo Chavez's efforts to create an anti-American alliance in Latin America. The 1999 Hart-Rudman Report on national security notes the special US interest in Brazil "because it is so large" and Mexico "because it is so close."[43] Attention to bilateral issues with Canada is a secondary priority under such circumstances. As one American diplomat commented, "when there's no fire, you don't send in the fire trucks."[44]

Of all the issues surveyed in this book, the Canada–US defence relationship in North America probably comes closest to Mahant and Mount's category of exceptionalism – distinctive policies toward Canada as an independent ally capable of affecting US interests significantly, whether through cooperation or neglect. This distinctiveness is derived from Canada's enormous geographic size and its physical proximity to the United States – so that maintaining or expanding Canadian defence capacities is a direct contribution to US national defence. The politics of exceptionalism are also visible in Canada–US law enforcement cooperation, which has become increasingly significant to the security relationship since 9/11, issues addressed in greater detail in Chapters 10 and 11.

A wide array of bilateral and binational institutions supports these functions. The Permanent Joint Board of Defense (PJBD), formed in 1940, provides a sounding board for a broad range of bilateral defence and security issues – reporting directly to the president and prime minister as well as to cabinet officers responsible for defence and foreign affairs. The North American Aerospace Defence Command (NORAD), formed in 1958 to create an integrated air defence capacity, has a binational command structure – with senior US and Canadian officers sharing command but reporting to their respective national governments. There are indications that after 9/11 the Pentagon approached Canada about the possibility of establishing a North American defence perimeter, which would have seen the expansion of NORAD responsibilities to include joint planning and command of all aspects of North American defence on a permanent basis. However, Mason suggests that, due to sovereignty and domestic political concerns, Ottawa would only agree to extend it to include maritime security.[45]

Jockel suggests that NORAD has survived periodic shifts in US and Canadian defence priorities and related threat perceptions because each country maintains parallel organizations that allow its government to pursue key objectives without requiring the other's participation or consent.[46] The emergence of a unified Northern Command (NORTHCOM) responsible for all aspects of US North American defence, and Canada Command, its Canadian counterpart, are merely the latest reflections of this phenomenon. These factors are also important in determining the occasions on which Canada–US defence cooperation is *binational* (stressing joint planning, command structures, and operational readiness) or *bilateral* (emphasizing parallel but organizationally and operationally independent military capacities and relationships).[47]

Both military commands seek to combine operational interoperability – the capacity to function together in a wide range of defence and security tasks – with the capacity for independent action. The Canadian navy has the greatest capacity for combined operations with its American counterpart, with Canadian ships having provided a command and support function in the Arabian Gulf during the 2003 Iraq War. When the US Coast Guard diverted much of its normal patrol capacity to the Gulf coast to assist in recovery from Hurricane Katrina in 2005, Canadian Coast Guard units assumed responsibility for patrolling much of the US east coast. When 37 percent of US Air Force F-15 fighters were grounded with airframe cracks in 2007, Canada's F-18 squadrons assumed responsibility for parts of US airspace.[48]

A side benefit of close military cooperation is access for Canadian defence industries and contractors – many of them owned by US-based firms – to US defence and aerospace contracts. Canada's defence spending is not large enough to make such industries viable in the absence of such access. Ek notes that Canada's participation in the US Joint Strike Fighter program, also open to other NATO allies, has generated substantial benefits for Canada's aerospace industries, whatever its problems in other respects.[49] However, the post-9/11 focus on domestic security has increased concerns over extraterritorial applications of US laws, including access to private information on Canadian citizens contained on databases linked to US computer servers under the US Patriot Act, the treatment of Canadian nationals suspected of terrorist links, and restrictions on the employment of certain dual nationals by US defence contractors, including those based in Canada. Most of these issues are managed by Canada's Washington Embassy through traditional channels of "quiet diplomacy."

Mason suggests that, forced to make the choice, US defence officials would probably encourage Canadian defence planners to focus on North American defence rather than support for US-led alliances in other theatres if budgetary and equipment constraints forced them to choose between the two.[50] Ottawa's expansion of Canadian defence capacities since 2004 has been explicitly calculated to avoid such a choice. However, the costs of maintaining interoperability with constantly evolving American military, naval, and aerospace technologies, and the long lead times for designing, purchasing, and acquiring new naval and aircraft systems, might prove difficult to accommodate within anticipated federal budgetary constraints driven primarily by economic policy priorities and domestic political considerations.[51]

The most politically significant issues in bilateral defence relations have involved Canadian participation in the siting, testing, and development of American missile systems. The Diefenbaker government's refusal to accept US Bomarc missiles in the early 1960s created a cabinet crisis that contributed to its defeat in the 1963 general election. The Trudeau government agreed to test "first generation" cruise missiles in Canada despite significant domestic opposition, and internal divisions and domestic political vulnerability led the Mulroney government to defer further missile tests during the late 1980s.[52] The Martin government's handling of US requests to support Ballistic Missile Defense tests in 2004-5 faced similar challenges. However, its mixed messages to Washington – initially signalling cooperation but then announcing its negative decision without prior warning – probably did more to erode its credibility with US policy makers than a straightforward refusal would have done. One Canadian diplomat framed the effect in this way:

> There's a golden rule in Canada–US relations. You don't blind-side the administration, particularly people who are considered allies ... When the prime minister rose in the House to announce the decision, he hadn't called the president. We all found out from watching Question Period. What really p----d off the president was that we caught them flat-footed.[53]

In contrast, Prime Minister Harper's announcement during the 2008 federal election (and the last month of the US presidential campaign) that Canada would not extend its combat commitment in Afghanistan beyond its previously scheduled 2011 deadline allowed Harper to present a *fait accompli* to the new president. It gave Washington two and a half years of notice to find replacement forces and sidestepped a messy domestic political debate over the declining political and military situation in Afghanistan.

These events point to the importance of domestic political considerations in managing appearances on formal defence relations and in developing or testing new weapons systems. In the absence of an actual emergency, Canadian governments are more likely to accede to American requests for cooperation that can be managed under the political radar, particularly if conducted under existing bilateral agreements. The greater the political novelty or visibility of such requests – whether substantive or mainly symbolic – the more likely Canadian governments are to avoid commitments requiring major investments of political capital, particularly if close to an election. Officials involved with ongoing coordination of security issues state that representatives of both countries are clearly aware of domestic political constraints and that such issues – including missile defence and Canadian assertions of sovereignty over Canada's Arctic waters – are "off the table" in working-level bilateral discussions.[54]

Decisions to conserve domestic political capital in this way correspondingly prevent Canadian governments from accumulating much international political capital on defence issues with Washington, though the absence of overt issue linkages allows them to compensate by pursuing parallel poli-cies in other areas.

Ottawa has sent signals of an expanded defence and security role in the western hemisphere as a long-term priority.[55] Although this decision has been welcomed in Washington, it is far from clear how growing fiscal pressures will affect Ottawa's ability or willingness to follow through.

The Civilian Dimension

> *The most important thing is not if there is a terrorist attack in the United States but a terrorist act that could have been prevented by you.*
>
> – *Confidential interview, US Department of State, 2005*

One aspect of bilateral political–security relations in which Canadian governments have made systematic and consistent efforts to influence American policies is that of border management and security. The border closures that followed 9/11 struck at a fundamental Canadian interest: secure access to US markets for much of its export trade, tourist business, and business travel. Taking the steps necessary to maintain trust in Canadian border management and security measures while facilitating low-risk trade and travel has been a top priority ever since.

Shortly after 9/11, Ottawa assembled a committee of senior officials to develop detailed proposals for a comprehensive bilateral agreement on border management and security. Drawing on several years of extensive bureaucratic contacts under the "Shared Border" process of the late 1990s, this process resulted in the Smart Border Accord, a thirty-point plan for cooperative border management and complementary security arrangements signed in December 2001.[56]

However, implementation of the accord also masked a complex and highly segmented series of processes, discussed at length in Chapter 10, that sought to establish Canada's credentials as a reliable security partner while maintaining varying levels of discretion on a program-by-program basis. The Smart Border Accord became the model for continuing border management negotiations as well as efforts by senior Canadian officials to ensure ongoing high-level contacts with the White House and cabinet officers in the Departments of State, Homeland Security, and Commerce.[57] Subsequent proposals for a "North American Initiative" to extend processes for shared border management, security, and trade facilitation ran afoul of the political chill that followed Canada's refusal to provide formal support in the Iraq War as well as White House preoccupation with the 2004 presidential campaign.

After the 2004 elections, the Bush White House reciprocated these gestures as part of a broader set of initiatives to restore relations with allied states and international organizations damaged by the Iraq War. The March 2005 summit of the three North American leaders initiated the Security and Prosperity Partnership (SPP) process that absorbed or paralleled a series of sectoral policy negotiations incorporating security issues, trade and travel facilitation, and, later, cooperation on assorted energy and environment policies. However, the SPP's highly technical character failed to sustain high-level political interest in Washington and aroused intense suspicions of a hidden agenda on North American integration from rejectionist interests in both countries.[58] The Obama administration suspended the SPP process in 2009, pending a broader review of its North American policies.

Conversations with Canadian officials suggested a highly segmented approach to security initiatives ranging from close cooperation on shared border measures involving full Canadian participation to parallel policies addressing legal, institutional, or technical policy differences between the two countries. American requests for cooperation sometimes evoked polite demurrals when compliance threatened to undermine Canadian policy discretion on major domestic policy issues, as discussed in Chapters 10 and 11. Ottawa's general approach was to avoid politicizing most of these issues – with the notable exception of the Western Hemisphere Travel Initiative (WHTI) – preferring to focus on technical responses that combined cooperation, respect for legal and procedural differences in each country, and increased operational effectiveness in reducing risks of terrorism and cross-border criminal activity while facilitating legitimate trade and travel.

The Obama administration's northern border policy review initially sought to reduce Canadian expectations of any significant changes to border policies. However, more recent diplomatic and security conversations have resulted in a US shift away from its "one border" policy toward a more flexible approach to conditions on the Canadian side in return for Canadian cooperation in completing the long-deferred entry–exit system for tracking foreign visitors to the United States.[59] I will address these issues further in Chapter 11.

Canada and Mexico in North America

The institutionalization of Canada–US defence and security relationships in NORAD and numerous other venues contrasts sharply with US (and Canadian) security relations with Mexico. The very different histories of coexistence and conflict in relations between the United States and its neighbours have entrenched dual bilateral approaches to security and defence issues. These dynamics are reinforced by the weakness (and on security issues the absence) of formal institutions for trilateral coordination and the very different priorities of each government.[60]

Mexico's long, unhappy relationship with the United States evokes historical memories that have strictly limited formal collaboration on military and security issues until recently. Since the 1970s, intermittent security cooperation between the two countries has reflected very different priorities attached to the cultivation and smuggling of illegal drugs, nationalist sensitivities in Mexico, and political attitudes toward large-scale Mexican migration to the United States. Despite periodic efforts to fight the growing influence of narcotics cartels, Mexico's historical sensitivity to military conflicts with the United States generally limited military cooperation until a growing narco-insurgency prompted a major policy shift symbolized by the Meridá Initiative of 2007.[61]

However, Canadian officials have strongly resisted US suggestions to include Mexican observers in bilateral defence-planning activities. Interviews with senior Canadian government officials under both the Martin and the Harper governments also suggested deep concerns over the possibility that US–Mexico disputes over immigration, drugs, and border management could prejudice Canadian interests in maximizing market access, trade, and travel facilitation with the United States.[62] The main exception to this well-entrenched pattern is in law enforcement cooperation, in which long-established Canada–US police links have been expanded to include Mexico in response to links between Canadian mobsters and their Mexican counterparts.[63]

The SPP process, discussed above, created a framework for annual summits of the three North American leaders, complementing the hemispheric

Summit of the Americas. These summits, interrupted after the demise of the SPP, have been reinforced by semi-annual meetings of the secretary of state with Canadian and Mexican foreign ministers, who have nominal responsibility (at least in the United States and Canada) for coordinating decentralized processes for bilateral and trilateral intergovernmental relations. Even so, the absence of formal institutions for trilateral coordination tends to privilege a dual bilateral approach in which both Canada and Mexico seek to maximize the benefits of their particular relationships with the United States, whatever the formalities of trilateralism.

The Politics of "Arctic Sovereignty"

The optics of managing Canada–US relations while "preserving Canadian sovereignty" require every Canadian government, however friendly toward the United States, to preserve at least one major issue on which it visibly and vocally chooses to disagree with American policies. Within days of winning the 2006 federal election, the Harper government signalled that it had chosen the defence of Canada's sovereignty in the Arctic to perform this important symbolic function.

The first significant bilateral dispute over the North arose in the late 1960s following the discovery of oil at Prudhoe Bay, Alaska. The US supertanker *Manhattan's* efforts to transit the Northwest Passage among Canada's Arctic islands raised questions of contested sovereignty – notably Canada's right to regulate passage on environmental and security grounds. The US government, while acknowledging Canada's sovereignty over the Arctic islands, viewed the passage as international waters, similar to major sea lanes adjoining various parts of Europe and Asia.[64] During the 1980s, in a pragmatic act of mutual accommodation, the Reagan administration agreed to inform Canada of American vessels' passage through these northern waters, and the Mulroney government agreed not to refuse their passage. Neither side conceded its position on the broader policy issues.

During this period, Canada strongly supported the UN Law of the Sea Treaty as a means of securing its claims to ownership and regulation of offshore and mineral resources and related environmental issues. Successive US administrations strongly opposed the convention until changes were made in the mid-1990s to accommodate international corporate interests. However, opposition in Congress precluded US accession to the treaty despite signs of openness from the Clinton and second Bush administrations. Even so, the Arctic has been marginal to US foreign and security policy interests since the ebbing of the Cold War.[65]

However, rapid increases in global energy prices since 2000, the rapid melting of the Arctic ice cap, the growing likelihood of rising shipping levels, the reassertion of Russian sovereignty claims within the region, and several related environmental issues have increased the Arctic region's relative political importance. With the approach of the 2005-6 federal election, the Conservatives selected the strengthening of Canada's Arctic presence as their major symbolic gesture toward Canadian nationalism, pledging significant increases in Ottawa's capacity to assert control over the region. A few days after winning the January 2006 federal election, Stephen Harper responded to an off-the-cuff comment from US Ambassador David Wilkins, which simply repeated traditional US policy, by bluntly asserting the traditional Canadian position and his government's commitment to defending Canada's Arctic sovereignty. Indeed, federal officials described Arctic policy as central to Canada's "Three A" foreign policy during the Harper government's first term: Afghanistan, Arctic sovereignty, and America.[66]

Conversations with federal officials suggested that the debate over the Northwest Passage masks a far wider range of technical issues related to Canada's assertion of its jurisdiction over the North, rules governing resource development in disputed areas of the offshore continental shelf, and the competing claims of other countries over rights to resource development and environmental regulation. Signatories of the Law of the Sea Treaty can file claims to the exploitation of offshore resources by 2012-13 based on mapping of undersea extensions of Arctic land masses and related areas of their continental shelf. Since 2008, Canadian and US Coast Guard vessels have cooperated in mapping the continental shelf in the Arctic Ocean as part of a broader process of establishing their respective claims to undersea territories for the purposes of resource exploitation and environmental management under international law. (Russia, Norway, and Denmark are engaged in similar processes.)[67]

Recent Canadian governments' approaches to these issues reflect a mix of quiet diplomacy and efforts to promote international cooperation through a variety of policy networks, including the Arctic Council and other circumpolar links involving Indigenous peoples from several countries.[68] Secretary of State Hillary Clinton has signalled support for this approach, largely continuing the Bush administration's policy toward the region though criticizing what some media reports characterized as Canadian efforts to sidestep the Arctic Council in favour of talks among Arctic coastal states.[69] Officials interviewed for this project suggested that, though US and Canadian governments can "agree to disagree" over the Northwest

Passage, there is considerable cooperation on several other issues in which national interests overlap. This cooperation is also reflected in broader dialogues among academics and policy makers to foster cooperation in ensuring that the progressive melting of the Arctic ice cap results in regulatory cooperation rather than a political free-for-all.[70]

Conclusion

Canada's management of the political–strategic dimension of its relations with the United States in recent years suggests four different approaches used in different circumstances – driven partly by domestic political considerations, partly by perceived national interests, and partly by the effective workings of the international system, in that order.

Canadian politicians and diplomats can seek to position Canada as a cooperative ally, generally in the context of multilateral commitments such as NATO, as reflected in Canada's participation in NATO's Kosovo intervention in the late 1990s and its commitments in Afghanistan and Libya since 2004. In such cases, Canadian governments' security priorities generally reinforce US interests, if not necessarily to the extent desired in Washington.

Alternatively, they can pursue policies that complement those of the United States, positioning Canadian diplomats to serve as brokers attempting to accommodate both American interests and those of allied or friendly nations. Examples of this approach include Canada's efforts in the late 1990s to secure the indefinite extension of the Nuclear Non-Proliferation Treaty[71] and the Harper government's more recent efforts to promote trade liberalization, human rights, and democratization in Latin America. Disparities of power ensure that American priorities are not constrained by Canada, and Canada can choose the extent to which its policies facilitate or parallel US interests as long as they do not provoke serious domestic controversy. In return, American officials tend to recognize that Canadian governments have greater freedom to cooperate with the United States when their actions do not attract significant publicity.[72]

In some cases, Ottawa might function as a reluctant ally, seeking to avoid antagonizing the United States while attempting to limit its cooperation with American actions – as in Paul Martin's decision to reject Canadian participation in the Ballistic Missile Defense program or the Chrétien government's acceptance of operational leadership of the NATO task force in the Arabian Sea just before the 2003 Iraq War while formally opposing US military action in Iraq. In such cases, domestic political considerations are likely to take priority over the public accommodation of US policy goals – though not precluding technical cooperation away from the public spotlight.

Although recent Canadian governments have occasionally opposed specific American policies outright, they have generally done so in a way associated with multilateral approaches to conflict resolution. However, senior Canadian policy makers tend to recognize that the more or less systematic expression of political sentiments hostile to the United States, or aimed at challenging its leadership and vital interests within the international system, is likely to result in reduced influence and the marginalization of Canadian interests in Washington. Such outcomes are most likely when Canadian governments engage in what Washington views as gratuitous, self-righteous posturing at US expense.[73] The greater the gap between rhetorical activism and the strategic, diplomatic, and humanitarian resources necessary to translate rhetoric into reality, the greater the likelihood that Canada's international policies will lack credibility not only in Washington but also with other major powers.

Under the Martin and Harper governments, Canada has generally been supportive of US initiatives that are broadly consistent with concepts of a liberal international order based on cooperation among states rather than the creation of authoritative international institutions. The latter, in particular, has demonstrated a capacity to appeal to Canadian interests and values – sometimes across partisan lines – in ways that strike the politically necessary balance between cooperating with US foreign and security policies and maintaining a degree of independence or policy discretion.

Opponents of such cooperation[74] suggest that Canada is unlikely to exercise much influence over US policies in such settings, and they are probably correct. Similarly, non-cooperation is unlikely to result in direct American retaliation, though it might reduce the likelihood of White House accommodation of Canadian priorities in other areas[75] – especially those that require congressional support.

Canada's effectiveness in engaging the United States, whether in bilateral, North American, or broader international settings, largely depends on its government's ability to set clear priorities and invest in what Thomas Axworthy has described as "power assets that [can] make Canada a player."[76] It also depends on the capacity of senior Canadian policy makers to maintain and strengthen their institutional access to American leaders, engaging their counterparts in the US executive branch with confidence, consistency, civility, and respect.

Canadian governments' political flexibility in pursuing these goals largely depends on the degree to which US global leadership is seen to be based on cooperation rather than unilateral action and on American leaders' capacity to exercise self-restraint and cultivate shared objectives when engaging the overlapping and often competing interests of both major powers and smaller states.

However, the biggest challenge of coming years will involve Canada's ability to triangulate among the pursuit of its broader interests within North America, which in recent years have been primarily economic, the challenges of engaging an American colossus that faces a period of strenuous economic adjustment, and the emergence of major new economic competitors likely to challenge as much as complement Canadian interests in the international economic system. Facing up to these challenges is the topic of the next chapter.

3

Multilevel Games
The Trade–Commercial Dimension

Relations with the United States have always loomed large for Canadian economic policies. However, they have become absolutely central to Canada's domestic economic policies since negotiation of the Canada–US Free Trade Agreement (CUFTA) in 1986-87. In contrast, Canada is relatively peripheral to *overall* American economic and trade policies and related political debates, whatever the importance of trade and supply chain linkages for many American-based firms, industry sectors, and communities.

These realities pose an interesting strategic challenge for Canadian officials and interest groups seeking to influence American trade and commercial policies toward Canada. These approaches are typically shaped by three broad perspectives. The first approach tends to be strategic and often emphasizes the pursuit of closer North American integration as a priority to be embraced or avoided – depending on the observer's interests or ideological perspective. In recent years, it has included debates over the extent to which Canada should balance its ongoing dependence on American markets with the development and expansion of new and emerging markets for trade and investment.

A second approach is more incremental – emphasizing the contingent and highly decentralized nature of Canada–US and broader North American economic relationships. This approach has often been criticized by others seeking the more assertive federal pursuit of deeper North American integration or, alternately, more diversified trade relations.

A third approach, typical of most business and interest groups as well as government officials with more specialized responsibilities, is to think primarily in sectoral terms. One senior Canadian foreign affairs official suggested that, "as soon as you recognize the limitations of the grand scheme of things, to go sectoral is to have a strategy."[1] The institutional structures that govern most aspects of Canada–US trade tend to be sector– or policy–specific. Therefore, engaging American policies toward Canada effectively requires an extensive knowledge of sectoral policy communities within the executive branch, Congress, and the interest group clusters that are virtually a fourth branch of government.[2]

The dynamic, decentralized, market-driven (or "bottom up") character of economic integration[3] leads economic and policy actors to emphasize the tactical dimension of trade–commercial relations within broader, multilevel policy frameworks discussed further in Parts 2 and 3 of this book. This tactical dimension is central to the work of Canadian diplomats and interest groups in the United States, whether by cultivating shared interests and alliances to "get things done" or, just as often, by keeping others from advancing agendas detrimental to Canadian interests.

Canada's dependence on the United States as its primary export market, though having declined during the past decade (see Table 3.1), increases the sensitivity of Canadians to US trade policy actions that affect them adversely, as demonstrated in case studies analyzed in Chapter 12. Canadian trade policies toward the United States are largely focused on protecting Canadian access to American markets and enhancing the international competitiveness of Canadian industries. However, the frequent focus of American trade policy debates on competitors and markets *beyond* North America makes the effectiveness of Canada's efforts to engage US policies largely dependent on understanding the domestic and international forces shaping broader American trade policies.

This chapter compares and contrasts the place of trade and commercial policies in the foreign and international economic policies of Canada and the United States – examining the latter in the context of American policies toward Canada. It considers the institutional arrangements that govern US international trade and commercial policy relations and their implications for Canadian governments when engaging their American counterparts. Finally, it explores emerging challenges arising from domestic political shifts in the United States and the broader global economy and Canadian governments' emerging responses to these challenges.

TABLE 3.1
Canada's evolving trade patterns, 2000-10

	2000	2002	2004	2006	2008	2010
Goods and services trade			(% of GDP)			
Exports	45.6	41.6	38.4	36.2	35.1	29.4
Imports	39.8	37.1	34.1	33.6	33.5	31.3
Total	85.4	78.7	72.5	69.8	68.7	60.7
Goods exports to US	33.4	30.0	27.2	24.9	23.1	18.3
Goods exports to rest of world	6.5	5.9	6.1	6.4	7.5	6.7
Goods trade surplus with US	8.7	7.9	7.8	6.6	5.5	2.3
Goods trade surplus with rest of world	−2.4	−2.9	−2.7	−3.2	−2.7	−2.8
Average Canadian dollar exchange rate (in $US)	0.673	0.637	0.768	0.882	0.938	0.971

SOURCES: Statistics Canada, *National Income and Expenditure Accounts*, Catalogue 13-001 (Ottawa: Statistics Canada, 2006-11); Statistics Canada, *International Merchandise Trade: Annual Review* (Ottawa: Statistics Canada, 2005-11); Bank of Canada; author's calculations.

A Tale of Two Countries: The Economic–Societal Context

Bilateral trade and commercial policies between Canada and the United States function in very different contexts rooted in their different approaches to the global, hemispheric, North American, and bilateral trade relationships.

The United States is the leading player within the global trading system – albeit one whose role has changed with the emergence of other major economic powers and the industrialization of large parts of Asia and Latin America. The United States is the world's largest importer and was the third largest exporter in 2010, after China and Germany. Canada remains the largest single-country destination for US exports, though exceeded slightly by the twenty-seven countries of the European Union. The United States retains a net surplus in its services trade, which accounts for about 30 percent of its overall exports. Overall US trade grew from 24 to 28 percent of GDP between 2000 and 2010. However, its trade deficit grew steadily from 1.4 percent of GDP in 1991 to 6.8 percent in 2006 before declining to 3.4 percent in 2010. Combined with low domestic savings rates and substantial foreign borrowing to finance chronic budget deficits, the

United States has become the world's largest debtor nation in recent years.[4] These realities reinforce the role of domestic politics in shaping American foreign economic policies. This is particularly true of the sectoral, micro-economic, and related regulatory policies central to the management of US–Canada bilateral relations.

For Canadians, physical proximity has made the United States their most important export market, their largest source of and destination for investment capital, and the central focus of broader economic and indus-trial policies since the mid-1980s. The development of integrated cross-border production networks and supply chains means that most Canadian provinces export more to other countries, primarily the United States, than to other provinces. Moreover, the intensity of trade among Canadian prov-inces and neighbouring American regions has become substantially greater than that with the United States as a whole – suggesting the emergence of cross-border economic regions.[5]

This reality reflects two major shifts in bilateral economic and trade re-lations since the 1980s, reflecting both market-driven factors and the policy choices of national governments. The first major shift, in the mid-1980s, was driven by three major factors. First, gradual trade liberalization and technological change contributed to the restructuring of Canada's manu-facturing industries and the closure of many foreign-controlled branch plants, reinforcing existing trends toward the integration of production and distribution processes across North America. Second, Canadian busi-nesses faced growing risks from US domestic protectionism, expressed through the exploitation by domestic business interests of domestic "trade remedy" laws. Third, the emergence of regional trading blocs in other parts of the world, especially Europe, threatened the competitiveness of Canadian manufacturers often dependent on small domestic markets.[6]

CUFTA addressed these issues by providing tariff-free access to US mar-kets for most Canadian exports. It gave security to Canadian energy ex-ports sought by oil- and gas-producing provinces and non-discrimination ("national treatment") for each country's businesses operating in the other country. A supranational dispute resolution mechanism provided an al-ternative to increasingly politicized US domestic trade remedy processes. Its signing followed a bitterly contested Canadian election in 1988 while scarcely raising a ripple in that year's US presidential race.

When Mexico entered free-trade talks with its American neighbour in 1990, Canada joined the negotiations to protect the gains in its relative se-curity of market access achieved through CUFTA. The resulting North

American Free Trade Agreement (NAFTA), which took effect in 1994, was a combination of trilateral measures affecting all three countries, "dual bilateral agreements," and sectoral opt-outs for each country. It also entrenched the dispute resolution system as a permanent feature of trilateral trade relations.[7]

Both US and Canadian governments saw advantages in pursuing parallel negotiations on CUFTA (and later NAFTA) and the multilateral Uruguay Round negotiations that led to the formation of the World Trade Organization (WTO) in 1994. American negotiators used bilateral and regional negotiations as a way of establishing precedents for the promotion of their global agenda, while Canada sought parallel advantages that would accommodate both export-oriented interests and others dependent primarily on domestic markets.

These policies were consolidated by the Clinton administration and the Chrétien government, reinforcing North American economic integration and an export-led boom. By 2000, exports – mainly to the United States – accounted for 45 percent of Canada's GDP. Both countries pursued hemispheric trade agreements through the Free Trade Agreement of the Americas (FTAA) process during the 1990s. Canada strongly supported the FTAA negotiations, seeing them as a way of avoiding "hub and spoke" economic relations with the United States.

The second major shift in American policies, under the Bush administration, intensified the pursuit of "competitive liberalization"[8] – the use of bilateral agreements to advance the US trade and economic agenda in broader multilateral negotiations in competition with other major economic powers – while making access to US markets largely conditional on trading partners' cooperation with US multilayered security measures after 9/11. Washington negotiated a series of bilateral and regional trade agreements, building alliances to advance its global and hemispheric trade agendas while rewarding countries that had cooperated with other aspects of American foreign policy – notably the "War on Terror" and the Iraq War. These policy shifts preceded the collapse of the FTAA talks in response to the irreconcilable agendas of the hemisphere's two largest economies, the United States and Brazil.

The North American focus of Canadian trade policies was sharply reinforced by the terrorist attacks of 9/11, which resulted in the temporary closing of the Canada–US border. The Chrétien and Martin governments cooperated with US freight and border security measures, if with growing reluctance, but it took some years for the stagnation of global trade talks to push the Harper government into pursuing a series of trade agreements parallel to those already signed by Mexico and the United States. Since 2006, the Harper government has signed treaties with Peru, Panama, Colombia, and, in 2011, Honduras as part of a broader Latin American strategy.[9] It has also initiated a series of trade negotiations aimed at diversifying Canadian trade and investment relations and reducing the potential for trade diversion resulting from competitive liberalization and the spread of preferential trade agreements.

Canada's economic restructuring within North America since 2001 has been complicated by two global economic trends. First was the resurgence of global commodity prices, particularly energy resources, driven by China's unprecedented economic expansion from generational lows during the late 1990s. The value of the Canadian dollar, whose floating exchange rate is sensitive to shifts in commodity prices and other terms of trade, rebounded from its record low of sixty-two cents in January 2002 to levels around parity in early 2008 – greatly increasing competitive pressures on Canadian manufacturers. Energy products' share of overall Canadian exports increased from 8.1 percent in 1999 to 15.2 percent in 2003 and 25.8 percent in 2008 – offset by sharp drops in automotive exports and forest products (see Table 3.2) – before the 2008-9 recession prompted sharp drops in commodity prices and overall trade in North America. These trends have reinforced the heavily regionalized character of Canadian trade, which in turn reflects significant differences in the goods- and tradable services–producing segments of provincial economies.

Second, these trends have produced major qualitative changes in the bilateral economic relationship. Rather than simply selling finished products or raw materials to one another, though this remains an important part of bilateral trade, Canada's manufacturing sector in particular has become integrated into cross-border supply chains involving networks of businesses – both related and unrelated. Intracorporate trade, exchanges among divisions and affiliated firms of corporate networks, was estimated at close to 50 percent of bilateral trade in a 2007 government report.[10]

These developments reflect ongoing economic restructuring involving the geographic dispersion of production functions and the creation of North American and global "value chains" characterized by specialized production of parts and components that Stephen Blank has characterized as "making things together" rather than "selling things to one another."[11] Similar exchanges of investment capital, whether by direct (or controlling) investments by corporations or financial institutions, have blurred traditional

TABLE 3.2
Canada's shifting export patterns, 1999-2010

	1999	2003	2007	2008	2010	1999-2010
	(% of Canadian merchandise exports)					
Automotive products	26.4	21.9	16.6	12.5	14.0	−12.4
Machinery and equipment	24.0	22.2	20.2	18.9	18.8	−5.2
Industrial goods and materials	16.2	16.7	22.6	22.8	23.8	+7.6
Forestry products	10.9	8.6	6.3	5.2	5.4	−5.5
Energy products	8.1	15.2	19.7	25.7	22.5	+14.4
Agricultural and fishing products	6.9	7.3	7.5	8.4	9.1	+2.2
Other consumer goods	3.8	4.3	4.0	3.7	4.1	+0.3

SOURCE: Statistics Canada, *International Merchandise Trade Annual Review,* Catalogue 65-208-XWE (Ottawa: Statistics Canada, 2005-11); author's calculations.

distinctions between Canadian- and American-based firms, rendering traditional Canadian regulatory strategies to control foreign investment increasingly obsolete outside a handful of "strategic" and protected sectors.[12] These trends enhance the challenges for governments of managing interdependence while maintaining the degree of political and policy discretion needed to balance competing interests and secure domestic political support for their policies.

Another effect of the asymmetrical interdependence noted earlier is that there is only limited awareness of the extent or nature of economic interdependence with Canada – whether among policy makers who do not specialize in bilateral relations or broader publics. Former Canadian diplomat Paul Frazer, now a well-connected Washington consultant, notes that "for most Americans who even think of NAFTA, it is a bilateral agreement with Mexico and has nothing to do with Canada."[13]

As a result, US trade and commercial policies toward Canada are often treated – particularly by Congress – as subsets of American domestic policies. Such realities limit Canada's capacity to influence strategic American trade policies. Instead, they lend themselves to the cultivation of bottom-up networks and coalitions using interest group politics to shape sectoral and issue-specific policy processes – reflecting former House speaker Tip O'Neill's dictum that "all politics is local."[14] A former Canadian official based in the southern United States noted that

It's difficult to get the message across about supply lines [sic]. You have to make it personal ... The secret is localizing. You can't generalize about a state-wide economy anymore. North Carolina isn't about furniture and textiles anymore. Life sciences and IT in the Triangle. Financial services in Charlotte. Automobiles and general manufacturing in upstate South Carolina. Aerospace and transportation in Charleston.[15]

The scale and scope of the Canada–US relationship, the challenges of effective policy coordination within both governments, and the practical effects of "intermesticity" largely ensure that "there is no single American policy towards Canada, but rather a number of policies applied at different times."[16]

American Policies toward Canada

The typology of American policies toward Canada discussed in Chapter 1 is clearly seen in the wide range of American trade and commercial policies. The first category, exceptionalism, suggests that American policies toward Canada are distinctive, reflecting the extent to which US- and Canadian-based businesses operate on both sides of the border and reinforcing the influence of cross-border interests and issues on bilateral relations. Canada was only the second country, after Israel, with which the US government negotiated a bilateral trade agreement before 2001. Although Washington subsequently negotiated a series of preferential trade agreements, Canada was one of only two countries, with Mexico, to secure more or less binding dispute resolution panels – a process conspicuously absent in more recent US agreements.[17]

Exceptionalist policies are also visible in a wide range of sectoral policies. Changes to US food safety policies, while clearly driven by American domestic interests following the 2003 discovery of BSE in cattle herds in both countries (see Chapter 12), recognized Canada as the first BSE-affected country to be allowed access to US markets as a "controlled risk" with effective domestic safeguards against contracting and spreading the disease.[18] Arguably, Canada's inclusion in the US government-led restructuring of Chrysler and General Motors in 2009 and the 2010 agreement on subnational government procurement fall into the same category.

The politics of exemptionalism are most visible in the fine-tuning of microeconomic or regulatory initiatives in the day-to-day activities of diplomats, interest groups, and policy makers on each side of the border so that

Canadian citizens or firms are exempted from the application of restrictive US rules applying to foreigners. As a result, exemptionalist policies tend to be visible primarily to policy specialists and diplomats responsible for the quiet negotiation of these exemptions.

For example, major publicly traded Canadian firms have had the right since 1991 to list their shares on US stock exchanges under Multiple Jurisdiction Disclosure System (MJDS) securities regulations without having to undergo detailed regulatory vetting by the US Securities and Exchange Commission – though comparable processes have subsequently been introduced for other foreign issuers. A more recent example is the agreement to negotiate "pre-clearance" of certain truck shipments destined for the United States as part of the "Beyond-the-Border" action plan released in December 2011.[19]

The category of policies toward allies is visible in the rapid growth of specialized international networks to coordinate or negotiate both technical policy and administrative arrangements. The concept of "alliance" is problematic in an international trading system whose major principles include "non-discrimination" among corporate citizens of national signatories to international treaties, though the US Department of State issues annual reports on the extent of cooperation of other countries with US policies promoting intellectual property rights and other policy goals.

However, it is relevant to a multipolar policy environment preoccupied with protecting international supply chains against risks of terrorism and international criminal activities. In recent years, these issues have included the pursuit of enhanced port and container security, air travel security, migration controls, and other policy processes in which national approaches to security are frequently "layered" based on the perceived willingness and capacity of other countries to cooperate with US security practices.

The early twenty-first century has also seen the emergence of China, India, Brazil, and other rapidly growing economies outside North America and the European Union along with the proliferation of bilateral and plurilateral trade agreements. These developments might complement the slow-moving multilateral processes of the WTO. However, they might also serve as forms of trade diversion that limit the capacity of medium-sized economies such as Canada's to diversify their trade and investment relations. Some observers have also suggested that relatively easy access to US markets has reduced the willingness and sometimes the skill sets necessary for major Canadian firms to expand and compete globally.[20]

Canada's relative economic dependence on the United States some-times invites unilateral assertions of American power. This can take the form of *force majeure* – a deliberate, unilateral assertion of power that com-pels Canadian compliance with American policy preferences. Alternatively, Canadian policy makers can negotiate compliance with US policy prefer-ences in ways that admittedly result in less than optimal policy outcomes in the perceived absence of politically viable alternatives. Arguably, the 2006 Softwood Lumber Agreement can be considered an example of *force majeure* in bilateral relations, albeit one cloaked by negotiations intended to frame the precise terms of Canadian compliance to American policy preferences.[21] Some aspects of US border security policies imposed since 9/11, discussed at length in Chapter 9, also fall into this category, though others were negotiated with Canadian officials. Another example, gov-erning the terms of access by Canadian businesses to US defence contracts, are the Department of State's International Trade in Arms (ITARs) restric-tions on the employment of certain dual nationals by US defence contract-ors, including those based in Canada.[22]

However, at a microeconomic level, the most frequent expression of American policies involves their inadvertent application in ways that affect domestic Canadian policy choices. Such actions are often by-products of US domestic bureaucratic processes or interest group competition reflected in congressional legislation. These inadvertent effects can often be modi-fied or countered by effective advocacy through technical, diplomatic, or congressional channels. However, the success of these efforts can depend on limiting the politicization of such issues, thereby avoiding accusations of interference in US domestic political processes or of changing the terms of American policy discussions.

The Institutional Dimension

A fundamental prerequisite of influencing American trade and commer-cial policies toward Canada is a basic understanding of the political dynam-ics and institutional underpinnings of the US trade policy regime. These features include reciprocity (rather than "free trade") as the core principle governing US international trade relations; institutional segmentation and decentralization of political and administrative responsibility for different aspects of US trade and commercial policies, involving all three branches of the US federal government, and often state-level policies; and the centrality of interest group politics in the ongoing dynamics of policy making, legislation, and policy administration.

These realities, reinforced by the relative openness and fragmentation of domestic political and policy processes and the institutionalization of special interest rent seeking,[23] apply even more in managing the trade–commercial dimension of bilateral relations than in broader political, diplomatic, and security relations. As Allan Gotlieb once quipped, "in Washington, a foreign power is itself only a special interest, and not a very special one at that."[24]

Reciprocity: The Basis of US Trade Relations

> *Canada is not a huge market. There's more moose than people up there.*
>
> *– Mike Boyd, US aviation consultant, 2008*[25]

The policy of reciprocity – the reduction of barriers to market access for imported goods and services in return for expanded access to (and security in) foreign markets for American goods, services, and, in some cases, investment – is the central pillar of modern US trade policy. A key feature of this strategy is the preservation of discretion, including "trade remedy" legislation, to guard against practices seen as conferring unfair competitive advantages. Another is the "bargaining tariff" (or regulatory measures with comparable effects) – the use of protectionist measures by Congress as tools to secure reciprocal concessions by foreign countries.[26]

This outlook leads many American policy makers to evaluate potential trade agreements either on their contribution to increasing market access for American exporters or on offsetting potential adjustment costs faced by domestic producers competing with lower-cost imports. It can also lead politicians to speak of "enforcing" agreements unilaterally when the behaviour of other countries or foreign businesses is seen to fall short of their political expectations.

The prospective growth of trade with Canada does not offer significant gains from expanding market access compared with many emerging economies. The growth of US trade with Canada has been only marginally greater than the average of that with other industrial economies since 1994, thus explaining the Bush administration's pursuit of greater market access in other parts of the world – primarily the Asia-Pacific region and Latin America. Large, entrenched trade deficits have also convinced many Americans that the rules of the international economic system are stacked against them – increasing the traditional importance of interest group politics in shaping American trade policies.

These outlooks create significant challenges for Canadian officials attempting to persuade American policy makers that closer cooperation with Canada – including the investment of significant political and bureaucratic resources in highly technical negotiations – is warranted by the scale of probable economic benefits. Much of the responsibility for making these arguments must be borne by US domestic groups whose interests happen to coincide with those of their Canadian counterparts.[27] Even when such negotiations do occur, as under the SPP and the more recent US–Canada Regulatory Cooperation Council processes, they are usually subject to the domestic constraints of participating agencies.[28]

The Diffusion of Power

The second core reality of engaging American trade and commercial policies is the diffused political and administrative responsibility for such policies. These responsibilities are distributed across numerous executive departments and agencies, congressional committees, and regulatory and judicial processes that are far from transparent and often bewildering to the untrained observer.

Gotlieb observes that these realities are rooted in the constitutional separation of powers in the United States and the "sub-separation of powers" among congressional committees and subcommittees, reinforcing congressional tendencies "to use domestic laws to achieve foreign [policy] goals" – particularly in supporting domestic economic interests.[29] Thus, the politics of trade help to blur traditional distinctions between the workings of domestic and international policy, transforming large elements of Canada–US relations into a series of hybrid, "intermestic" policy relationships in which American policies toward Canada are often subsets of US domestic policies.

Constitutional responsibility for trade policies and commercial legislation is vested in Congress. Congress organizes its functional responsibilities by functional area of specialization – in hundreds of committees and subcommittees (see Chapter 8). The power to initiate tariff changes is vested in the House Ways and Means Committee. However, dozens of other committees and subcommittees claim jurisdiction over various aspects of trade-related policies – particularly those relating to overlapping areas of domestic regulation. Legislation and the appropriations (spending) necessary to implement it generally require separate legislative authority – thus allowing key senators and representatives to fine-tune, or even obstruct, implementation through their respective committees in response to special interests or their own personal agendas. In recent years, these opportunities have also been exploited by alliances of US and Canadian interests to delay the implementation of several restrictive measures harmful to both, including funding of country-of-origin labelling (COOL) and regulations to implement the WHTI passport initiative (see Chapter 11).

Although both parties sought to recentralize power somewhat in recent years, especially in the House of Representatives, the effects of these changes are much greater on major legislative measures than on the microeconomic and regulatory issues that preoccupy most areas of bilateral relations from day to day.

As a result, former Canadian ambassador Frank McKenna comments that foreign governments must often negotiate with two distinct American governments, the executive branch and Congress, neither of which is a unitary actor.[30] American political scientist Judith Goldstein observes that support by a specific institution for more open trade generally increases with the size of its members' constituencies, being greatest with the White House, followed by senators (especially from large coastal states that benefit most from trade). Members of the House are often the most parochial and protectionist. "The result is a log-roll in which all interests are accommodated; the cost is a sub-optimal collective policy."[31]

To impose some order on this process, Congress periodically delegates the right to negotiate trade agreements to the president, subject to terms defined in enabling legislation. Such agreements are usually submitted to Congress as executive agreements, thus requiring only a majority vote of each House rather than the two-thirds Senate vote required for treaties.[32] To limit special interest pressures to renegotiate such agreements, it can also extend Trade Promotion Authority (TPA), also known as "fast track," to allow an "up or down" vote (without amendments) within ninety days of their formal submission to Congress. Periodic trade bills usually extend TPA for fixed periods – as with the October 1987 deadline for submission of CUFTA to Congress.[33]

The presence of TPA permitted the negotiation of several major trade treaties between 1975 and 1994, culminating in NAFTA and the Uruguay Round treaty, and again between 2002 and 2007. However, the domestic political backlash against globalization and NAFTA led Congress to withdraw fast-track authority between 1995 and 2002, reflecting the growing strength of protectionist coalitions within Congress and the American public.[34] The Democratic-controlled Congress elected in 2006 withheld TPA from President Bush, forcing him to renegotiate two trade treaties and reducing the likelihood of others. I will discuss the implications of these developments later in the context of future US trade policies in North America.

Responsibility for trade and commercial policies within the executive branch is fragmented still further. The Office of the US Trade Representative (USTR) coordinates negotiations on international trade agreements – whether multilateral (through the WTO), regional, or bilateral. The sprawling Department of Commerce oversees trade promotion, administration of trade laws, as well as negotiation of technical regulatory provisions under working-group processes established under NAFTA and later the SPP. However, the four main bureaus of the Department of Commerce – Commercial Services (trade commissioners and diplomats); Import Admin- istration (enforcing trade remedy laws and other import regulations); Manufacturing and Services (further divided by economic sector and in- dustry); Market Access and Compliance (negotiating and implementing trade agreements) – usually function autonomously from one another. As one official commented, "you can work for thirty years in one component of Commerce and not interact much with the others."[35] The Canada Desk, located in Market Access and Compliance, deals with many aspects of trade policies relating to Canada.

Responsibility for other regulatory policies affecting trade is widely dis- tributed among and within particular executive departments. Commerce officials have limited leverage with other departments in promoting broad- er policy objectives, reflecting the relative weakness of interagency process- es relating to Canada and the deference generally given to "subject matter experts" in other departments.[36]

New regulatory initiatives must conform to rules established by the Office for Information and Regulatory Affairs (OIRA), located within the Office of Management and Budget. These processes are enforceable by stakeholders through the federal courts. Related requirements for stakeholder consulta- tions provide extensive opportunities for interest groups (and foreign gov- ernments) to engage federal regulatory processes.

These groups often resort to litigation as a tactic to strengthen their standing within regulatory processes or secure judicial support for their policy goals. Repeated special interest litigation has been a consistent factor in stringing out regulatory processes for numerous cross-border projects, ranging from the reopening of borders to Canadian cattle exports in 2003-5, to ongoing battles over the building of the Keystone XL pipeline in 2010-12, and to the "megaloads" controversy regarding the shipping of components for oil sands expansion.[37]

Responsibility for domestic trade litigation rests with the Department of Commerce, subject to review by the US Court of International Trade or, for Canada and Mexico, binational dispute resolution panels formed under NAFTA's Chapter 19 for most trade disputes and Chapter 11 for investment-related disputes. Both US domestic legislation and trade remedy rulings are also subject to varying degrees of recourse under WTO dispute resolution processes, though such recourse is uncertain, slow, and subject to extended negotiations and political foot-dragging.[38]

Taken together, these complex institutional structures contribute to a kaleidoscopic montage of policies, rules, processes, and related political dynamics that require extensive specialized knowledge to navigate effectively. These realities reinforce tendencies to decentralize responsibility for managing cross-border policies within the Canadian government, often making them situational and dependent on close working relations with American counterparts from the cabinet level to working levels of the bureaucracy.[39]

On major disputes, Canadian prime ministers might attempt to circumvent these cumbersome processes by appealing directly to the White House, often with the intention of initiating high-level negotiations to resolve such problems. However, though such appeals can be successful, there is no guarantee that American presidents and their senior advisers will put a high priority on the accommodation of Canadian interests.

Interest Group Politics

These realities ensure that, despite the general commitment of most presidents and their senior trade policy advisers to trade liberalization, these policies are open to challenges by numerous domestic interests facing increased foreign competition along with stagnant or declining American living standards since the late 1990s.[40]

These reservations are at the heart of US domestic "trade remedy" legislation and contemporary "fair trade" campaigns seeking to force foreign producers to accept regulatory requirements comparable to those facing American producers. Similar measures have been proposed to limit imports that fail to meet US domestic environmental standards. Although such pressures are predictable responses to declines in the business cycle, they reflect the widespread public perception that borders should be reinforced in the name of "economic security" or "levelling the playing field."

US trade laws have institutionalized elaborate processes for consulting with Congress, state governments, and major stakeholders on ongoing international trade negotiations. Domestic producer interests might pursue relief from increased international competition by resorting to trade remedy laws or lobbying Congress for increased protection. Such actions are typically related to levels of domestic economic activity and major variations in import volumes facing specific industries, though some interest groups, such as the sugar lobby and coastal shipping industry, are so deeply entrenched in the rent-seeking game that they resist any threat to their privileges.[41] Of course, Canadian supply management policies attract similar criticisms from Canadian consumer groups and foreign competitors.

As a result, any Canadian strategy to engage American trade or regulatory policies must include provisions for identifying and mobilizing particular interest groups and policy advocates, whether in Washington or "beyond the beltway," to engage in parallel advocacy and lobbying of the executive branch, Congress, and state governments. Paul Frazer, a veteran Washington observer of cross-border policy, noted that "the government can't do it alone. It needs the private sector. People on the Hill expect people to come in and talk to them. But they need to do their homework. And it's helpful if they come in as part of a Canadian–US business coalition."[42]

However, this is only one dimension of the ongoing game of special interest rent seeking within Congress and different parts of the executive branch. The politics of American trade policy – and of a great many related regulatory issues – is a highly competitive arena in which Canadian governments and economic interests are often engaged. The next section examines some of the processes by which Canadian interests seek to influence the American political process.

US Government Responses

The global and North American contexts for Canadian governments attempting to engage US trade policies have changed fundamentally since the late 1990s – notwithstanding the continuing realities of economic interdependence and bottom-up economic integration.

Rising resource prices, a Canada–US exchange rate hovering at or near parity, and growing Asian competition have fundamentally changed the competitive context for many Canadian industries. Unsustainable fiscal and economic policies and growing political polarization have seriously undercut the elite political consensus on international trade liberalization in the United States without replacing it with a viable alternative. Ongoing domestic conflicts over immigration policies and concerns over the effects of Mexico's narco-insurgency on US border management policies have shifted the focus of Canadian political and economic elites toward an emphasis on "dual bilateralism" rather than the SPP's incipient trilateralism in the years 2005-8.[43] Minority parliaments between 2004 and 2011 largely precluded Canadian governments from pursuing grand policy visions, but so have the competing interests of provincial governments, which retain constitutional authority over the development of natural resources and serve as powerful advocates of regional industries on trade, investment, and other economic development issues.

Combined with the progressive decentralization of policy processes in both countries discussed in Chapter 1, these pressures have tended to privilege incremental, sector-specific approaches to cross-border policy relations. This section summarizes the approaches taken by Canadian governments and societal interests, especially major business groups in managing the two-level and multilevel games of policy relations in an increasingly globalized context.

Strategic and Sectoral Initiatives

The federal government might have an evolving strategy for projecting Canadian interests in bilateral and North American economic relations – a process that includes influencing American policies toward Canada. However, it has not always been readily apparent to officials who have responsibility for the implementation of its different components – or to large segments of the "Canada policy community" in the United States.[44] Discerning the nature and priorities of such a strategy requires moving beyond the rhetoric of public engagement on bilateral or North American issues and engaging the many government officials and stakeholders actually engaged in these processes.

Arguably, the priorities of Canadian governments in bilateral trade relations have been fairly consistent since 2001 – even though their means of engagement might have evolved. Maintaining Canadian access to US markets has been the most important priority for the Chrétien, Martin, and Harper governments, particularly in response to the risks of border closings or "thickening" as a result of assorted American security and regulatory measures. As discussed in Chapter 11, the policy tools used to support this objective have been highly contingent, sector-specific, and responsive to conditions shaping or limiting the capacity for cross-border coalition building. In many cases, these policies have involved close cooperation with major business groups with substantial interests in maintaining and enhancing access to US markets.

However, notwithstanding rhetorical debates surrounding the SPP, no Canadian government has embraced business proposals for comprehensive negotiations leading to significantly deeper integration.[45] The US–Canada Regulatory Cooperation Council created in June 2011, while providing opportunities to "break down regulatory barriers" between the two countries, appears to be a continuation of the incremental approach.[46] Its effectiveness is likely to be linked to that of President Obama's regulatory review process announced the previous month.[47]

Successive governments have embraced the selective coordination of regulatory and other policy initiatives, usually at the subsectoral or micropolicy level, to facilitate the workings of integrated production and distribution networks. However, they have also sought to maintain political and policy discretion in many areas to manage the asymmetries between the two countries – including major differences in their economic structures and federal systems. At an operational level, as discussed in Part 2, the Martin and Harper governments have expanded Canada's diplomatic capacities in the United States as part of an increasingly systematic effort to identify US domestic actors whose interests or policy goals overlap sufficiently with those of Canadian governments to serve as allies in engaging American domestic policy processes.

Central to these efforts have been the use of "summit diplomacy" to facilitate transgovernmental cooperation on key policy and regulatory issues, discussed in Chapter 5; an expanded emphasis on public diplomacy in the United States, discussed in Chapters 7 and 8; cooperation on border security issues aimed at facilitating cross-border trade and travel, addressed in Chapter 10; and the broadening of bilateral and regional trade agreements in response to US and Mexican strategies of competitive liberalization.[48] Provincial governments have also played a growing role since the 1990s through cross-border networks of premiers, governors, and legislators, discussed in Chapter 9. However, these initiatives must often compete with the pressures of political crisis management: the resolution of major cross-border irritants that threaten to undermine or derail broader efforts at cooperation.

The Smart Border Accord of December 2001 was an effective response by the Chrétien government to trade disruptions caused by post-9/11 border closings and slowdowns. However, its positive effects in facilitating border management were limited by the complexities of security politics in both countries and bilateral conflicts over the Iraq War.[49] The accord later provided a model for closer political and transgovernmental cooperation through the SPP process initiated in 2005. However, the latter suffered from bureaucratic agenda overload, a lack of sustained political commitment from national leaders, inadequate processes for agenda management, and widespread public suspicion arising from its lack of transparency before it was suspended by the Obama administration in early 2009. However, it created ongoing processes for summit diplomacy and regular cabinet-level meetings that provide useful outlets for managing bilateral and sometimes trilateral policy issues.

The Washington Declaration of February 2011 on perimeter security and regulatory cooperation and the subsequent Action Plans released in December 2011 are the latest iterations of this process. However, their effectiveness remains heavily contingent on domestic political trends in each country – not least the willingness of both national leaders to invest significant political capital in political as well as bureaucratic initiatives to advance these agendas.[50]

Promoting greater American awareness of the benefits of economic interdependence with Canada, both in general and in highly specific geographical and sectoral terms, has become a central focus for Canadian public diplomacy in the United States, as discussed in Part 2. The Harper government has done a better job than its predecessors in managing the "two-audience problem" – the tendency of Canadian politicians visiting the United States to confuse the management of bilateral relations and domestic politics by emphasizing messages primarily of interest to domestic Canadian audiences.

This process is complicated by the politics of crisis management: the tendency of a single, major irritant in cross-border relations to become the principal focus of Canadian diplomacy in the United States and public attitudes to bilateral relations in Canada. During the past decade, these realities were reflected in the WHTI passport debates of 2004-9 (see Chapter 11), the protracted softwood lumber dispute of 2001-6, and the Buy American controversy of 2009-10 (see Chapter 12) despite the overall decline in bilateral trade disputes since the end of the 2001-2 recession.[51] Table 3.3 notes the declining frequency of US trade remedy cases during the past

TABLE 3.3
US trade remedy investigations and actions, 2000–10

	Initiation		Preliminary ruling		Final ruling		Duty order imposed	
	World	Canada	World	Canada	World	Canada	World	Canada
2000-2	187	11	145	10	143	9	89	6
2003-6	96	4	74	2	69	2	42	0
2007-10	97	1	62	1	61	1	53	1
Total	380	16	281	13	273	12	184	7
Canada as percent of world								
2000-2		5.9		6.9		6.3		6.7
2003-10		2.6		2.2		2.3		1.1

SOURCE: Import Administration, US Department of Commerce, "Antidumping and Countervailing Duty Investigations Initiated after January 01, 2000" (Washington, DC: Department of Commerce, n.d.); author's calculations.

decade. Indeed, only one trade remedy dispute was initiated against Canada under US law between 2006 and 2011 (concurrently with a 2008 case against China). When placed in the broader contexts of each country's trade policies and flows, these debates illustrate the degree to which bilateral relations can be distracted by the side effects of domestic American political debates and reveal the relatively limited constituency in Washington for closer North American integration except, perhaps, as a by-product of ongoing market forces.

However, the bilateral economic relationship is much broader than this focus on recurring sectoral trade disputes. Perhaps the most significant development in the trade–commercial dimension of Canada–US relations in recent years has been their growing integration with broader trade and economic negotiations and emerging global governance structures. This trend is visible in the two countries' cooperation in several international settings, including the G-8, the G-20, and the Major Economies Forum.

Since taking office in 2006, the Harper government has attempted to play "catch-up" with the Bush administration's strategy of competitive liberalization in broader international trade relations – negotiating a series of bilateral trade agreements with the European Free Trade Association, Peru, Panama, Colombia, Jordan, and Honduras. In 2009, it initiated wide-ranging talks with the European Union on trade and related regulatory issues, with a treaty signing expected in 2012. Additional negotiations have been initiated with South Korea, India, the Caribbean Community, the Dominican Republic, the "Central American Four," Singapore, and the Trans-Pacific Partnership.[52] With the exception of the EU and TPP negotiations, most of these arrangements have limited economic significance in the short term. However, they address a fundamental challenge arising from competitive liberalization: the emergence of "hub and spoke" trade relations that increase the costs of administering trade conducted through complex supply chains due to complex rules of origin.

Micropolicy Engagement

The reality of bilateral trade and commercial relations is rooted in the extensive interaction and interdependence of the two countries' citizens, businesses, and governments at different levels that will be addressed in greater detail in subsequent chapters: intergovernmental relations with both the executive branch and Congress; public diplomacy inside and beyond the Washington beltway; cross-border initiatives between provincial and state governments; and cross-border cooperation among business and other societal groups.

The absence of effective interagency coordination on cross-border issues in either government has usually resulted in the substantial devolution of degrees of responsibility for managing bilateral issues to officials of line (or executive) departments and agencies: Industry (and Commerce), Energy (and Natural Resources), Public Safety (and Homeland Security), Environment, Transportation, Agriculture, and so on. The task forces on border and regulatory coordination issues arising from the Washington Declaration of February 2011, which were led initially by Privy Council Office and US National Security Council staff, respectively, are partial exceptions to this pattern. The effective management of bilateral relations requires ongoing efforts by politicians and senior and working-level officials to cultivate close relationships with their American counterparts to manage issues at a technical level wherever possible, limit the politicization of disputes, identify political boundaries or "no go" zones, and establish areas in which political intervention is necessary to secure politically and administratively viable compromises on contested issues.

These processes call for considerable political and institutional awareness and tactical skills in engaging each country's very different political and bureaucratic culture. The open and contested character of American political processes – particularly those involving Congress – ensures that, even if issues are managed successfully through one electoral cycle, they can resurface if supported by persistent societal interests or advocates in Congress. These realities require constant attention to political and policy intelligence by cultivating policy networks and prospective "friends of Canada" as long-term investments in political goodwill and policy capacity that transcend the short-term political horizons of elected officials.

Shifting Directions for Trade Relations?

Economic and policy trends during past decades might have made Canadian trade and investment policies more *outward* looking – whatever the effects of minority Parliaments on Canadian governments' willingness to take significant political risks. However, they have had the opposite effects on US trade policies and, more importantly, the domestic political climate that shapes those policies, suggesting the emergence of the third major shift in the broader environment for bilateral trade and economic relations since the 1980s.[53] Major contributing factors include a decade of rising trade deficits (until 2008), growing economic insecurity among Americans, and intense partisan and societal polarization during the Bush and Obama years. The entrenched power of protectionist interests in Congress, the puncturing of the credit bubble of the Clinton–Bush era, and sharply increased economic intervention under the Obama administration have reinforced these trends. Although these shifts are not directed at Canada as much as at redefining US economic relations with the rest of the world, they have profound implications for Canadian interests, which often depend on securing a place in the American economic tent while adapting to broader global trends.

Decentralized American policy-making processes within both the executive branch and Congress, along with the checks and balances that often impel policy makers to negotiate differences in priorities and interests, suggest that proposed policy changes are likely to be negotiated sector by sector as dictated by the balance of competing interests within the administration and a divided Congress. However, the ideological polarization of American politics could result just as easily in an extended period of partisan gridlock. Absent significant changes in the American domestic political climate, these realities are likely to leave other industrial nations, including Canada, on the outside looking in. Negotiating room on specific issues or the potential for policy parallelism – the pursuit of similar policies characterized by common goals but different mixes of policy instruments reflecting different national political environments[54] – will largely depend on the degree to which their interests and priorities are similar to those driving US policies. This pattern, which has characterized the Obama administration's term in office, is likely to continue through the next electoral cycle – whatever the outcome of the 2012 elections.

On some issues, the traditional US commitment to reciprocity in international economic policies provides opportunities for complementary or parallel Canadian policies that accommodate differences between the two countries' economic and regulatory structures.

The Obama administration's insistence that national responses to the financial crisis of 2008-9 be rooted in national policy decisions reflecting different institutional realities, rather than the creation of a global regulatory system advocated by European leaders, won strong Canadian support – if only because of benefits seen to result from existing differences in financial markets and regulatory structures. The decision of the Bush and Obama administrations to bail out and supervise the restructuring of bankrupt General Motors and Chrysler prompted the Harper government to secure a coordinated response based on a proportionate investment to protect the Canadian industry against the prospect of unilateral American action. More challenging, however, will be engaging the unpredictable evolution of US environmental and energy policies, discussed in Chapter 13.

The conventional wisdom in Canadian trade and economic policies is that prospects for further growth in Canada–US trade are largely linked to greater regulatory harmonization, embracing a variety of policy fields somewhat distant from traditional notions of trade policy and subject to independent congressional initiatives, oversight, and review. However, it is unclear how the newly formed US–Canada Regulatory Cooperation Council will engage or overcome the insecurity and defensiveness of congressional and public opinion, let alone entrenched (and bipartisan) resistance within Congress to sacrificing the latter's institutional prerogatives.[55]

These trends offer little encouragement to Canadians who seek to renew the special relationship of the postwar years – at least in ways that would allow for widespread adaptation of American policies or institutional processes to Canadian preferences.[56] The postwar special relationship emerged from a position of unprecedented American strength relative to the rest of the world, reinforced by shared worldviews and policy goals among senior policy makers and the mutual advantage to be gained by countries at different stages of economic development. It is hard to discern comparable conditions for a new special relationship amid the economic insecurity, relative weakness, and special-interest-dominated politics that currently constrain

American capacity for global economic leadership and the pursuit of mutual advantage with both larger and smaller powers in the global economic system. The United States is undoubtedly capable of transcending such challenges, as it has in the past. However, such developments will require a new political and economic synthesis that provides more credible answers to domestic and global challenges than those currently on offer from America's deeply polarized political classes.

Ultimately, Canada's capacity to engage American policy makers effectively will depend in part on the kind of cross-border diplomacy, private and public, discussed in Parts 2 and 3 of this book. It will also depend on its ability to expand what Sands describes as its "third country" connections: initiatives that strengthen policy and economic linkages with other countries. Such measures can complement American policies while contributing to a rules-based framework for international economic relations beneficial to Canada as a trade-dependent nation. Alternatively, they can provide Canadians with broader policy choices that allow the negotiation of overlapping policy goals rather than unilateral compliance with US policy preferences.

The Harper government's decision to negotiate a network of trade agreements with countries in the Western hemisphere and beyond, most of which already have trade agreements with the United States and/or Mexico, falls into the first category. The absolute value of these agreements in diversifying trade is limited. However, they facilitate a potential future negotiating framework for a common North American external tariff that would enable the relaxation of many costly customs measures when political conditions in Washington become more accommodating to such objectives. Wide-ranging discussions on trade and regulatory issues with the European Union are likely to address many technical issues that are increasingly the subject of multilateral trade negotiations, just as past Canada–US trade negotiations provided workable policy options for multilateral trade negotiations. Just as important in the long term, if not more so, are discussions with India and China on reciprocal investment protection agreements to provide greater legal transparency for Canadian companies doing business in those countries and, more controversially, state-sponsored entities from those countries doing business in Canada.

Such initiatives might enable Canadian businesses to expand their international networks amid the ongoing evolution of the global economy. However, trade and investment agreements might enable but are not a substitute for the building of organic relationships among businesses that allow for the enduring growth of trade and investment. "Bottom-up" supply chain linkages that create international communities of interest usually take longer to forge than do formal trade agreements, especially when bridging significant geographical and cultural barriers.

Such a strategy – reinforced to a degree by shifts in exchange rates and terms of trade discussed above – can help to reduce American perceptions that Canada is sufficiently dependent on US markets to be an economic dependent of the United States and thus taken for granted in its trade relations. However, given the geographic proximity and economic integration already present between the two countries, it is not a substitute for the nurturing of close bilateral relations.

This analysis suggests that the diverse and decentralized character of American trade and commercial policies invites a multitracked set of Canadian responses – purposeful enough to strengthen and diversify trade links inside and outside North America but flexible enough to anticipate and respond to the multiple issues and competing interests striving for influence in the American political system.

4

Neighbo(u)rs, Friends, and Strangers
The Psychological–Cultural Dimension

A central element, and truth, is that we don't understand
the United States: how its society works or how its system of
government works. We imagine the Americans think about
us but they don't.

– David Dyment, Doing the Continental, *2010*[1]

One of the greatest challenges of Canadian politicians and diplomats attempting to influence US policies toward Canada is that of dealing with public opinions and expectations in each country as reflections of significantly different political cultures. As noted in previous chapters, Canada is largely an afterthought of the American political classes except for the relatively small number whose political or economic interests are directly and substantially affected by cross-border relations. But American political, economic, and cultural influences are inescapable realities of Canadian life, provoking emotions and responses ranging from attraction and selective emulation to revulsion, resentment, and self-absorbed claims of moral superiority.

Recognizing and finding ways to compensate for differences in size and power are central to managing bilateral relations on economic and security issues that have shaped Canada–US relations during the past generation. However, these differences are even more acute in dealing with what Doran has characterized as the "psychological–cultural dimension" of the relationship: the historical and contemporary outlooks of each country toward itself, its place in the world, and its relations with other countries, as reflected in the influence of domestic politics on each country's foreign policies and other cross-border relationships.[2]

Both Canadian policies toward the United States and US policies toward Canada are profoundly influenced by domestic politics, political cultures, and attitudes toward the other – but in very different ways. As a result, how Canadian politicians and diplomats address bilateral issues or dealings within broader international institutions is often heavily influenced by their expectations and perceptions of domestic publics' responses.

Even so, there are significant parallels in the domestic political contexts that shape bilateral relations in both countries, whatever the differences in the attention that each country's policy makers or citizens pay to the other. There is broad popular support in both countries for maintaining both the forms and the substance of political sovereignty and policy discretion rather than delegating extensive authority to supranational institutions. Each country's relative political and economic openness to the other reflects relative levels of economic security and perceived risks of social dislocation from broader economic trends.

However, both countries' policy makers and citizens often project domestic political norms and conflicts into their expectations of their neighbour's behaviour. With the complacency of assumed familiarity with "the other," such attitudes can often take the form of smug self-absorption and self-righteousness – particularly among those who seek to exploit such differences in the pursuit of ideological conflicts in their own country. Critics of such attitudes have frequently labelled them the "narcissism of small differences."[3]

This chapter compares and contrasts Canadians' profoundly ambivalent and often conflicted attitude toward their southern neighbour with official and societal attitudes toward Canada in the United States. It notes the effects of political culture as a constraining or enabling variable in determining the consideration or exclusion of political options. Using published polling data from each country, it summarizes the contexts in which relevant attitudes have evolved in recent years, reflecting different trends in political and societal relationships and policy cycles of relative closeness and alienation.

The chapter examines the realities of mutual insecurity that dominated bilateral relations after the 9/11 terrorist attacks and how these realities interacted with economic insecurities that were encouraging growing protectionism even before the credit crisis and recession of 2007-9. Finally, it suggests ways that governments can engage the cultural and psychological similarities, differences, and sensitivities in each country to cultivate a political environment conducive to both cooperation and mutual accommodation while working within their distinctive political systems and cultures.

Communicating within and across Political Cultures

A central theme of this book is the reality of Canada–US relations as a two- or multilevel game in which each country's government must build domestic coalitions capable of promoting its view of the national interest on particular issues while building cross-border coalitions with like-minded institutions and interests.

Acknowledging the similarities and differences of political cultures – the principal attitudes, beliefs, and values that shape the workings of political systems – in each country is critical to this process. "Playing the game" is central when trying to shape a viable policy consensus, injecting particular interests or policy objectives into an emerging consensus, or seeking ways to block specific measures until the system accommodates such interests. However, doing this first requires policy diplomats, policy makers, and interest groups to determine the nature of the "games" in question.

Navigating these cultural patterns is often complicated by institutionalized differences in the legislative, administrative, intergovernmental, and interest group cultures of Ottawa and Washington that are only dimly understood, if at all, by Canadians who lack experience in engaging the American political system.

Political culture has always been a major constraining or enabling variable in determining the consideration or exclusion of political options in bilateral relations – especially in Canada. It has shaped the foreign and security policy balancing acts between relative autonomy and influence in engaging US foreign and security policies, the means chosen to expand and secure trade and investment relations in different political eras, the interaction of water and other environmental policies, and the symmetries and asymmetries of transportation systems, policies, and networks, to name only a few.[4]

In Canada–US relations, and more specifically Canadian efforts to influence American policies toward Canada, the effects of political culture are often expressed as psychological expectations of and responses to the other at multiple levels. The multilevel and multidimensional nature of political cultures can be seen in the similarities and differences among broader societal attitudes in the two countries, their exploitation to serve partisan political interests or agendas on particular issues, distinctions among popular outlooks and those of governing elites, and the relevance of bureaucratic cultures to the "below the radar" elements that dominate transgovernmental relations between the two countries.

The workings of cross-border relations also reflect the reality that neither country is typically a "unitary actor" on most aspects of bilateral relations. Both public attitudes and bureaucratic interactions take varied forms that reflect the very different practical and symbolic value of the relationship to the citizens of each country as a whole and the specific mix of opportunities, assets, risks, and threats involved in particular issues and initiatives. Just as Canada and most Canadians place greater relative importance on the bilateral relationship than do the United States and Americans, Canadians attempting to influence US government policies toward Canada must acknowledge that Canada per se is of limited relevance to American political culture. Even so, many aspects of American political culture – including public attitudes toward the outside world, the roles and limits of governments, public participation in decision making, the constitutional prerogatives of various institutions, and the domestic contests over political power and ideology – are vital in determining whether American policy priorities accommodate or challenge particular Canadian interests, along with Canadians' sometimes fragile self-esteem. The next section explores some major ways in which these cross-cutting realities frame the Canadian domestic contexts for cross-border relations.

Canadian Attitudes toward the United States: Identity, Attraction, and Differentiation

> *It is not the U.S. that is the problem, but how we think about the U.S. Our relationship is not about them as much as it is about us.*
>
> – David Dyment, Doing the Continental, 2010[5]

The salience of domestic politics in both countries is critical for Canadian governments attempting to engage and, to some extent, influence American policies toward Canada. This reality has always been central to Canadian domestic political dynamics as a reflection of the belief systems of Canadians and especially political and cultural elites. It has been said that "Canadians are the original un-Americans." Indeed, a certain strain of moral superiority, mixed with smugness and insecurity, is central to Canadian political culture as it relates to the United States.[6]

These attitudes can also be seen in recurring cycles of insecurity and self-assertion when dealing with its giant American neighbour. Charles Doran has noted the importance of these cycles in the broader contours of the relationship, with both decision makers and publics in each country alternating between more outward- and inward-looking, optimistic and defensive, perspectives.[7] The latter have been most prominent during periods of relative American assertiveness, particularly in foreign and security policies, especially if reinforced by the relative decline of American global economic leadership – as in the late 1960s and 1970s or under the leadership of George W. Bush during the prolonged US conflict in Iraq (2003-9). At other times, American insecurity can prompt efforts by Canada to pursue more secure economic relationships – as in the aftermath of the 1981-82 recession or after the 9/11 terrorist attacks in New York and Washington. Allan Gotlieb has described this sometimes simultaneous approach to pursuing shared interests and "value-driven" policy differentiation as the "bipolar" impulse in Canadians' views of Canada's place in the world.[8]

This pursuit of a distinct political and/or cultural identity should not be confused with anti-Americanism – a more or less systematic mistrust of or bias against the United States[9] – though both realities have long coexisted in Canadian political culture. Such sentiments can be seen in what Mark Milke describes as the "Loyalist myth" of Canada's founding or in Reginald Stuart's description of the efforts of successive generations to establish a society that has both small and often significant differences from the United States, particularly those of political and social institutions, and extensive similarities, especially in matters of popular culture and social interaction.[10] Nationalist attitudes exist independently of attitudes toward the United States but can be strongly reinforced by them, especially if driven by political or ideological goals currently out of favour in the American political system.

The politics of identity is closely linked to nationalist discourses that have asserted the promotion of strong sovereign national (or governmental) institutions that enable Canada's federal (and sometimes provincial) governments to secure effective policy autonomy, often explicitly *from* American political influence or control.[11] Such policies can promote a particular view of the national interest (and the related interests of specific people, companies, and groups embedded within it) or sometimes the pursuit of difference for its own sake. This discourse can be philosophical or explicitly ideological, emphasizing Canadian distinctiveness (or American untrustworthiness) as a bearer of liberal, social democratic, or other values in domestic and/or international politics. Leading examples include Pierre Trudeau's "third national policy" of 1980-82, Minister of Foreign Affairs Lloyd Axworthy's efforts to promote Canada as a "norm entrepreneur" in international relations during the 1990s, and persistent opposition by organized labour and assorted activist groups to economic globalization and North American integration.[12]

Political leaders might attempt to exploit such sentiments for partisan advantage – often by castigating their opponents as beholden to American interests (or "American" ideas) or insufficiently attentive to "Canadian" ones – as if these ideas and policies can be neatly packaged in ways that serve the interests of all or most Canadians. On some occasions, these differences might reflect genuine conflicts over the national interest. At others, they are driven by short-term political calculations and opportunism.[13] Of course, campaigns can be driven by both sets of calculations. High-profile examples include attacks by public sector unions (and their acolytes) on supporters of greater competition as advocates of "American-style" health care; or the delight with which supporters of domestic oil and gas development stigmatize their opponents as financially dependent on American foundations and environmental lobbies intent on undermining Canada's national economic interests.[14]

At the same time, Canadians have long sought to take advantage of their proximity to the United States to get the most they can from the relationship – whether in investments, markets for their products and services, recognition of their contributions to international peace and security, or the opportunities for favoured treatment that often come from "friendship" with a great power. Tensions between these twin preoccupations have long been the source of conflicts *within* Canada and the ambivalent attitudes of many Canadians toward the United States. The efforts of governments and senior political leaders to cultivate close, mutually beneficial relations can often conflict with popular or interest group demands that they "stand up to the United States" or to particular policies or interests that, in the minds of some Canadians, momentarily serve as proxies for the American political system.

Depending on the issue, about 20 percent of Canadians persistently display attitudes that can be described as "pro-American" in the sense of being

TABLE 4.1
Cross-border sociocultural value differences

	BC	AB	SK, MB	ON	QC	NB, PEI, NS, NL
Northeast	8.0	7.5	*6.0*	5.5	8.0	*4.0*
Midwest	8.5	7.0	7.0	5.5	9.5	4.5
Southern	13.0	9.6	7.6	9.3	12.0	6.7
Western	*6.3*	*4.6*	7.3	*5.3*	*7.6*	6.3

NOTE: Using 1990 and 2000 data from the World Value Survey, the Policy Research Initiative calculated for each region the average percentage of respondents who agreed with each of thirty-two different questions representing seven sociocultural dimensions. The results presented in the table are the percentage point differences between the regions indicated for all questions. The lower the number, the more similar the sociocultural values of regions compared. *Italic type* indicates closest correlation for each pair of regions.

SOURCE: Christian Boucher, "Toward North American or Regional Cross-Border Communities: A Look at Economic Integration and Socio-Cultural Values in Canada and the United States," working paper (Ottawa: Policy Research Initiative, 2005).

strongly favourable to the United States (or emphasizing the similarity of Canadian and US interests) over an extended period. Between 20 and 30 percent of Canadians consistently manifest views suggestive of a mix of strong nationalist and variably anti-American perspectives. The latter might be rooted in political hostility to an incumbent American president or to an international economic system driven by American policies and interests.[15] This reality has enforced an unwritten political rule that Canadian prime ministers should be seen to have close but not excessively cordial, "cozy," or enthusiastic relations with their American counterparts.[16] The frequently opportunistic or ideologically driven nature of identity politics can also be seen in the willingness of many of its practitioners to identify with American policy initiatives and personalities when it serves their interests or policy goals.[17] Both federal Liberals and New Democrats have close links with Democratic Party operatives in Washington, and PCs and Conservatives have frequently worked with Republican counterparts.

Dunsky, Adams, and others suggest that the growth of economic integration has led to a shift from emphasizing distinctions based on the two countries' political systems to those based on differences in value systems.[18] However, the diversity of individual and regionally varied attitudes and perspectives in both countries makes it risky to draw broad generalizations. Biette and Goold contend that, "while Canadians as a whole are probably more liberal than Americans, in sharp contrast to the 1930s and 1940s, internal value divergences in each country are probably more important than overall difference between the two countries."[19]

TABLE 4.2
Canadians and Americans: "The same" or "different"?

	Essentially the same	Mainly the same	Mainly different	Essentially different	Don't know
2008	13	37	30	19	1
2006	6	44	32	17	1
2004	12	32	23	31	2
2002	7	34	29	28	2
1999	8	44	23	24	1
1990	12	37	26	25	–
1989	13	43	24	19	–

NOTE: In response to the question: "Would you describe Canadians and Americans as essentially different, mainly different but with some similarities, mainly the same but with some small differences, or essentially the same?"

SOURCE: The Strategic Counsel, *Globe and Mail,* and CTV News, June 2008. Reproduced with permission.

This perspective is supported by research, summarized in Table 4.1, that points to significant regional differences in public attitudes that cut across national boundaries. It suggests that Quebecers and Atlantic Canadians have fairly similar sociocultural attitudes to residents of the US northeast and midwest, and attitudes of Ontarians and Albertans are most similar to those of US west coast residents. Not surprisingly, the biggest gap in sociocultural attitudes is between residents of the American south and those of Canada's four largest provinces, especially British Columbia and Quebec.

This diversity of outlooks is also supported by longitudinal polling data summarized in Table 4.2 indicating that at least half of Canadian respondents view cultural differences between Canadians and Americans to be fairly limited, an outlook that has remained fairly consistent, despite ebbs and flows in political cycles, since the late 1980s.[20] Public opinion polling since 2000 suggests that Canadians are generally supportive of "a stronger economic relationship" with the United States, somewhat less supportive of "free trade," and verging on skeptical of "closer North American integration" – though public perceptions of the relative benefits of these arrangements tend to ebb and flow with overall levels of economic activity. A 2010 comparative survey suggests that Americans are generally more favourable to closer relations than Canadians but that skepticism of "Canada–US integration" is inversely proportional to familiarity with the other country among both publics.[21] This "permissive consensus"[22] on globalization can be disrupted momentarily by popular and interest group reactions to specific events, as discussed in the next section, but is sufficiently durable that few serious Canadian politicians feel at liberty to challenge it except at the margins of political debate. However, these expectations – which some American observers suggest verge on a sense of entitlement[23] – can easily trigger a political backlash when confronted with the realities of special interest politics in Washington or American security policies.

Cyclical Factors

Cyclical attitudes toward the United States tend to reflect four broad factors that can reinforce or offset one another. Most significant in recent years have probably been Canadian public responses to US foreign and security policies. Negative attitudes toward US foreign policies are most deeply entrenched on the Canadian political left and in Quebec – reflecting the nationalism of small nations and their instinctive skepticism toward the military activities of major powers.[24] These constraints are less apparent when US foreign policies are seen to be oriented more consistently toward collaboration with other major powers and working through international organizations – as under the Clinton and Obama administrations.

However, the Bush administration's intense unpopularity in Canada, particularly during the Iraq War, substantially limited successive Canadian governments' political flexibility in dealing with Washington because of the political risks of being seen to be "too close" to the unpopular president. Although this reality was most visible in the Martin government's 2005 decision not to cooperate with the US Ballistic Missile Defense (BMD) initiative despite extensive behind-the-scenes cooperation on defence issues, it had a broader, more persistent effect on bilateral relations.[25] Indeed, though the Harper government sought to reverse the chill after taking power in 2006, it generally sought to avoid appearances of excessive closeness to the Bush administration to deflect partisan and ideological attacks identifying the latter's policies with its own.[26]

Two other related factors that affect public and elite attitudes toward the United States are the relative (if varied) success of the American economic model compared with that of Canada, often framed in terms of higher average living standards (per capita GDP), and the degree to which closer economic cooperation, mediated largely through market forces, is seen to enhance the economic opportunities and living standards of ordinary Canadians. Higher US living standards and, during certain periods, faster rates of economic growth have often proven attractive not only to Canadian economic elites but also to ordinary citizens. Conversely, the American model becomes significantly less attractive when the United States experiences severe economic shocks, when its less extensive welfare state visibly fails to cushion large numbers of Americans from personal calamity or economic downturn, or when US domestic political conflicts threaten to destabilize economic activity in other countries, especially Canada.

The effects of economic interdependence often take different forms in different regions – depending on the relative importance of investment by US-based firms to local and regional economic development and the degree to which growth is driven by heavy dependence on US markets. Even so, high-profile cases of regulatory barriers or protectionism such as the protracted softwood lumber dispute, the BSE-related closing of US borders to Canadian cattle exports in 2003-5, or the Buy American provisions of the 2009 US stimulus bill can provoke a backlash from citizens and businesses. In such cases, many Canadians naively presume that American presidents have as much power over domestic legislative or regulatory measures as Canadian prime ministers. For example, more than 30 percent of Canadians polled in a 2009 Ekos study thought that the election of Barack Obama would make a "fundamental" and positive difference to bilateral relations despite significant indications to the contrary in the recently concluded US election campaign.[27]

On balance, cross-border cooperation among economic, social, and economic interests can be seen as beneficial to the extent that it is seen to serve the interests of ordinary Canadians. However, public acceptance of such arrangements is likely to be greatest when they are portrayed as products of "choice" – allowing for the accommodation of significant national or regional differences through Canadian political and administrative processes.

A third factor that affects attitudes toward the United States – and Canadian governments' relative political flexibility – is the impact of American political trends on Canadian public opinion. Milke notes that the responses of Canadian political and opinion leaders to these trends are closely linked to the extent to which they reinforce or constrain their domestic political agendas. Liberal and social democratic politicians, academics, and pundits who respond to a Ronald Reagan or George W. Bush as they might to the discovery of toxic waste in their backyards will also attempt to take advantage of the political appeal of a Kennedy, Clinton, or more recently Obama.[28] This reality might explain the almost total absence of debate over the Canada–US relationship from the 2011 federal election campaign despite Obama's joint announcement two months earlier with Prime Minister Harper of intentions to pursue a Canada–US security perimeter (discussed further in Chapter 11).[29] Right-of-centre politicians might appeal to the examples of US counterparts when they are demonstrably successful in improving policy outcomes but usually find it necessary to distinguish themselves in other ways – as in Harper's high-profile assertion of Canada's claims to Arctic sovereignty.[30] However, most Canadians appear to be able to make the distinctions between the policies of individual presidents and the broader sentiments of cultural aversion that often characterized different variants of nineteenth-century anti-Americanism.

Finally, both the political positions and the rhetorical attitudes of Canadian governments toward the United States are largely a function of their relative security or insecurity in domestic politics. Although many US policy makers appear to recognize this reality, blatant political appeals to anti-American sentiments in Canada – as opposed to civil disagreements over particular policy issues – do little to enhance the receptiveness of American policy makers to Canadian interests in cross-border policy discussions.[31]

However, Canadian governments must also find ways to work with or around the principal currents of *American* public opinion, whatever the prevailing Canadian public attitudes toward closer bilateral cooperation, in order to influence American policy makers within the context of American political cycles.

Enabling and Constraining Variables in American Attitudes toward Canada

> *The fact of the matter is that Canada will never be a top-of-mind issue for the Americans. Get used to it. They still think of us as nice neighbours.*
>
> *– Confidential interview, Privy Council Office, 2005*

American public attitudes toward Canada reflect a general goodwill that allows Canadian governments to engage American political processes in ways that might be risky for countries whose governments are widely viewed as indifferent or hostile to US interests. However, like its Canadian counterpart, this "permissive consensus" is relatively shallow and subject to manipulation on specific issues by interest groups in the service of domestic political agendas. A 2011 public opinion survey indicated that 92 percent of Americans have a favourable view of Canada (compared with 72 percent of Canadians toward the United States) but that only 39 percent viewed Canada as being "vitally important" to US interests. (The three countries viewed as more important to US interests were China, Iran, and North Korea – scarcely enviable company given American public opinion toward these countries!)[32]

Canadians and Canadian interests are of interest to Americans primarily to the extent that they are seen to complement American interests, values, and priorities – or those of particular groups that attempt to shape those priorities to their own advantages. On most bilateral issues, there is probably some segment of American society whose interests and objectives overlap with those championed by Canadian governments as well as those of other Canadians whose interests or policy goals might work at cross-purposes to those of the current government.

As a result, generic American attitudes toward Canada are less important than those of particular clusters of interest groups and policy makers responsible for designing and implementating US policies. This reality is reinforced by the fragmentation of American policies toward Canada and their tendency (noted previously) to emerge as subsets of American domestic (and occasionally foreign) policies.[33] Similarly, American media coverage of Canada and Canadian issues is most likely to surface on issues relevant to particular media markets or personalities.[34]

Accordingly, cultivating general public goodwill is less important to Canadian diplomacy in the United States than cultivating shared interests and values among American decision makers and interest groups that have the most to gain or lose as a result of particular policy decisions. Consequently, an understanding of the different layers of American political culture and its capacity to empower or constrain the actions of major decision makers is vital to the success of Canadian efforts to influence American policies toward Canada.

Friends, Yes, but Particularly if You're Like Us

Americans just do not see us as different from themselves. You know, one hamburger, one hot dog, one culture, one boundary. There is a good side to this. If the U.S. goes around bashing

someone, they don't bash us. But there is a negative side. When
we do something different, Americans feel betrayed. They don't
see us as foreigners but as perverse Americans.

– Allan Gotlieb, The Washington Diaries, *2006*[35]

American attitudes toward Canada are shaped by a long history and widely shared perceptions of shared cultural origins and broadly shared values. A 2008 survey suggests that about 70 percent of Americans perceive Canadians as "essentially" or "mainly" the same as Americans – about 20 percent more than Canadian perceptions of Canada. As noted in Table 4.3, these figures have remained fairly stable in recent decades.

During the 1990s, American public opinion generally endorsed the conclusion of the US Commission on National Security in the twenty-first century that "if the United States has a best friend ... and partner ... it is Canada."[36] More recently, Canada's public standing in the United States has been closely linked to its relative support for American foreign policies. Although a majority of Americans perceive Canada as a "close ally," second only to Britain since 9/11, as noted in Table 4.4, this standing declined somewhat after Canada's refusal to support American military action against Iraq – only to rebound as Canada's combat commitment in Afghanistan became more widely known. Not surprisingly, this commitment featured prominently in a 2006 Canadian government advertising campaign in the Washington, DC, subway system (see Figure 4.1), with billboards prominently located at stops frequented by US military personnel and government employees.

TABLE 4.3
American attitudes toward Canadians

	Essentially the same	Mainly the same	Mainly different	Essentially different	Don't know
2008	24	46	15	6	9
1999	19	52	12	8	9
1990	26	43	14	10	7
1989	18	60	15	6	1

NOTE: In response to the question: "Would you describe Americans and Canadians as essentially different, mainly different but with some similarities, mainly the same but with some small differences, or essentially the same?"
SOURCE: The Strategic Counsel, *Globe and Mail*, CTV News, June 2008. Reproduced with permission.

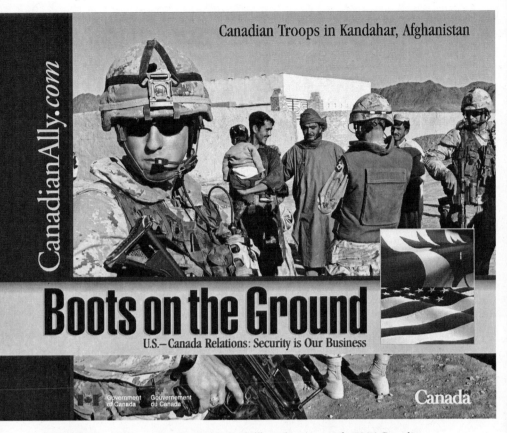

FIGURE 4.1 "Boots on the Ground." This billboard was part of a 2006 Canadian government advertising campaign in the Washington, DC, subway system, displayed at stops frequented by US military personnel and government employees. [*Source:* CanadianAlly.com. Reproduced with permission]

American public attitudes toward Canada and Canadians, who are generally viewed as "much like us," except in the most assertively conservative and "exceptionalist" circles, contrast sharply with those toward Mexico, as demonstrated in Table 4.4. Although American political and economic elites generally support US cooperation with both countries, much of the broader public views Mexico as a threat to its interests – whether as a result of competition from "low wage" labour under NAFTA, large-scale immigration (especially if illegal), or police corruption that hinders cooperation with American law enforcement agencies.[37] These attitudes tend to reinforce the preference of Canadian government officials to work directly

TABLE 4.4

US public perceptions of other countries

		2002	2003	2004	2005	2006	2007
Canada	Close ally	60	57	51	48	64	57
	Friendly but not ally	27	27	29	37	27	31
	Not friendly or enemy	6	10	10	12	8	10
Britain	Close ally	64	74	70	74	74	70
	Friendly but not ally	22	12	14	18	11	21
	Not friendly or enemy	6	6	6	4	11	7
Australia	Close ally	43	53	45	44	61	54
	Friendly but not ally	34	24	32	36	26	28
	Not friendly or enemy	9	8	10	9	9	11
Israel	Close ally	37	44	43	41	47	42
	Friendly but not ally	28	25	26	31	28	26
	Not friendly or enemy	22	19	20	19	20	27
Mexico	Close ally	29	33	29	27	31	27
	Friendly but not ally	41	39	44	47	42	39
	Not friendly or enemy	21	20	16	20	23	31
France	Close ally	28	13	15	17	19	20
	Friendly but not ally	36	33	35	38	35	38
	Not friendly or enemy	25	43	42	41	44	38

SOURCE: Humphrey Taylor, *The Harris Poll # 78* (Harris Interactive, 6 August 2007); Geoffrey Hale, "Managing Alternate Realities," *Canadian–American Public Policy* 71 (2007): 16. Reproduced with permission.

with their American counterparts rather than pursue the greater emphasis on trilateralism often preferred by senior US government officials and policy experts as a way of managing both relations with Mexico and "North American" policies as a whole.

These attitudes became much more important after 9/11 as American public discourse came to be defined by significant levels of insecurity, initially due to risks of terrorism, subsequently due to economic insecurity resulting from widespread income stagnation and the decline of American manufacturing industries. A mid-2004 Pew survey reported that Americans viewed "protecting the jobs of American workers" (84 percent) as almost as great a priority as "protecting against terrorist attacks" (88 percent).[38]

However, deepening partisan divisions in American society provided little comfort for Canadian policy makers. Growing numbers of voters, particularly Republicans, became significantly less accepting of overt displays of anti-Americanism, and growing numbers of Democrats were inclined to blame "free trade" – especially NAFTA – when income levels failed to reflect steady economic growth after the recession of 2001 despite high levels of employment. If anything, skepticism toward trade liberalization increased, and support for "enforcement of trade agreements" based on domestic American standards increased sharply across party lines with the financial crisis and subsequent recession of 2007-9.[39]

However, a series of studies suggests that public attitudes toward trade also track partisan divisions and relative levels of trust toward the incumbent administration. For example, net Republican support for "free trade" increased from +10 in September 1997 to +47 in September 2001 (subsequently fluctuating with economic conditions), following the election of George W. Bush, whereas net Democratic support dropped from +27 to +4 between 1997 and 2004.[40] Similarly, net support for trade agreements among Democratic voters jumped from −16 in early 2008 to +13 following the election of Barack Obama. However, "dealing with global trade" ranked near the bottom of public priorities. Another survey taken in early 2009 indicated that more Americans viewed trade as a "threat to the economy from foreign imports (47%)" than as "an opportunity for economic growth through increased U.S. exports (44%)," with limited differences in the responses of Republican, Democratic, and "independent" voters.[41] These findings suggest that, even without public hostility toward Canada, American public opinion imposes significant constraints on broad policy options likely to be considered by senior policy makers even before the pervasive influence of interest group politics and partisan polarization of Congress are taken into account.

Public opinion plays a similar, if more volatile, role in energy and environmental policies, as discussed in Chapter 12. Widespread public concerns over US energy security after 9/11 led Canadian governments (especially Alberta) to promote Canada as a reliable and politically secure source of energy imports in much of their public diplomacy – though one wonders how much of this information percolates down to the average voter. However, the shift of power between 2006 and 2008 from a Bush administration closely allied to conventional energy sector interests to a Democratic majority more strongly aligned with environmental groups led to parallel shifts in debates over energy and environmental policies. Even before the

2008 elections, powerful interest groups with close links to congressional leaders sought to limit imports of "dirty oil" from Canada's oil sands as part of a broader strategy to force the conversion of US energy and transportation systems to renewable fuels. However, their capacity to translate these agendas into actual legislation has been constrained by the same kinds of competing regional interests as in Canada.

These factors, combined with the spread of the "urban myth" that some of the 9/11 attackers arrived in the United States from Canada, have increased the attention paid by Canadian diplomats to the American media, along with periodic efforts to promote Canadian messages to selected audiences through the cultivation of American media outlets. These issues are discussed at greater length in Chapter 8.

Elite Attitudes toward Canada

> *Canadians should talk with Americans on things that are of interest to Americans.*
>
> *– Paul Frazer, seminar remarks, 2006*[42]

Public discussions of Canada–US relations are often very different from the private discussions of government officials. Former US ambassador to Canada Paul Cellucci has written about the "profound difference between the optics and the reality of Canada–United States relations. The optics seemed to be all about conflict, disagreement, and tension. The reality was continued cooperation and a significant progress on issues of mutual concern."[43]

Cellucci's comments were echoed by many officials in both embassies, Canadian and US federal departments, and agencies interviewed for this book. However, the psychological–cultural dimension of bilateral relations among policy makers is both very different from and far less transparent than the differences between the two countries' political cultures. These realities reflect the broad distribution of responsibilities for cross-border relations among departments and agencies of both governments noted in previous chapters. Institutional awareness of Canadian sensitivities tends to be greater in the US executive branch, or at least those parts of it whose officials deal regularly with their Canadian counterparts, than in Congress. However, such awareness is limited to the relative handful of people whose careers or personal backgrounds have given them a reason to acquire substantial knowledge of or familiarity with Canada or cross-border issues. Even then there is often limited understanding of the differences between the two countries' political and institutional cultures that structure the terms of cooperation or conflict management.

A 2004 handbook prepared for officials of Canada's federal government notes the importance of "personal diplomacy" for "line department" officials whose responsibilities involve dealings with counterparts in the United States.[44] These observations were reiterated by mid-ranking and senior officials interviewed for this book. Officials at all levels are encouraged to get to know their counterparts in the United States to be able to "pick up the phone" and discuss issues before they become politically sensitive. Contacts are facilitated through routine meetings and by the existence of cross-border working groups on numerous issues, many formed before or during the implementation of NAFTA.[45]

However, the effectiveness of personal contact also depends on the ability of Canadian politicians and officials to demonstrate a degree of sensitivity to US interests even while seeking to advance Canadian interests or secure their accommodation within the American political system. Heynen and Higginbotham stress that successful engagement with US counterparts requires Canadian officials to understand the policy preferences of multiple actors within the American political system and "how an issue of importance to Canada will play out in U.S. domestic politics." It is necessary not only to "know your U.S. counterparts" but also to know the "powers, constraints and limitations they face."[46]

Paul Frazer also warns against taking approaches that discount US political or policy sensitivities or project a self-centred "set my widgets free" approach to bilateral relations. Speaking in early 2006, he noted that, "if the PM and his advisers had a better handle on how the US government functions, it would affect how they deal with Washington and how they speak about issues in play," though he later described both Ottawa and Canadian Embassy responses to the evolving political scene in Washington as more "agile and adaptable."[47]

Although policy conflicts occur periodically, they can be smoothed when individual departments have comparable goals – even if they are sometimes pursued in different ways. One Canadian official commented thus:

> Personal relationships are not a means to an end. In the big picture, it doesn't make that big a difference. On difficult issues, it can make a big difference. Neither one of us is going to give the other a free ride. If you

have a good personal relationship, it's easier to strike a balanced exchange than if you don't.[48]

Similar comments were offered by an American diplomat:

The relationship is often defined by the personal relationships at a high level. For example, the relationship between [a senior Customs and Border Protection official] and [his Canadian counterpart, later promoted within the federal government] ... That relationship was very beneficial for facilitating things at a grand policy level that Canada wanted to achieve and that CBP wanted to achieve. For example, on a handshake between the two, without much paperwork, the two agencies agreed on an exchange of people to work in one another's countries on maritime and container security. You couldn't do this in France or Japan.[49]

A positive relationship between the prime minister and president can facilitate the management of certain issues – as with President Bush's overt support for the reopening of the US border to shipments of Canadian beef after the discovery of BSE in a Canadian cattle herd in May 2003. However, the vast majority of issues are managed at much lower levels of the executive branch, with political oversight provided by cabinet officers responsible for line (or executive) departments rather than White House officials. A signal from the White House might facilitate problem solving but is rarely sufficient to work out the practical details necessary for a workable solution. Conversely, a chill in high-level relations has little effect on most day-to-day relationships. But it is more likely to create barriers to resolving problems requiring high-level political engagement.

Some career officials have an advantage in being able to cultivate relationships with American counterparts relatively early in their careers that allow for long-term familiarization with their personalities and priorities over an extended period. Such relationships can be facilitated by common patterns of socialization, as with defence and security issues, based on common agency mandates and cultures. Although it is more difficult to build such relationships with elected officials, the greater frequency with which state-level politicians make the transition to national politics gives Canadian diplomats posted outside Washington incentives to cultivate relationships on issues of shared interest as a long-term investment in bilateral relations.

Good personal relationships can facilitate cooperation when particular departments share common policy objectives. However, they have only limited value when major policy goals or, in the security field, perceptions of potential threats diverge. In such cases, transparency is important to cultivating or maintaining trust. American decision makers, diplomats, and officials might strongly disagree with particular decisions of foreign governments, including Canada's. However, such disagreements are easier to deal with when communicated up front, professionally, and without attempts to embarrass American counterparts.

Both American and Canadian officials noted three major decisions that soured bilateral relations under the Chrétien and Martin governments: the former's refusal to accommodate US insistence on a "carve-out for Korea" in the 1997 International Land Mines Treaty, a process that prompted tart observations from officials for more than a decade; Ottawa's decision not to provide direct support to the United States in the Iraq War; and the Martin government's February 2005 decision to withhold symbolic Canadian support for the US BMD program. In all three cases, officials noted that the substance of the decision was less important than the way in which it was made.

Officials made similar comments about the Martin government's exploitation of bilateral disputes to score domestic political points at the expense of the Bush administration. In contrast, officials from both countries noted the care taken by Prime Minister Harper and his senior advisers to manage disagreements carefully, provide advance notice of "bad news," and respect the confidentiality of private discussions with senior administration officials. Harper's announcement during the October 2008 federal election that Canadian combat troops would not remain in Afghanistan beyond 2011, while reaffirming the outcome of a cross-party vote in the House of Commons, was received in Washington as advance notice of a decision by an ally that had already contributed more than most countries to the NATO effort.

At the same time, American officials who deal only peripherally with Canada are often surprised at what they view as disproportionate Canadian responses and sensitivities to perceived slights or American policy measures harmful to Canadian interests – particularly when Canadian officials fail to prepare the relational groundwork for such disputes. One former Bush administration official described internal perceptions of a "Canadian negotiating style" in dealings with Washington: "Every game is [like] game seven of the World Series." There is "a perception that the Canadian side will always end up being scanted in its relations with the United States. That means that the Canadians are always 'sliding into third with their spikes high' because they're afraid they will lose if they don't come in hard."[50]

An alternative Canadian approach described by American officials is to anticipate US policy processes and attempt to engage senior decision makers before they are "paying attention" or have framed a broader policy approach to the issues in question.

> The Canadian side will serve up ideas that sound procedural or just "good government," but as they play out over time they are surprisingly advantageous to Canada ... There is a tendency for the Canadian side to try to make as much progress towards its goals as you can before the Americans are paying attention. "We can do this because they are not focused, so let's nail down as much as possible before they do focus while we're just talking as friends."[51]

Much of the latter approach is tacitly acknowledged by some Canadian officials and sometimes publicly advocated by some close observers of bilateral relations in Canada who perceive any major policy departure as depending on Canadian initiatives that attempt to address US policy goals in ways favourable to Canada. At other times, however, officials complain that they have difficulty getting ministers and senior departmental officials to engage their concerns because of either domestic political preoccupations or perceptions that their American counterparts might not be able or willing to engage on terms potentially favourable to Canada.

Administration officials are also sensitive to perceptions that Canadian diplomats might "game the system" by negotiating with counterparts in the executive branch while seeking different policy outcomes by lobbying members of Congress. These perceptions, which contributed to a significant cooling of Canada–US relations on border security during the latter years of the Bush administration, and the challenges of working "both ends of Pennsylvania Avenue" will be discussed further in Chapter 5. Although dealing with Congress is a central element of Canadian diplomacy, Canadian officials must walk a fine line between engaging Congress and appearing to end-run their counterparts in the executive branch.

Conclusion

The 2008 election of President Barack Obama – combined with the departure of George W. Bush, probably the most unpopular American president in recent Canadian history – created circumstances necessary for renewed alignment in the cycles of Canada–US relations. However, the broader realities of American domestic political cultures have limited the extent to which these shifts enable closer cooperation on major bilateral issues. Moreover, successive minority federal Parliaments (until May 2011) significantly constrained Ottawa's willingness to consider taking major political risks in bilateral relations, whatever the similarities between the broader agendas of Harper's Conservatives and Michael Ignatieff's Liberals. (Harper's mid-2009 appointment of retiring Manitoba NDP premier Gary Doer as Canada's new ambassador in Washington illustrated the broad, "permissive" character of this consensus and its careful incrementalism.) President Obama's initially overloaded domestic and foreign policy agendas – and the challenges of managing a fractious Democratic Party coalition in Congress – pushed bilateral issues with Canada and broader North American issues in general well down the political agenda.

The Harper government remained a carefully interested spectator in American domestic debates relevant to bilateral relations but without an invitation to participate in an institutional framework within which it could address both the executive branch and Congress on broader American policies affecting Canada. However, the decision of the Obama administration to move away from its predecessor's trilateral approach to North American relations, and other policy shifts to promote trade and economic growth after the 2010 congressional elections, created a window of opportunity for closer cooperation on cross-border security and regulatory issues.[52]

The Beyond-the-Border and Regulatory Cooperation Council action plans negotiated during 2011 suggest some willingness to pursue closer cross-border and interagency coordination on issues whose management had been heavily segmented among line departments and agencies. Winning a parliamentary majority in the May 2011 federal election has given the Harper government far more latitude to pursue these negotiations. However, it is far from clear whether current political and economic conditions will allow for the consolidation of these processes in the United States. Whatever the outcome of the 2012 presidential election, they might require further changes in the leadership of Congress to allow for the development of a viable cross-partisan agenda for renewed American leadership in international economic and environmental relations. However, as Christopher Sands notes, cultivating bilateral networks might give Canada a source of competitive advantage to the extent that both governmental and societal

interests can build on "a myriad of ties: family relationships, business relationships, alumni networks, and basic friendships."[53]

Thomas Axworthy has effectively summarized the conditions for engaging the United States during an earlier period of national introspection
and self-absorption:

> As an ally ... you must never threaten their definition of the[ir] national
> interest ... You must have excellent intelligence to understand how an issue
> is developing before the decision gels; ... you can offer arguments or sup-
> port for one side of the debate, if they are inclined to listen to you; and ... if
> quiet diplomacy fails, you can try to persuade the American public. But ...
> to influence, you must have an audience willing to listen.[54]

Under these circumstances, Canadian governments must continue to
work with the current administration, both parties in Congress, and
regional interests across the United States to identify shared and overlapping interests capable of supporting a new bilateral or North American
agenda. At the same time, they must frame such issues domestically in
ways that identify them with broader Canadian interests recognizable by
the general public and not just policy elites. Although such an agenda is
not likely to emerge without clear presidential leadership, such leadership
still depends on cultivating a bilateral (or North American) agenda that
complements a broader American international agenda and with it the pursuit of American strategic interests in a stable international order adaptable
to emerging trends.

Such a balancing (or perhaps "juggling") act can emerge incrementally
over time. However, chances are that it will depend on an alignment of domestic political conditions in both countries that allows each government
the flexibility to pursue its own interests in ways that complement the interests of its neighbour.

PART 2

Tactics and Strategies

Political and Procedural Dimensions

5

Governing from the Centre?

Political and Policy Coordination in the
Management of Canada–US Relations

Previous chapters have described Canada–US relations as a series of multilevel games shaped by the broader strategic priorities of both governments,
their respective sectoral policy goals (interacting with one another), bureaucratic politics, transgovernmental relations, and the competing efforts of
a myriad of interest groups to influence each government's policies at multiple levels. The challenges of policy coordination are shaped by major differences in the relative importance and current preoccupations of the bilateral
relationship to policy makers in both countries and by their very different
constitutional systems and institutional structures.

In Canada, prime ministerial leadership is both an enabling and a constraining variable for officials responsible for managing bilateral relations.
Such leadership is vital in providing the political will, bureaucratic mandates, and resources to engage American policies at strategic or sectoral
levels. Prime ministerial priorities determine whether Canadian governments take a proactive rather than reactive or incremental approach to
cross-border policy relations. These choices both shape and depend on Canadian officials' capacity to engage the attention of their American counterparts on an ongoing basis so that senior policy makers in both governments
are prepared to take advantage of the relatively brief openings of what
American political scientist John Kingdon has described as "policy windows": institutionalized or ad hoc opportunities to address specific policy

challenges within the constraints imposed by each leader's political calendars, domestic institutions, and international goals and commitments.[1]

The willingness and capacity of both governments to recognize, let alone take advantage of, such opportunities depend partly on the relative political salience of particular issues, the extent to which national (or sectoral) policy goals coincide or overlap, and the relative political security or insecurity of each government. They also reflect political or institutional obstacles to the negotiation of mutually beneficial outcomes and the extent to which political actors are motivated to achieve full or partial resolution of the issue before windows of opportunity close, perhaps for an extended period.

Kingdon describes the opening of policy windows as being contingent on the convergence of three independent "streams." The first or *problem stream* involves the recognition of a problem by the public, relevant interest groups, policy entrepreneurs, or authoritative decision makers.

Interest groups or other members of the relevant policy community might perceive certain issues to be problems worthy of governmental attention. However, these issues must also become part of the second, *political stream*, defined by Kingdon as the "governmental agenda" or list of issues or problems to be resolved. In bilateral relations, the shared or complementary recognition of a problem – first as something of national or bilateral significance, second as something amenable to resolution or management through governmental action – is necessary for the problem stream to become an occasion for bilateral cooperation. Such common recognition can take place at the level of senior officials with the administrative authority to engage a particular problem ("transgovernmental relations"), of cabinet officers with complementary responsibilities, or, failing agreement at lower levels of authority, between the president and prime minister (with their closest advisers).

The third or *policy stream* involves the development of specific measures capable of effective implementation in one or both countries. The more similar the interests and institutional frameworks involved in engaging particular issues in both countries, the greater the likelihood that they can be managed through policy collaboration or coordination between departmental or agency counterparts (see Chapter 1). The greater the diversity of interests (and conflicts among them), the greater the likelihood that policy shifts will be managed either by the intervention of senior political decision makers (if highly salient to one or both governments) or through a series of incremental changes over time.

The greater the complexity of the problem – or the collateral issues affected by it – the greater the need for internal coordination within governments and, in the United States, between the executive branch and Congress. As a result, effective cross-border diplomacy requires an unusually high degree of internal or intergovernmental policy coordination within Canada. Major examples include the Continuing Committee on Trade Negotiations during the free-trade negotiations of the 1980s and the ad hoc committee created after 9/11 to assemble the components of the Smart Border Accord. At the same time, successful cross-border cooperation on major issue sets depends on the capacity of relevant US and Canadian government actors to mobilize support from the White House, executive branch, relevant committees of Congress, and related stakeholders among American interest groups in and beyond the Washington beltway. Thus, Canadian governments' capacity to exercise influence in Washington depends in part on the domestic context for Canadian policy processes and on how it affects the ability of Canadian governments to engage the very different policy processes and institutional structures of the American political system.

This chapter examines the coordination of bilateral relations with the United States by Canada's federal government, particularly as it relates to influencing American policies toward Canada. It contrasts the practice of "single point diplomacy" centred on relations between national leaders with the considerable decentralization of relations at sectoral and departmental levels. It also considers the implications of the ways in which these processes interact for the "multilevel games" involving a mixture of strategic, sectoral, and microlevel tactical approaches that often characterize bilateral policy relations. The chapter examines key institutions for coordinating and managing cross-border relations in Canada and how they have adapted in recent years to major institutional differences between the two countries. Finally, it explores the growing relevance of international governance institutions in shaping the context for bilateral relations and the need for Canadian governments to coordinate and sometimes "triangulate" the domestic, North American, and broader international dimensions of public policies to maintain the flexibility to address Canadian interests and objectives.

Proactive and Reactive Policy Management

Conventional wisdom in Canada–US relations suggests that, for Canadian governments to exercise effective influence in Washington, they must first take the initiative in engaging US policy processes on issues of *shared* interest – preferably at the highest political levels.[2] As with much received wisdom, there is an element of truth to such analyses. Canada was the *demandeur* in initiating trade negotiations that led to the Canada–US Free Trade Agreement (CUFTA) of 1988. Canadian officials, after recovering from their initial shock at American border closures, mobilized their expertise with remarkable speed and effectiveness to enable Deputy Prime Minister John Manley to negotiate the Smart Border Accord with his White House counterpart Tom Ridge after 9/11. More recently, Ottawa responded effectively to congressional Buy American legislation in 2009 to present a response that became the basis for a bilateral agreement on subnational procurement in early 2010 – albeit one vulnerable to further policy shifts in Washington.[3] The Harper government's Beyond-the-Border initiative of 2011 builds on earlier efforts to update the Smart Border Accord.

Another school of thought suggests that these measures, and many others, were really defensive reactions to American policy initiatives taken with little or no regard for Canadian interests.[4] Indeed, major proactive initiatives that are not essentially reactions to American policy actions – whether those of the White House, executive agencies, or Congress – are relatively few and far between, whatever the periodic proposals that emanate from think tanks or business groups in both countries. As noted in Tables 5.1 and 5.2, only two major initiatives, CUFTA and the Security and Prosperity Partnership (SPP) of 2005-9, could be described as essentially proactive Canadian initiatives, with the latter involving the bundling and repackaging of hundreds of sectoral and microregulatory initiatives from other processes. The 2011 Beyond-the-Border and Regulatory Cooperation processes might be viewed as a bilateral repackaging of unfinished business carried forward from the SPP.

Since 2001, most major bilateral negotiations have been sectoral reactions to American initiatives, as noted in Tables 5.1 and 5.2. The main priorities of bilateral prime ministerial diplomacy since 2003 have been sectoral or issue-specific expressions of the overriding priority of maintaining access to US markets for Canadian products and services as part of a more or less integrated North American market. Examples noted in Table 5.2 include the reopening of US borders to Canadian beef and cattle exports after the BSE outbreak of 2003; the resolution of the protracted Canada–US softwood lumber dispute, which dominated bilateral relations in 2005-6; the partial accommodation of Canadian interests in the US implementation of the Western Hemisphere Travel Initiative (WHTI) in

TABLE 5.1

Horizontal initiatives in bilateral relations

Issue or agenda item	Relative salience		Overlapping/ coinciding goals?	Window(s)	Political will	Outcome
	Canada	US				
CUFTA (Canada proactive)	High	Low-moderate	Moderate overlap	Electoral cycle (both); expiry of US fast-track authority	Canada, very high; US, modest but bipartisan	Successful negotiation of CUFTA
NAFTA (Canada reactive)	Low	Moderate-high	Moderate overlap (defensive/dual bilateral)	Extended over 1992 presidential election	Canada, moderate; US, moderate-high	Successful negotiation of NAFTA and "side agreements"
Post-9/11 border restrictions (Canada reactive → proactive)	Very high	Very high	Overlap (market access/security)	Do something!	Canada, high; US, very high	Successful negotiation of Smart Border Accord
North American Initiative (2003-4)	Moderate	Low	No	Derailed by Iraq dispute, electoral cycles in Canada, US	Canada, tentative; US, low	Deferral until after 2004 presidential election

▼ TABLE 5.1
Horizontal initiatives in bilateral relations

Issue or agenda item	Relative salience		Overlapping/ coinciding goals?	Window(s)	Political will	Outcome
	Canada	US				
Security and Prosperity Partnership (2005)	Moderate	Initially moderate	Negotiated but limited	New presidential term (2005); limited by minority/divided governments in Canada and Mexico (US after November 2006)	Canada, modest and declining; US, modest and declining	Diminishing returns after 2006 US elections
Beyond-the-Border and Regulatory Cooperation	Moderate	Low	Overlap (parallel US regulatory reforms; mutual accommodation on security, trade facilitation)	Beginning of 2012 presidential campaign	Canada, high; US, initially moderate	To be determined

TABLE 5.2
Sectoral initiatives

Issue or agenda item	Relative salience		Overlapping/ coinciding goals?	Window(s)	Political will	Outcome
	Canada	US				
BSE border closings (Canada reactive)	Moderate-high	Moderate (sectoral)	US admin, yes; Congress, no	Shared economic pain, constrained by courts	Canada, high; US, moderate	Negotiated reopening of border
NORAD renewal (2005-6)	Low	Low	Yes, but different priorities	Expiry of previous agreement	Canada, moderate; US, moderate	Modest extension of NORAD mandate
Softwood lumber US initiative (2005)	High but conflicted	Low	No	Martin government vulnerable, defeated in Parliament	Canada, low; US, low	No deal
(2006)	High	Moderate	Modest	Canada, get it over with! US, avoid constitutional challenge	Canada, high; US, moderate	Negotiated Softwood Lumber Agreement III (suboptimal)

▼ TABLE 5.2
Sectoral initiatives

Issue or agenda item	Relative salience		Overlapping/ coinciding goals?	Window(s)	Political will	Outcome
	Canada	US				
Western Hemisphere Travel Initiative (2005-8) (Canada reactive)	Moderate-high	Security high, facilitation (conflicted)	Competing priorities both administration and Congress	Annual congressional appropriations cycle; 2008 presidential election	Canada, moderate-high; US, low (Congress lead)	Modest adjustment of US policies to Canadian concerns
Auto industry bailout (Canada reactive)	High	Very high	Yes	Looming GM/ Chrysler bankruptcy	Canada, moderate	Canada integrated in US bailout package
Buy American/ subnational procurement (Canada reactive)	High	Low-moderate	Administration, yes; Congress, no	Before stimulus funds exhausted	Canada, very high	Negotiated short-term agreement; platform for future negotiations
North American cap-and-trade agreement (2009-10)	Moderate	Low	Administration, yes; Congress, no	No opening for negotiations on bilateral agreement	Canada, moderate; US, none	Incremental executive cooperation on regulation, research

2005-8; the Harper government's successful "slipstreaming" of the Obama administration in the bankruptcy, bailout, and reorganization of General Motors and Chrysler in 2008-9; and its successful negotiation of a bilateral agreement on subnational procurement to resolve the dispute over congressional Buy American legislation in 2009-10.[5] The routinization of North American summit diplomacy, initially under the SPP process described by Kirton and Guebert,[6] has been a way of institutionalizing these discussions – albeit with limited success, as noted by Clarkson's evolving views on the subject. As noted later in this chapter, North American policy relations remain firmly rooted in the reality of "dual bilateralism," whatever the desire of certain policy advocates to expand trilateral governance structures.[7]

Domestic political considerations have also influenced other diplomatic processes ranging from ongoing climate change negotiations, to Canada's NATO-related involvement in the protracted war in Afghanistan, to its agreement to disagree with Washington over Iraq, and to its ongoing engagement in Haiti. Most of the sectoral bilateral debates (softwood lumber notably excepted) have resulted from American domestic initiatives responding to other domestic and external concerns rather than specifically targeting Canada.

Since the early years of the Bush administration, the political environment in both countries has been far more conducive to the conduct of quiet diplomacy than to large-scale political or economic initiatives. No Canadian government enjoyed the secure parliamentary majority and internal political cohesion necessary to pursue such initiatives between Jean Chrétien's decision to retire in mid-2002 and Stephen Harper's victory in the May 2011 federal election. The Canadian public's growing hostility to the Bush administration limited the willingness of successive governments to pursue closer North American integration, though not to the extent of undermining support for existing arrangements, as noted in Chapter 4. Such conditions have limited the potential convergence of domestic problem and political streams in Canada and the opening of policy windows for major policy departures in bilateral relations, particularly since these openings require the consent and engagement of political leaders in both countries. The persistent polarization of American domestic politics, institutionalized congressional power over domestic (and many "intermestic") policies, and the generally higher political salience of US–Mexican relations make it far easier for American presidents to manage bilateral relations with Canada on a case-by-case basis than to entertain proposals for broader policy change.

These realities, which have characterized both the Bush and the Obama administrations, have been central to Canadian government calculations and the multilevel game of managing cross-border relations in recent years, notwithstanding the Harper government's effort to exploit the opening of policy windows in Washington to talks on perimeter security and regulatory coordination after the 2010 congressional elections. The post-9/11 shift in American policies from a relatively confident emphasis on progressive North American economic integration to much greater congressional defensiveness on economic and security issues convinced senior Canadian officials of the need to increase domestic capacity to coordinate cross-border initiatives and to expand Canada's diplomatic capacity in the United States.

These initiatives came from senior Foreign Affairs officials in 2002-3. Initial steps involved efforts to cultivate a shared institutional approach to managing transgovernmental relations in internal government publications, cataloguing the myriad of bilateral policy processes involving dozens of federal and provincial departments and agencies in Ottawa. Other measures, discussed in Chapters 8 and 9, were aimed at enhancing Canada's diplomatic capacities in the United States, expanding its "network diplomacy" with the involvement of other actors in the broader policy community, and laying the groundwork for what became known as the Enhanced Representation Initiative (later North American Platform) after Prime Minister Paul Martin took office in December 2003.[8]

The effectiveness of transgovernmental relations has depended largely on the political priorities of the prime minister and his senior advisers, their overall approach to coordinating and managing bilateral relations, and related cabinet-level diplomacy to manage specific issues that might emerge periodically. Although overall approaches to bilateral relations have varied more in tone than substance, the managerial and leadership styles of the later Chrétien, Martin, and Harper governments have varied substantially, creating very different environments for engaging and attempting to influence American policies toward Canada.[9] These processes are the subject of the next two sections.

Managing from the Centre

The formal organization of Canada's federal government has remained relatively stable in recent years after substantial gyrations in the late 1970s and early 1980s and the wholesale consolidation and reorganization of government departments in the early 1990s. However, the progressive consolidation of power at the "centre" – the term used by Donald Savoie to describe the constellation of prime ministerial power based in the Prime Minister's Office (PMO), the Privy Council Office (PCO), other central agencies, and the prime minister's discretionary exercise of power – has increased the already substantial importance of the prime minister's political and managerial style in setting priorities and coordinating policies.[10] However, this centralization of political power coexists with the significant *decentralization* of policy making and administrative processes across a wide range of federal departments and agencies.

The scale and scope of the bilateral relationship, combined with the diffusion of policy processes in Canada (and the United States), allow little time for senior policy makers to focus on all but a handful of major policy initiatives. Moreover, "bolts of electricity"[11] from the centre are necessary to activate (or circumvent) the channels of bureaucratic power and inter-agency coordination to trigger major policy changes. Initiating such changes, building public support for them, and then implementing them successfully so that they actually achieve their objectives are often difficult within a single country and order of government. It becomes exponentially more difficult when similar initiatives must bridge two national governments, with substantially different policy processes, priorities, and internal (or external) systems of checks and balances, let alone broader international governance processes.

As a result, prime ministers must "pick their spots" in bilateral relations, balancing the need for varying degrees of collaboration and cooperation across a wide range of policy fields, as exemplified by the cluttered agendas of North American and multilateral diplomacy, with decisions over the few issues that prime ministers have time to emphasize in their periodic meetings with presidents.

Sending Signals, Setting the Tone

These realities can be seen in several distinct aspects in the centre's approach to Canada–US relations, including its major sectoral and policy elements (see Figure 5.1). The most visible, if not necessarily the most important, is the public stance taken by the prime minister toward the president and administration of the day for both partisan and policy purposes. As noted in Chapter 4, a prime minister's political and rhetorical style might not be a reliable indicator of the substance of the broader relationship. However, it sends signals to cabinet colleagues and to the public servants who manage most day-to-day aspects of bilateral relations about

FIGURE 5.1
Governing from the centre

The Politics and Coordination of Canada–US Relations

• Priority and rhetorical style given to the relationship by the prime minister and his senior advisors and ministers
• Organization (centralization/delegation) of governmental functions
• Engagement of provincial governments (extent/consultation vs. participation)
• Frequency, content, and public presentation of meetings between prime minister and president
• Prime minister's public diplomacy in the United States

Limits to Prime Ministerial Power

• Time and the need for a focused domestic and international agenda
• The persistence of minority parliaments (until 2011)
• The "outward" drift of power to international negotiations, institutions, and provincial governments
• The need to accumulate and manage political capital in cross-border relations
• Competing priorities and political constraints in Washington

---

the broader political context that should guide their pursuit of new policy initiatives and implementation of existing measures.[12]

Available historical evidence suggests that there have been significant differences in prime ministerial leadership styles on national security and defence issues and on economic issues since the Trudeau era, with the centre's engagement with broader foreign policy issues gyrating between the two poles of centralized activism and decentralized incrementalism depending on circumstances. Although Canadian governments have often reacted to broader American initiatives in both settings, prime ministerial leadership on economic issues has tended toward various forms of engagement, while on defence issues it has often tended toward various forms of avoidance.[13]

The quiet collaboration of Jean Chrétien and Bill Clinton on economic issues enabled them to pursue several incremental bureaucratic initiatives during the 1990s without requiring either government to invest much political capital in the public relationship. Chrétien's standoffish approach to the Bush administration, especially after the initial post-9/11 shock wore off in Canada and disputes over Iraq became more prominent, enforced a cautious incrementalism among civil servants – whether in dealing with security-related pressures from Washington or pressures from Canadian business groups to pursue closer integration within the American security umbrella. Although these signals did not preclude close cabinet-level collaboration on specific issues, they did lead to a cooling of the overall political relationship.

Paul Martin's efforts to restore the bilateral relationship after taking office in December 2003 were reflected in his centralization of policy – not just political – control over bilateral relations as much as in specific policy choices. However, the Martin government's domestic political insecurity after losing its parliamentary majority in the 2004 election and the growing internal divisions between its "accommodationist" and "nationalist" wings contributed to a series of mixed messages that undercut both domestic policy coherence and its credibility in Washington.[14] This reality was most visible in his handling of proposals to participate in the US Ballistic Missile Defense initiative, as noted in Chapter 2.

Although the Harper minority governments of 2006-11 faced a similar balancing act, Prime Minister Harper carefully avoided the sorts of rhetoric described by some observers as self-righteous posturing while attempting to cauterize or resolve outstanding irritants with the Bush administration. This approach was visible in Harper's 2006 decision to negotiate a truce in the softwood lumber war, discussed further in Chapter 12; his restrained public approach to the ongoing dispute over US WHTI passport requirements and other American security measures, discussed in Chapters 10 and 11; and his efforts to work closely with the Obama administration in a variety of international contexts. Although Ottawa had invested considerable political capital in support of the Keystone XL pipeline project that would connect the Alberta oil sands to Texas refineries, Harper demonstrated similar restraint when, in November 2011, Obama sought to sidestep political controversy over the project by deferring a decision until after the 2012 presidential election.[15]

The cyclical character of Canada–US relations and the challenges of balancing domestic political requirements with those of managing bilateral relations can reinforce tendencies toward incremental policy management. So do the complex processes of coordinating international and transgovernmental policy relations.

Coordinating International and Transgovernmental Relations

The centralization of domestic political power in the PMO and PCO is reflected in some aspects of cross-border relations but definitely not in others.

Dealings with other foreign leaders, always a prime ministerial prerogative, have been further institutionalized in regular "summit diplomacy," a
process intensified since the 1990s through the G-8, G-20, hemispheric
Summit of the Americas, and North American leaders' summits.

Bilateral or trilateral summits provide useful tools for domestic, bilateral, and North American policy coordination to the extent that line departments have the opportunity to project their priorities (or problems) on
to leaders' agendas where feasible, in cases of consensus with American
and/or Mexican counterparts or conflict – where prime ministerial intervention might be necessary to secure high-level American attention to a
particular problem.

The elaborate bureaucratic mechanisms for organizing the agendas for
larger leaders' meetings are probably less important for Canada than the
opportunity for its leaders to be at the table with their global counterparts.
Such gatherings allow prime ministers to build personal relationships that
might be turned at some point to serve Canada's interests and to broker
formal or informal international agreements that accommodate Canadian
interests and priorities. The proliferation of so-called summit diplomacy in
recent years has given prime ministers opportunities for repeated personal
contact with American presidents above and beyond the limited contacts
afforded by bilateral meetings. Seven of Stephen Harper's eleven meetings
with Barack Obama between early 2009 and late 2011 came in multilateral
settings.

The proliferation of summit diplomacy and the spread of transgovernmental relations among line departments and agencies have complicated
the role of Foreign Affairs and International Trade Canada (DFAIT) in
managing bilateral relations. DFAIT retains responsibility for the day-to-
day management of Canadian diplomacy, international treaty negotiations,
and trade relations, including the operational management and coordination of Canada's diplomatic missions in the United States.

However, four major factors constrain its capacity to provide actual
leadership in this role. First, as noted above, prime ministers set the tone of
the relationship and determine when and how to intervene on specific
issues. They might be guided by the advice of the foreign or trade ministers
and their senior officials on these issues. Details of such relations can leak
out through the news media or surface years later through insider memoirs
such as those of former ambassadors Allan Gotlieb and Derek Burney.[16]
However, on issues requiring high levels of government intervention,

Canada's delegations to Washington are more likely to be led by the clerk of the Privy Council, sometimes supported by the prime minister's chief of staff, than by the deputy minister of Foreign Affairs.[17] On security and defence issues, several observers have noted the presence of institutionalized competition, if not conflict, between DFAIT (and its predecessor departments) and the Department of National Defence in which both the tone and the substance of policy (and consistency between public statements and "below the radar" cooperation) are vitally dependent on the balance between prime ministerial leadership, temporizing, and evasion.[18]

Second, Canada's ambassador to Washington is a prime ministerial appointment who, since the 1980s, has generally been a senior political or bureaucratic figure capable of maintaining close and direct ties to the PMO independent of his formal chain of command through DFAIT (see Chapter 2). The responsibilities of ambassadors require them to engage the American political system as a whole rather than conducting traditional "single point" diplomacy with foreign ministry counterparts, as in most other countries. However, though relatively independent, they (and Embassy officials) must also provide political support to the bilateral contacts and initiatives of line departments and agencies – and related ministerial visits.

Third, the growth of the highly decentralized processes of transgovernmental relations during the 1990s, documented by Mouafo and colleagues and described by Higginbotham and Heynen as part of Canada's "network diplomacy" in the United States,[19] also limits DFAIT's ability to exercise centralized control over bilateral relations, though its approval is usually required to negotiate formal international agreements. However, the requirement for such approval does not extend to the multitude of "soft law" arrangements that might be concluded by line departments and agencies or even by provincial governments.

Fourth, the relative importance of these factors and how they interact with one another are highly contingent on the management styles of individual prime ministers. Jean Chrétien delegated operational responsibility for most key issues to individual cabinet ministers while retaining the right to intervene on any issue at any time. His delegation of cross-border relations to Deputy Prime Minister John Manley after 9/11, with a mandate to coordinate border and security-related issues across departmental boundaries, was a classic expression of a prime ministerial "bolt of electricity," as was his 2002 decision to challenge US policies on Iraq in a speech to the Chicago Council on Foreign Relations.[20]

Paul Martin assigned responsibility for coordinating bilateral relations to a special cabinet committee, closely supported by the Privy Council Office. The PCO moved beyond its normal coordinating role to manage several key files from the centre, including proposals for large-scale regulatory coordination and border management and later the management of the SPP process.[21] Martin's interventionist management style could also be seen in the PCO's development of a comprehensive national security policy in April 2004, the international policy statement of 2005, and the SPP process that emerged from the leaders' summit of March 2005. All three initiatives were carefully calibrated to complement American policies with a well-glossed veneer of "Made in Canada" rhetoric.[22] In the eyes of some, the function being performed at the centre was catalytic. The launch of the Security and Prosperity Partnership was seen as going well beyond what the Departments of Foreign Affairs and Industry could handle, with over twenty departments involved and an agenda dealing with domestic as much as foreign policy issues. What people at a distance might see as a hands-on function looks more like a coordination function from the centre.[23]

However, this personal style had its drawbacks. Public servants engaged in the process observed that Martin "didn't have a focus – he had too many priorities – but he wouldn't empower anybody else to do it."[24] This unfocused activism sometimes backfired, as with DFAIT's division into its separate diplomatic and trade components, disrupting its efforts to coordinate advocacy activities in the United States and elsewhere. This reorganization was rejected by Parliament and later reversed by the Harper Conservatives.

Stephen Harper's management style for bilateral relations appears to have evolved into a blend of his predecessors' approaches. Shortly after taking office in 2006, his newly appointed clerk of the Privy Council, Kevin Lynch, announced the transfer of responsibilities for all major bilateral policy files to their relevant line departments and agencies: regulatory coordination to the Treasury Board, border and security issues to Public Safety Canada, and most other microeconomic issues to Industry Canada, while the Privy Council returned to its traditional "coordination and challenge" function within the government.[25] This pattern largely persisted until the Washington Declaration of February 2011 created the necessity for more centralized PCO coordination of negotiations on perimeter security and selected regulatory issues. Most cross-border files have been managed by relevant line ministers, particularly David Emerson (Trade), Stockwell Day (Public Safety, Trade), Jim Prentice (Industry, Environment), and later, Vic Toews (Public Safety), enjoying the prime minister's personal confidence. Ministers who failed this test were moved into less sensitive portfolios (Rona Ambrose from Environment, Peter Van Loan from Public Safety). The Prime Minister's Office was directly consulted and closely engaged on all major policy decisions, but detailed (as opposed to strategic) policy leadership typically came from ministers and their senior officials.

At the same time, the Harper government centralized its communications function to an unprecedented extent. All public communications were vetted from the centre, though this process has usually been fast-tracked for senior ministers and ambassadors and relaxed somewhat since 2006. This micromanagement has constrained the capacity of Canadian diplomats in the United States to engage in public diplomacy. However, these constraints have been balanced since 2009 by intermittent PMO efforts to cultivate favourable media coverage in the United States.[26]

As with most domestic issues, the more directly particular questions of cross-border relations engage the government's core priorities, the more likely they are to involve some degree of central coordination. Technical and administrative issues are far more likely to be dealt with through the decentralized processes of transgovernmental relations unless they become the subject of political controversy – at which time ministers (or ambassadors) discover the extent to which they enjoy "the boss's" confidence.

Bringing in the Provinces – or Not

After the growth of international and bilateral transgovernmental relations, the most substantive change in the domestic and institutional character of Canada–US relations since the 1990s has been the growing role of provincial governments, whether expressed through the ongoing channels of federal–provincial relations, expanded provincial–state relations, or DFAIT's networking with provincial governments in its cross-border advocacy activities.

The need for federal–provincial policy coordination in Canada–US relations is most visible in conducting ongoing bilateral and multilateral trade negotiations. Christopher Kukucha has detailed the evolution of the federal–provincial C-TRADE process on trade consultations since the 1970s.[27] Several factors have expanded the political incentives for Ottawa to engage provinces in ongoing policy discussions relevant to their core interests. They include the continuing impact of the 1937 *Labour Conventions* ruling, which limits Ottawa's power to enforce international treaty commitments unilaterally in areas of provincial jurisdiction, the regional character of the Canadian economy, and the trend of international trade negotiations to engage spheres of microeconomic regulation traditionally within provincial jurisdiction.

In reality, Ottawa's engagement of provincial premiers and governments in cross-border relations is highly uneven, even though it has grown substantially since the turn of the century. Department officials suggest that Pierre Pettigrew, who served as trade minister in the Chrétien government (1999-2003) and as Paul Martin's foreign minister (2004-6), was pivotal in fostering DFAIT's more consultative approach to the provinces.[28] Prime Minister Martin invited the provinces to set up representative offices within the Canadian Embassy in Washington as a sign of openness and goodwill upon taking office in 2003, though to date only Alberta has been willing to pay the hefty price tag associated with the privilege.[29] Ottawa actively engaged the provinces in ongoing discussions leading to the negotiation of the 2006 Softwood Lumber Agreement while maintaining control over the actual negotiations and wording of the eventual agreement.[30] Minister of International Trade Stockwell Day's ability to mobilize a consensus among premiers on reciprocal access to subnational procurement was vital to initiating and completing negotiations to limit the application of expanded Buy American laws to Canadian exports in 2009-10. However, Ottawa has maintained a much more arm's-length relationship on cross-border aspects of energy and environmental policies for reasons discussed in Chapter 13.

A key departure in Ottawa's diplomatic approach to the United States, begun under the Chrétien government but gradually expanded under the Martin and Harper governments, has been to encourage growing provincial involvement in these processes. Working independently of Ottawa, provinces have developed a growing range of formal and informal contacts with state-level counterparts since the 1970s. All provinces bordering the United States now participate to varying degrees in formal cross-border networks, attend meetings of regional governors' associations, and maintain links with state legislative networks. Cross-border issues now surface regularly on the agendas of premiers' meetings. Ottawa's willingness to take advantage of these growing cross-border networks, discussed in Chapter 9, is a significant departure from traditional approaches to diplomatic advocacy.

Prime Ministerial Diplomacy: Traditional and Public

Prime ministerial diplomacy, whether formal or informal, is a major element of managing bilateral relations, though one whose importance should be neither underestimated nor overestimated. Presidential time and attention are, if anything, even more constrained than prime ministerial time and attention. For that reason, close observers of the process suggest that high-profile state visits, a form of public theatre, are probably of less importance to the ongoing relationship than the capacity to cultivate relations of mutual respect that serve the interests of both parties, though "working visits" are often more productive.[31]

Compared with most other foreign relationships of the US government, the Canada–US transgovernmental relationship is sufficiently broad and deep that it can be facilitated or constrained by the cyclical nature of political relationships between the two governments, but working-level relations continue as a matter of practical necessity.[32] Bilateral or trilateral meetings serve as a way of concentrating the attention of senior officials – policy windows that enable them to secure high-level approval of ongoing policy initiatives or discussion of policy roadblocks of major significance to each government. As such, they can serve as signalling devices to senior officials within each government's bureaucracy of the need to accommodate the interests of the other or to expedite the mutually satisfactory resolution of specific problems.[33]

Close relationships do not guarantee the resolution of particular problems, as with the persistence of the acid rain dispute during the 1980s and softwood lumber disputes over five separate presidencies. Nor does a cooling of bilateral political relations mean that certain irritants might not be addressed effectively. This reality was demonstrated by Secretary of State George Shultz's initiation of quarterly meetings with his Canadian counterparts during the early 1980s and President George W. Bush's quiet support for the reopening of the American border to Canadian beef exports after the 2003 closure despite disputes over other foreign and defence policies.[34] Similarly, Canadian diplomats in Washington work assiduously to smooth rough patches in the relationship by advising Ottawa on the most effective ways of managing the sensibilities of particular American decision makers and by advising American officials of the domestic constraints facing their political masters, as, of course, do American diplomats in Ottawa.[35]

However, relations suffer when prime ministers or their senior advisers are seen to exploit bilateral meetings for domestic political advantage at the president's expense – for example by leaking the contents of discussions to the Canadian media that reflect adversely on the president, as during the Martin years – or when prime ministers are seen to exploit domestic anti-Americanism for partisan political purposes. Such behaviour contributed to a substantial cooling of the political relationship under the Martin government.[36] In contrast, Prime Minister Harper and his officials have been careful to observe normal diplomatic conventions in their dealings with both the Bush and Obama White House.

The Harper government's approach to personal diplomacy has evolved with the broader political climate in bilateral relations. During the Bush administration, its first priority was to resolve major ongoing irritants – notably the softwood lumber dispute and processes for WHTI implementation – while restoring Canada's political capacity in Washington and simultaneously attempting to limit domestic perceptions of excessive closeness to the highly unpopular president.[37]

As discussed in Chapter 4, Canadian leaders' approach to their American counterparts is often conditioned by the latter's relative popularity among Canadians. Barack Obama's phenomenal popularity in Canada has made it easier for Stephen Harper to cultivate closer working relations on many issues than was possible during the Bush administration. Harper has sought to dispel the widespread perception that bilateral relations are a by-product of partisan and ideological affinities – or the lack thereof – between the two governments. Canadian diplomats have generally been supportive of US government initiatives in international settings, with the significant exception of American (and European) proposals for a global bank tax in response to those countries' bailouts of major financial institutions during the financial crisis of 2008-9.[38] The two leaders' February 2011 announcement of negotiations leading to the development of a North American security perimeter, a phrase that had been politically off-limits in Canada during the previous decade, also illustrates this reality.

These positions reflect the government's economic priorities and its view of Canada's national interests. However, its decision to work more closely with Washington on issues fairly marginal to Canadian interests, such as support for expanding NATO membership to include Ukraine and Georgia, suggests a desire to accumulate political capital for use in Washington's highly transactional political culture. A less immediately obvious but more intriguing dimension of prime ministerial diplomacy under the Harper government has been its approach to public diplomacy.

Talking to Americans, Promoting Canada

> *Public diplomacy ... is meant to impress the constituents of*
> *legislators of the wisdom of not taking action against*

> *Canadian interests. Not because such action is not nice, but*
> *because it hurts specific American interests.*
>
> *– Allan Gotlieb, cited in Henrikson, 2005*[39]

Canadian diplomacy in the United States reflects the underlying reality of bilateral relations as a two- or multilevel game in which domestic political actors simultaneously attempt to build supportive coalitions for current and proposed policies within their own domestic political spaces as well as in dealings with foreign governments. However, pressures for public input into "intermestic" policy processes increasingly require national governments to take foreign public opinion and the activities of related nongovernmental actors into account, whether in building closer relations with or contesting the policies of their international trading partners. As a result, traditional forms of diplomacy focusing on state-to-state relations are increasingly supplemented by "public diplomacy."[40]

Public diplomacy can be defined as the targeting of foreign audiences by governments of another country in order to build relationships and promote their short- and long-term foreign policy objectives. It can take a variety of forms, ranging from systematic efforts at "strategic public relations" or "branding" (the crafting of clear, consistent public relations messages to complement a state's political objectives), to the cultivation of elite and stakeholder networks favourably disposed to one's country and its interests, to academic and cultural outreach activities, and to routine media relations. It is distinguished from traditional state-to-state diplomatic relations since it specifically seeks to cultivate relationships with non-state actors in foreign countries.[41] This aspect of public diplomacy, central to Canada's diplomatic activities in the United States,[42] is addressed in greater detail in Chapters 8 and 9.

Canada's media relations in the United States have often been a marginal and relatively ineffective component of Canada's public diplomacy, regardless of the best efforts of Canadian diplomats, with the possible exception of Allan Gotlieb's colourful tenure in Washington during the 1980s. All foreign governments, including that of Canada, share the challenge of securing favourable attention in the highly competitive American media market and engaging the popular (as opposed to elite) media on matters central to their interests.

This inherent challenge is reinforced by what Canadian journalists and diplomats described as the "two audience problem." Canadian political leaders visiting Washington are usually more interested in Canadian media coverage of their activities than in securing peripheral coverage in the American media. Canadian journalists in Washington – for whom prime ministerial visits, in particular, are "big news" – often reinforce these incentives. However, though American diplomats recognize politicians' intrinsic tendency to "play to their constituents," the greater the gap between the contents of private discussions and public statements, the less likely they are to give credence to the former in ongoing policy discussions.[43]

The Harper government's approach to public diplomacy during its first three years in office was characterized by the hyper-cautious micromanagement that often characterized its domestic public communications during the same period – much to the frustration of Canadian diplomats attempting to obtain clearance for speeches to interest groups and other public relations activities.[44] Although the pressures of minority government and President Bush's unpopularity in Canada certainly influenced this low-profile approach, this caution was reinforced by extensive media publicity given to off-the-record comments by Chief of Staff Ian Brodie in March 2008. His comments, based on diplomatic reports of conversations with a senior Obama adviser, drew unwanted attention to Obama's cynical exploitation of anti-NAFTA sentiments among union organizers and voters – a key Democratic constituency – in his pursuit of the party's presidential nomination. Although Harper took advantage of the April 2008 NAFTA leaders' summit to remind Americans of their dependence on imported oil from Canada, he subsequently kept a studious distance from the presidential election campaign – even warning ministers to avoid meeting with Republican candidate John McCain on his visit to Ottawa in June 2008.[45]

Although President Obama has been less responsive to protectionist sentiments among his supporters than candidate Obama, Prime Minister Harper has taken almost every opportunity to use his periodic meetings with the president to speak directly to the American people "based on themes that we expect to permeate the Canada–US relationship on a longer-term basis."[46] The result has been a series of carefully orchestrated interviews with national and financial media outlets – speaking to Americans through Americans – to promote the relative success of Canada's economic and regulatory policies, especially in the financial sector, and warn against a reversion to protectionist policies in the United States. These interviews are typically linked to bilateral leaders' meetings, international summits, and other major media events, such as the 2010 Winter Olympics in Vancouver. As part of this process, Harper's advisers retained two former presidential press secretaries, former Clinton aide Mike McCurry and former Bush spokesman Ari Fleischer, for project-based advice on strategic relations with media networks spanning the American political spectrum.[47]

Although bilateral meetings provide the context for some of this activity, the issues under discussion are increasingly addressed in broader international contexts. Rather than a unipolar environment in which Canada seeks to cultivate a special relationship with the United States, many aspects of bilateral economic relations must also be engaged in the multipolar context of international economic discussions and negotiations.

Engaging Washington in Global Policy Streams

As discussed in Chapter 2, Canada's engagement of US policies necessarily involves both bilateral dimensions and broader policies toward allies and competitors in the international arena. The growing internationalization of many policy fields traditionally treated as domestic policies in both countries – and the inevitable overlap of such activities – increase the premium on policy coordination without necessarily ensuring that it happens. These processes reflect the reality of multilevel governance: the interaction of national (and/or subnational) government agencies with international counterparts at multiple levels – political, senior, functional, and operating levels of departmental and agency bureaucracies.

The federal Department of Finance has come to play the leading role in coordinating Canada's international economic policies, whatever DFAIT's formal and functional roles in the leadership of trade negotiations and the resolution of trade disputes. Finance plays the lead role in dealings with a wide range of specialized international economic organizations, from ministerial meetings through G-8 and G-20 processes to the International Monetary Fund and several other organizations responsible for the coordination of financial sector policies (except securities regulation).

However, the proliferation of other international organizations whose activities can have significant impacts on Canadian domestic policies increases the importance of the centre's role in ensuring appropriate international coordination. Under both Prime Ministers Mulroney and Chrétien, Canada's participation in international environmental organizations functioned more or less independently from domestic economic or energy policy considerations despite the significant potential domestic impacts of Canada's commitments under the Rio and Kyoto Protocols. These contradictions became increasingly apparent during the Martin years, giving way to an explicit if evolving mandate for internal policy coordination under the Harper government.[48]

Similar effects are visible in the field of border, container, and airline security policies discussed in Chapters 10 and 11. Direct responsibility for these policies is broadly distributed among Public Safety Canada (and its Canada Border Services Agency), Transport Canada, and DFAIT through its oversight of Passport Canada. However, commitments made under the Smart Border process of 2001-3 have contributed to decentralized networks for international policy coordination involving the International Civil Aviation Organization (ICAO) on passport standards and security, the World Customs Organization on container security, as well as formal and informal networks of national police, intelligence, and immigration officials.

Although these networks generally operate below the radar, they become more politically salient when specific crises force political leaders to acknowledge expectations for international coordination while attempting to protect or accommodate national discretion in policy making dictated by constitutional requirements, public expectations, or differing national circumstances. Decision making from the centre can either empower or constrain the departments responsible for transgovernmental relations – as shown by the ongoing leadership role of federal finance ministers and their senior officials in international economic relations and the implicit mandate given to Minister of Environment Jim Prentice and his successor, Peter Kent, since 2008 to incorporate provincial and sectoral concerns over industry competitiveness and regional redistribution into Canada's domestic and international climate change policies.[49]

These realities increase the importance of transgovernmental relations among specialized cross-border and international bureaucratic networks but also of effective communication and cooperation among Canadian diplomats and other officials responsible for managing bilateral relations and their counterparts in line departments and agencies.

Canada–US Relations as Multilevel Governance

National political leaders continue to play a vital role in overseeing and directing Canada's relations with its American neighbour, whether in the specific context of bilateral relations or policies toward allies. However, the often segmented and decentralized character of transgovernmental relations has contributed to the outward drift of responsibility and influence, if not necessarily of power, from the centre to clusters of intergovernmental, economic, and societal networks with specialized and often discrete responsibilities and functions.

These networks represent what some observers have described as a shift from "government" (the authoritative exercise of power based on delegated legal responsibilities functioning independently of societal actors but subject to direct control by elected officials) to "governance" (the sharing of responsibility for various aspects of policy making and administration among governmental and societal actors, often cutting across formal political jurisdictions).

In few areas of Canadian life are the concepts of "network governance" more applicable than in the multiple policy communities associated with Canada's efforts to influence American policies toward Canada. These relationships function at multiple levels, but for the sake of simplicity they can be condensed to three interlocking sets of relationships. First, Canadian diplomats in Washington, DC, parallel the coordinating role of the political and bureaucratic centre in domestic Canadian politics as they engage the American political process, including the White House, other executive departments and agencies, the complex beehive of Congress, and the networks of interest groups and societal interests. Second, Canadian diplomatic activity in the United States involves growing federal and provincial networks of activity outside the Washington beltway. These networks involve formal and informal engagement with state governments, provincial–state networks, and overlapping societal interests. Third, intertwined with these activities are the cross-border networks of Canadian and American economic and other societal interests – sometimes cooperating, often competing, with one another. This honeycomb – or labyrinth – of activity is the focus of the next three chapters.

6

Network Diplomacy
Engaging the Executive Branch

How do we settle our differences – economic, commercial, political, environmental – with a country in which political power is so broadly diffused throughout the entire system of governance? ... Foreign policy towards Canada might well not be foreign policy at all but simply an aggregation of domestic policy thrusts.

– Allan Gotlieb, I'll Be with You in a Minute, Mr. Ambassador, *1991*[1]

The past generation saw a fundamental shift in the patterns and processes of bilateral policy relations between the United States and Canada. Rather than reflecting traditional forms of international diplomacy conducted between national foreign ministries or between national political leaders, the two countries' extensive economic integration requires Canadian governments to engage the American political system as a whole.

This process necessarily extends formal primacy to relations between the political executives of each country, not just the president and prime minister but also senior political and bureaucratic advisers to each leader and cabinet officers responsible for comparable federal departments and agencies. The executive branch – the White House and executive departments and agencies – of the US federal government remains the primary focus of transgovernmental relations between the two countries, whether among political leaders, diplomats and senior policy makers, or working-level officials.

However, any US federal policy subject to legislative authorization, funding, or oversight invariably engages the attention of relevant members of Congress, their professional staff advisers, and the many interest groups inside and outside the capital beltway that compete to influence these policy decisions and the related allocation of public funds and/or regulatory authority. Regulatory policies are subject to judicial oversight, frequently making courts and judges the arbiters of political disputes initiated by citizens, interest groups, other governments, or agencies over the application of US federal laws and administrative processes. As a result, managing bilateral relations often resembles a two- or multilevel game *within* the United States as Canadian officials engage the cross-currents of the American political system.

This chapter outlines the relationship between Canada's federal government – in particular as moderated by the Canadian Embassy in Washington – and the development of American domestic policy processes affecting Canada. It contrasts traditional diplomatic forms with the functional roles played by Canada's ambassador and Embassy officials in engaging the executive branch, providing political and technical guidance to policy makers in Ottawa, and facilitating cross-border dealings between cabinet-level officials and their senior advisers in both countries. (The Embassy's broader functions in engaging Congress, conducting public diplomacy and interest group relations within the beltway, and coordinating and monitoring related activities beyond the beltway are addressed in Chapters 7 and 8.)

These dynamics – and Canadian diplomats' engagement with them – vary significantly depending on whether they relate to the strategic dimension of bilateral or North American relations, sectoral (or major subsectoral) policies, or the multitude of micropolicy dynamics in day-to-day interactions between the two countries.

The Washington Embassy in Canada–US Relations

> *Diplomacy isn't just saying nice things in public. It is doing your homework, being smart, and knowing what you want so that you can chew through the hard-to-resolve issues and make gradual progress on them.*
>
> – *Paul Frazer, seminar remarks, 2006.*[2]

The imposing marble façade of the Canadian Embassy in Washington, DC, fronts on Pennsylvania Avenue a few short blocks from Capitol Hill. Built in the early 1990s, following a move from its long-time Embassy Row location on Massachusetts Avenue NW, it symbolizes a central reality of bilateral relations. Canadian diplomacy in Washington must deal with the American domestic political system as a whole, not just traditional diplomatic functions of engaging heads of state, foreign ministry counterparts, and heads of executive departments primarily responsible for economic relations.

As such, the Embassy is a structural heretic within both countries' political systems. Embassy officials, and their colleagues in Canada's network of consulates across the United States, carry out all the traditional "eyes and ears" functions of foreign diplomatic and commercial representatives. They engage in quiet advocacy and promotion of their country's interests associated with traditional concepts of diplomacy, reflecting the policy priorities and positions of the government of the day. They also identify and interpret political and economic opportunities for and risks to Canadian interests at multiple levels of analysis: strategic, sectoral, subsectoral, and microlevel. However, the two countries' extensive social and economic integration ensures that Canada's cross-border diplomacy is also heavily influenced by the "intermestic" dimension of bilateral relations across multiple policy fields in which US domestic initiatives (executive or legislative in origin) can enhance or disrupt bilateral economic and social relations between the two countries and their citizens.

As a result, the Embassy provides an important staff function for central agencies, Foreign Affairs and International Trade Canada (DFAIT), and numerous line departments in Ottawa. Its officials relay information on American domestic initiatives and the varied political and bureaucratic processes that shape them. They advise and, in some cases, work closely with senior Ottawa policy makers on the framing and timing of ongoing bilateral policy discussions to insert Canadian priorities into American "problem streams" discussed in Chapter 5, identify opportunities in both executive and congressional calendars to advance these initiatives, and support the regular stream of federal Canadian cabinet ministers travelling to Washington to meet with their American counterparts and institutionalize sectoral policy conversations. More recently, the Embassy has also played a growing role in engaging provincial government interests in Washington.

However, the Embassy also plays several important line functions in engaging the American political system. Although formal negotiating processes on specific agreements are often managed from Ottawa, senior Embassy officials can be directly tasked with negotiating on sensitive political issues – including those leading to the Softwood Lumber Agreement of 2006 and the accommodation of Canadian priorities in periodic US energy bills under consideration by Congress. Embassy officials actively network with US executive departments and agencies, congressional committees and the staff who support them, domestic interest groups, and think tanks. A significant part of this process, common to any professional government relations function, is to identify actors whose agendas might overlap, complement, or conflict with those of the Canadian government or major Canadian domestic interests on particular issues. They can also serve as advocates for private Canadian interests in dealing with the administration and Congress on matters consistent with DFAIT's broader mandate to promote open trade and investment flows within and beyond North America.

These activities have been known to cause offence among American diplomats and administration officials, especially when directed at cross-purposes with some aspect of administration policy.[3] Depending on the circumstances, they can also be deeply offensive to some Canadian nationalists, who bridle at the thought of governments engaging in a foreign country's special interest politics – at least to the extent that doing so creates similar incentives for American interests and diplomats in Canada.[4] However, they also speak to the reality of "intermestic" relations between the two countries – the blurring of traditional distinctions between foreign and domestic policies and politics on numerous issues.

Formally, Canada's diplomatic missions in the United States report to Ottawa through the assistant deputy minister responsible for North America, or the Americas, depending on the latest iteration of DFAIT's organizational chart. In recent years, as discussed in Chapter 5, the Canadian ambassador in Washington has been a political appointment, generally with direct access to the prime minister and his closest advisers. His officials provide vital intelligence and analytical and support functions to numerous Canadian government departments and agencies and to Canadian businesses and advocacy groups with extensive cross-border interests. Together with the nationwide network of consulates and their growing interactions with the cross-border activities of provincial governments, discussed in Chapter 9, the Embassy is engaged in multiple diplomatic networks and policy communities whose activities directly or indirectly affect the interests of millions of Canadians.

Under such circumstances, the behaviour of varied governmental actors on both sides of the border is often contingent on the expected responses of other key stakeholders. Coordination between governments, whether formal or informal, can include "mutual enlightenment" on participants' policy goals and intentions, "mutual reinforcement" of policy goals to overcome domestic or foreign opposition, "mutual adjustment" involving adaptations of national policies to reduce conflicts, or "mutual concessions" in which policy adjustments by one state are conditional on reciprocal adjustments by another.[5] However, in Washington's complex, often opaque political environment, a key function of the Embassy is to identify the actual nature of the game and the set of rules by which it is being played.

Priority Setting, Risk Management, and Crisis Management
The range of issues associated with bilateral relations – corresponding to Kingdon's "problem stream" – is generally far larger than can absorb the attention of senior decision makers and diplomats – Kingdon's "political stream." Moreover, as noted in Chapter 2, the substantial differences between the scale and scope of problem and political streams between Canadian and US governments mean that bilateral issues of critical importance to Canadian interests are often peripheral to senior American decision makers with whom they deal.

As a result, both Ottawa policy makers and Canadian diplomats in Washington must establish their priorities and identify appropriate means of securing political recognition by relevant American political actors to secure a hearing and obtain substantive relief or accommodation through American political processes. Such processes and the decision-making contexts within which they function are often far from transparent. So are the "policy windows" that provide occasions to translate these agendas into authoritative actions or to prevent other political actors from doing so at the expense of Canadian interests.

Discussions with Canadian officials in Ottawa and Washington during the past several years suggest that they have pursued a relatively consistent set of priorities in cross-border relations. Most of these priorities are "defensive," responding to perceived political risks or threats to Canadian interests from within the American political system – something far broader than administration policies. However, they can also reflect proactive approaches intended to secure the ongoing recognition and accommodation of Canadian interests within American policy processes to the extent that domestic political conditions in Canada enable such approaches.[6]

These priorities tend to reflect "issue clusters" based on broad policy objectives: economic advocacy, both maintaining US market access for Canadian goods and services and combatting economic protectionism, and security issues, ranging from the facilitation of bilateral cooperation on security and law enforcement issues, to combatting perceptions of Canada and the northern border as security risks, to debates over implementation of the Western Hemisphere Travel Initiative (WHTI; see Chapter 11). More recently, overlapping energy and environmental issues have taken an increasingly important place in bilateral relations, though one that varies with shifting economic circumstances and constellations of power in Washington.

In addition to these issues, the Embassy facilitates ongoing conversations with Department of State and White House officials on broader foreign policy issues, particularly those relating to cooperation with the United States in the international arena. These discussions have generally involved ongoing issues such as US and NATO engagement in Afghanistan, nuclear security and proliferation, as well as Canadian engagement in Latin America and the Caribbean.

The roles played by the president and senior White House staff on bilateral issues depend on several factors, notably the management styles and priorities of individual presidents, the formal and informal interagency processes used by different administrations to coordinate policies, and the ability of Canadian ambassadors to secure regular access to senior advisers enjoying access to and the confidence of the incumbent president.[7] The tone of personal relations between individual presidents and prime ministers can contribute at the margins to facilitating or hindering the broader management of bilateral relations or the resolution of particular issues. Individual presidents can direct executive agencies to accommodate Canadian interests in ways not prejudicial to those of the United States or withhold support that might otherwise reduce institutional barriers to such arrangements. However, such directives rarely result in actual policy reversals in the absence of broader policy changes resulting from changing circumstances or national priorities.

As noted by Bow[8] and others, a key priority in managing bilateral relations is to avoid linkage politics – the explicit connection of US concessions or accommodations in one issue area with Canadian policy concessions in an unrelated field. Two exceptions to this rule – tacit or explicit – have emerged in recent years. As discussed in Chapter 2, relatively unfettered Canadian access to US export markets has been closely tied to *general* cooperation with US security initiatives *within* North America if not to Canadian compliance with specific US security measures. And during the 2008 US presidential primaries, the Harper government clearly linked unfettered US access to Canadian energy exports to the preservation of market access guarantees under NAFTA.[9]

Within the three issue clusters noted above – economic access, security, and energy/environment – and often dominating them are specific issues or irritants that absorb disproportionate amounts of political attention as they come to symbolize a particular aspect – and sometimes dysfunction – of the broader relationship.

During the months and years following 9/11, a critical priority of Canadian governments was to maintain American confidence in Canadian security cooperation through implementation and extension of the Smart Border Accord. Although Canadian diplomats were relatively successful in sidestepping congressional protectionism during and after the 2001 recession, the softwood lumber dispute came to dominate political agendas and Canadian public perceptions of bilateral economic relations after the 2004 presidential election. As noted elsewhere, resolving this dispute became a critical priority in unblocking the broader political agenda for cross-border cooperation. The security and economic agendas came together between 2006 and 2008 in debates over the implementation of congressionally mandated WHTI and other requirements for secure identification both within and when entering (or re-entering) the United States. These debates largely obscured bureaucratic cooperation on numerous issues, including those bundled in the Security and Prosperity Partnership (SPP) process.

Shifts in Washington's balance of power arising from Democratic victories in the 2006 congressional elections and Barack Obama's rise to the presidency in November 2008 increased the salience of protectionist outlooks on multiple fronts – culminating in congressional Buy American legislation passed as part of the stimulus bills of early 2009. Although the Obama administration has lived up to neither the hopes of organized labour and other protectionist interests nor the corresponding fears of Canadian governments and business interests, Canadian interests remain vulnerable to a wide range of protectionist measures, often tacked on to broader legislative initiatives whose contents are negotiated in the back rooms of Congress.

The result is a series of overlapping but usually discrete two-level games in which Canadian government (including Embassy) officials work with administration counterparts on a wide range of technical issues while

Embassy officials engage in networking activities with interest groups, members of Congress, and their staffs to identify and recruit support for different Canadian objectives.

At the centre of this networking is the Canadian ambassador and a small cluster of senior officials responsible for political, economic, congressional, and defence-related liaison activities within the Embassy.

Role and Personality of the Ambassador

> *If the ambassador is the right person, it unlocks a whole other warp speed. If the guy at the top has the vision and has the access and the drive, and both McKenna and Wilson have that, it makes a difference.*
>
> – *Confidential interview with Canadian diplomat, Washington, 2006*

The modern era in Canadian diplomacy in the United States arguably began with the appointment of Allan Gotlieb, formerly the professional head of the Canadian foreign service (Undersecretary of State), as Canada's ambassador in Washington in 1981. His long tenure (1981-89), active engagement of Congress, and skilled use of political connections and back-channel diplomacy in both Washington and Ottawa established the standard for what Gotlieb later described as the "New Diplomacy" to be conducted by Canadian ambassadors.[10]

Most of his immediate successors came from the same mould – senior foreign service officials who had developed close links with the prime minister of the day in prior responsibilities and maintained those links after moving to Washington: Derek Burney under Brian Mulroney, Raymond Chrétien and Michael Kergin under Jean Chrétien. Both Paul Martin and Stephen Harper reinforced the overtly political nature of the ambassador's role by appointing veteran political leaders: former New Brunswick Liberal premier Frank McKenna (2005-6), Mulroney-era finance and trade minister Michael Wilson (2006-9), and serving Manitoba NDP premier Gary Doer (2009-). However, neither appointment process has been a guarantee that the ambassador would not be undercut by the prime minister's political advisers.[11]

The ambassador is the principal contact with senior members of the administration and of Congress – though his principal deputies, the deputy chief of mission and the ministers (senior officials) responsible for political and economic affairs and congressional relations, are also actively engaged in dealing with mid-ranking officials in the executive agencies and members of Congress. However, much of the day-to-day activity is carried out by sector specialists who usually deal with technical counterparts in relevant executive agencies, congressional staff, and interest group or corporate representatives.

Gotlieb, uniquely in recent history, served three prime ministers and governments with varied agendas. He has long contended that the ambassador's role is "the art of penetrating concentric intersecting circles of influence" to secure access to senior decision makers in the White House, executive branch, and Congress, and the political power brokers with whom they interact, and to ensure that Canadian interests are taken into consideration in US policy decisions affecting Canada.[12] However, credibility depends on the extent to which the ambassador is seen to speak for the government of the day. Former ambassador Michael Kergin observes that "if you have access to the prime minister, it's amazing how many people want to talk to you."[13]

Canada's last four ambassadors have come to the job with different backgrounds, management and diplomatic styles, and approaches to engaging their own governments – reflecting their role at the centre of the two-level game of balancing political realities in Ottawa and Washington. All have had extensive personal networks among senior American and Canadian decision makers that they cultivated and expanded during their time in Washington. Some ambassadors, notably Gotlieb and McKenna, have taken a relatively high-profile approach to public relations, actively seeking US media interviews to promote Canada's image in the United States and, in the latter case, refuting urban myths such as the false perception that some of the 9/11 terrorists entered the United States from Canada. Others, such as Kergin and Wilson, have concentrated more on influencing media personalities behind the news – especially in the heavily polarized Washington environment of the post-9/11 years.

McKenna, a gregarious, highly political personality, sought a relatively high public profile in Washington as part of a deliberate strategy of public diplomacy intended to help Canada's image in Washington recover from the cooling of official relations over Iraq – albeit with mixed results for reasons discussed in previous chapters. Wilson combined a dignified personal and public style with a hands-on approach to policy issues reminiscent of his style as a senior cabinet minister. Both were highly regarded by their officials as demanding, highly engaged, hard-working personalities deeply committed to the Embassy's mission. One senior official commented that

> Each ambassador has his own style and his own relationship with the prime minister. Ambassador Wilson came in here as a godfather ... in the Conservative cabinet. He was seen as almost a senior minister [while ambassador], and he acted that way. And Michael Wilson being Michael Wilson, he also acted as a senior deputy minister. We'd get into detailed policy issues and send back recommendations to Ottawa.[14]

Gary Doer, appointed across partisan lines by the Harper government in mid-2009, brought a somewhat different approach and style to the position, quickly attuning himself to the political nuances of Washington after a decade of cultivating state-level networks through his participation in national and regional governors' conferences.

In Washington, the greatest challenge of an ambassador is to secure the attention of (and access to) senior decision makers and other "persons of influence" in an exceptionally competitive global capital with 156 different embassies. Ambassador Gotlieb was well known for his public entertainment at the Embassy during the 1980s, though his most significant relationships were usually cultivated in small private dinners and social events with cabinet secretaries, their senior advisers, and senior White House staff.[15] Although his successors have typically had lower public profiles, each one has brought a slightly different style to outreach activity.

Both Wilson and Doer have made frequent use of "outreach dinners" on particular topics of interest to the Embassy to cultivate relationships with Washington decision makers, business executives, think tank specialists, and other groups. They have also exposed visiting policy makers from Canada to a cross-section of Washington insights. Depending on the topic and purpose of such gatherings, invitation lists are carefully crafted with senior political and bureaucratic decision makers, senior business executives, think tank and interest group representatives, and academics with the desired combination of influence and expertise.

Although diplomatic disputes can arise occasionally, there are risks in allowing Canadian responses to become personal or to send a message that the two countries' interests are seriously at odds. For example, one senior US government official noted that, when Ambassador Wilson issued a strong public rebuke of Janet Napolitano's statement in a televised interview in

April 2009 that some of the 9/11 terrorists had entered the United States from Canada, "you lost 90 percent of your diplomatic advantage by emphasizing that you are a foreign country with different interests."[16] However, Canadian diplomats had been under firm instructions for some time to respond firmly, directly, and publicly to such allegations, which had become a widely circulated urban myth following the Chrétien government's failure to take related media reports seriously in the aftermath of 9/11.[17]

The sectoral character of cross-border relations, with an emphasis on the cultivation of direct contacts between cabinet-level officers and their senior officials in both countries, expands the ambassador's potential range of influence as the Canadian government's senior "eyes and ears" on the ground in Washington. One senior Canadian diplomat noted that "our ambassador ... can develop a relationship with most members of the Canadian cabinet. When you have cabinet ministers coming here regularly – which we do – and when you have an effective ambassador, as we do, they can develop effective relationships with the politicians."[18]

The appointment of senior political figures to the Embassy has facilitated this process. Politicians are more likely to relate to one another than to senior officials – whether on a personal level as veterans of the political trenches or in addressing questions of small-p political tactics and the political opportunities and constraints facing their US counterparts.[19]

Engaging the Executive Branch

> *The success of the relationship depends on relationships:*
> *understanding each other, knowing each other, respecting*
> *each other.*
>
> – *Anne McLellan, comments in the roundtable*
> *New Leadership in U.S.–Canada Relations, 2006*

The US government is not a unitary actor. Rather, it is a collection of agencies whose functions and objectives often overlap and conflict and whose leaders often compete for power, resources, political attention, and preferment. The priorities of cabinet secretaries and their senior officials, whether political appointments or career civil servants, often reflect their backgrounds and priorities, including the agendas of their political patrons, the institutional interests of their particular organizations, and the societal interests that these agencies are expected to promote, support, or regulate.[20] These realities are central to differences in the political cultures of the two countries that Canadian policy makers and diplomats must factor into their calculations in managing bilateral relations.

Formal cross-border relations are defined by two fundamental realities: each country's very different roles in the international system, noted in Chapter 2, and the two governments' very different institutional structures. Canada is rarely an object of strategic or government-wide policy initiatives in the United States. As suggested by Doran, Sands, and others, the asymmetries of bilateral relations contribute to the asymmetries of policy approaches on several levels.

Strategic policy initiatives by Canada must first engage the attention of the US executive branch and then be accommodated within a broader set of strategic or economic initiatives potentially applicable to global or hemispheric "allies." Any strategic policy initiative by Canada must compete for scarce political and bureaucratic resources both at the centre and in the line department or agency tasked with primary responsibility for bilateral (or, since NAFTA, potentially trilateral) negotiations. However, Canada generally needs to invest substantial political capital and bureaucratic resources both prior to and during any such negotiation. In contrast, American commitments tend to be more contingent, reflecting the different priorities and agendas of the White House, the relevant lead agency, and relevant committee leaders of Congress.

Any strategic initiative must eventually engage the relevant committees of Congress to secure a legislative mandate for effective bilateral or trilateral action. Securing such a mandate is likely to be contingent on the accommodation of particular domestic interests with congressional patrons holding senior positions on relevant committees or subcommittees of the US House or Senate. Winning the ongoing support of key Senate and House committee chairs (and preferably ranking minority members) is vital to the political success of any strategic or major sectoral policy initiative. These issues are discussed further in Chapter 7.

The Security and Prosperity Partnership of 2005-9 was specifically designed to avoid engagement with Congress, working instead on issues that could be managed within the existing jurisdictions of US, Canadian, and Mexican federal governments. Although this approach might have made a virtue of necessity, given the reality of minority (or divided) governments in Canada and Mexico, it also reflected President George W. Bush's disinclination to invest waning political capital in North American issues even with a Republican-controlled Congress. The failure of his efforts at bipartisan outreach on immigration reform – a vital priority in managing relations with Mexico and a key condition for integrating security concerns along American borders with broader economic priorities – also signalled the limits of political support for the SPP's broader efforts to achieve greater trilateral (or dual bilateral) cooperation on economic and security issues.[21] Some observers have suggested that processes announced in early 2011 to secure closer regulatory cooperation between the two countries, paralleling President Obama's domestic regulatory review process, face many of the same challenges.[22]

Mexico's political and economic opening to the United States since the 1980s – combined with the shift in demographic and economic power toward the American south, southwest, and west coast – has greatly complicated Canada's historical pursuit of a special relationship with its giant neighbour. Any strategic Canadian initiative in dealing with the United States must increasingly acknowledge the political relevance of US–Mexico relations and have the potential or capacity for application or extension to Mexico in some form. Processes aimed at creating an expanded security perimeter encompassing the United States and Canada, announced in early 2011, have been an exception to this rule, at least in the short term.

These factors have greatly increased the complexity of designing complementary strategies to promote Canadian interests in cross-border relations. As a result, Canadian governments have tended to emphasize the pursuit of sectoral strategies to limit Canada's vulnerability to "joint decision traps" – the need to secure the support of multiple decision makers, each with an actual or potential veto on policy change – built into American political processes.

In contrast, bilateral relations are most consistent at the transgovernmental level, in which career public servants deal with their counterparts over an extended period on operational issues affecting interactions between the two countries and their citizens. Relations can be informal or structured through the exchange of memoranda of understanding (MOUs) that establish protocols for specific interactions between officials of the two federal governments or state and provincial governments. Mundane examples include the mutual recognition of drivers' licences, mutual assistance among emergency responders in the two countries, or hundreds of other arrangements. In addition to DFAIT, most line departments – particularly those whose operations are affected by cross-border economic relations or regulatory or operational cooperation – maintain independent international relations units that enable them to deal directly with middle management and working-level counterparts in the United States.[23]

Relations are more unpredictable, however, at the political level and higher levels of management. Electoral cycles in each country are rarely synchronized. There is a significant turnover of cabinet-level officials (ministers and secretaries) and even more so of subcabinet-level officials – associate and assistant secretary positions in the United States, deputy and assistant deputy ministers in Canada – who are generally responsible for shaping official positions on major policy issues within their jurisdictions. The election of a new president in the United States generally results in the wholesale turnover of senior and many mid-ranking officials, not just cabinet secretaries. The election of a new government in Canada, of course, produces wholesale turnover in the cabinet.

Paradoxically, the capacity to develop effective personal relations at the levels of cabinet and subcabinet officials becomes a critical factor in managing bilateral policy relations on a departmental or sectoral basis. As a result, the cultivation and even institutionalization of such relations have become major elements in managing Canada–US relations in recent years.

Such dealings can be conducted independently from the Embassy in Washington. However, in practice, there is frequently close cooperation, particularly on issues that cut across departmental jurisdictions in either country or in which American interest group (and congressional) politics are significant factors in bilateral policy relations. This section explores the reality of "distributed diplomacy" and its implications for bilateral relations.

Cabinet-Level Relations

> *I think we should have ministers down here frequently because it's the best way to get the administration and the Congress involved with Canadian issues.*
>
> *– Confidential interview, DFAIT, 2006*

One of the more significant developments in bilateral relations in the years since 9/11 has been the broadening and deepening of cabinet-level relations between the governments of the two countries. As noted in Chapter 2, Secretary of State George Shultz initiated such meetings with his Canadian counterparts during the early 1980s as a way of "weeding the garden" or helping to defuse the tensions that had emerged between the two countries due to ideological conflicts between the third Trudeau government and the Reagan administration.[24]

Although these quarterly meetings were discontinued after 1989, cabinet-level contacts grew on a variety of issues during the 1990s – particularly on issues of economic and border policy coordination. These contacts became particularly significant after 9/11, when cross-border security cooperation became vital to both US and Canadian interests. The creation of the SPP process in 2005, which cut across numerous departmental functions traditionally viewed as domestic, created both political and bureaucratic frameworks for regular cabinet- and subcabinet-level contacts not only between the principal ministers responsible (Industry/ Commerce and Public Safety/Homeland Security) but also among a broader range of their colleagues. This process was reinforced by the Harper government's early decision to decentralize the management of bilateral policy files, shifting the initiative to individual ministers of line departments.

Regular cabinet-level meetings are an extension of what Allan Gotlieb has described as "consultative functional mechanisms"[25] or regularly scheduled meetings of cabinet officers, senior departmental officers, or responsible operating-level officers from both countries to discuss specific bilateral issues. Such activities can range from cooperation through regular information sharing, the lowest level of cooperation, to intergovernmental coordination of related policy agendas in different institutional or governmental contexts, to efforts at collaborative policy making involving a variety of policy instruments and processes – as discussed in Chapter 1.[26]

The deliberate limits imposed on the development of NAFTA-wide institutions, noted in Chapter 3, increase both the political and the institutional importance of cabinet-level contacts as well as lower levels of professional and bureaucratic cooperation. With limited exceptions, such as North American defence and some aspects of homeland security, cross-border relations with Canada are often relatively marginal to senior US government decision makers, except as they might relate to the expectations or demands of particular American domestic interests. Institutionalizing regular, usually semi-annual, bilateral meetings of cabinet-level officials creates a formal bureaucratic process for "putting content" into such meetings, developing an ongoing agenda of shared activities and negotiations for which officials will be politically accountable, and creating a political forum in which problems or differences can be managed or resolved.

However, there are two effective conditions to maintaining such meetings over the medium term. First, there needs to be enough substance to agendas – so that officials of both governments continue to see value in meeting – rather than merely adding to already busy schedules. Second, broader political relations need to be sufficiently constructive that cabinet officers perceive them as something more than an opportunity to be badgered by their counterparts. Poor political relations are not necessarily an obstacle to the maintenance of these consultative functions if individual cabinet officers perceive value in maintaining open communications to work around existing irritants. However, in the absence of willingness to engage in substantive discussions, these dialogues are unlikely to continue over the long term.

The incremental process of institutionalizing cabinet-level meetings has spread under the Obama administration to include semi-annual meetings of ministers and secretaries responsible for trade, public safety (Homeland Security), environment, and energy. There are less publicized ad hoc meetings of numerous other cabinet-level officials. Senior economic ministers (e.g., finance ministers and treasury secretaries) tend to meet on the margins of broader international meetings such as the G-8 and G-20.

Some of these processes are more extensively institutionalized than others. Relations among defence department officials have been heavily institutionalized through NATO, NORAD, defence procurement, and a wide variety of joint training agreements that have evolved over many years, together with the location of defence attachés with extensive liaison responsibilities in Embassies in Washington and Ottawa. Similar relations have developed between Public Safety and Homeland Security bureaucracies since the formation of these departments in 2003 – though both liaison functions governed by several formal and informal arrangements among police, border services/protection, and intelligence agencies have evolved over the longer term. Canada and the United States have negotiated a variety of energy-related agreements in addition to relevant chapters of CUFTA and NAFTA – supplemented by a variety of consultative arrangements between the two countries, some of which have been expanded more recently to include Mexico. Although there has been cross-border cooperation on environmental issues for many years, activity in this area has grown substantially under the Obama administration, with regular meetings of environment and energy ministers, ongoing cooperation on "clean energy" research, and increased coordination of environmental regulations, though Canada appears to have been more of a "policy taker" than an active participant in cross-border policy development on a number of these initiatives.

The nature of these ongoing sectoral contacts depends on the extent to which they involve incremental changes to existing policies, significant policy departures – actual or prospective – in one country or the other, reactions to policy changes from the "other end of Pennsylvania Avenue," or a form of "purposeful incrementalism" aimed at coordinating and, in some cases, harmonizing federal policies within the jurisdictional discretion of each government.

The greatest challenges in bilateral relations generally arise from major sectoral policy shifts in the United States that are usually the products of domestic policy forces. During the 1980s, in addition to CUFTA, such changes included large-scale economic deregulation in the highway, air, and rail transportation sectors that had major implications for Canadian businesses involved in cross-border commerce, along with more gradual regulatory shifts in US federal regulation of the oil and gas sectors. During the 1990s, these changes spilled over into electricity regulation, with significant implications for Canadian electrical utilities, as well as ongoing changes to financial sector regulation that sparked significant regulatory and market shifts in Canada. Since 2001, major unilateral changes to US homeland security and related immigration regulations, along with significant and intensely contested changes to US energy and related environmental regulations, have led to regular cross-border conversations given the highly integrated realities of the two countries' economies.

Some of these regulatory changes have been initiated by the executive branch, raising the potential for substantive intergovernmental discussions, especially when the cross-border integration of major economic stakeholders creates parallel pressures for mutual adaptation in each country. As discussed in Chapter 1, these shifts can take the form of policy parallelism, in which Canadian governments adapt independently to US policy trends while maintaining freedom of action to deal with distinct domestic political conditions, mutual recognition of different technical standards, or adaptation of similar or identical standards in recognition of the extent of industry integration in both countries. Ottawa's active cooperation with Washington in bailing out General Motors and Chrysler in 2009, and its subsequent alignment of tailpipe emission standards and CAFE (Corporate Average Fuel Economy) automotive mileage requirements, are highly visible examples of the latter approach.

However, most major changes in US regulatory policies during the past thirty years have been either initiated by or negotiated with Congress. The greater the extent to which Congress chooses to assert its constitutional prerogative of domestic policy leadership, the greater the degree to which US domestic interest group politics becomes a major factor in shaping policy trade-offs and legislative decisions. Such forces necessarily push foreign governments and related interests to the margins of US domestic policy processes unless they can ally themselves with major US domestic stakeholders (including elements within executive departments and agencies) to carve out a share of the contested policy territory that allows for recognition of their interests. Alternatively, they can engage in the kinds of "niche" diplomacy that allow for the practice of exceptionalism and exemptionalism on technical issues, as discussed in previous chapters.

Major differences in the legal, budgetary, and regulatory contexts and cultures of US and Canadian governments often mean that processes for policy coordination or the management of irritants arising from regulatory differences in the two countries are often drawn out and inconclusive. Officials in each country must deal with different institutional histories, clusters of interest groups, and cross-cutting political pressures. Just as Congress serves as a practical check on the autonomy of particular departments and agencies, the independence of provincial governments often imposes comparable checks on Canadian government officials. Conversations with officials in both countries suggested that a lack of familiarity with the other government's legal, technical, and procedural requirements is often a barrier to effective cooperation or resolution of policy differences.

Under such circumstances, regular cabinet-level meetings can provide a vital impetus to address policy roadblocks, particularly when the interests of both governments – and those of major interest groups in both countries – are similar or complementary. Canadian officials report that the appointment of Nebraska governor Mike Johanns as George W. Bush's secretary of agriculture made a major difference in expediting the process for reopening the US border to Canadian beef exports following the BSE crisis of 2003. Conversely, the replacement of Secretary of Homeland Security Tom Ridge, a former Pennsylvania governor and congressman from a district bordering on Canada, with former New Jersey prosecutor and Department of Justice official Michael Chertoff contributed to a period of diverging priorities along the border.[27] Similar considerations can also apply to major sub-cabinet appointments.

The greatest challenge to bilateral relations tends to come from changes to administration policies driven largely by domestic political or special interest pressures that might or might not be specifically targeted at Canada. The most effective way of dealing with such challenges, especially on economic issues, is to identify policy options beneficial to Canada that serve the interests of key American domestic constituencies whose support or activities are valued by relevant policy makers. Gotlieb's dictum that Canadian responses "need to be fashioned according to circumstances," reflecting both "the source of the threat and the character of the players" involved, typically shapes the approach taken by Canadian diplomats. "What is essential is that there be a specially tailored microstrategy requiring a combination of public diplomacy, legal skills, alliance seeking and plain old fashioned lobbying."[28]

Such approaches tend to be less successful, however, when they deal with a central US policy goal, enjoying strong domestic support, that applies across a wide range of allies and trading partners and is not contrary to international commitments. Under such circumstances, such as debates over intellectual property, the legal status of the Northwest Passage as an "international strait," or the extraterritorial application of US security rules governing American citizens or military contracts, securing accommodation is usually a long, slow, and uncertain process.

Operating at the Margins

Timing is everything in lobbying.

– Confidential interview, DFAIT, 2010

Canadian diplomats and government officials in Washington face four major challenges in dealing with the different components of the executive branch. First, they are not only outsiders to the workings of individual departments and agencies but also representatives of a foreign government. Such considerations are more important during periods of intense domestic political conflict, and of real or perceived external threats, than at others. They can be mitigated by senior policy makers and working-level managers' recognition of shared interests and policy goals and cultivation of personal relationships. However, in the absence of such mutual trust, or where there are clearly differences in policy priorities between the two governments, intergovernmental relations are often characterized by high levels of opacity and uncertainty.

Second, as outsiders, Canadian officials frequently lack the detailed knowledge of internal policy processes, histories, and legal and interest group dynamics central to the workings of individual departments and agencies. This limited familiarity, which, as noted above, is shared by Americans toward Canadian government processes and cultures, is reinforced by the fact that Embassy staff typically serve for three- or four-year terms – some portion of which is spent "learning the ropes" in Washington, even if they might have specialized issue expertise or previous career expertise from serving in the United States. Senior Ottawa-based officials typically have even less awareness of US policy processes unless they have spent significant portions of their careers in cross-border relations although the Embassy now sponsors two- and three-day programs to introduce senior department officials to "how Washington works."[29] This problem can be mitigated, especially at senior levels of the Embassy, by appointing ministers with senior departmental experience in Ottawa that has familiarized them with both the technical details of issues and many of the personalities involved. Among numerous examples, Paul Frazer, who served as public affairs minister in the Embassy early in the Bush administration, had been in charge of departmental media relations for Minister of Foreign Affairs Joe Clark and Director of Communications to the prime minister, as well as ambassador to the Czech Republic and Slovakia and several other positions relevant to cross-border relations. Colin Robertson, the Embassy's high-profile minister of congressional relations under Frank McKenna, was previously Canada's consul general in Los Angeles. Paul Robertson, minister of economic affairs under Ambassadors Wilson and Doer, served as the assistant deputy minister for North America within DFAIT's trade section.

The local knowledge gap can also be bridged by retaining local staff or, in certain cases, converting career foreign service officers to long-term contract staff with specialized responsibilities within the Embassy to create (or preserve) an institutional memory. However, though many such officials have provided valued service, there are also risks involved in this process. A serious leak within the Embassy that contributed to unwelcome publicity on internal memoranda on the anti-NAFTA tactical positions taken by presidential candidates Barack Obama and Hillary Clinton in early 2008 was later traced to a contract staff person with personal connections to a senior congressional Republican.[30]

Third, new arrivals in the Embassy, most of whom are steeped in Canadian bureaucratic cultures, must acculturate themselves to the very different, diverse, and often more free-wheeling policy environments of Washington. At one level, such an approach involves learning how to speak to Americans on issues that are of interest to Americans, often recognizing that the most important issues to Canada in a particular policy cluster might be the tenth or fifteenth most important issues to American officials and interest groups involved in the same policy community. At another level, such an approach involves familiarization with the broader range of policy instruments – the direct or indirect policy tools available for translating a policy goal into action – available to US federal officials and members of Congress and the context in which each can be used in particular settings. Such issues are directly related to the need to become sensitized to nuances of timing and tactics. Gotlieb and his numerous acolytes frequently emphasize the need to develop a separate microstrategy for each issue, in the manner of domestic government relations professionals, taking into account the political and institutional contexts, actors, and interests peculiar to each issue or issue cluster.[31]

Fourth, compared with other foreign governments, especially those of Japan, Great Britain, and a number of Middle Eastern countries, the Canadian Embassy makes relatively limited use of professional lobbyists, media, and government relations advisers in its dealings with the executive branch and Congress. Such contracts or retainers, which must be disclosed under the US Foreign Agents Registration Act (FARA), are used more frequently by provincial governments or specialized agencies of the Canadian federal government seeking specialized US legal advice and policy perspectives independently of the Embassy.[32] As such, they will be addressed in Chapters 8 and 9.

Questions of timing can relate to electoral cycles and related turnover in management personnel, which might be more predictable in the United States but which are rarely synchronized with those in Canada – especially during periods of minority government. They also require an awareness of varied executive branch and congressional processes, familiarization with legal and regulatory constraints facing individual departments and agencies on particular issues, and engagement with special interest groups as active players within policy processes. These processes look very different from within the Embassy and from the perspective of American participants in the same policy communities who deal with them – though it is rare for either group to appreciate fully the political or bureaucratic context in which the other operates.

Washington-based officials are not the only ones who must come to terms with these technical and tactical nuances. They are also important to Embassy officials' interactions with Ottawa-based counterparts in the Privy Council Office, DFAIT, and line departments whose macrotactical judgments might be at variance with political realities in Washington.

This reality can be seen in the timing of Canadian ministerial visits to Washington for which adequate groundwork might not have been laid with American counterparts and their officials. For example, the Harper government's initial pursuit of negotiations on a comprehensive agreement on climate policy in the early weeks of the Obama administration in 2009 ignored the reality that very few of the officials whose cooperation was needed for such an initiative had been confirmed by Congress – a necessary step in enabling them to carry out their functions. Those who had been confirmed were overwhelmed with the administration's 100-day agenda, including negotiations with Congress on the contents of the budgetary stimulus package that would provide financial support for numerous administration initiatives. Ottawa-based officials fundamentally misread the extent to which the administration was prepared to provide a clear policy lead to Congress on these issues and senior members of Congress were prepared to accept such leadership.

Following President Obama's February 2009 visit, the Harper government's strategy shifted. Cabinet ministers with cross-border responsibilities "flooded" to Washington during the spring and summer of 2009. Most visits had little substantive content but, in the words of one observer, were intended to "connect to counterparts, get some profile, and put Canada on the radar screen of the Obama administration."[33] A side benefit of all this travel, as in previous years, was to strengthen personal relationships between the ambassador and various members of cabinet, thus strengthening the Embassy's capacity to play a coordinating role at the Washington end of the relationship.[34]

With the prospect of American cap-and-trade legislation receding into the distance by the fall of 2009, Canadian officials had negotiated a number of more modest processes focusing on information sharing, the funding and sharing of promising technological developments, and selected microregulatory coordination with counterparts at the Environmental Protection Agency and the US Department of Energy. However, congressional support for a more broadly based initiative had dissipated, and the administration chose to invest much of what was left of its political capital in securing passage of significant health care and financial sector reforms in the run-up to the 2010 congressional elections. Similar challenges – limited political attention spans and shifting political calculations – are likely to affect any major cross-border initiative, including those resulting from the February 2011 Washington Declaration.

These issues are relevant when the broad policy objectives of the US and Canadian federal governments are broadly aligned. They become even more challenging when Canada's policy priorities are at cross-purposes to those of the administration or its specific departments and agencies.

Although it is not necessary for the policies of the two countries to be closely aligned for close relations to develop, development of the interpersonal trust central to such relations is closely linked to the perceptions of senior Washington officials that the two countries share common or fairly closely related priorities and objectives. Among US executive departments, the closest alignment has probably been found at the Department of Energy, for reasons related to Canada's status as a secure energy supplier with closely integrated energy markets and industry interests. The same can generally be said of the Department of Agriculture, with selected exceptions in the fields of international wheat marketing and periodic disputes over farm subsidy programs in each country. The range of competing interests represented by the Department of Commerce, noted in Chapter 3, contributes to a more diverse set of relationships, contingent on the political visibility of major issues.

The similarity of broader US and Canadian foreign and international economic policies in recent years has contributed to generally positive relations with the Department of State, despite a certain degree of diplomatic reserve over Canada's aggressive lobby against WHTI, discussed in Chapter 7.[35] Although there has been a greater convergence of broader foreign policy objectives during the latter years of the Bush administration and under the Obama administration, some issues are more difficult to resolve. Canadian claims to sovereignty over navigable waters surrounding its Arctic islands (e.g., the Northwest Passage) have been fundamentally at odds for more than forty years with the two-century-old American policy of promoting freedom of the seas, including passage through "international straits."[36] It has taken years of discussions for US and Canadian officials to work out functional arrangements over these issues without either government conceding its core principles.

The extraterritorial applications of US national (or homeland) security laws to American property and American government contracts – most recently International Trade in Arms Regulations (ITAR) and Secure Flight rules governing passenger information sharing on foreign overflights of US territory – are subjects of perennial sensitivity given their potential to affect the rights of foreign, not just US, citizens. Disputes over WHTI contributed to a significant cooling of bilateral relations between Homeland Security and its Canadian counterparts between 2006 and 2009, reflecting Canadian reactions to constantly shifting "goalposts" in the relationship and related American perceptions of erosion in post-9/11 levels of trust and cooperation between the two countries.[37]

Under such circumstances, relations with Canada, as with other countries, tend to be governed by the principle of reciprocity. A decline in trust or perceptions of diverging interests can also lead to greater decision-making centralization, making the exercise of operating-level discretion at least partly contingent on Canadian cooperation on related issues. As one US government official commented, "I want to know what anyone who comes to meet with us wants from us – across the board – and what we want from them. I never want to go to a meeting and be asked for things without having something to ask for in return."[38]

The growing importance of US (and, to a lesser extent, Canadian) services trade to each country's longer-term prosperity has made the protection of intellectual property an ongoing focus of American (and European) trade policy pressures on Canada, which are often difficult to accommodate in the context of Canadian domestic politics. The cross-border environmental effects of each country's domestic policies remain potential flash points, whether on long-term issues such as the Garrison and Devils Lake diversion projects, actual and potential pollution of US boundary waters by Canadian resource producers and processors, or the risk of Asian carp migrating to the Great Lakes – an issue that unites Ontario and Great Lakes states in a shared alliance to pressure Washington-based officials.

Much of the Embassy's work involves a wide variety of microeconomic and regulatory issues arising from the normal workings of American regulatory agencies and their interactions with various committees of Congress. As such, Embassy staff must have detailed familiarity with both Canadian and American regulatory systems and the capacity to communicate these details effectively to American counterparts. In some cases, especially those relating to areas of provincial jurisdiction and key provincial economic interests, such brokerage can also involve some engagement with provincial governments and their representatives in Washington.

Managing and, where feasible, institutionalizing relations between the two federal governments remain central elements of influencing American policies toward Canada, and Canadian governments ignore them at their peril. However, the evolution of the American political system since the 1970s means that, though necessary, positive relations with the White House and executive departments and agencies of the US federal government are no longer sufficient due to the role of Congress as an equal and coordinate branch of government within the American system of checks and balances.

As in many other areas, Allan Gotlieb summarizes a fundamental reality of managing bilateral relations: "The fact that the basic principle of international law that all official business must be conducted through the Executive Branch of government is no longer an acceptable basis for the conduct of diplomacy in Washington."[39] Whether on foreign, security, and international economic policy issues or on matters of "intermestic" relations, influencing American policies toward Canada requires that Canadian diplomats actively engage the domestic policy processes of Congress.

7

Canada and Congress

Foreign government lobbying in Washington lies at the
interface of public and traditional diplomacy. It has become
an essential component of contemporary diplomatic
technique.

> – *Charles Doran and Joel Sokolsky,* Canada and
> Congress, *1985*[1]

Canadian governments' engagement of the US Congress, societal interests, and indeed the broader American political system is rooted in the constitutional, political, economic, and societal realities of both American and North American life. This chapter examines Canadian governments' interaction with Congress. It explores the context of Canada's involvement with American domestic political networks centred on the decentralized processes of Congress, the methods used to build relationships on Capitol Hill, and the challenges of developing effective lobbying microstrategies on specific issues or clusters of issues while avoiding public accusations of "meddling" in American domestic politics.

As with many other aspects of Canada–US relations, Allan Gotlieb provides both a theoretical and a practical understanding of what he has called the "New Diplomacy."[2] Canada's economic integration within North America and extensive interaction between the two countries' citizens and businesses transcend formal intergovernmental relations. However, the political and bureaucratic dimensions of bilateral relations are mediated through very different sets of institutions and processes in each country.

First and most important, the US Constitution – reinforced by more than 200 years of evolving political practice – has entrenched a separation of powers between the executive branch and Congress. It gives members of Congress an independent role in initiating legislation, and multiple opportunities to challenge or obstruct executive branch policies, thus creating the equivalent of a second, equally decentralized, executive branch within the US federal government. These forces are reinforced by the decentralization and relatively weak internal discipline of the American party system, the incentives offered and constraints imposed by overlapping two-, four-, and six-year election cycles, and the diverse constituencies of members of Congress. All these factors, and the popular expectations that go with them, create strong incentives for Congress to respond to the diverse interests of Americans as well as broader expressions of the popular will. No Canadian government can afford to ignore these cultural and institutional differences between the two countries when attempting to influence American policies toward Canada.

A second dimension of this reality is the "sub-separation of powers" within Congress, Gotlieb's phrase for the decentralization of power and jurisdiction among hundreds of House and Senate committees and subcommittees, noted in Table 7.1.[3] The congressional committee system divides the exercise of congressional power along functional (policy field–related), geographic, and partisan/ideological lines. The interaction of these political fiefdoms depends in large measure on personalities, constituencies, and agendas of congressional committee chairs, ranking members, and their key lieutenants. Committee chairs are usually powerful, ambitious, and procedurally skilled legislators, often with decades of legislative experience, as noted in Table 7.3.

Ideological polarization and related efforts to centralize leadership power since the 1980s have somewhat reduced the autonomy of committee chairs, especially in the House of Representatives. However, House speakers and Senate party leaders are rarely able to impose undesired legislative outcomes on senior colleagues within their committees' areas of jurisdiction.

Third, the dispersed character of congressional leadership is reinforced by the frequently diverging cultures and agendas of the Senate and House of Representatives, whether or not the same party (or the president's party) controls both houses. This diffusion of power creates multiple points of access in which organized interests (including foreign governments) can seek the privileging or accommodation of their own agendas – whether on particular policy issues or in congressional spending mandates. Conversely, it also provides multiple choke points in the legislative process in which well-placed senators or representatives can extract concessions – and sometimes exert vetoes – on matters that run afoul of their personal agendas or the interests of key constituents.[4]

Fourth, these underlying realities both enable and are strongly reinforced by the centrality of special interest politics in Washington and their interaction with local interests championed by key members of Congress. The competition and collusion of organized interest groups are critical to the development and interpretation of legislation and the allocation and distribution of public funds and regulatory authority to serve their interests. Interest group competition also contributes to the reality of congressional politics as an exchange process on several levels. Depending on the relative openness of (and number of competing interests in) particular policy systems and subsystems, this process can harden into an "iron triangle" in which groups with well-placed allies in Congress and the executive branch effectively shape the terms whereby other interests can participate in specialized policy processes.

Many organized interests have developed close working relations with members of Congress and their staffs. They deploy extensive lobbying resources, assist members to raise campaign funds, and, in some cases, help to mobilize voter turnout. These factors have reinforced the longer-term trend toward more candidate-centred parties in many parts of the United States, though party discipline has generally been stronger in the House than the Senate in recent years.

These structural realities can serve or accommodate Canada's interests in some settings. Close cross-border collaboration among electric utilities, dating from the 1960s and institutionalized under US federal rules during the 1990s, facilitated the design of shared electricity reliability rules after a major blackout in 2003. Strong cross-border unions enabled steel interests to incorporate a NAFTA exemption into protectionist tariffs imposed during the 2002 economic downturn, even though these measures were subsequently ruled in violation of American WTO commitments. However, the more far-reaching the issue, the greater the diversity of interests typically engaged and the more likely that congressional log rolling will marginalize Canadian interests unless US domestic interest groups with similar interests are central to the policy calculations of key members of Congress.

All four dimensions help to structure the role of Congress in "intermestic" policy questions in which effects on Canadian-based interests or broader cross-border relations are often subsets of American domestic political debates. The relative importance of various actors and the options available to Canadian governments and diplomats are likely to vary at different levels of policy analysis in each country: major questions of US or Canadian national interest, sectoral issues without broader systemic implications, or micropolicy questions affecting relatively small numbers of people or even individual businesses.

Engaging Congress

> *Foreign interests have no senators, no congressmen, and no staffers to represent them at the bargaining table. They have no votes and no political action committees. That is why a foreign government or interest often lives or dies by its capacity to find domestic allies that do enjoy these estimable assets.*
>
> – *Allan Gotlieb,* I'll Be with You in a Minute, Mr. Ambassador, *1991*

Congress possesses primary constitutional jurisdiction over US international economic relations. This fundamental reality, together with the "sub-separation of powers" noted above, makes engagement with Congress an essential focus of Canadian diplomacy in the United States. Much of the work of the US Senate and House of Representatives is conducted through their 217 committees and subcommittees, noted in Table 7.1, each with its respective chair and ranking minority (party) members. Jurisdiction over major legislation can be spread over several committees. Congress not only makes policy passing legislation – a process that often requires the reconciliation of separate House and Senate bills – but also does so through separate, decentralized House and Senate appropriation processes to authorize the more or less specific expenditure of public funds and by exercising operational oversight of executive departments and agencies with the assistance of arm's-length agencies such as the Government Accountability Office (GAO).

TABLE 7.1
Congressional committees and subcommittees, 2010

	Senate	Joint	House	Total
Committees	20		22	42
Subcommittees	68		102	170
Joint committees		5		5
Total	88	5	124	217
Members	100		435	535

SOURCES: http://senate.gov/; http://house.gov/; author's calculations.

As a result, congressional processes are complex, frequently opaque, and subject to extensive bargaining among members – especially in the Senate. Although ideological polarization has contributed to greater party discipline since the mid-1990s, legislative and appropriation processes often involve complex patterns of bargaining within parties and across party lines that require careful monitoring by government relations professionals, lobbyists, congressional liaison staff of executive agencies, and foreign diplomats. In addition, they foster an intensely transactional approach to procedural and substantive legislative negotiations among members of Congress that is far more difficult to track.

The distinctive culture of congressional politics, intersecting at multiple points with policy making and the day-to-day operations of an equally decentralized executive branch and with the multi-billion-dollar industry of interest group politics inside and outside Washington, creates major challenges for Canadian diplomats. After all, Canadians do not vote in American elections, and Canadian business, advocacy, and other interest groups are marginal, if not irrelevant, to the funding of American elections.

This section examines the key external functions of the Canadian Embassy in attempting to influence congressional policies toward Canada along with Canada's "good neighbour diplomacy" in attempting to build relationships and "make Canada relevant" on Capitol Hill.

The Congressional Relations Function
Canadian diplomats interviewed for this book described five key functions of the Embassy's congressional relations function. Embassy staff track proposed legislation for its potential effects on Canada and Canadian interests.

They organize databases and information management systems to permit the tracking of statements and positions taken by members of Congress on relevant issues and the documentation of economic linkages to Canada in every state and congressional district – often down to the firm and community level. They attempt to build relationships with members of Congress to demonstrate Canada's contribution to the economic well-being of their constituents, and they explain the actions and priorities of Canadian governments on issues of interest to individual members. They also build linkages with think tank, advocacy, and other interest groups both inside and beyond the Washington beltway as part of broader processes of public diplomacy discussed in Chapter 8.[5] However, on issues of high political salience and priority, the Embassy might go into "crisis management" mode, attempting to mobilize all available resources to influence congressional (and related executive branch) decision-making processes.

Tracking Legislation

> *Typically, we're not the direct target of legislation. There's usually a bigger issue lawmakers are trying to get at. In trying to get at those issues, they sideswipe us. So we try to get to the right members of Congress and the right committees. When we get an early warning, we work with key stakeholders in the United States who have a direct stake in these issues and can do something about them.*
>
> *– Confidential interview, DFAIT, 2006*

A key function of Embassy staff (and their provincial counterparts in Washington) is the tracking of legislation and resolutions introduced in Congress that can have an effect, intended or otherwise, on American policies toward Canada or on specific Canadian interests. As with private members' bills in Canada, the introduction of legislation is often of public relations value for members of Congress in their dealings with constituents and contributors. It is a signal that the member is "doing something," whatever the likelihood of a bill being passed into law. Table 7.2 notes the number of bills and resolutions introduced in each house of Congress since 2005 and the number and percentage that have actually been passed into "public laws." Bills and resolutions can range from purely symbolic gestures

TABLE 7.2
Congressional legislative activity, 2005-10

	House measures introduced		Senate measures introduced		Public laws passed	
Congress	Bills	Resolutions*	Bills	Resolutions*	Number	%†
111th					383	5.7
2010	2,158	940	1,829	367		
2009	4,371	1,287	2,910	460		
110th					460	6.2
2008	2,423	815	1,210	373		
2007	4,913	1,264	2,531	509		
109th					482	7.4
2006	1,800	666	1,933	349		
2005	4,632	1,050	2,172	449		

* Includes joint and concurrent resolutions and resolutions introduced separately in each house.
† Public laws as a percentage of bills and joint resolutions introduced in the House of Representatives.
SOURCES: http://thomas.loc.gov/home/; author's calculations.

and one-line revisions, to tariff or customs legislation introduced on behalf of particular industry "clients," to massive omnibus legislation thousands of pages long.

Tracking legislation includes more than its contents or progress through Congress. It also includes identifying the identities and objectives of congressional sponsors and the political and professional interpretations of congressional staff, many of whom play significant political as well as technical roles in advising their political principals on each side of the partisan divide. Beyond that, tracking legislation also involves the identities of relevant interest groups and stakeholders who might have policy or material interests in different aspects of a bill and the extent to which these interests might coincide, overlap, or conflict with those being promoted by the Embassy or Canadian provincial interests in Washington. These factors coincide with Kingdon's concepts of "political streams" and "problem streams" noted in Chapter 5.

The greater the complexity of legislation, the greater the need for information on its political context to identify the objectives of its sponsors, the positions and relative influence of interest groups engaged in behind-the-scenes and public debates on the measure, the degree to which the current administration is engaged in the debate (and in what ways), and the implications of these findings for specific measures of interest or significance to Canadian interests and officials.

These findings play a significant role in the crafting of Embassy microstrategies to engage the issue, the timing and targets of political intervention, and the degree to which Canadian efforts will be conducted behind the scenes or with varying degrees of publicity. They also involve assessments of the potential risks and benefits of formal political intervention by the ambassador, senior Canadian cabinet ministers, or even the prime minister.

The greater the scale and complexity of specific bills, the greater the likelihood that their specific provisions of interest to Canada will be only a small part of the whole – potentially opening the door to behind-the-scenes deal making. For example, Canadian officials identified five specific measures in the Energy Bill of 2005 that directly affected Canadian interests. First, Alaska energy interests had been lobbying for a price floor, or implicit subsidy, for Alaska natural gas shipments that could have placed Canadian interests, especially those related to the prospective Mackenzie Valley pipeline, at a competitive disadvantage. Second, Canadian interests, including MDS Nordion and Atomic Energy of Canada, were lobbying for greater accommodation in existing rules governing US exports of enriched uranium used in their medical isotope business. Third, technical language provided for mandatory electricity standards that would have affected both cross-border electricity trade and the formal regulatory jurisdictions of provincial governments. Fourth, the creation of national renewable energy portfolio standards for utilities, overriding state measures, could have put Canadian hydroelectric exports at both a regulatory and a competitive disadvantage. Fifth, Canada opposed proposals to allow oil and gas drilling in the Arctic National Wildlife Refuge (ANWR) because of the potential environmental impacts on caribou herds along the Yukon-Alaska border.[6]

Each of these issues involved separate clusters of interests on each side of the border, in each house of Congress, and within the administration. In some cases, a certain degree of political and legal creativity could provide for a technical "fix" of the issue. In others, policy outcomes would require hard bargaining involving a number of competing US domestic interests with varied agendas. Bush administration officials were supportive of some Canadian positions, neutral on others, and opposed to others. The eventual outcomes on all five points were viewed as acceptable, given the range of interests in play, but with the recognition that the next Congress would probably revisit each issue, necessitating a new round of negotiations and coalition-building efforts with relevant interests.[7]

The willingness of key committee chairs and senior members of their committees to accommodate Canadian interests in their legislative proposals is no guarantee that their bills will actually come to a vote in either or both houses of Congress. However, the potential for such legislation to affect Canadian interests – as with the ultimately unsuccessful immigration legislation of 2005-6 or the different House and Senate climate change bills of 2009-10 – requires that Embassy officials actively engage these processes.

The frequently opaque character of congressional processes means that legislation can evolve substantially between the time of its introduction, its passage through relevant committees, its approval by one house, and possible negotiations in "conference" to reconcile differences between Senate and House versions of the same legislation. It also means that measures that fail to pass in one form can often resurface in another context – whether in the same or a subsequent session of Congress.

Congressional leaders can make "side deals" with colleagues to add specific amendments to legislation that might or might not be directly related to the original bill. They can also pursue a single legislative objective by using different procedural techniques as part of different committees' legislative, appropriation, or oversight processes. Such legislative "tacks" are difficult to monitor and often very difficult to remove, especially when they have authoritative sponsors. Alternatively, Canadian diplomats might seek to recruit support from within the executive branch on issues in which Canadian objectives coincide with those of the administration. One official commented that "it's very difficult to engage on the hill, precisely because it is subterranean. My colleagues deal with people at various administrative departments, especially where proposals would be especially disadvantageous to Canada or inconsistent with the ostensible objectives of the measure."[8]

Two prominent examples of this technique during the past decade include the Western Hemisphere Travel Initiative (WHTI), which imposed passport requirements on all persons entering or re-entering the United States, and environmental groups' ongoing efforts to restrict oil sands imports from Canada. The WHTI initially passed Congress in December 2004 as an amendment to the omnibus Immigration Reform and Terrorism

Protection Act. The measure resulted from a deal between Chair of the House Judiciary Committee James Sensenbrenner and the House Republican leadership to strengthen border controls as part of a broader plan to control illegal immigration – including the widespread habit of overstaying legitimate visas.[9] An independent commission had identified the failure of procedures to detect and control the latter as a key security breakdown that had facilitated the 9/11 terrorist attacks. Sensenbrenner's efforts, which reopened a decade-long debate over border controls and travel documents,[10] resulted in four years of lobbying by border business interests and the Canadian government before its eventual implementation in amended form in June 2009, as discussed in Chapter 11.

Similarly, in late 2007, Chair of the House Energy and Commerce Committee Henry Waxman (D-CA) inserted a measure into the fine print of the Energy Independence and Security Act (EISA) limiting US government purchases of unconventional fuels with higher than average "life cycle" emissions of greenhouse gases. Given the higher-profile measures contained in the bill, Section 526 survived a complex three-way bargaining process among House, Senate, and White House interests.[11] Although Waxman suggested that the measure was aimed at American synthetic oil shale fuels rather than Canadian oil sands imports, the Harper government viewed the measure as the first shot in a war by US environmental groups to block oil sands exports to the United States and has made ongoing efforts to secure its repeal.[12]

These are only two of many examples of the low-level lobbying operations conducted by Embassy officials at any one time to head off, modify, or repeal technical legislation with the potential to affect specific Canadian interests and signal broader regulatory shifts that could put Canadian interests at a significant disadvantage in their largest market. This activity is reinforced by targeted lobbying by provincial government representatives, particularly Alberta, Manitoba, and Quebec, all of which have ongoing representation in the American capital. As a result, assembling political intelligence on members of Congress, their positions on particular issues, and the effects of Canadian trade, tourism, and investment on their states and districts becomes a major priority in Embassy officials' dealings with Congress.

Profiling Members of Congress and Their Constituencies

A second major part of the congressional relations function involves the tracking of positions taken by individual members of Congress on issues of importance to Canada, their state's or district's macro- and microeconomic linkages with Canada, and the related benefits to (and sometimes problems for) their constituents. Political data can be drawn from public statements, votes on legislation, meetings with Embassy officials, and a variety of other sources. Economic and other statistical data in the cutely named GOCART system are assembled from public records as well as firm- and industry-level data compiled by DFAIT officials, Statistics Canada, the US Department of Commerce, and other public agencies.[13]

These tracking functions are vital given that the roughly sixty profes-sionals who comprise the political, economic, and congressional relations branches of the Embassy are constantly interacting with members of Congress and their staffs on multiple and varied issues. Although senior officials suggest that internal coordination in the Embassy has improved in recent years, such coordination is necessary to ensure that its different segments are not working at cross-purposes – or seen to be doing so – in dealings with members of Congress.

Embassy officials also monitor closely the appearances of administra-tion officials before congressional committees. These discussions provide substantive evidence of the political and administrative priorities of execu-tive departments and agencies and how they interact with various mem-bers of Congress, providing clues about their relative openness to Canadian priorities and concerns.[14]

A truism of congressional relations is that members of Congress have no permanent friends, no permanent enemies, only political and constituent interests that can evolve over time. Embassy officials necessarily deal with senators on a wider range of issues than members of the House of Repre-sentatives. Particular senators or representatives might be allies on one issue in which their legislative agendas or constituents' interests overlap with those of related Canadian interests, opponents on others, and rela-tively disinterested parties on still others. One veteran observer commented that "there's a man who would be an ally of Canada on economic and trade matters but not such an ally on drug policies. Those are the kinds of things that need examination. But with 435 districts, that's a lot of work."[15]

Table 7.3 notes senior committee chairs and ranking minority members in each house with jurisdiction over major issues of cross-border relations and their major interests in dealings with Canada. As noted in the next section, it is vital for Canadian diplomats to maintain ongoing relations without regard to partisan affiliation, particularly in the Senate, where chairs and their minority party counterparts often work closely together on

TABLE 7.3

Key congressional committee chairs and ranking minority members, 112th Congress (2011-12)

Senate	House of Representatives
·Finance Committee Max Baucus (D-Montana) • Elected 1978 (House 1974-78); chair 2001-2, 2007-present. • Champion of state's lumber, cattle, and energy industries; persistent foe of Canada on softwood lumber issues. Orrin Hatch (R-Utah) – RMM • Elected 1976; RMM 2011. • Former chair, RMM Judiciary committee; moderate-conservative Republican. • Strong supporter of stronger intellectual property rights legislation.	*Ways and Means Committee* Dave Camp (R-Michigan) • Elected 1990; chair 2011. • Strong supporter of trade agreements and Michigan farm and automotive sectors. Sander Levin (D-Michigan) – RMM • Elected 1982; chair 2010. • Suburban Detroit representative; his brother chairs Senate Armed Forces Committee. • Moderate protectionist on trade policies as champion of auto industries and related union interests; strong opponent of Ontario garbage exports to Michigan.
Energy and Natural Resources Committee Jeff Bingaman (D-New Mexico) • Elected 1982; chair 2001-2, 2007-13. • Champion of state's energy (oil, uranium), aerospace industries; moderate environmental legislation. • Generally supportive of cross-border energy trade. Lisa Murkowski (R-Alaska) – RMM • Appointed 2002; daughter of longtime senator. • Influential champion of state's energy industries, energy trade with Canada.	*Energy and Commerce Committee* Fred Upton (R-Michigan) • Elected 1986; chair 2011. • Ranking member, Subcommittee on Energy and Environment (2007-10). • Opponent of cap-and-trade legislation. Henry Waxman (D-California) – RMM • Elected 1974; chair 2008-11. • Champion of climate change legislation, alternative energy industries, restrictions on oil sands imports (e.g., Section 526).
Homeland Security and Governmental Affairs Joe Lieberman (I/D-Connecticut) • Elected 1988; chair 2001-2, 2007-13. • Centrist Democrat; national security "hawk."	*Homeland Security* Peter King (R-New York) • Elected 1992; chair 2005-7, 2011-present. • Centrist Long Island Republican; homeland security "hawk."

▶

◀ TABLE 7.3

Key congressional committee chairs, 112th Congress (2011-12)

Senate	House of Representatives
Susan Collins (R-Maine) – RMM • Elected 1996; chair, 2003-7. • Centrist Republican. • Strong supporter of Maine lumber interests, border security, improved regional border infrastructure; generally open to cross-border cooperation.	Bennie Thompson (D-Mississippi) – RMM • Elected 1993; chair 2007-11.
Agriculture, Nutrition, and Forestry Debbie Stabenow (D-Michigan) • Elected 2000, chair 2011 (House 1997-2001). • Liberal upstate Democrat.	*Agriculture* Frank Lucas (R-Oklahoma) • Elected 1994; chair 2011. • Conservative Republican; rancher. • Champion of regional agricultural interests, wheat growers.
Pat Roberts (R-Kansas) – RMM • Elected 1996 (House 1981-97). • Conservative Republican. • Supporter of agricultural trade liberalization.	Collin Peterson (D-Minnesota) – RMM • Elected 1990; chair 2007-11. • Centrist Democrat. • Champion of farm subsidies, ethanol sector.
	Rules Committee David Dreyer (R-California) • Elected 1980; chair 1999-2007, 2011-13. • Conservative, Southern California Republican. • Strong supporter of free trade, regional high-tech industries, border security.
	Louise Slaughter (D-New York) – RMM • Elected 1986; chair 2007-11. • Liberal Democrat. • Strong supporter of local interests along US–Canada border.

RMM – Ranking Minority Member: senior member of minority party on committee; varies with party control of each house of Congress.

SOURCES: Michael Barone, Richard E. Cohen, and Grant Ujifusa, *The Almanac of American Politics: 2012* (Washington, DC: National Journal Group, 2011); US Senate; US House of Representatives; confidential interviews, DFAIT, 2006-10.

technical issues. Such relations are always important but become even more so when congressional elections result in shifts in partisan control of each house – as in the Senate in 1994, 2001, 2002, and 2006 and in the House in 1994, 2006, and 2010.

Proximity to the Canadian border can contribute to better understanding of and greater sympathy to Canadian interests – particularly when they overlap with significant domestic constituencies in specific states or districts. However, it is certainly no guarantee of a supportive hearing, especially when the constituency interests of committee chairs and other senior members compete with Canadian priorities. Such interests tend to trump political partisanship and transcend geography. For example, northern border state senators and members of Congress often worked across party lines to support a wide range of constituent and Canadian interests on WHTI- and border-related issues in 2006-9. However, responding to a combination of constituent and partisan pressures, most border state senators actively opposed the border's reopening to Canadian cattle exports in 2004-5, whereas southern senators (from both parties) often indifferent to Canadian concerns were among the strongest supporters of border reopening. These divisions typically reflected the size, scale, and relative export orientation of each state's cattle industry; the relative influence of meat-packing interests, which strongly supported border reopening, on individual senators; and the nature of each state's broader agricultural trade relations with Canada.[16] Senior Embassy officials noted that most farm-related legislation involves considerable log-rolling, with competing interest groups lobbying for regulatory measures that can have the effect of creating barriers to Canadian agricultural exports.[17]

Comparable divisions could be seen in long-standing disputes over softwood lumber. One Canadian diplomat commented that

> The Senate is an interesting body. It is a minoritarian place. You don't need sixty senators to get action on an issue. All you need is five or ten who are prepared to be obstructive and have a willingness to get involved in the issue. On softwood lumber, you have about a dozen – and the administration has listened to them.[18]

These comments reflect a long-standing view of interest group politics: relatively narrow, cohesive interests tend to have a significant political advantage over broadly based groups whose interests are more diffuse and who have fewer incentives to mobilize on relatively technical policy or legislative issues.[19]

However, the same principle can be made to work for Canadian interests that have developed close relations with counterpart groups across the border. The microlobbies on the 2005 Energy Bill, noted above, are one example. Another is the success of border community chambers of commerce and related business groups, strongly supported by regional lobbies such as the Pacific Northwest Economic Region (PNWER), and selected state governments in promoting the enhanced driver's licence as a viable alternative to US passport requirements under the WHTI – despite an initially lukewarm response from the Embassy and other cross-border business interests.[20]

The interests of committee chairs can be wider or narrower depending on circumstances. John Dingell, former chair of the House Energy and Commerce Committee, who has represented his Detroit-area district since 1955, reportedly kept a map of the world prominently displayed in his office as a signal of his jurisdictional ambitions. The Senate Finance Committee and the House Ways and Means Committee exercise broad jurisdiction over a range of economic issues, including different aspects of trade policy, with partisan and ideological differences being less prominent in the Senate. However, both these and other committees face major competition over and fragmentation of their jurisdictions. For example, in 2009-10, three major House committees – Energy and Commerce, Ways and Means, and Agriculture – fought over separate "mark-ups" (the right to make clause-by-clause amendments) to climate change legislation, while competition among at least five committees prevented the Senate from bringing its versions of such legislation to votes. At last word, more than 100 separate congressional committees and subcommittees – about 47 percent of the total – claim control over some aspect of the jurisdiction and operations of the Department of Homeland Security (DHS)!

Under these circumstances, the central challenge facing Canadian diplomats (federal and provincial) is to identify the economic and societal interests most relevant to specific members of Congress on each issue – especially when supportive of Canadian interests. The Embassy has prepared economic fact sheets on each state, detailing its specific economic links to Canada, the number of jobs related to exports to Canada, major investments by Canadian firms, and their related employment in the state.[21] However, even though Canada is the largest export market for thirty-five states, and the second largest market for most others, this economic activity amounts to only 1-2 percent of GDP in most states. As a result, the Embassy tracks specific investments and industry clusters down to the congressional district level in order to identify the major employers and communities that benefit directly from Canadian trade, investment, and tourism. Such information enables senior Embassy officials to make a case for open borders and trade facilitation that directly addresses the interests and incentives of individual members of Congress.

Building Relationships/"Working the Hill"

> *Our access is pretty good. We can see pretty well anyone*
> *we need to see. But our success depends on ... how we can*
> *structure the issue to show the potential impact on*
> *congressmen personally.*
>
> – Confidential interview, DFAIT, 2006

Senior Embassy officials, whether the ambassador or senior ministers responsible for political, economic, and congressional relations, walk a fine line in their advocacy activities on Capitol Hill. They must secure access to key congressional decision makers and their senior staff advisers in order to promote Canadian interests and policy goals. At the same time, there are political risks in being seen to interfere in primarily domestic policy debates – a fine line that becomes more challenging when the Canadian position is opposed by the White House or other elements of the executive branch.

The direct advocacy function has three major elements. First, embassy officials seek to build relationships with members of Congress that enable them to identify prospective supporters on relevant issues, based on a combination of the member's policy views and constituency interests. Second, they engage in lobbying to secure accommodation of Canadian interests on domestic legislation, often engaging committee staff directors who play a vital advisory role to committee chairs.[22] On many issues, these interests are peripheral to broader debates. As a result, such interventions are often technical and procedural. On others, they might be more overtly political. Third, they might seek to promote legislation amending or repealing previous measures that harm Canadian interests or place them at a competitive disadvantage.

Published reports suggest that Canada was the fourth most active government on Capitol Hill, with 1,328 separate contacts, including meetings, telephone calls, and direct email contacts with members of Congress between July 2007 and December 2008 – after Turkey (2,268), the United Arab Emirates (1,957), and the Republic of Congo (1,538). However, unlike most other countries that have invested heavily in professional lobbying capacities in Washington, Canadian governments rely primarily on their professional staffs.[23]

The relationship-building element of congressional engagement, as suggested earlier, is very much about identifying common interests – both policy related and constituency related. One diplomat commented that "people here are busy. They like Canada. They're disposed to receive a Canadian official. But everybody wants to know what it's about. They don't have time for idle chit-chat. We're going to talk to them in a focused way on something that's important to us."[24]

At the same time, Canadian officials must be careful to demonstrate the ways in which Canada's position or policy requests address the policy priorities of targeted senators and members of Congress, or the interests of their constituents, rather than take a primarily self-interested approach. As former Canadian diplomat Paul Frazer, now a Washington government relations consultant, put it, "you can't run to the hill and say, 'no, no, no, you can't do that – we're Canada.'"[25] Former ambassador Michael Kergin commented that "I was surprised at how much access I had to John McCain on security issues – until I found out that Canada was the largest foreign investor in Arizona."[26]

Relationship-building efforts with Congress are largely proactive. Canadian diplomats and government officials try to get ahead of specific issues – both policy measures that are potentially helpful to Canadian interests and those that might harm them. On some issues, this process requires gentle reminders that "Canada is a separate country" rather than assumptions of similarity or "congruence of interests" between the two countries.[27] In such cases, Doran and Sokolsky note the importance of avoiding any appearance of anti-Americanism or attacking the United States for particular actions when Canadian governments might engage in similar behaviour.[28]

On security issues, a key priority under both Republican and Democratic administrations since 9/11, Embassy officials have made extensive efforts to demonstrate a strong Canadian commitment to American security, including ongoing efforts to strengthen border management, though these efforts were undercut to some degree in 2005-8 by ongoing disagreements over immigration and identification issues, especially the WHTI. One former diplomat noted that, following the expansion of Canada's combat mission in Afghanistan, he made a point of visiting Capitol Hill accompanied by a defence attaché in full uniform as a way of drawing attention to Canada's military commitment.[29]

The ambassador and other senior Embassy officials make regular visits to Capitol Hill to rebut political attacks or charges against Canada that arise from the day-to-day workings of partisan or interest group politics.[30] Following the uncovering of a "homegrown" terrorist conspiracy – the "Toronto 18" case – in mid-2006, the Embassy made a point of flying senior Canadian police and security officials to Washington to meet with senior members of Congress to demonstrate the seriousness of Canada's counter-terrorism commitment as well as brief senior administration officials.[31]

Lobbying campaigns can be proactive or reactive, depending on the issues in question and whether Canadian officials are seeking to head off proposed congressional legislation or promote amendments to existing legislation adverse to Canadian interests. Canadian officials noted that Canada is often "sideswiped" by partisan political debates in the United States that either have little to do with Canada or in which Canadian interests become a proxy for broader domestic conflicts.[32] Effective lobbying often involves "finding solutions to bilateral problems where the costs, if any, are shared and where the benefits are not conspicuously in favour of one partner."[33]

Threats to Canadian interests are far more likely to emerge from the personal agendas of members of Congress and their obligations to service constituents, key stakeholders, and political donors than they are from the actions of the executive branch. Such challenges are as likely to result from the unintended consequences of domestic special interest politics as they are from direct hostility to Canadian interests.[34]

Special interest pressures on members of Congress are increased by the rising costs of financing both primary and general election campaigns. These realities reinforce the relative (and expected) disparity of influence between foreign governments and US domestic interest groups who broker political support and campaign contributions in return for accommodating their political, economic, and regulatory interests.

This phenomenon can be seen in debates over border security, in which an initial focus on border and container security spread to concerns over the US northern border – partly to rebut accusations of anti-Hispanic prejudice among members of Congress attempting to curb illegal Mexican immigration. It is visible in efforts of small ranchers' and farmers' groups to limit Canadian beef and pork exports to the United States, reflecting a broader reaction against low farm margins, competitive pressures from large agribusiness interests, and assorted import competition.

Embassy officials note that "part of the challenge is to keep Canadian issues from being matters of congressional concern. The more Congress gets involved, the more likely it is to create problems for Canada."[35] The extended debate over the Keystone XL pipeline since 2009, discussed later in Chapters 8 and 13, demonstrates the risks to Canadian interests of being caught in partisan and ideological crossfires, whether in Congress or executive-congressional relations.

Canadian interests are often most vulnerable to special interest pressures from the House of Representatives, in which tighter party discipline and procedural rules designed to limit legislative debate can expedite the passage of legislation favoured by party leaders and whose members' localized interests often contribute to more protectionist outlooks, as noted earlier.[36]

These underlying political realities meant that the shift in partisan control of both houses of Congress after the 2006 congressional elections was more significant for bilateral relations in the House than the Senate, in which a super-majority of sixty votes is often required to pass major legislation. One business lobbyist, speaking in early 2009, characterized the House Democratic leadership as "a lost cause ... on a lot of issues important to Canada."[37] For that reason, the Republicans' recapture of the House in November 2010 was welcomed by Canadian energy interests if not by most environmental groups. However, such partisan or ideological polarization can often be detrimental to Canadian interests by creating zero-sum political contests in which the pursuit of partisan political advantage can trump the achievement of more substantive policy outcomes.

Conversely, the Senate is characterized as "very much a trade-off kind of place," in which the ability to negotiate an amendment to legislation can require its sponsor(s) to "agree to six other things" that are important to their committee colleagues or party leaders, regardless of which party controls the Senate.[38] For example, Michigan senator Carl Levin persuaded colleagues to include provisions restricting Canadian garbage exports to his state in an otherwise unrelated environmental bill in 2005, while border state Senate veterans Patrick Leahy (D-Vermont), Byron Dorgan (D-North Dakota), and Ted Stevens (R-Alaska) combined to insert strict conditions for implementation of the WHTI into the 2006 Homeland Security

Appropriations Bill in response to pressures from constituents and business interests in border communities – despite strong opposition from counterparts in the House.[39] Although the Embassy can sometimes be successful in securing changes to proposed legislation without "outside" support, it has become standard procedure since the 1980s for Canadian diplomats to work closely with businesses and other relevant interest groups to pursue their goals.

A key factor in many of these debates is the willingness of the administration to engage the issue – whether sending signals that a Canadian government position enjoys the support of the administration, that the administration has no objection to congressional action in response to Canadian concerns (a more hands-off approach), or that the administration has different goals altogether. After US and Canadian agriculture officials agreed on measures to reopen the US border to Canadian cattle imports in 2005, with similar approaches to ensuring food safety in each country, the Bush White House clearly signalled that it would veto a congressional resolution that would have kept the border closed. Although such a resolution narrowly passed the Senate, the Republican chair of the House Agriculture Committee refused to take up the measure.[40] However, if a cohesive group of senators whose votes are needed to pass major legislation favoured by the administration demands certain concessions in return for their votes, the White House will often make concessions on narrower issues to secure its broader objectives. Under such circumstances, Embassy officials need to display tactical flexibility and a sense of proportion – working with individuals or groups that can extract an acceptable compromise from key decision makers, recognizing that the issue might well resurface during the next congressional session under more auspicious political circumstances.

Most of these issues involve fairly routine legislative matters, even though some might be particularly important to specific Canadian interests. However, on three occasions since the mid-1990s, the Embassy has deployed all available resources to pressure Congress and the administration, up to and including the White House, to secure legislative outcomes or policy or administrative changes to protect open borders and trade relations – a core objective of Canadian economic policies.[41] The first two episodes – the Section 110 debates of 1996-2000 and the WHTI debate of 2005-8 – involved requirements that Canadians (and Americans) entering the United States carry passports or "other secure documents." The third episode involved Canadian efforts to reverse or secure exemptions from congressional Buy American legislation passed as part of the 2009 budget's stimulus package. These debates are addressed in greater detail in Chapters 11 and 12, respectively.

On such occasions, while "business as usual" continues among the Embassy's front-line professional staff, the bulk of its lobbying resources are focused on this key priority. Such decisions usually require the active support of the prime minister and relevant cabinet minister, both in defining the issue as a key national interest and in raising it at every opportunity with their counterparts in the White House and US executive departments. Such initiatives must take account of specific political conditions in Washington to avoid the fairly common accusation that Canadians are "overreacting" to a congressional initiative. For example, the very different political environments for border security before and after 9/11 imposed different tactical responses on Canadian officials, as discussed in Chapters 10 and 11, as did the substantial leverage with Congress enjoyed by organized labour and other protectionist interests during the 2008-9 recession. Ottawa must come up with a specific "ask" of both administration and congressional leaders that is politically and administratively feasible as well as consistent with broader US interests.[42] And in some cases, while avoiding linkage with unrelated policies, it might identify policies that provide for reciprocal treatment or accommodation of each country's citizens and interests – an approach that generally benefits Canada given its disproportionate economic dependence on access to US markets.

Although the congressional gridlock on climate change policies since 2006 has kept environmental and related energy issues from achieving the same "quasi-crisis" status in Canada–US relations, Ottawa has made considerable efforts to work with the Obama administration on regulatory and "clean energy" issues in an effort to create a political "firewall" against the potential for hostile congressional action. At the same time, Embassy officials (and those from energy-producing provinces, especially Alberta) have worked closely with sympathetic members of Congress on both sides of the partisan aisle to promote recognition that US energy security substantially depends on secure energy supplies from Canada. Alberta officials note that more than 80 percent of the oil consumed in northern states such as Michigan and Minnesota comes from Canada. This message has brought Canada into conflict with major environmental groups, whose influence increased substantially after House Democrats replaced long-time Energy and Commerce Committee chair John Dingell, a champion of automotive sector interests, with California Democrat Henry Waxman in late 2008.[43] The political context for these debates has shifted with the Republican recapture of the House in 2010, the ongoing debate over the Keystone XL pipeline, and GOP efforts to turn Keystone into a major partisan issue in the 2012 presidential campaign.[44] These issues are addressed at greater length in Chapters 8 and 13.

The greatest risk of Canadian involvement in congressional processes, whether in mounting relatively targeted lobbying efforts or an all-out campaign to achieve particular objectives, is that these efforts can be perceived as "foreign meddling" in US domestic politics. Although such "meddling" is unavoidable given American political realities and the interdependence of the two countries, Canadian diplomats can use a variety of tactics to avoid or defuse such accusations, depending on political circumstances.

Lobbying without "Meddling"

> *The method and context of congressional and public lobbying are affected profoundly by the position of the Administration on the issue in question. If the Administration is strongly opposed to the position of the foreign government, the potential is high for a foreign lobbyist both to increase resistance and breed resentment in the Administration's midst and to contribute to a backlash on the Hill ... It can also "play into the hands of the opposing special interests" – making "Canada" the issue.*
>
> – *Allan Gotlieb*, I'll Be with You in a Minute, Mr. Ambassador, *1991*

American academics writing about bilateral relations sometimes observe that Canada has a somewhat privileged position in Washington of which its officials tend to be highly protective.[45] Although many Canadians working in Washington might contest the first observation, it is often echoed by American government officials who note the uniqueness of their relations with Canadian counterparts compared with those from other countries viewed as US friends or allies.

Canadian officials in Washington often view their dealings with Congress as a constant struggle to protect Canadian interests amid the crossfire of special interest politics. However, their ability to draw on extensive networks of shared and complementary cross-border interests actively engaged in lobbying in Washington constitutes a significant advantage available to relatively few other countries. This reality is recognized by senior US government officials and accepted within certain limits. As one put it, "the Canadians ... tend to work the political system. They can have meetings with anybody on the hill. They can meet with all the senators, the representatives, and all the trade associations. If the Chinese did that, the US would be hopping mad. But if Canada does it in moderation, you can get away with it."[46]

Most Embassy officials whom I interviewed acknowledged the risks of being seen to interfere in US policy processes, though the extent of the two countries' interdependence makes the risks of not engaging members of Congress potentially much greater. As a result, Canadian microstrategies in lobbying Capitol Hill – or in going back and forth between the hill and relevant executive departments, depending on circumstances – are often heavily reliant on cooperation with domestic American interests and elements of the administration.

Although coordinating positions with the current administration is no guarantee of avoiding partisan attacks in Congress, as Allan Gotlieb discovered on several occasions during the 1980s, Canadian diplomats usually attempt to find allies on both sides of the partisan divide. In many cases, they can do so by sharing information with sympathetic lobby groups. Such lobbying is usually more effective if seen to be done in concert with the administration.[47] For example, in its efforts to secure the reopening of the border after its BSE-related closure to Canadian cattle exports in 2003, the Embassy "worked very closely with the American Meat Institute, the National Cattlemen's Beef Association, [and] the beef-processing plants ... to convince members of Congress that there's a problem there that they can't afford to ignore."[48] Consular officials outside Washington actively worked with local interest groups to broaden the range of US domestic interests pressuring Washington on the issue. However, these efforts followed concerted and largely successful efforts by Agriculture Canada officials to establish a common front on international food safety issues with the US Department of Agriculture (USDA). With the administration's general support, it was substantially easier to recruit the support of Agriculture Committee leaders in Congress.

However, the risks of being seen to "interfere" in American domestic politics become substantially greater when Embassy officials work at cross-purposes with the administration. One Canadian diplomat commented that "we undermine ourselves if it's Canada driving the issue on the hill. It's more beneficial to us if it is lawmakers who recognize that there are real shortcomings in the process. We may end up causing ourselves real problems with the administration. Better to have that coming from lawmakers than from Canadians."[49]

These sentiments were echoed by US Department of State officials whom I interviewed, especially with regard to the Embassy's persistent efforts to persuade Congress to change the provisions of the WHTI.

> I don't have a problem with Canada lobbying Congress. I don't think they do all that good a job of it. I more draw the line not at lobbying Congress but in two areas – the tone, the assertion that "the US just can't do this." Because ultimately it is our decision at all times who and at what times people can enter the United States.[50]

The Embassy's two-and-a-half-year lobby of Congress on the WHTI, and its support for US border communities whose interests diverged significantly from those of both DHS and Department of State officials responsible for the passport policy, contributed to a chilling of bilateral border security relations for a time – at least in dealings between respective line departments. President George W. Bush took a more conciliatory if hands-off approach when Stephen Harper first visited the White House in July 2006, commenting that, since Congress had passed the original law, it was up to Congress to change it, if desired, to provide greater "flexibility."[51]

Although under no illusion that they could prevent the WHTI from proceeding in some form, both the Embassy and Public Safety Canada sought to engage DHS officials on a variety of issues related to program design and implementation. The Canadian mantra, from Harper himself in periodic speeches to American audiences to Ambassador Michael Wilson and his senior officials, was "let's take the time to get it right."[52]

However, the success of border interests, often supported by the Embassy, in persuading Congress in mid-2007 to push back the policy's implementation date on land borders beyond the 2008 presidential elections convinced DHS officials that the Embassy was actually trying to kill the measure through incremental delays, a common enough tactic in congressional politics. Both published reports and interviews with DHS officials suggested that, combined with impasses in a series of operating-level discussions, the Embassy's WHTI lobby helped to erode mutual trust and created frustration resulting from declining political support in Congress.[53] One commented that "there was the perception that Canada was really working the system. They pushed it off longer than we wanted to put it off. Nothing gets people annoyed like getting beaten."[54] These issues will be addressed at greater length in Chapters 10 and 11.

As noted in Chapter 4, a frequent American critique of Canadian diplomacy targeting both the executive branch and Congress is that Canadian responses tend to be disproportional – whether in reacting to American initiatives or by focusing significant lobbying resources on issues seen to be peripheral to Canadian interests. One veteran Canada watcher observed that,

> Where I find it offensive in some ways is when Canada becomes very public with its internal debate when items are relatively peripheral to Canada's interests. There was a very public campaign against ANWR [Arctic National Wildlife Refuge] drilling. A foreign diplomat asked me whether ANWR was a shared refuge between the two countries. I said no. Also when Canadian cabinet ministers use a venue in the US for attacks on US domestic policy, that is over the edge.[55]

Given conventional diplomatic norms, these observations are not overly surprising.

However, the cross-border activities of Canadian diplomats and government officials in recent years have been less likely to stir up congressional or public controversy than in the 1980s or 1990s, when both Democratic and Republican members of Congress were often quite assertive in challenging what they perceived to be interference – and occasionally high-level influence peddling – in American domestic politics.[56]

In summary, Canadian officials in Washington tend to be guided by a few basic rules when engaging Congress.

- Always work with, and if possible through, domestic interest groups and networks or cross-border coalitions to ensure a "domestic echo" when engaging Congress on issues affecting Canada, whether large or small.[57]
- Do not neglect the executive branch when engaging Congress: a two-track strategy is usually more effective and provides some insulation against accusations of "interfering" in US domestic politics.[58]
- Affirm, whenever possible, shared interests and policy goals between the two countries (and/or the constituents of particular members of Congress) rather than focusing on uniquely Canadian concerns – an approach that can be seen as "whining."

- Whenever possible, present a clear "ask" that is within the legal authority, and consistent with the broader political interests, of the interlocutor – whether in Congress or the executive branch.
- Be willing to accept half a loaf – a technical compromise or procedural stop-gap measure – when political conditions do not allow for a "clear win"; chances are that there will be future opportunities to pursue the issue – as well as future challenges by competing interests.
- Be persistent: competing interests are hard-wired into the American political system; yours might as well be among them.

When all else fails, remember that "an ambassador (and his staff) [are] paid to intervene in the domestic affairs of the United States. If he does it badly, he can get into trouble; if he does it well, he can get into an equal amount of trouble."[59] Although Canadian diplomats should not go looking for trouble, and can often avoid it with tact and skill, conflict is built into the highly competitive world of congressional and interest group politics. Looking for allies in that world and identifying messages that help to shape the terms of debate on issues that can affect Canada are essential parts of Ottawa's public diplomacy – and the central focus of the next chapter.

8

Canadian Public Diplomacy in the United States

———— Promoting Canadian Interests, Fostering Networks of Influence

There are three cardinal rules in the war of ideas. Know yourself; know your enemy; know your audience. It is important not to confuse these three. Or you may become your own worst enemy and end up talking to yourself.

– Robert R. Reilly, *"The Battle for Hearts and Minds,"* 2006[1]

Canadian governments dealing with the United States face two basic challenges in attempting to influence the policies of their giant neighbour. First, they must attempt to foster the development of a domestic political consensus, however limited, on the objectives, limits, and details of particular policy goals. Second, as "just another special interest" in Washington, they need to identify those American domestic groups whose interests complement or conflict with policy goals pursued by Canadian governments in cross-border relations – looking for ways to cooperate with the first and conciliate or work around the second. These objectives complement Canadian governments' dealings with both the executive branch and Congress by seeking to foster a domestic echo for Canadian policy goals and concerns within the American political system while gathering effective political intelligence on the opportunities, risks, and limits associated with particular goals and tactics.

As discussed in previous chapters, many cross-border issues are treated by American politicians, governments, and interest groups primarily as subsets of US domestic policies. They are also pragmatic responses to the growing role of public opinion and non-governmental actors in international relations, whether as constraining factors on governments' activities or as sources of expertise and possible political support in navigating the technical details of complex policy issues. National governments must often take foreign public opinion and the activities of non-governmental actors into account, whether in building closer relations with or in contesting the policies of their international trading partners. As a result, traditional forms of diplomacy focusing on state-to-state relations are increasingly supplemented by "public diplomacy" – the targeting of foreign audiences by governments of another country to build relationships and promote their short- and long-term foreign policy objectives.

This chapter considers the role of public diplomacy in Canadian governments' efforts to advance their interests in the United States in engaging both specific policy communities in Washington and relevant policy networks and public opinion "beyond the beltway." It explores Canadian diplomats' interactions with the American news media and the challenges of managing media relations when politicians and senior diplomats speak to domestic audiences as much as or more than Americans. The chapter notes the complementary and sometimes conflicting roles played by Canadian business and other interest groups in Washington and cross-border politics. It assesses the strengths and limitations of Ottawa's alliance-building efforts in the United States and the practical implications of such tactics for future policy making by Canadian governments.

Public Diplomacy in Theory and Practice

> *The "premise" of public diplomacy is that "democracies try overtly to influence each other's policy from inside."*
>
> – *Charles Doran and Joel Sokolsky,* Canada and Congress, *1985* [2]

Public diplomacy takes a variety of forms. Both Canadian diplomats in the United States and their American counterparts in Canada regularly attempt to cultivate public opinion. Public diplomacy is distinguished from traditional state-to-state diplomatic relations, or from public relations and propaganda, in that it seeks to cultivate relationships with non-state actors in foreign countries. Its core objective remains the development of "direct relations with people in a (foreign) country to advance the interests and extend the values of those being represented" by their national governments.[3]

These relationships should contribute to the recognition of shared or overlapping interests and values between the officials of a foreign government – and often major stakeholder groups among its citizens – and citizens and interest groups of the host country. Over time, these perceptions can deepen into a foundation of mutual understanding that shapes broader policy agendas, not just opportunistic issue or policy coalitions.

More recently, public diplomacy has also come to embrace Canadian (and other) expatriates in the United States and the ways that they participate in American social networks and political processes. Effective public diplomacy requires an ongoing capacity to adapt themes, messages, and practices to social, cultural, and political trends within the countries whose policies it is seeking to influence. As such, it is subject to the evolving constraints imposed by public opinion when seeking to influence the policies of the host country's government, even as it often involves efforts to shape public opinion in that country. As discussed in Chapter 4, Canadian public diplomacy faces the additional challenge of having to work within the constraints of public opinion in Canada, which is often based on different assumptions or priorities than those shaping American public (or elite) opinion.

Although active Canadian public diplomacy in the United States predates the 1987 signing of the Canada–US Free Trade Agreement by several years, Canada's growing economic integration in North America since the 1980s has greatly increased its relevance to the management of bilateral relations. A veteran Canadian official responsible for crafting Canada's public diplomacy in the United States characterized it as

A program that undertakes to engage targeted contacts based on themes that we expect to permeate the Canada–US relationship on a longer-term basis. These are not issues demanding immediate attention. Rather, they are key underlying themes that we know will come to the surface in the public policy form in the US and where Canada will need well-informed US allies to explain US interests.[4]

The relational dimensions of public diplomacy are most relevant to dealings with targeted audiences generally composed of influential members of society. Its next stratum involves economic, social, and political networks, which are often organized on a sectoral or local basis, whose priorities and interests can be affected by general trends or specific issues related to Canadian governments' core priorities in cross-border relations. On occasion, it can include leaders of American academic and cultural networks that overlap with Canada – though one former Embassy official described these groups as the "least likely to be amenable to a structured engagement that can be directed to a specific end."[5]

Influencing broader public opinion, even at the margins, also requires governments to engage in "strategic public diplomacy" – the crafting of clear, consistent public relations messages to complement a state's political objectives or to respond to unforeseen policy shocks.[6] Part of this process involves building "a body of expertise among the US media so that they are innately skeptical when an inaccurate story is filed concerning Canada – and so that we have ready access."[7] The failure of the Chrétien government to perform these functions effectively after 9/11, which led to the unchallenged emergence of the urban myth that the terrorists had entered the United States from Canada,[8] prompted more systematic efforts to engage American journalists, interest groups, members of Congress, and other shapers of opinion.

In both contexts, effective communications require that public diplomacy must "have foreign rather than one's own perceptions as a starting point"[9] – just as people attempting to sell a product or service are well advised to first understand the existing preferences and perceptions of their audiences. In this context, an excessively narrow focus on one's own interests, characterized by Paul Frazer as the "set my widgets free"[10] approach, can be counterproductive.

Effective public diplomacy thus requires an ongoing capacity to adapt themes, messages, and practices to social, cultural, and political trends within the countries whose policies it is seeking to influence. Public diplomacy need not, and often does not, lead to a convergence of political interests and objectives. Rather, it cultivates a level of mutual understanding capable of enhancing bilateral relations and reducing potential levels of friction between countries. Achieving these results, however, can be impaired by the actions of governments, politicians, or other societal actors that are intellectually dishonest or transparently inconsistent with the strategies or messages used to cultivate influence in the target country.[11]

Writing in 1985, Doran and Sokolsky noted Canada's relatively limited visibility in Washington compared with other countries with extensive diplomatic, military, or economic relationships in the United States. They attributed this "structural under-attention"[12] to Canada to American assumptions that the interests of the two countries are similar and to the greater priority traditionally given to defence issues in US foreign relations. This theme was picked up in the late 1990s by Mahant and Mount in their book *Invisible and Inaudible in Washington*.

However, the combined effects of NAFTA and, more particularly, American responses to the terrorist attacks of 11 September 2001 focused policy makers' attention on the extent to which the assumptions underpinning Canada's previously unique relationship with the United States could no longer be taken for granted. As noted by Sands[13] and others, Canada's so-called special relationship with the United States, born of shared experiences and close cooperation among senior decision makers during the Second World War and the building of postwar alliance and economic systems, became increasingly distant and formal during the 1970s and early 1980s whatever the short-term effects of Brian Mulroney's subsequent cultivation of close personal relationships with Presidents Ronald Reagan and George H.W. Bush.[14]

The same period also saw a progressive shift of demographic, economic, and political power from northeastern and midwestern American states with relatively close economic and social links to Canada to southern and western states whose external orientation, if any, was likely to be toward Mexico, Latin America, or the vast expanse of the Pacific Rim. The advent of free trade with Mexico in 1994, which formally incorporated Mexico into several economic and administrative relationships previously considered unique to US–Canada relations, and the rapid growth of Hispanic and Mexican American communities since the 1980s, have also tended to reinforce the southward focus of US hemispheric policies.

One senior official commented that, "after 9/11, it was a shock to Canadians to see the rapidity with which borders were shut." Canadian policy makers also became increasingly aware of the reality that "there's just too much going on in this abundant society for Americans to need or want to focus on their relationship with Canada" and that many aspects of American politics (as in Canada) remain intensely local.[15] The result has been an expansion of Canadian diplomatic activity across the United States – both inside and outside the beltway – in efforts to strengthen and extend networks and relationships inside and outside government.

Public Diplomacy in the United States: Actors, Targets, Processes

To engage the different layers of American society and political processes that shape American policies toward Canada, both directly and indirectly, Canadian public diplomacy needs to be a multilayered process. Just as the scale, scope, and diversity of the Canada–US relationship precludes effective centralization of its control within DFAIT or other agencies of Canada's federal government, the diversity – and diverse preoccupations – of American society require the capacity to use what Allan Gotlieb and others have described as a "multiplicity of instruments"[16] – the willingness of Canadian governments to enable and even encourage multiple actors to engage different elements of the American political process as long as their messages are relatively consistent.

Contemporary Canadian public diplomacy involves multiple actors: visiting Canadian politicians – federal, provincial, and sometimes municipal; the ambassador and Embassy officials in Washington; Canada's network of consulates across the United States; provincial offices in Washington and major American cities; and a variety of official and societal cross-border networks. In addition to enabling transgovernmental relations between Ottawa and Washington, these networks include the cross-border networks of provincial and state governments, economic networks conducted among horizontal business groups and sectoral associations, and networks of academics and societal actors, including labour, environmental, and more targeted "single issue" organizations. These intergovernmental, economic, and societal networks provide much of the "hidden wiring"[17] of the broader Canada–US relationship. They intersect with a multitude of comparable domestic networks in the United States – some internal to the different branches of the US government, others involving the intersection of US domestic political and societal networks.

Both economic and societal groups function independently of governments, though some degree of coordination can take place on an issue-by-issue basis. The relevance of economic and other societal actors to the public diplomacy of governments stems from their capacity to reinforce or counteract the messages of governments to counterpart groups in the United States and to broader publics.

Canadian public diplomacy involves multiple targets as well – both inside and outside Washington. Activities within and beyond the beltway are intended to complement one another in creating a "societal echo" for general themes that reflect the medium- and longer-term priorities of Canadian diplomacy in the United States as well as specific "messages" intended to influence public debates on specific issues.

Writing in the early 1990s, Allan Gotlieb described the interest group and advocacy industries in Washington as the "third house of Congress."[18] The Center for Responsive Politics reports that there were 12,967 active lobbyists registered under US federal disclosure legislation in 2010 – 2.5 times as many as reported by Gotlieb in the late 1980s – incurring $3.51 billion in direct lobbying expenses, not including political contributions to members of Congress and candidates for federal office.[19] In contrast, the Canadian Embassy employed sixty-two professional staff (diplomats and locally hired officers) in its political, economic, congressional, and federal–provincial relations offices in mid-2011. Unlike other foreign governments that have invested heavily in Washington lobbyists, Canadian governments typically spend modestly on outside public and government relations advice – though some provinces have retained outside government relations advice in recent years, as noted in Table 8.1.[20]

Canadian public diplomacy in Washington is heavily focused on building and maintaining contacts with think tanks and interest groups actively engaged in cross-border economic issues and sectoral policy debates of direct interest to Canada. Within the Washington beltway, this activity is focused on major think tanks, the Canada policy community, and more specialized industry and civil society groups whose priorities overlap with those of the Embassy.

The presence of hundreds of think tanks – policy research and advocacy organizations – in the Washington area also provides another avenue for outreach: the (co-)sponsorship of conferences, seminars, and other events on issues of interest to Canada. Although these activities must compete with the agendas of thousands of domestic interest groups, all attempting to catch the attention of policy makers and/or the media, they are an important part of expanding what might be called the Canada policy community in Washington.

Many foreign governments attempt to create networks of interests and individuals whose activities complement these governments' policy agendas and contribute to creating a climate of opinion more receptive to their policy goals. Some governments, including those of Israel and Mexico, actively cultivate the support of American citizens based on shared ethnic origin and/or cultural and religious sympathies. Others, such as Saudi Arabia, are reputed to engage in large-scale "chequebook diplomacy" in which former government officials are often retained as consultants on large retainers. Others, such as Japan and Great Britain, finance major economic lobby organizations to promote positive trade relations.

Table 8.1 summarizes the countries with the most significant presence on the US Foreign Agent Registration system. If anything, these listings substantially overstate the relative dependence of Canada's federal government and its diplomats on the Washington public affairs and government relations community.

More significant are the business interest, think tank, legal, and academic networks that provide a forum for cross-border cooperation and the cultivation of shared outlooks on many issues that complement the advocacy activities of Canadian diplomats. Since issues related to Canada tend to be peripheral to the activities of most Washington think tanks, only a handful of groups, such as the Canada Institute of the Woodrow Wilson Center and more recently the Hudson Institute, have had dedicated expertise related to Canada. At the Brookings Institution, US–Canada relations have been treated as a subset of US urban and regional policies in recent years as part of the Metropolitan Policy Program.

Since most policy institutes tend to be relatively specialized in their expertise, the Embassy or other Canadian interests work with American think tanks to foster ongoing dialogues on issues of mutual interest. However, the sheer number and diversity of specialized think tanks in Washington create major challenges for Embassy officials. One veteran Canada watcher commented that

> It's an overwhelming task to reach out to the think tank community in Washington because you have think tanks around every set of issues and every political orientation. This has got to be the world capital of think tanks. I think it's a really hard thing to do. The Embassy spends a lot of time just dealing with incoming Canadian visitors ... They don't have the time to do serious, long-term consultation and relationship building.[21]

DFAIT, the Embassy, and Canadian consulates outside Washington are also actively engaged in promoting academic outreach and related forms of public diplomacy, including partnerships between American and Canadian

TABLE 8.1
Foreign agent registrations, by country, 2010

	National government or related agency	Other government	Private sector/ other	Total
Japan	19	7	9	35
Canada	5	15	3	23
Great Britain/ United Kingdom	4	7	9	20
South Korea	11	1	7	19
United Arab Emirates (especially Dubai)	12	–	7	19
Iraq	3	9	5	17
Taiwan	15	–	1	16
Mexico	10	2	2	14
India	7	1	5	13
China	3	–	8	11

SOURCE: US Department of Justice, Foreign Agents Registration Unit; author's calculations.

policy researchers. These efforts have the effect of promoting the expansion of a knowledge base about Canada in the United States and about various aspects of bilateral relations in Canada. Much of this engagement is a long-term investment in academic and policy networks, including the Association for Canadian Studies in the United States, parallel efforts by the government of Quebec, and regional networks in the Pacific Northwest. The long-running Canada–US Fulbright program funds international research and study by academics, graduate students, and, more recently, undergraduate students by Canadians in the United States and Americans in Canada. The Embassy can also provide direct and indirect assistance to medium-term research by American think tanks that directly address important bilateral issues.

These activities complement the activities of Washington-based think tanks and other organizations that are part of the Canada policy community in Washington. For example, the Wilson Center provides regular venues for Canadian and American academics and policy practitioners to present research and topical discussions on bilateral and North American issues. The Hudson Institute's Christopher Sands is deeply networked within academic and policy communities engaged on bilateral issues. The Center for

Strategic and International Studies uses adjunct scholars for research on North American and hemispheric issues – particularly security and energy issues – that touch on both Canadian and Mexican perspectives. However, most American academics are reluctant to be seen as active protagonists in networks dependent on funding by foreign governments – linked as they are to the active promotion of private and foreign interests.

Embassy officials liaise regularly with other major think tanks such as the Brookings Institution, especially when Democrats are in power, and the Heritage Foundation to network with Republicans. However, much of the social cross-pollination between Canadian and US interests takes place at the level of interaction among policy institutes, general business or industry-specific groups, labour organizations, and environmental groups – each functioning within its respective policy communities. The Council on Foreign Relations has close relations with major horizontal business groups in Canada and Mexico that contributed in 2005 to the publication of a significant "independent task force" report suggesting paths toward North American integration.[22] It also maintains expertise on "energy security" issues of direct relevance to bilateral relations. Similar cooperation – if aimed at competing policy objectives – is visible among major labour federations across North America[23] as well as the remaining large international unions such as the United Steelworkers of America, which has been led by Canadian Leo Gerard since 2001.

Among business groups, there are extensive linkages between major horizontal business groups in each country, such as the Canadian and US Chambers of Commerce, which have published several recent policy reports on border management and other major cross-border issues, national manufacturers' associations, and organizations representing different business (or agriculture) sector interests. The energy sector, led by the Canadian Association of Petroleum Producers and its larger members, has played an active role in raising Canada's profile as the largest supplier of oil, natural gas, uranium, and other energy resources to the United States. The Canadian–American Business Council provides a regular venue for visiting Canadian speakers and serves as a vehicle for major companies with substantial cross-border operations to focus on issues that are often below the radar of larger horizontal or sectoral business groups.

The Embassy has been less successful in cultivating relationships with American environmental groups in the polarized environment of beltway politics, though there has been cooperation on more regionally focused issues. The strategic priorities of Canadian governments – including maintaining and expanding US market access for Canadian hydrocarbon and hydroelectric energy exports – have been fundamentally at odds with those of several major environmental lobby groups, including the powerful Natural Resources Defense Council (NRDC). These groups have sought to promote shifts to alternative energy sources through regulatory barriers to the expansion of hydrocarbon and large hydroelectric production in North America. However, the regional diversification and provincial ownership of most energy resources in Canada, combined with memories of the deeply divisive federal–provincial battles over energy policies of the 1970s and 1980s, have reinforced the long-standing commitment to a relatively market-oriented, decentralized approach to energy policies in Canada, as discussed in Chapter 13.

Former US ambassadors to Canada also play an ongoing role as advocates for positive cross-border relations – often for specific clients who wish to draw on their expertise, insights into Washington policy processes, and networks of contacts to advance their interests in the American capital. One prominent Washington law firm heavily invested in Canada–US relations has actually established an advisory council, composed of all former American ambassadors to Canada and Canadian ambassadors to the United States, that serves as a significant hub of influence on bilateral relations, especially under Democratic administrations. More recently, the governments of Saskatchewan and Alberta have retained the law firm of former US ambassador David Wilkins to provide them with strategic government relations advice.[24]

During 2009, Prime Minister Harper's communications advisers retained two former presidential press secretaries – Mike McCurry (Bill Clinton) and Ari Fleischer (George W. Bush) – for communications advice and support in obtaining national television exposure for the prime minister related to major international conferences also attended by President Obama. However, Canadian governments have generally been cautious about this kind of contact since being caught up in the legal difficulties of former Reagan White House adviser Michael Deaver during the 1980s.[25] However, some veteran Washington observers suggest that the centralization of media relations functions in Ottawa has made the Embassy less effective than it might be in seeking to engage national media coverage of key bilateral issues and events in Washington.[26]

A more common approach involves cooperation with interest groups in both Canada and the United States on issues in which Canadian interests are engaged. Embassy officials are actively engaged in monitoring many different policy processes and legislative initiatives. As discussed in Chapter 7, exchanging information with interest groups and other participants in the relevant policy communities is important to monitoring and engaging American policy processes affecting Canadian interests. Other activities include hosting visits by American policy makers, including legislators and their staffs, journalists, and other "influentials," to locations in Canada associated with current policy issues. Among the most prominent venues for such visits have been major border crossings and the Athabasca oil sands.

Canadian public diplomacy outside the beltway is more eclectic. Each consul general and consul is responsible for developing personal relations with at least 100 key persons of influence within his or her territory. Consuls and their staffs, including both foreign service officers and locally engaged personnel, develop contacts with state governments, legislators, key business, industry, and other advocacy groups, as well as academic networks involved in the study of Canada. Ottawa has gradually expanded the network of honorary consuls in smaller centres that serve as sources of information on issues relevant to bilateral relations and provide entrees to local political and business networks of importance to Canada's interests in each region.[27] The expansion of Canada's consular network since 2003 will be discussed further in Chapter 9, together with the activities of provincial governments and regional cross-border networks.

However, the Embassy's ongoing efforts at public diplomacy also intersect at many points with the need for coherent and consistent efforts at public and media relations in the increasingly fragmented media markets of the United States.

Public Diplomacy and Media Engagement

The media and public relations dimension of Canadian public diplomacy is a constant challenge: how to create the "right kinds" of visibility in a highly competitive marketplace for news and information in which visibility frequently invites controversy.

American media coverage of Canada is sporadic and generally attuned to the interests of its primary markets. As with other aspects of the bilateral relationship, cross-border issues and Canadian initiatives in the United States receive far greater media coverage in Canada than in comparable American markets. For example, visits by national leaders and the appointment of new ambassadors – from either country – are usually front-page news in Canada. They rarely qualify for more than a brief mention, if that, in the White House or diplomatic columns, respectively, of Washington newspapers – even less beyond the beltway. Even with extensive cultivation of the American media, a major domestic or international news story – such as the response of the White House to Egypt's pro-democracy demonstrations in February 2011 – can easily steal the public spotlight from national leaders' efforts to highlight cooperation in bilateral relations.[28]

This reality provides strong incentives to Canadian politicians to play to domestic audiences rather than foreign ones when visiting the United States.[29] An amusing example can be seen in Prime Minister Harper's opening of his public remarks in French at the same White House press conference in 2011, only for the Fox News anchor to cut away from his coverage of the event with the comment "Fox don't do French."[30]

Canadian governments' engagement of the US media is both proactive and reactive. The former can take the form of efforts to promote or showcase prime ministerial visits to the United States – often in conjunction with White House visits or other international meetings, as noted in Chapter 5, but also in speeches, usually to business groups, in major American cities. The latter engagement frequently occurs in response to unexpected events that place Canada in the news, including comments by American politicians or public relations campaigns by US-based interest groups challenging the policies of Canadian governments.

With the decline in the number of US media outlets with correspondents located in Canada – in mid-2011, only the Associated Press and the *Wall Street Journal* maintain a full-time presence – efforts to generate "earned media" have required more systematic outreach either to national American media outlets or to more specialized business media. However, much media relations activity takes place behind the scenes as the ambassador of the day and senior Embassy officials develop personal relationships with journalists, columnists, and media executives. Such relationship building can allow them to obtain access to national media when necessary – such as after the arrests of the Toronto 18 terrorist conspirators in 2006 – but also to develop relations of mutual trust that allow them to provide background information on developing stories and avoid public "ambushes" by prominent media personalities.[31]

The proliferation and decentralization of news media, reinforced by the Internet, create significant challenges for managing public diplomacy. On the one hand, this trend facilitates targeting information to particular market segments more likely to be receptive to particular messages conveyed by foreign governments or interests. On the other, it can increase the difficulty of communicating to a wide audience through traditional media.

FIGURE 8.1 "Fight Fear." CanadianAlly.com is a website developed by the Canadian Embassy in Washington to promote American public awareness of the Canada–US defence and security relationship – including Canada's engagement in Afghanistan. This photograph from 2008 is part of a broader public relations effort to highlight Canada's combat role in Afghanistan. [*Source:* CanadianAlly.com. Reproduced with permission]

A significant innovation in the Canadian Embassy's public diplomacy during the past decade has been its use of issue-specific websites and other non-traditional media to "narrow-cast" messages to particular American audiences. For example, CanadianAlly.com promoted Canada's military commitment alongside US and NATO allies in Afghanistan (see Figures 8.1 and 8.2). However, some sources suggest that the Harper government has downplayed such approaches to diplomacy in favour of the cultivation of interest group networks inside and outside the Washington beltway.

Another technology-driven innovation is Connect2Canada, a "virtual network" for Canadian expatriates in the United States and "friends of Canada" launched in 2005; it provides a vehicle "to exchange news and ideas" and "find out what is happening in the U.S. related to Canada."[32] The

FIGURE 8.2   "Remembering 9/11: Friends, Neighbors, Ally." This picture from the CanadianAlly.com website provides a softer public relations message intended to reinforce the often "warm but fuzzy" attitudes of Americans towards Canada. [*Source:* Canadian Ally.com. Reproduced by permission]

program combines website- and email-based communications that function as tools for transmitting key themes and messages to participants, gathering information, and promoting events intended to "get Canada's message out" to particular, self-selected communities in the United States. The US Embassy in Ottawa uses similar techniques.

Persistent efforts by US environmental groups to target Canadian oil sands imports have prompted growing involvement by both Canadian private sector interests, discussed later in this chapter, and federal and provincial governments to engage US media markets. Major environmental groups such as the Natural Resources Defense Council have attacked the growth of Canadian oil sands imports since at least 2006.[33] This campaign has supported broader efforts to increase the share of renewable fuels in US energy markets by restricting new oil and gas exploration and production while externalizing the costs of adapting to climate change. In 2010-11, oil industry interests, construction unions, and supporters of "energy security," supported by the Canadian and Alberta governments, championed a major counter-lobby of the Department of State and other agencies involved in the regulatory process.

When fifty members of Congress signed a letter to Secretary of State Hillary Clinton asking her to block regulatory authorization for expansion of the Keystone XL pipeline carrying Canadian oil to refineries in Oklahoma and Texas, the Alberta government ran a half-page ad in the *Washington Post* with the headline "A good neighbor lends you a cup of sugar. A great neighbor supplies you with 1.4 million barrels of oil per day."[34]

This ad was part of an ongoing public relations campaign in support of the province's energy industries that has included sponsorship of a month-long Alberta display in the Smithsonian Folk Festival on the Mall in Washington, DC, in July 2006, regular cross-border visits by Alberta premier Ed Stelmach and his senior ministers, the sponsorship of dozens of prominent visitors annually to the oil sands in Fort McMurray, and more recently promotion of Alberta's efforts to achieve greater environmental sustainability in oil sands production.

Canadian public diplomacy is complicated when Canadian governments use bilateral issues to seek tactical advantages in domestic political contests, though most Canadian governments resort to such tactics from time to time. The credibility of public diplomacy is impaired when governments send mixed or conflicting messages – as in the Martin government's private hints to Washington that Canada would support the proposed US Ballistic Missile Defense system, only to reject it later, or in its private efforts to seek a negotiated end to the protracted softwood lumber dispute while Martin publicly fulminated against American bad faith in successive legal proceedings on the issue.[35]

Technological changes that have strengthened trends toward media decentralization also increase the avenues available for message contestation and "push back," whether by private (including media) interests that seek to exploit a particular event or story to advance their own agendas or by competitive public diplomacies, when one government seeks to exploit policy inconsistencies of another to challenge its political agendas. For example, Prime Minister Martin's efforts to make the Bush administration's opposition to the Kyoto Accord an issue in the December 2005 Canadian election campaign backfired when US Embassy staff gleefully circulated statistics demonstrating that Canadian CO_2 emissions had increased substantially faster than US emissions since 2001.[36] Greater visibility for public diplomacy also expands opportunities for parallel or adversary discourses independent of traditional media that individuals and interest groups can use to challenge or attempt to discredit "mainstream" political and media discourse.

These realities increase the challenges facing Canadian public diplomacy in the United States. However, if anything, they also increase its importance, particularly in managing "intermestic" policy processes in which traditional distinctions between domestic and foreign policy discourses and processes have become increasingly blurred.

Both US and Canadian mass media tend to engage bilateral issues in the context of domestic political (and ideological) competition in their respective countries – providing a useful platform for major media personalities or domestic interest groups in both countries to promote their agendas, often at cross-purposes with their national governments. One Canadian diplomat noted that "Fox News comes after us on occasion. But when Bill O'Reilly goes on a rant about Canada, we should substitute Democrats for Canada. He tells his viewers they have a choice between having a clear, no-nonsense choice and the wishy-washy view of Democrats."[37] (Others offer similar comments about coverage of bilateral issues by the CBC.) More recently, conservative American journalists have repeatedly cited the past successes of Canadian Liberal governments in reducing federal deficits to discomfit the Obama administration.[38]

Conversely, ultranationalist groups in both countries have demonized the Security and Prosperity Partnership (SPP) processes of 2005-9 as a conspiracy to sell out national sovereignty and form a "North American Union,"[39] and Canadian expatriates used the media to challenge Obama's proposed health-care reforms.[40] These factors increase the challenges for Canadian governments in engaging American media markets on those occasions that northern cross-border issues gain momentary significance for particular journalists.

A 2007 study of print media coverage of Canada in the United States indicated that an average of 9.8 stories relating to Canada were printed monthly by each of seventeen major national and regional newspapers studied between 2003 and mid-2007, most in communities served by

TABLE 8.2

Coverage of Canada in selected US newspapers, 2003-7

Topic	Total	%	2003	2004	2005	2006	2007*
Bilateral political relations	222	2.8	2.1	4.1	2.9	3.1	2.7
Trade, economic, business issues	2,368	29.9	23.4	36.8	37.3	23.7	32.5
Homeland security, public safety	1,357	17.1	11.9	12.9	18.2	22.7	**32.8**
Defence, national security	764	9.6	8.8	11.6	3.9	**16.6**	4.6
Public health, food safety	1,043	13.2	**24.8**	11.0	10.4	*3.1*	*2.7*
Canadian domestic politics, policies	449	5.7	3.9	5.4	7.7	7.3	5.5
Social policies	344	4.3	6.7	4.3	3.7	2.4	*1.7*
Energy policies	389	4.9	**8.2**	2.8	4.5	4.1	*1.8*
Environmental policies	314	4.0	3.2	3.1	3.7	5.4	5.6
Immigration issues	212	2.7	*1.3*	3.5	2.9	**4.3**	2.6
General interest articles	468	5.9	5.9	4.6	4.8	7.4	7.5
Total articles	7,930	100	2,538	1,772	1,469	1,495	656

NOTES: **Bold** type signifies a significant increase in levels of coverage; *italic* type a significant decrease.
* First six months of 2007.

SOURCE: Geoffrey Hale and Jamie Huckabay, "Canadian Public Diplomacy in the United States: Which Public? How Diplomatic?" paper presented at the meeting of the Association for the Study of Canada in the United States, Ottawa, ON, 15 November 2007.

Canadian consulates – despite a steady overall decline in news coverage of Canada during this period. Issue emphasis varied widely, both between publications and from year to year, as demonstrated in Table 8.2. (Proximity to the border was rarely a factor given the relative prominence of Canadian coverage in cities such as Miami and Houston.) Although trade, economic, and business issues received the most continuous and extensive coverage, homeland security and public safety issues became more prominent toward the end of the period, and public health and food safety issues received extensive coverage in 2003 due to the SARS epidemic in Toronto and the discovery of BSE in an Alberta cattle herd.

These findings reaffirm the suggestion, noted above, that Canada rarely provides "top of mind" issues for Americans and that Canadian efforts to engage US media outlets depend on their ability to address issues that interest Americans. However, when such issues surface, as with the June 2006 arrests of eighteen alleged "would be" terrorists in Toronto, Canadian officials need to deal with them effectively to avoid being caught in the crossfire of American domestic politics.

Canadian officials were sensitized to this problem when the *New York Times* and other media outlets reported rumours that some of the 9/11 terrorists had arrived in the United States from Canada. Although these rumours were later proven false, the Chrétien government's failure to address them at the time allowed the story to spread widely, becoming an urban legend repeated as late as 2009 by Secretary of Homeland Security Janet Napolitano.[41] Even so, its persistence reflected the concerns of American (and some Canadian) security officials that Canadian immigration and refugee policies had significantly increased security risks to the United States.[42] After the Martin government took office in 2004, it instructed Canadian diplomats to respond within twenty-four hours to any false or misleading story relating to Canada, including comments by any American public figure giving credit to the 9/11 myth. Canadian diplomats also worked assiduously to keep Canadian border issues separate from long-standing concerns over illegal immigration and drug smuggling along the US–Mexican border.

Engaging US Policies toward Canada: Business and Societal Responses

The increasingly "intermestic" environment of trade and economic policies has reinforced the growth of cross-border relations among societal groups, particularly those representing various business sectors but also environmental groups, organized labour, and other sectoral policy interests. Corporate structures and business interest groups in particular are increasingly organized and networked across national borders, often blurring traditional distinctions between American- and Canadian-based firms – though the density of these networks varies widely by industry sector.

These trends are contributing to the growth of sectoral trade strategies that are often complementary if not fully integrated within North America, as demonstrated by extensive, market-driven integration in the automotive, steel, chemical, oil and gas, aerospace, and information technology sectors, among others. Several industries are actively pressuring governments to move toward common external trade policies for their sectors.[43]

Economic integration is contributing to business pressures for improved regulatory coordination within and across national borders, particularly with regard to a wide range of microeconomic regulations affecting particular industries – as reflected in the Joint Action Plan for the Regulatory Cooperation Council announced in December 2011.[44] However, such initiatives are heavily dependent on the support of major interests most likely to be affected as well as the positions of national and subnational governments and agencies in both countries – many of which are naturally protective of their jurisdictions and prerogatives. The greater the need to enlist congressional or provincial support for regulatory changes, the greater the likelihood that these proposals will run afoul of competing societal and governmental interests.

Interest group networking takes place at a variety of levels, though such networks are often segmented by policy field and economic sector. The horizontal networking of business interests is visible through the regular meetings of groups such as the Canadian Council of Chief Executives, which has played a leading role in promoting deeper North American integration, the Canadian and US Chambers of Commerce, and national manufacturers' associations. The extent of cross-border coordination depends on the level of corporate concentration within particular industries in each country, the significance of cross-border operations to major firms, and the degree to which the political activities of particular industry sectors and subsectors are coordinated or "firm specific." As noted in Chapter 6, the cross-border integration of automotive, steel, and meat-processing industries has played a significant role in the management or resolution of major cross-border policy issues in recent years.

The greater the level of decentralization and internal competition within particular industries, the more fragmented and competitive their interests are likely to be in the political marketplace as well. Washington-based business observers suggest that this reality is reinforced by the understandable tendency of individual business and association executives to focus on "microissues" of direct interest to their members,[45] by the lobbying styles of individual organizations,[46] and by their positions as relative insiders and outsiders within their particular policy communities.

Apart from major manufacturing groups, Canada's energy industry probably has had the greatest visibility in Washington of any set of Canadian economic interests in recent years. Energy production and transmission interests in Canada are closely integrated with counterpart organizations in the United States; this is not surprising given the extensive integration of their major firms and operations. The Canadian Association of Petroleum Producers (CAPP), which represents both major integrated oil and gas producers and independent operators, provides a much greater degree of industry coordination than its more fragmented American counterparts, though major firms engaged in cross-border operations maintain independent lobbying capacities. In 2008, CAPP hired Tom Huffaker, formerly the US consul general in Calgary, to be its executive vice-president of policy and environment – reflecting the enormous importance to its members of maintaining secure access to US markets. Members of the Canadian Electricity Association work closely with their counterparts at the Edison Electric Institute – the industry association for shareholder-owned electric utilities, serving about 70 percent of the US market – as well as through regional (cross-border) electricity reliability organizations, as discussed in Chapter 13.

As in domestic politics, cross-border cooperation also takes the form of special purpose coalitions designed to address particular policy challenges, such as the Coalition for Secure and Trade-Efficient Borders, formed to address border management issues after 9/11, and the BESTT coalition of border community and tourist sector interests formed in 2005 to promote alternatives to the WHTI's passport requirements.[47] Unique among these groups for its persistence and multisectoral character is the Pacific Northwest Economic Region (PNWER), a public–private sector organization spanning the five westernmost Canadian provinces and territories and five northwestern American states, bringing together executive, legislative, private sector, societal, and academic stakeholders for annual and semi-annual meetings on a wide range of issues.

After the signing of NAFTA, horizontal and sectoral business interests were incorporated into a series of sectoral working groups, some more active than others, to address technical regulatory and trade issues. Several NAFTA sector committees were subsequently absorbed into the short-lived SPP process. These groups parallel the work of sectoral advisory committees that are a continuing feature of trade consultation processes in both the United States and Canada, though they have been criticized as "forums to 'talk and talk' without any mechanism to bring closure to an issue."[48] The creation in 2006 of the North American Competitiveness Council (NACC) – a trilateral body bringing together a cross-section of business groups and corporate interests in all three NAFTA countries – was intended to provide some degree of coordination and focus to an otherwise diffuse process comparable to similar bodies that advise national governments on trade negotiations. NACC's activities lapsed with the demise of the SPP process in 2009. However, much of its work is continued by the bilateral Regulatory

Cooperation Council (and related working groups) established in 2011. Composed of government officials, its mandate includes provisions for semi-annual "stakeholder engagement" sessions and publication of work-plans and reports.[49]

Formal initiatives for policy coordination, particularly those involving business groups, have aroused the never particularly latent antagonism of organized labour and nationalist interests that remain deeply hostile toward the existing structures of NAFTA and other aspects of economic globalization – let alone more far-reaching initiatives, real or imagined.[50] Some of these criticisms reflect hostility toward the entire process of North American economic integration. Others reflect legitimate concerns over the absence of a broader range of societal voices in a wide range of technical issues that can be addressed in the absence of detailed legislative oversight. The overlap among interest group networks, particularly those associated with the Canadian Council of Chief Executives, has blurred distinctions between Ottawa's avowedly incremental approach and the pursuit of much deeper levels of integration sought by some business groups and policy entrepreneurs.[51]

As noted previously, institutions for intergovernmental or interagency coordination in both Canada and the United States, let alone across national borders, tend to be highly segmented and decentralized to the extent that they exist at all.[52] As a result, neither US nor Canadian governments generally possess the capacity necessary to coordinate the extensive regulatory initiatives championed by some business groups and feared by their ideological opponents. The US–Canada Regulatory Cooperation Council, whose creation was announced by President Obama and Prime Minister Harper in February 2011, could conceivably evolve into such a body. But the precedents of more than fifteen years of glacially incremental bureaucratic change suggest otherwise to many observers.[53]

These realities tend to reduce the transparency of policy processes to many stakeholders and, especially, to broader publics, raising questions of democratic legitimacy. They also provoke suspicions that such processes are likely to promote the interests of stakeholder groups invited by governments to participate while discounting those of societal and economic groups not so favoured. These concerns, reinforced in the United States by the continuing ideological polarization of partisan politics and the stagnant or declining standards of living of many lower- and middle-income Americans, are likely to become a significant barrier to further integration unless new approaches are developed to engage and win the trust of citizens on both sides of the border.[54]

Conclusion

Canadian governments' efforts to "ramp up" public diplomacy in the United States since 9/11 have been broadly successful in the sense of reinforcing generally favourable public attitudes toward Canada and of broadening and deepening networks for projecting Canadian economic interests in US domestic policy debates, particularly outside Washington.

Public diplomacy is unlikely to be successful when the interests of the two countries are fundamentally at odds or necessary when they are perfectly aligned. But the nature of continuing interdependence suggests that the normal realities of bilateral relations are likely to fall between these two poles. Thus, the systematic cultivation of groups with shared outlooks and interests will remain central to Canadian public diplomacy.

The two most significant developments in Canadian public diplomacy during the past decade have been the growth of Canada's diplomatic capacity outside the Washington beltway and the systematic engagement of provincial governments and regional economic interests in cross-border diplomacy – often with Ottawa's active encouragement. These developments are the subject of Chapter 9.

9

Beyond the Beltway

Federalism, Regionalism, and
Cross-Border Relations

The political legitimacy of growing North American economic integration in Canada, as in the United States, hinges largely on two related but potentially conflicting variables: the economic benefits to be derived from increased trade and specialization of labour, and the perception that each country's political system is able to maintain the capacity and discretion to respond effectively to its own citizens' interests and concerns.

Each country's distinctive processes of federalism – the division of powers between separate orders of government with the effect of facilitating the representation of geographically defined interests – are central to this trade-off. The dynamics of federalism – whether played out within each country's federal government, in dealings between central governments and state or provincial governments, or in both – are vital to the multilevel game of integrating and balancing domestic and North American policy relationships. Building on a concept popularized by James Rosenau, Anderson and Sands have characterized these realities as the politics of "fragmegration": the interaction of integrating and fragmenting forces at multiple levels of social, economic, and political interaction.[1] The institutionalization of regional representation – and regionally important sectoral interests – in federal and intergovernmental decision-making processes provides multiple points of access for economic and societal interests in both countries. In some cases, cross-border cooperation among these interests can reinforce processes for policy convergence within North America.

In others, decentralized policy processes can either impose constraints on economic integration or provide an environment that shapes the terms under which the integration of policies and economic activities takes place.[2]

This chapter examines the efforts of Canadian governments to engage the American political system beyond the Washington beltway. It explores the relevance of federalism and regionalism for cross-border relations – particularly as the reflection of different federal structures and sharing of jurisdictions and the projection of regional interests in each country. The chapter examines the role of Canada's consular network in public diplomacy and advocacy activities, the growing engagement of provincial governments with state-level counterparts, and the resulting uses of "network diplomacy" involving state and local US interests to advance Canadian interests in the United States. Finally, it ponders the implications of these approaches for the future of North American integration.

Federalism, Regionalism, and Cross-Border Relations

Some early studies of North American integration suggested that pressures from corporate interests for more standardized rules conducive to economic integration would contribute to a greater centralization of power in Canada – similar to that which occurred in the United States after its Civil War – as well as the substantial harmonization of public policies between the two countries. However, others have argued that the effects of globalization and North American integration on "the institutions and practices of intergovernmental relations" have been relatively small and incremental.[3] These trends are seen to "reinforce and exaggerate tendencies already present in domestic societies and politics, rather than fundamentally to change and reorient them."[4] Divergent responses to "intermesticity" reflect the "compatibility of values, interests, and self-interest of policy actors" along with persistent differences in "governance structures, traditions, expectations, and processes"[5] among jurisdictions and policy sectors.[6]

Although CUFTA and NAFTA have generally facilitated the bottom-up, market-driven processes of economic integration discussed in Chapter 3, neither has provided much room for the kinds of bilateral or North American institutions that allow for formal policy coordination among national governments.[7] These realities are driven largely by the concerns of political leaders in all three countries to maintain political sovereignty and the democratic capacity to respond to competing domestic interests, including their regional and local dimensions.

The dynamics of federalism and regionalism in the context of bilateral relations and North American integration have several major dimensions. The formal division of powers between federal and subnational governments – provinces (and territories) in Canada, state and local governments in the United States – has institutionalized significant asymmetries between federal and subnational responsibilities in each country. Even where federal governments possess effective jurisdiction, entrenched legal requirements and cultural expectations for consultation enforce the need to negotiate major policy changes with cross-sections of political and societal stakeholders. These realities reinforce institutional pressures discussed in Chapters 6 and 7 to decentralize decision making along sectoral lines.

As noted in Chapter 8, American demographic shifts since the 1950s have favoured southern and southwestern regions of the United States, with fewer social and economic linkages with Canada. These trends have contributed to major shifts in political power, making the cultivation of relations with political and economic actors in these regions a growing priority of Canadian governments under both Democratic and Republican administrations. The importance of these relationships is reinforced by the related tendency of both American elite and public opinion to view North American relationships in the context of linkages and tensions with Mexico.

Moreover, Canadian provinces have become increasingly active participants in cross-border relations. Most provinces bordering on the United States have active international relations functions, centring primarily on promoting or protecting their economic (and often environmental) interests. Growing exports provided a safety valve for most provincial economies during the domestic retrenchment of the 1990s. During the 1980s, Ontario and New Brunswick were the only provinces that exported more to other countries (mainly the United States) than to other provinces. Between 2003 and 2008, international exports of eight provinces, mainly to the United States, consistently exceeded their interprovincial exports, with Manitoba and Prince Edward Island hovering around parity.[8] These trends gave most provincial governments a significant interest in cross-border economic relations along with US federal or state government policies that might affect them disproportionately.

In contrast, Kukucha has noted that trade with Canada accounts for a much smaller proportion of the economies of most American states and that growing trade since the 1980s, while significant, did not fundamentally change most previous economic relationships between American states and Canadian provinces.[9] However, three major factors have contributed to

TABLE 9.1

US state merchandise trade with Canada, as percent of US gross state product (GSP), 2008, 2010

	Exports to Canada		Imports from Canada		Two-way trade	
	2008	2010	2008	2010	2008	2010
United States	1.83	1.58	2.38	1.88	4.21	3.46
More than 10 percent of GSP						
Vermont	6.6	7.9	11.1	9.6	17.7	17.5
Michigan	6.4	5.7	12.0	10.6	18.4	16.3
Montana	2.0	1.4	16.5	11.9	18.4	13.3
New Hampshire	1.1	0.9	12.3	9.6	13.4	10.5
North Dakota	4.5	4.5	7.5	5.5	12.0	10.0
5-10 percent of GSP						
Illinois	2.3	2.3	6.3	4.6	8.6	6.9
Ohio	4.3	3.6	3.5	3.0	7.7	6.6
Maine	1.9	2.0	4.4	4.5	6.2	6.5
Kentucky	3.8	3.6	2.7	2.5	6.5	6.1
Washington	2.8	2.0	5.2	4.0	8.0	6.0
Indiana	4.0	3.9	2.2	2.2	6.2	6.0
Delaware	1.5	4.6	1.0	0.7	2.4	5.3
Minnesota	2.2	2.0	6.2	3.1	8.4	5.1
Tennessee	2.6	2.8	3.9	2.2	6.5	5.0
Fluctuating						
Kansas	2.1	2.0	1.8	2.6	3.7	4.6
Iowa	2.9	2.4	3.0	2.0	5.9	4.4
Wyoming	0.8	0.6	9.1	3.7	9.9	4.3

NOTE: Numbers may not add precisely due to rounding.

SOURCES: US Bureau of Economic Analysis, "News Release: GDP by State" (Washington, DC: Bureau of Economic Analysis, 2009, 2011); Foreign Affairs and International Trade Canada, "U.S. State Trade Fact Sheets" (Ottawa: DFAIT, 2009); US Census Bureau, *State Trade Data* (Washington, DC: Census Bureau, 2011).

ongoing shifts in the balance of trade between individual American states and Canada since 2002: the appreciation of the "loonie" against the "greenback," the volatility of energy prices, and the after-effects of the 2009 recession, which reduced two-way merchandise trade by 20.3 percent. By 2010, twenty-five states reported merchandise trade surpluses with Canada (versus eighteen in 2008). Five states had two-way trade with Canada of more than 10 percent of gross state product (GSP), compared with two in 2003, while nine states, including four at some distance from Canada, had two-way trade over 5 percent of GSP (see Table 9.1).

TABLE 9.2

Comparing federal division of powers in Canada and the United States

	Canada		United States	
	Federal	Provincial	Federal	State
International trade	●	○	●	
Economic development	○	●	●	○
Primary industries/land use		●	○	○
Food standards	●		●	○
Energy	○	●	●	○
Environment	○	○	●	○
Border management	●		●	
Related infrastructure/highways		●	●	○
Immigration	●	○	●	
Labour mobility		●	●	
Corporate governance/ securities regulation	○	●	●	○

● = sole or primary jurisdiction; ○ = concurrent or partial jurisdiction.

Source: Adapted from Geoffrey Hale, "Canadian Federalism and the Challenge of North American Integration," *Canadian Public Administration* 47, 4 (2004): 500.

Jurisdictional Issues

Significant differences in the structures and styles of federalism are central to the politics of federalism and "intermesticity" in each country. Compared with American states, Canadian provinces possess significantly greater jurisdiction, fiscal resources, and political legitimacy in representing regional interests. Direct provincial spending accounted for 46.6 percent of overall government expenditures in Canada in 2010, compared with 28.6 percent for the federal government, though federal transfer payments characterized by little or no conditionality remain an important source of provincial revenues.[10]

A series of judicial rulings since the nineteenth century has given Canadian provinces significantly greater jurisdiction and discretion in policy fields ranging from economic development to regulation of labour relations, capital markets, and natural resource development (see Table 9.2). Moreover, though the 1937 ruling of the Judicial Committee of the Privy Council in the *Labour Conventions* case[11] allows Ottawa to negotiate treaties in areas of provincial jurisdiction, it effectively precludes their enforcement without provincial consent. These patterns contrast sharply with more than 180 years of centralizing precedents in Supreme Court interpretations of the "commerce clause" of the US Constitution.

As a result, the formal and informal structures of Canadian federalism tend to privilege interstate federalism – the brokerage of regional interests through negotiations between or among federal and provincial governments – over intrastate federalism: the negotiation and coordination of regional differences through the internal processes of federal governments. These patterns have been reinforced by persistent regional weaknesses of major Canadian political parties that limit their perceived capacity to represent all regions of the country when holding federal public office.[12]

In contrast, the processes of American federalism entrench patterns of intrastate federalism, especially since they are mediated through the constitutional prerogatives and decentralized processes of Congress. The US federal government accounted for the bulk of both overall revenues (47.5 percent) and direct expenditures (49.3 percent) in 2010-11.[13]

Managing Bilateral Jurisdictional Differences

The most significant jurisdictional differences between the two countries, at least for purposes of bilateral relations, fall into the areas of energy, natural resource, environmental, transportation, and labour policies.[14] In Canada, the ownership and regulation of most energy and natural resources fall under provincial jurisdiction, whereas in the United States there is a patchwork of governmental and private ownership and federal and state regulation. Although Ottawa carefully guards its jurisdiction over international trade and other negotiations, US government officials – particularly in the Department of Energy – often take into account the position of Alberta and other energy-producing provinces on oil- and gas-related issues. Similar considerations arise on issues of electricity regulation, where six provinces have extensive interties with American regional energy grids, though the US Federal Energy Regulatory Commission (FERC) has taken a more proactive role in this area.[15]

The interim resolution of the long-running softwood lumber dispute between the two countries in 2006 hinged on the ability of the US Office of the United States Trade Representative (USTR) to craft a proposal that could bridge differences among the very different industry and regulatory structures of British Columbia, Ontario, Quebec, and the Maritime provinces.[16] The first three provinces held de facto vetoes over the implementation of any prospective softwood lumber agreement negotiated by Canadian federal officials.

On environmental issues, the US federal government has regulatory primacy, while state and local governments retain important residual and supplementary rights on both environmental and related land-use issues. As a result, California often plays a leading role in regulations affecting air quality – and more recently climate change – while state governments bordering Canada play important roles in water quality issues.

Under the Boundary Waters Treaty of 1909, bilateral issues on boundary waters – lakes, rivers, and streams shared with or flowing into the other country – are formally within the jurisdiction of the International Joint Commission (IJC), a binational agency of federal appointees from both countries whose actions are based on joint references by the two central governments. Since the 1930s, any such references on disputes over the interpretation or application of the treaty have depended on the ability and willingness of the two governments to agree on specific terms of reference.[17] However, in practice, both governments tend to defer to the political sensibilities of states and provinces if the latter are functioning within their respective jurisdictions. For that reason, Washington deferred to North Dakota interests in the dispute over that state's proposed diversion of water from Devils Lake into the Red River watershed (2004-6) despite strong protests from Manitoba. Subsequently, Ottawa refused to intervene when the government of British Columbia turned a deaf ear to the outcry of Montana's federal and state political leaders over proposed natural gas drilling in the upper Flathead River (2006-8), which forms the western boundary for Glacier National Park in the United States, though British Columbia later reversed its decision. Canadian federal officials whom I interviewed formally denied any linkage between the two disputes. However, the failure of bilateral processes in the first dispute might well have contributed to Ottawa's greater deference to provincial rights in the second. In a third issue, the Canadian federal government's cession of its ownership share of the headworks of a water diversion pipeline between the St. Mary and Milk Rivers to Alberta has effectively ceded policy leadership to that province in dealing with Montana's request to reapportion water rights under the treaty.[18]

Jurisdictional issues can also complicate the management of cross-border transportation projects. Stanley[19] notes that, though 21 percent of the value of US international merchandise trade was carried by truck in 2001, truck shipments accounted for more than 64 percent of American trade with its NAFTA partner. The challenges of interjurisdictional cooperation can be seen from the effects of local litigation that effectively delayed more than 200 large truck shipments of equipment for the Kearl Lake oil sands project for more than a year in 2010-11 despite the negotiation of substantial infrastructure upgrades with governments in Idaho, Montana, and Alberta.[20]

Major border crossings in the heavily populated Great Lakes region often involve the building of bridges, reorganization of traffic flows in urban areas, and related neighbourhood and environmental impacts that can mobilize numerous stakeholders.[21] Even though federal governments regulate border crossings in both countries, differing patterns of infrastructure ownership, and provincial/state control over access roads and related land-use regulations, can make any major redesign or expansion an adventure in intergovernmental relations. Ownership of border infrastructure is widely distributed among multiple federal, provincial, state, and even municipal agencies along with private ownership of the Ambassador Bridge between Detroit and Windsor.[22]

Highway construction and maintenance are a shared responsibility in the United States but primarily a provincial responsibility in Canada. Diffused jurisdictions for land use and environmental assessment and decision making among provincial, state, and local governments complicate the approval, design, and construction of major "gateway" and "corridor" projects between the two countries, especially when these projects are located in major urban or environmentally sensitive areas.[23] Provincial-state relations in these issues are most deeply institutionalized between British Columbia and Washington and between Maine and New Brunswick. The development of efficient transportation corridors has become a central topic in provincial governments' encouragement of cross-border regional networks.

The depth and quality of cross-border relations between state and provincial governments are central to the efficiency of these processes. They also depend on the ability and willingness of federal and state/provincial decision makers to coordinate complex budgetary, environmental assessment, and land-use processes in each country. For example, the planning of a new Detroit–Windsor international crossing requires the coordination of separate processes in four jurisdictions. When the 2009 recession threatened to derail Michigan's participation in the project, Ottawa offered the cash-strapped state government $550 million to finance its share of a new Detroit–Windsor bridge.[24] However, intensive lobbying and a high-profile publicity campaign against the new crossing financed by the owners of the Ambassador Bridge has prevented newly elected Governor Rick

Snyder from securing legislative approval for the project through the end of 2011.[25]

Conceptualizing and Building the North American Platform

> *Diplomacy – like politics – must be "local" to succeed.*
>
> *– Colin Robertson, "CDA_USA 2.0," 2008*[26]

The growing integration of national economies since the 1980s has reinforced trends toward "intermesticity," as noted previously. Although this phenomenon is most pronounced in Canada, it is also directly relevant to American political and policy processes and the ways that Canadian governments engage those processes.

Four core realities relevant to federalism and regionalism have shaped the advocacy activities of Canadian diplomats in the United States during the past decade. First, as discussed in Chapter 7, congressional primacy in domestic policy processes greatly increases the importance of building political coalitions *inside* the United States as part of the broader two-level game of mobilizing domestic political forces in both countries to support cross-border initiatives. Both North American integration and political resistance to it are by-products of market forces interacting with crosscutting economic and societal interests organized on a sectoral, regional, or even local basis. These processes argue for a bottom-up approach to coalition building and interest brokerage that directly engages these actors to develop the advocacy microstrategies necessary to project relevant Canadian interests in Washington.

Second, demographic changes in the United States have resulted in significant shifts of populations, economic activity, and political power away from economic regions bordering Canada toward the American south and southwest, as noted above. Table 9.3 outlines the evolution of the US Electoral College's regional composition between the censuses of 1960 and 2010.

Third, these trends have been reinforced by the growing presence of Hispanic Americans across the United States, especially in regions distant from the Mexican border during the 1980s and 1990s. The US Census Bureau estimated the number of Hispanic Americans at 50.5 million in 2010, almost half again as large as the total population of Canada – more than double the 22.4 million counted in the 1990 census. About two-thirds

TABLE 9.3
Regional shifts in the Electoral College, 1964-2020

	Electoral votes (out of 538)						Percent change
	1964-68	1972-80	1984-88	1992-2000	2004-8	2012-20	1964-2020
New England	37	36	36	35	34	33	−10.8
Mid-Atlantic	105	101	93	87	83	79	−24.8
Midwest	129	126	119	112	107	101	−21.7
Plains states	27	26	25	23	23	23	−14.8
Pacific Northwest	22	22	24	25	25	26	+18.2
Sub-total: North	320	311	297	282	272	262	−18.1
Southeast	119	120	124	128	132	135	+13.4
Southwest	55	58	66	70	75	82	+49.1
California–Hawaii	44	49	51	58	59	59	+34.1
Sub-total: South	218	227	241	256	266	276	+26.6
For states bordering Canada	164	158	149	140	134	129	−21.3
% of total electoral vote	30.5	29.4	27.7	26.0	24.9	24.0	

NOTE:
Columns reflect congressional redistribution following each decennial census through the 2010 redistribution.
New England: Connecticut, Maine, Massachusetts, New Hampshire, Rhode Island, Vermont.
Mid-Atlantic: Delaware, District of Columbia, Maryland, New Jersey, New York, Pennsylvania.
Midwest: Illinois, Indiana, Iowa, Michigan, Minnesota, Missouri, Ohio, Wisconsin.
Plains states: Kansas, Montana, Nebraska, North Dakota, South Dakota, Wyoming.
Pacific Northwest: Idaho, Oregon, Washington State, Alaska.
Southeast: Alabama, Arkansas, Florida, Georgia, Kentucky, North Carolina, Louisiana, Mississippi, South Carolina,
   Tennessee, Virginia, West Virginia.
Southwest: Arizona, Colorado, Nevada, Oklahoma, New Mexico, Texas, Utah.
California–Hawaii: California and Hawaii.

of Hispanic Americans are of Mexican origin, many having immigrated to the United States during the past twenty years in response to Mexico's rocky transition toward economic modernization before and after its entry into NAFTA.[27]

Fourth, demographic shifts have contributed to a growing American preoccupation with Mexico. In some cases, they have created incentives for greater "trilateralization" of policy relations, though this trend has been reversed under the Obama administration. They have also fed a substantial public backlash against illegal immigration from Mexico and a related emphasis on border security that substantially affected American relations with Canada, even before 9/11.[28]

The Enhanced Representation Initiative

Ottawa responded to these trends and the political shocks from 9/11 by expanding its diplomatic representation, particularly in opening consulates outside traditional regional centres such as New York, Boston, Chicago, Detroit, Buffalo, Minneapolis, Seattle, and Los Angeles.[29] These initiatives sought to restore some of the capacity lost to budget cuts in the 1990s, reorganize the functions and "territories" of Canada's consular network across the United States, and redeploy staff from Ottawa (and elsewhere) to activities in the field. One official noted that "the formula that the Privy Council Office [PCO] proposed was that, if DFAIT could come up with twenty-five cents of every dollar required, and matched it by twenty-five cents from other partners, PCO would match that fifty cents to make a dollar."[30]

Beginning in September 2002, DFAIT officials sought to expand their reach, particularly in the southern and southwestern regions. Recognizing the growth of other federal departments' cross-border activities, they also reached out hoping to secure "partners" in funding and staffing consulates general by allowing participating departments and agencies to influence their business plans and priorities.

The result was the Enhanced Representation Initiative (ERI) of 2003-4, subsequently rebranded as the North American Platform in 2007. Six departments and agencies, including Industry Canada, Agriculture Canada, the National Research Council, and three regional development agencies, joined the temporarily separated Departments of Foreign Affairs Canada and International Trade Canada in funding the project.

A new consulate general was established in Denver. Six new consulates were located in Anchorage, Phoenix, Philadelphia, Miami, Raleigh, and San Francisco. Separate suboffices focused on important economic sectors within their states were established in Houston (reporting to the Dallas consulate general), Princeton (New York), Tucson (Phoenix), San Diego (Los Angeles), and San Jose (San Francisco). These locations reflected the growing diversification of regional economies and DFAIT's continuing emphasis on trade promotion.

The initiative authorized eighty new positions in the United States, including both career diplomats and locally hired staff; twenty-one positions were redeployed from other American posts. Treasury Board provided the initiative with an additional $3.5 million for advocacy and $5 million for business development in 2005-6, not including budgets for salaries and office space.

Discussions with senior DFAIT officials suggested that ERI was meant to focus as much on business development in the United States (export promotion and partnership development) as on advocacy. One key priority has been to promote technology partnerships between Canadian firms and American technology clusters: specialized networks of industry groups with concentrated expertise in particular areas.

Consuls general and their political officers – including locally hired staff with substantial business and political expertise – play a significant if usually low-key role in their advocacy functions. Consuls general are expected to identify and get to know 100 of the most important people in their territories in major regional and local industries, state governments, staff officials of senior members of Congress, major societal and economic interest groups, key media personalities, and policy experts. Complementing the activities of the Embassy in Washington, consular officials regularly plan trips for policy makers and congressional staff to familiarize them with Canadian dimensions of issues relevant to their states and regions. In recent years, these arrangements have included regular trips to inspect the Athabasca oil sands, border facilities (including meetings with front-line law enforcement officials), and academic study tours intended to promote engagement with Canada by American academics.

Consulates also identify community leaders in "second tier" cities of political and economic importance for appointment as "honorary consuls" to serve as "eyes and ears – American citizens paid a stipend to do what the consul general wants them to do." Identifying and responding to state and local initiatives that can facilitate or obstruct Canadian trade and investment complement the trade promotion functions of the consular network. Consulates also provide an important supporting role in engaging regional interest networks on major advocacy issues on the Embassy's current agenda. Examples in recent years have included networking with regional interests on border management issues and fostering closer linkages among industry, research organizations, and governments on "clean energy" research and related technology partnerships.

Canadian consulates play several other important roles. They help to familiarize Canadian diplomats with regional cultures and interest networks beyond the Washington beltway and cultivate relationships with government officials that can pay dividends in later years. State politicians are more likely than their Canadian provincial counterparts to move into federal politics. Time spent in building positive relationships with state governors and key legislators, and helping them to become more familiar with significant local and regional cross-border linkages with Canada, can pay dividends in later years when such individuals assume cabinet or congressional leadership positions in Washington. The Harper government's 2009 appointment of Gary Doer as Canada's US ambassador was influenced by his broad familiarity with American political personalities and cross-border issues through his engagement with conferences of the Western Governors Association, the Western Climate Initiative, and other networks during his decade as premier of Manitoba.

More prosaically, consulates regularly help to target Canadian federal funds to support cross-border networks of businesses, academics, policy specialists, and societal groups whose activities increase Canada's profile in the United States or foster collaboration on issues of priority to Canada.

Such networks are useful in contributing to greater local awareness of the interdependence of Canadian and US economies and other policy fields, reinforcing the activities of Canadian diplomats in Washington and broadening networks to support the broader advocacy microstrategies discussed in Chapters 6 and 7. However, these networks are subject to growing budget constraints as Ottawa shifts funds to support its diplomacy and growing trade promotion activities outside North America. These realities give added significance to the activities of provincial governments in building political and economic networks across the United States.

Provincial Engagement with State Counterparts

Provincial cross-border engagement is nothing new. Provincial governments, particularly Quebec, have maintained international offices to promote international trade and investment since the early twentieth century, though most provinces reduced their international presence in response to fiscal constraints during the 1990s.[31] As noted by Kukucha and others, the shifting emphasis of international trade negotiations since the 1970s from tariff reduction to efforts to regulate and reduce non-tariff barriers helped to institutionalize federal–provincial consultations through what later became DFAIT's C-Trade Committee process.[32]

As a result, federal advocacy in Washington and broader international settings often affects provincial economic and trade interests. Ottawa negotiated the Auto Pact of 1965 to protect Ontario's substantial investment in the industry. Similarly, the two governments worked hand in glove in 2008-9 to ensure that the Obama administration's restructuring of the troubled US automotive sector did not result in the significant displacement of employment or production capacity in Canada.[33] CUFTA's and NAFTA's energy clauses directly reflected "pressure from Alberta"[34] following the Mulroney government's dismantling of the National Energy Program. Ottawa's negotiation of the 1986 and 1996 Softwood Lumber Agreements largely reflected British Columbia's interests and agenda, as did its 2001 termination of the latter.[35] The 2006 Softwood Lumber Agreement brokered conflicts among British Columbia, Ontario, and Quebec lumber interests. Ottawa's trade diplomacy has also supported Alberta cattle interests following the BSE-related border closings of 2003, still defends Quebec's asbestos interests against health- and safety-related challenges, and has secured congressional support to prevent oil and gas drilling in Alaska's Arctic National Wildlife Refuge (ANWR) on behalf of local First Nations (2003-8). It continues to respond to ongoing challenges to the development of Alberta's oil sands.

Similarly, provinces have long maintained informal relations with neighbouring states on numerous commercial, regulatory, and environmental issues of mutual interest – described by Kukucha as "functional relations."[36] However, excepting Quebec, whose government has sought to translate its constitutional jurisdiction over economic and cultural matters into more formal international representation since the 1960s, these contacts remained fairly ad hoc outside the area of trade relations until the past ten or fifteen years.

Quebec's assertion of the "Gérin-Lajoie doctrine" of 1965 – named after the deputy premier who asserted that, "in all areas of its full or partial (constitutional) jurisdiction, Quebec intends from now on to play a direct role, consistent with its character and to the full extent of its rights"[37] – triggered strong resistance from federal officials to direct provincial representation in international relations for the next thirty-five years.

This resistance began to thaw after 2001 under the influence of Pierre Pettigrew, international trade minister at the time and later foreign affairs minister and a former chief of staff to Quebec premier Robert Bourassa. This background made Pettigrew more receptive to the recognition of significant provincial economic interests in international relations and to consulting extensively with provinces when engaging the growing number of international issues overlapping with their jurisdictions.[38] Prime Minister Martin signalled Ottawa's growing openness to direct provincial engagement in bilateral relations on taking office in December 2003 by inviting

Alberta premier Ralph Klein to open an Alberta office within the Canadian Embassy in Washington. This pattern has continued under the Harper government, though officials from each order of government are prone to view such dealings through opposite ends of the proverbial telescope.

Provincial engagement with American states and promotion of trade and investment beyond North America has oscillated widely for some years. Political interest and bureaucratic capacity to pursue coherent trade policies, trade promotion, and, more recently, environmental relations vary widely by province – often fluctuating significantly depending on domestic political and fiscal conditions.[39]

Quebec has long maintained the most extensive and continuous international relations presence as part of a broader strategy of asserting its "international personality" under both Liberal and Parti Québécois governments. Mouafo and colleagues note that Quebec had over 200 agreements and arrangements with US state governments, cities, and other public organizations in 2004, including seven missions (six in 2009) to promote trade and/or tourism.[40] Michaud and Boucher report that the Quebec Ministry of International Relations had a staff of 613 in 2004-5 – including 253 employed in twenty-five international diplomatic, trade, cultural, immigration, and tourism missions around the world.[41] However, departing from past practices, the Charest government has encouraged the co-location of several trade and immigration offices in federal embassies and consulates.

Quebec also asserts its political and cultural identities within the United States. Its Washington office has promoted Quebec interests for several decades, regularly sponsoring academic and cultural events, and is a regular contributor to and sponsor of seminars and conferences through the Canadian policy community in Washington (see Chapter 8). Quebec's public diplomacy includes a strong outreach program to American and other foreign academics, promoting academic and student exchange programs. More than most provinces, Quebec maintains an active outreach to state governments outside its immediate cross-border region as a member of or observer in multiple regional organizations, including the Council of Great Lakes Governors and the Western Climate Initiative. Quebec's engagement in cross-border regionalism will be discussed further in the next section.

Apart from Quebec, Alberta maintains the strongest outreach program beyond its immediate cross-border region.[42] Provincial officials participate actively in regional organizations of US state governments, cross-border

TABLE 9.4
Provincial government international offices, 2011

	Worldwide	United States
Quebec	26*	6
Ontario	10*	2
Alberta	10*	1
British Columbia	9	1
Manitoba	1	1

* Some offices co-located with federal government offices abroad.
SOURCES: Provincial government websites; interview, government of Manitoba, 2007.

trade, and trade corridor networks. Its Washington office maintains an active network of contacts in support of the province's "petro-diplomacy" and agricultural interests. The Alberta-based oil industry also maintains extensive lobbying and outreach activity in the United States – often in partnership with American oil and gas interests – which periodically draw attention to Canada's contribution to US energy security (see Figure 9.1). Alberta's Washington office plays an important symbolic role in asserting the province's right to protect and promote its resource industries, whose activities and markets are functionally integrated across North America, in broader international settings. It also plays a practical role in networking with sympathetic and complementary interests in Washington and other parts of the United States. Alberta has also played a leading role in the Pacific Northwest Economic Region (PNWER) since its inception in the early 1990s.

Ontario's international relations are more issue-specific and ad hoc despite having 125 agreements of different kinds in force with US state governments in 2004.[43] Although Ontario long maintained (and, in recent years, has resurrected) its network of international trade offices, its political presence in the United States is fairly modest. Ontario premiers and senior officials meet regularly with the governors of neighbouring states, particularly Michigan and New York. In addition to sharing interests in the automotive sector and the Great Lakes, Ontario engaged Michigan for almost a decade over the potential complications of a unitary business tax, finally passed in 2007, as a way of taxing the global operations of international businesses that created significant concerns in Ontario. Both Ontario and Quebec are signatories to the Great Lakes–St. Lawrence River Basin Water Resources Compact of 2005 together with eight US states bordering the

Great Lakes that had ratified the agreement by the end of 2008. The agreement provides all signatories with vetoes over proposed water diversions into other watersheds.[44]

British Columbia's cross-border relations have often reflected the personalities and priorities of different premiers – frequently conflictual in the 1990s under New Democratic governments, more collaborative since 2001 under the Liberal government of Gordon Campbell. Premier Campbell worked closely with west coast governors on climate issues. British Columbia joined the Western Climate Initiative on cap-and-trade and other measures regulating greenhouse gases. The BC cabinet meets annually with its Washington state counterpart, having developed cooperative strategies on transportation, environmental issues, tourism promotion (especially for the 2010 Olympics), and travel facilitation through enhanced drivers' licences (see Chapter 11). British Columbia's approach to cross-border irritants emphasizes bilateral contacts with American state counterparts – either directly or through various forums for regional coordination, including PNWER, the Western Governors' Association, and the Council of State Governments-WEST (CSG-WEST).

Manitoba and Saskatchewan have maintained dialogues with neighbouring state governments in recent years, particularly Minnesota, North Dakota, and Montana. They also engage business groups promoting trade corridors southward through the Dakotas. Relations between Manitoba and North Dakota were soured for some years by the lengthy Devils Lake dispute,[45] though efforts to improve relations have led to annual meetings with legislators in Minnesota and the Dakotas in recent years. Saskatchewan has actively engaged its southern neighbours, especially Montana, in pursuing cross-border partnerships to provide markets for its carbon capture technologies and to ship carbon dioxide to be used for enhanced recovery in the latter's oilfields.[46] Many of these activities support the cross-border networking activities of business groups, such as the Winnipeg Chamber of Commerce, and major municipalities, especially Winnipeg. The interaction

◀ **FIGURE 9.1** Canada's contribution to US energy security. This full-page newspaper advertisement from August 2008 responds to ongoing attacks by environmental groups on rising oil sands imports from Canada as part of the ongoing debate over climate change and US "energy security." Canadian governments work closely with cross-border energy interests to promote and protect US market access for what has become Canada's largest export industry. [American Petroleum Institute. Reproduced with permission] of these groups can be seen in Manitoba's creation in 2009, with federal financial support, of Centreport Canada, a major intermodal freight terminal linking truck, rail, and air transport facilities, "anchored" on Winnipeg's international airport.[47]

Among the Atlantic provinces, New Brunswick has been the most active in managing cross-border relations, reflecting its greater export dependence, extensive cross-border infrastructure with Maine, and efforts to become an energy hub for the upper New England states.

Provincial governments and their respective agencies also participate in a number of sector-specific institutions related to law enforcement, energy policies and the operation of interconnected electricity grids, boundary waters, coastal fisheries, and other policies. Some of these initiatives, such as the Cross-Border Crime Forum and cross-border infrastructure planning projects, function under federal leadership in both countries.

Three major challenges affect all forms of cross-border relations for provincial governments. First, political inertia arises from the predominantly domestic and local orientation of state (and provincial) politics, and cross-border issues are usually peripheral to the daily business of governing and running for re-election. This reality is particularly important in most border states, whose major population centres are either at some distance from the border or whose major border cities (e.g., Detroit, Buffalo) are much larger than their Canadian neighbours. Brunet-Jailly has noted the relative weakness of cross-border connections in major urban regions straddling the Canada–US border, particularly in the Great Lakes region.[48]

Second, the lack of alignment between state and provincial electoral cycles narrows the windows of political opportunity for effective cross-border cooperation and for building working relationships with counterparts in neighbouring jurisdictions. These challenges are compounded with the regular turnover of state governments, including governors, cabinet officers, and senior members of their administrations, which can inhibit the development of institutional memories in managing many cross-border issues.

Third, both state and provincial governments usually depend on federal action to deal with significant cross-border issues. Major infrastructure investments or regulatory interventions to facilitate or coordinate cross-border activities usually require direct federal involvement in each country. These realities are most visible in managing major transportation projects, coordinating border security and trade facilitation, and ensuring collaboration among public and animal health officials to deal with potential outbreaks of communicable diseases while reducing the risks of border disruptions. They have also been reinforced by the "thickening" of the Canada–US border since September 2001 and related American preoccupations with security issues.[49]

One major response to these realities, which are embedded within their respective political cultures, has been for political entrepreneurs in each country to encourage the development of cross-border regional organizations capable of bridging institutional gaps between neighbouring governments and encouraging greater cross-border cooperation on shared priorities and concerns.

The Development of Cross-Border Regionalism

Growing economic integration and the related increase of regulatory issues with implications crossing jurisdictional boundaries have meant an increase in cross-border economic, political, and administrative linkages among regional interests and subnational governments.

The concept of cross-border regionalism is contested both theoretically and empirically – as, indeed, is the imprecise, multilayered notion of regionalism. The Policy Research Initiative, an internal think tank in Canada's federal government, notes the proliferation of cross-border networks and organizations since NAFTA that "work together on issues of mutual interest with the ultimate aim of problem-solving or creating local edges for success in the larger North American and global economies."[50] However, the density and nature of linkages vary widely in different border regions, ranging from primarily bottom-up and market driven in much of central Canada and the Great Plains region to deeper and more institutionalized on the west coast and, to a lesser degree, in the New England–Atlantic–Quebec region.[51]

Another significant factor shaping these relationships is the relative depth and intensity of supply chain networks and related avenues for policy and administrative cooperation related to particular sectors. The greater the degree to which particular industry sectors or societal interests in each country see one another as direct competitors rather than a broader community of interest crossing national borders, the weaker regionalism's claim to create a community of interest based on geographically defined distinctions of interest and/or culture. These factors result in substantial differences in border effects across provinces and in the relative integration of provincial economies with those of neighbouring states – as opposed to the United States as a whole.[52] Localized border effects are smallest in Quebec,

Ontario, New Brunswick, and, surprisingly, Saskatchewan but significantly greater in other provinces.

The effective integration of regional markets is closely related to the density of industrial clusters and supply chains straddling national borders, especially the automotive and auto parts industries of southern Ontario, Michigan, and the US midwest. New Brunswick's export markets are centred primarily in the New England states. Provinces whose principal exports consist of bulk commodities, whether unprocessed or semi-processed, tend to have much more broadly distributed American markets, though the primary markets for most Atlantic provinces are distributed along the US eastern seaboard.

Cross-border regional linkages are becoming more significant as means of sharing information on common problems and coordinating provincial and state governments' interactions with their respective federal governments. Mouafo notes four major varieties of cross-border linkages: multi-state, multisector institutions; bilateral initiatives and agreements; multi-state, sector-specific institutions; and binational, sector-specific institutions, usually involving both federal and subnational government participation.[53]

The most visible cross-border networks are those of provinces and neighbouring states working through multijurisdictional institutions. As noted above, provincial premiers often attend meetings of the US National Governors' Association or its regional affiliates. Quebec and Atlantic premiers have met with the Council of New England Governors since 1973. Ontario and Quebec are associate members of the Council of Great Lakes Governors. British Columbia and Alberta have played leading roles in PNWER since the early 1990s. Saskatchewan joined PNWER in 2009, reflecting the Wall government's pursuit of closer policy collaboration with its western neighbours.[54] In recent years, Manitoba has become a more active participant in the Midwest Council of State Governments and meets annually with legislative counterparts in Minnesota and the Dakotas.

These and related developments have persuaded federal officials of the potential of provinces' cross-border networks to reinforce their efforts to influence American policies toward Canada. Border-state governors and legislators whose interests overlap with broader Canadian interests have greater influence over their senators and members of Congress than do foreign diplomats. Significant examples of such lobbying include the acid rain issue during the 1980s, the development of successive Great Lakes water-quality agreements, and post-9/11 disputes over enhanced identification requirements at the border.[55]

The PNWER model – which brings together elected legislators, provincial (and often federal) cabinet ministers, senior public servants, major business groups, and some other societal interests in semi-annual meetings that rotate around the region's ten member jurisdictions[56] – is probably the most effective. Although PNWER's operations are consensus-driven, ongoing sectoral task forces are generally oriented toward pragmatic administrative measures to facilitate cooperation among governments and other interests rather than attempt to coordinate high-level policy making. Its "legislative academy" also provides important information on the differences in political, administrative, and regulatory systems among member jurisdictions. More recently, PNWER has formed an "energy academy" to familiarize the region's legislators with the workings of diverse energy markets and regulatory systems. The organization's greatest strength is the continuity of its leadership, which helps to offset the losses in institutional memory noted above resulting from turnover of elected and senior officials.

The informal nature of many provincial–state contacts makes policy cooperation more reliant on the cultivation of personal relationships. However, as noted above, turnover among senior officials can be a major constraint on policy continuity – particularly since senior state administrators are often political appointments with limited terms in office. Even more important is the tendency for border effects to increase with the distance of major population centres from the border. Provincial–state collaboration is usually closest in those regions whose major cities are closest to the border, involving extensive social as well as economic contacts and creating strong political constituencies for intergovernmental cooperation.[57] Conversely, a disproportionate number of cross-border conflicts seem to take place with US plains and mountain states.

The number and disparity of provincial–state linkages and the range of relevant cross-border issues make it difficult to evaluate the effectiveness of such links in enabling subnational governments to manage such issues independently of Washington and Ottawa or to work together to influence them to reach mutually satisfactory alternatives. As with most issues, the greatest likelihood of success is found in issues whose political salience is limited to particular clusters of states, especially in cases in which flexible (or decentralized) administrative responses can be devised that do not trigger conflicting responses from other sectors or regions. The introduction of enhanced drivers' licences in 2007-9 as a form of secure identification under the Western Hemisphere Travel Initiative (WHTI), discussed further in

Chapter 11, is a good example of both criteria. Although regionalized responses to climate change have suggested the potential for bottom-up approaches to cross-border policy challenges characterized by significant regional differences, it remains to be seen how these measures will interact with different political processes in each country, discussed in Chapter 13.

Provincial Activities in Washington

Most provinces maintain a relatively limited and sporadic presence in Washington, either respecting federal primacy in international relations or retaining legal counsel and lobbyists to maintain a watching brief over major provincial interests and engage specific political or legal challenges as required.

Quebec has maintained an office in the US capital since 1978, and Alberta opened its offices in the Canadian Embassy, led successively by former provincial cabinet ministers Murray Smith (Energy) and Gary Mar (Environment), in March 2005. Ontario announced plans to follow Alberta's example but had not done so at the time of writing. The roles of both offices are similar: to monitor US political developments with the potential to affect major provincial interests; to cultivate networks of influential contacts in Congress, the current administration, think tanks, and the media; and to promote business contacts for their provinces' major industries.[58] Manitoba maintains a one-person office led by a former Canadian Embassy official who performs most of the same functions – with a particular emphasis on building relationships with congressional decision makers from neighbouring states.[59]

Since 2001, the activities of all three provinces and their representatives have generally aligned with federal priorities: positioning themselves as reliable partners in security issues and reliable contributors to US energy security. With its extensive hydroelectric resources, Quebec has been the more active participant in climate change issues, while Alberta has worked closely with industry interests in response to real and perceived environmental challenges related to its development of the oil sands, which have evolved from a political asset to a potential liability as political winds have shifted in Washington.

Manitoba worked closely with Ontario and Quebec between 2006 and 2008 in lobbying for alternatives to passports mandated under the WHTI (see Chapter 11). Ongoing changes in federal electricity policies are also important to the "Keystone Province," a major electricity exporter integrated

TABLE 9.5

Registrations filed by Canadian entities under the US Foreign Agents Registration Act, 2001-10

	2010	2009	2008	2007	2006	2005	2004	2003	2002	2001
Federal government	1	1	1	2	4	2	4	5	1	3
Federal agencies	4	6	4	4	5	5	5	4	4	3
Provincial governments	15	14	11	10	11	6	5	8	9	8
Private sector	1	1	2	–	–	–	6	3	5	2
Other	2	1	1	1	1	4	4	3	4	4
Total	23	23	19	17	21	16	24	23	23	20

SOURCES: US Department of Justice, Foreign Agents Registration Act database, http://www.fara.gov/; author's analysis.

with the US midwestern regional grid. One close observer described both Alberta and Manitoba offices as "good news offices" – "telling the Americans what's good about their provinces and why it should matter to the United States."[60]

A review of the US Foreign Agents Registration Act database indicates both the intermittent and the issue-specific character of government relations and lobbying activities by other provincial governments. Registrations by Canadian provincial governments averaged 8.3 between 2001 and 2003 at the beginning of the most recent softwood lumber dispute, slipping to 5.5 in 2005-6, rising to 10.7 in 2006-8, and climbing to a record 14.5 in 2009-10 in response to the Obama administration's policy activism (see Table 9.5). Governments can retain professional advisers either on narrow, sector-specific briefs – as with Ontario's long-standing monitoring of issues related to transboundary air pollution and waste exports – or to deal with broader economic issues and monitor ongoing political trends.

Canadian premiers have become regular visitors to Washington in recent years. They can generally obtain a sympathetic business audience through the auspices of groups such as the Canadian-American Business Council. However, close observers of bilateral relations generally note that premiers are often viewed in the same context as state governors in Washington, visiting dignitaries who are outsiders to the Washington political process and who have substantially less capacity to confer political favours on or withhold them from key decision makers.[61]

Conclusion

Federalism and regionalism remain key dimensions of Canada–US relations. Americans remain largely ignorant of Canada's political system and, when made aware of it, are often bemused at its relative political, administrative, and economic decentralization. However, these features have contributed to the building of constructive cross-border relationships where provincial interests do not directly conflict with one another or with those of neighbouring states, enabling the federal government to champion regionally significant interests in their cross-border relations without engaging in zero-sum games over jurisdiction or the (re)distribution of wealth or economic activity *within* Canada. Such an approach to regional differences remains critical to Ottawa's constructive management of cross-border relations. So does its willingness to serve as an honest broker among sometimes competing provincial interests, along with the willingness of provinces to practise self-discipline and mutual accommodation in cross-border relations. It remains to be seen what effect the possible return to power of a separatist government in Quebec will have on the quality of federal–provincial cooperation on cross-border issues.

Jurisdictional asymmetries between US and Canadian federal systems can indeed buffer the deeper asymmetries of power inherent to the broader bilateral relationship. On issues important to all or most provinces, Ottawa has demonstrated both a capacity and a willingness to mobilize coalitions of supportive provincial governments – as initially during CUFTA negotiations or in seeking reciprocity on access to American subnational procurement markets in response to Buy American provisions contained in 2009 US federal stimulus legislation.[62]

Neither federal government has the political capacity to act unilaterally on issues that involve cross-cutting pressures from different domestic sectoral and regional interests. Just as the White House often uses the need to obtain congressional support or approval as a way of "putting off" Canadian importunities on particular issues, the constitutional and political limitations on unilateral Canadian federal action in areas of provincial jurisdiction restore a measure of reciprocity to an otherwise lopsided relationship.

A standard claim of Canadian business groups seeking the removal of regulatory barriers to closer economic integration with the United States is that Canada's decentralized federal system often serves as an obstacle to closer regulatory harmonization. However, the validity of such objections depends in part on the extent to which governments in both countries share similar views of the broader public interests to be served by such policies. It also depends on the ability of each country's political and regulatory systems to generate policies that accommodate the varied economic and social interests characteristic of large, continent-spanning democracies without producing the kinds of log rolling and favouritism to special interests that can often lead to policy incoherence sometimes described as the "garbage can theory" of policy making.[63]

It is probably futile to expect that horizontal policy processes designed to serve a multitude of US domestic interests will achieve much more than accommodating particular Canadian interests at the margins rather than legislating for a diverse cross-section of North American interests. The challenge of North American policy making, except on relatively narrow sectoral issues, increases exponentially when Mexico's highly competitive, increasingly decentralized, and "anti-majoritarian" political processes are added into the mix.

The laboratory of federalism can often provide opportunities for domestic or even cross-border policy innovation when economic and social relations are geographically segmented, market driven, and bottom-up in character. However, such organic developments are inimical to the politics of "grand visions." Given the contemporary divisions in all three societies, it might be that the "fragmegration" that accompanies federalism and regionalism in North America provides a relatively practical balance of diversity and cooperation on which Canadians, Americans, and, where desired, Mexicans can continue to build to the extent that it suits their varied interests.

PART 3

Specific Policy Fields

10

Smart Borders or Thicker Borders?
Homeland Security and Public Safety Policies

Few policy fields illustrate the central features of Canada–US relations, or the interactions of their political–strategic, trade–commercial, and psychological–cultural dimensions, as well as the overlapping fields of homeland security, border management, and public safety. Once described as the world's "longest undefended border," the Canada–US border now appears to have very different qualities in the eyes of American and Canadian governments and publics.

During the past decade, public or homeland security policies in each country have been driven by overlapping but somewhat different agendas and threat perceptions that have enabled significant cooperation but also limited the two governments' willingness and ability to develop fully integrated security policies and systems. These differences increase the likelihood that governments will insure themselves against both particular threats and the possibility of inadequate cooperation by other governments in addressing them.[1] This reality was visible in the institutionalization of post-9/11 security policies by the Bush administration and Congress and their extension under the Obama administration.

These differences also contribute to greater levels of "intervulnerability," as noted by Doran – the concept that shared or overlapping risks from foreign countries tend to increase without cooperative efforts to reduce them.[2] Security analyst Stephen Flynn describes this phenomenon as the "hardened border paradox." He notes that unilateral efforts to insulate nations from risks posed by neighbouring countries or their residents increase the likelihood of countervailing efforts by other governments, by citizens of other countries (ordinarily law-abiding or otherwise), and indeed by people and groups within their own countries, to protect their interests and accustomed forms of behaviour from what they view as arbitrary actions.[3]

American homeland security policies are driven primarily by domestic policy imperatives, whatever the genuine risks posed by ideologically motivated terrorist groups and agents of foreign governments. These policies stem from a core function of democratic governments – protecting their citizens from avoidable harm – a central justification for any country's assertion of national sovereignty. They reflect competing priorities among domestic bureaucratic institutions, especially those of the sprawling Department of Homeland Security and other law enforcement agencies. The policies also respond to competition among American domestic interest groups and to intensive media coverage of threats to public safety or public order, including the relative adequacy of government responses. In addition, US border management policies have been linked to ongoing concerns over illegal immigration, drug trafficking, and related violence – especially along its southern border with Mexico – though migration levels have declined since 2005.

In Canada, the pursuit of these objectives is filtered through another priority: its dependence on secure access to US markets and transportation systems for its citizens' economic well-being. This reality is central to Canadian governments' efforts to engage US homeland security and border management policies. Canada shares a fundamental interest in protecting the security of the American public, both as a good neighbour and to avoid the potential for retaliatory action should some future incident be seen to have resulted from its government's negligence or indifference or the hostility of anti-American elements within Canada. As one US diplomat put it, "the most important thing is not if there is a terrorist attack in the United States but a terrorist act that could have been prevented by you."[4]

In sharp contrast to the 1990s, security issues have generally "trumped trade"[5] in shaping Americans' attitudes toward cross-border relations since 9/11. These factors increase the importance of maintaining the confidence of American policy makers and the American public that Canada and Canadians are reliable partners in securing their northern border against potential threats. In practice, Canadian officials must also work closely with US domestic interests whose well-being depends on efficient border management – not just enhanced security – to cultivate and maintain a political climate supportive of cooperation on security and border management issues.

This chapter examines the politics of border security and its implications for bilateral relations. It compares institutional and societal paradigms for homeland security in the United States and Canada, considers competing security paradigms informing American policies, and assesses their applications to five broad policy areas: external trade, especially container and other cargo security, cross-border travel, cross-border security collaboration, immigration and visa policies, and border infrastructure. Three case studies related to issues discussed in this chapter – the Container Security Initiative, the land preclearance project, and ongoing issues related to proposed US entry–exit controls – will be elaborated in Chapter 11.

Homeland Security and Border Management

> *Each definition [of homeland security] represents a set of interests that claims a niche in the homeland security ecosystem.*
>
> – Christopher Bellavita, "Changing Homeland Security," 2008[6]

US and Canadian governments have overlapping institutions and approaches to define and manage homeland security or public safety. Their security policies are driven by several factors: institutional interests, expanding political mandates, and competition for financial, personnel, and (often unproven) technological resources that have not expanded as fast as the policy mandates that they are intended to implement.[7] Canadian efforts to influence American homeland security policies toward Canada attempt to balance collaboration on broader security goals, sector-by-sector cooperation in program design and implementation affecting citizens of both countries, and protection of Canadian interests where "security first" measures create disproportionate risks to Canadian and related US societal interests.

Congress created the Department of Homeland Security (DHS) in November 2002 from elements of twenty-two "legacy agencies" – the largest US government reorganization since the creation of the Department of

Defense in 1947. DHS's mandate defines the dominant approach to homeland security in the United States. Its evolution can be seen by comparing the 2003 and current (2008) versions.

> We will lead the unified national effort to secure America. We will prevent and deter terrorist attacks and protect against and respond to threats and hazards to the nation.

[2003:]
> We will ensure safe and secure borders, welcome lawful immigrants and visitors, and promote the free flow of commerce.[8]

[2008:]
> We will secure our national borders, while welcoming lawful immigrants, visitors and trade.[9]

The 2010 Quadrennial Homeland Security Review introduced a number of changes in emphasis from the 2007 Homeland Security Strategy – suggesting progress in the thinking of senior policy makers from an all-consuming emphasis on counterterrorism to an all-hazards approach to their functions. After the shock of 9/11, DHS priorities were driven by security-first perspectives that lent themselves to prescriptive, "command and control" approaches to regulation and relations with societal stakeholders and other (including foreign) governments.[10] These approaches are gradually evolving toward an all-hazards perspective on public safety. This perspective reflects the principle that public safety and emergency management bureaucracies should plan for and organize to reduce the likelihood of, or manage the consequences of, a broad range of foreseeable and often interrelated hazards likely to place people and property at significant risk but in more collaborative ways that combine greater operational decentralization with improved information sharing among relevant agencies. The evolution of dominant homeland security policy doctrines also responds to pressures for more efficient border operations to promote greater economic security and protect civil liberties. Table 10.1 summarizes DHS's key objectives as outlined in its 2008 Strategic Plan and the 2010 Homeland Security Review.

Although preventing terrorism remains DHS's first priority, policy emphasis appears to have shifted toward acknowledging its interdependence with other functions, including effective border management, administration of the immigration system, cyber-security (an emerging form of

TABLE 10.1

Strategic goals: US Department of Homeland Security, 2008, 2010

Objectives (2008)	Mandates (2010)
1 Protect our nation from dangerous people. 1.1 Achieve effective control of our borders. 1.2 Protect our interior and enforce immigration laws. 1.3 Strengthen screening of travellers and workers. 1.4 Enhance security through improved immigration services.	1 Preventing terrorism and enhancing security. 1.1 Prevent terrorist attacks. 1.2 Prevent the unauthorized acquisition or use of chemical, biological, radiological, and nuclear materials and capabilities.
2 Protect our nation from dangerous goods. 2.1 Prevent and detect radiological/ nuclear attacks. 2.2 Prevent, detect, and protect against biological attacks. 2.3 Prevent and detect chemical and explosive attacks. 2.4 Prevent the introduction of illicit contraband while facilitating trade.	2 Securing and managing our borders. 2.1 Effectively control US air, land, and sea borders. 2.2 Safeguard lawful trade and travel. 2.3 Disrupt and dismantle transnational criminal organizations.
3 Protect critical infrastructure. 3.1 Protect and strengthen the resilience of the nation's critical infrastructure and key resources. 3.2 Ensure continuity of government communications and operations. 3.3 Improve cyber-security. 3.4 Protect transportation sectors.	3 Enforcing and administering our immigration laws. 3.1 Strengthen and effectively administer the immigration system. 3.2 Prevent unlawful immigration.
4 Strengthen our nation's preparedness and emergency response capabilities. 4.1 Ensure preparedness. 4.2 Strengthen response and recovery.	4 Safeguarding and securing cyberspace. 4.1 Create a safe, secure, and resilient cyber-environment. 4.2 Promote cyber-security knowledge and innovation.

▶

◀ **TABLE 10.1**
Strategic goals: US Department of Homeland Security, 2008, 2010

Objectives (2008)	Mandates (2010)
5 Strengthen and unify DHS operations and management.	5 Ensuring resilience to disasters.
5.1 Improve departmental governance and performance.	5.1 Mitigate hazards.
5.2 Advance intelligence and information sharing.	5.2 Enhance preparedness.
5.3 Integrate DHS policy, planning, and operations coordination.	5.3 Ensure effective emergency response.
	5.4 Rapidly recover.

SOURCES: United States, Department of Homeland Security, *One Team, One Mission, Securing Our Homeland: U.S. Department of Homeland Security Strategic Plan, Fiscal Years 2008-2013* (Washington, DC: DHS, 2008), 6-24; United States, Department of Homeland Security, *Quadrennial Homeland Security Review* (Washington, DC: DHS, 2010), x.

unconventional warfare and conflict with growing societal implications), effective emergency management, and the related promotion of societal resilience. These trends reflect an awareness that, though "preventing a terrorist attack in the United States remains the cornerstone of national security ... [it] does not capture the full range of interconnected threats and challenges that characterize today's world" (see Table 10.2).[11]

The emerging discipline of homeland security studies suggests that these objectives can often be reconciled by integrating counterterrorism goals within day-to-day operational processes that serve the interests of a wider range of government agencies and societal groups.[12]

This perspective seems to be reflected in the 2010 Quadrennial Homeland Security Review:

Three key concepts that are essential to, and form the foundation for, a comprehensive approach to homeland security:

Security: Protect the United States and its people, vital interests, and way of life.

Resilience: Foster individual, community, and system robustness, adaptability, and capacity for rapid recovery.

Customs and Exchange: Expedite and enforce lawful trade, travel, and immigration.[13]

US border management policies are therefore a subset – or, more accurately, several different components – of more comprehensive homeland

TABLE 10.2
Threats, hazards, and long-term global challenges and trends

Threats and hazards	Global challenges and trends
• High-consequence weapons of mass destruction • al Qaeda and global violent extremism • High-consequence and/or wide-scale cyber-attacks, intrusions, disruptions, and exploitations • Pandemics, major accidents, and natural hazards • Illicit trafficking and related transnational crime • Smaller-scale terrorism	• Economic and financial instability • Dependence on fossil fuels and the threat of global climate change • Nations unwilling to abide by international norms • Sophisticated and broadly available technology • Other drivers of illicit, dangerous, or uncontrolled movement of people and goods

SOURCE: United States, Department of Homeland Security, *Quadrennial Homeland Security Review: A Strategic Framework for a Secure Homeland* (Washington, DC: DHS, 2010), viii, Table ES-1.

security policies that attempt to combine security measures to regulate migration, ensure compliance with trade agreements and other commercial regulations, and combat criminal activities. These policies also seek to provide "layered security" to defend against potential terrorist attacks while attempting to facilitate or encourage the efficient processing of low-risk trade and travel across national borders. The underlying concept of layered security is that, perfect security being unattainable in any real-world setting, the existence of complementary layers of security at, within, and beyond national frontiers makes it progressively more unlikely that potential foreign terrorists can penetrate each successive layer without greatly increasing the likelihood of detection.[14] This concept is sometimes referred to as "pushing out the border" by attempting to screen goods and travellers before they arrive at ports of entry. This risk management philosophy is reflected in the joint declaration and subsequent action plan on border and security issues released by President Obama and Prime Minister Harper in 2011.[15]

Evolving US homeland security policies since 9/11 reflect an ongoing competition of ideas and priorities that has also informed Canada's *National Security Strategy* since its publication in 2004.[16] However, respective emphases on counterterrorism and all-hazards preparedness and response in each country have reflected the initial "focusing events" that framed the political and administrative contexts for their respective security policies.

Three key events helped to define these policies in the United States. Most important were the terrorist attacks of 9/11 and political responses to them, including the creation of DHS, as discussed in Chapters 2 and 4. The bipartisan 9/11 commission report pointed to internal flaws in domestic security and coordination systems that made 9/11 possible. It made forty recommendations that became the basis of congressional legislation. However, only two of these recommendations directly addressed questions of border security.[17] Media and public responses to the escapades of the "underwear" bomber in December 2009 suggest that, whatever official policies, US security officials remain subject to high public expectations in preventing mass casualty terrorist attacks.

DHS's shambolic response to the devastation caused by Hurricane Katrina in August 2005 was another key event. It revealed the extent to which counterterrorism concerns had diverted resources and management attention away from other key homeland security functions. Subsequent American media coverage of disaster responses suggests significant improvements in interagency cooperation and gap filling.

A third dynamic resulted from the bitter debate over the breakdown of US immigration policies that gridlocked Congress between 2005 and 2007 and continues to preclude substantive reforms to these policies. The earlier debate was driven by the rapid growth in the number of illegal immigrants, largely from Mexico and Central America, from roughly 8 to 12 million people between 2000 and 2007, though subsequent annual migration flows have dropped sharply.[18] Related political pressures resulted in attempted crackdowns along the US–Mexican border and legislation, such as the REAL-ID Act of 2005, aimed at strengthening the security of "foundational" identification documents and limiting access to them to legal US residents. Congress has also attempted to control illegal immigration through the construction of security fences, supported by new electronic monitoring technologies, along heavily populated stretches of the border.

Many border security advocates ask why the "porous" northern border with Canada should be treated any differently from that with Mexico.[19] These outlooks, sometimes described as the "One Border policy,"[20] contributed to legislation requiring all persons entering the United States to carry passports or "other secure documents" under the Western Hemisphere Travel Initiative (WHTI). They also led to the mandatory fingerprinting of aliens entering the United States (not yet including most Canadians, except visa holders) under the partially implemented US–VISIT entry–exit screening program.[21] These issues – and Canadian efforts to influence related US government policies – are discussed át greater length in Chapter 11.

A fourth, offshore trend, the proliferation of nuclear technologies in rogue states such as North Korea and Iran, along with Pakistan's continuing instability, has raised significant concerns over risks that terrorist organizations such as al Qaeda could obtain nuclear weapons for attacks against American territory.[22] Such fears have led to more extensive screening of shipping containers destined for the United States and Canada.

Each of these factors has had implications for border management with Canada. 9/11 and its resultant border closings demonstrated Canada's vulnerability to US responses to actual and potential terrorist events, leading to the changes to Canadian security policies.[23] 9/11 also highlighted the need for closer cross-border collaboration to reduce these vulnerabilities; such collaboration was embodied in the December 2001 Smart Border Accord between the two countries and subsequent measures.

Three other focusing events have identified the risks of overlapping but poorly coordinated security measures in and with Canada. The "rendition" in 2002 of dual Canadian-Syrian citizen Maher Arar to Syria by US security officials, based largely on "overstated" information provided by the RCMP, temporarily had a chilling effect on the sharing of intelligence information.[24] Its more permanent effect was to subject Canadian police and security measures to tighter legal and judicial protections for civil liberties.[25]

The WHTI legislation of December 2005 further shifted the balance between security and border facilitation for tourists and residents of border communities. The resulting two-year lobby to delay its passage and broaden the range of "secure" identification acceptable to DHS was successful but at some cost to mutual trust on other initiatives.[26]

The June 2006 arrests of eighteen aspiring young *jihadis* in Toronto on charges of plotting terrorist attacks in Canada, eleven of whom were ultimately convicted, drew intense public attention to the risks of "homegrown terrorism" on both sides of the border, partly validating US security concerns and demonstrating the importance of effective intelligence and police cooperation. So have a series of less visible arrests and prosecutions in Canadian courts[27] and the trial of a Canadian travel agent in Chicago charged with providing logistical support for terrorism abroad.[28]

These events have shaped the contexts for homeland security and border management policies in each country. However, day-to-day policy making and implementation are the products of substantially different institutional structures.

Institutional Contexts

The years since 9/11 have seen an institutionalization of homeland security policies in the United States. However, the cross-cutting efforts of the White House, competing domestic agencies, and diverse elements of Congress have contributed to the development of what one observer describes as "an environment [that] is more complex, both organizationally and politically," than the well-established global and regional command structures of the US Department of Defense.[29]

Five main sets of institutions shape this process: the National Security Council (NSC) and its supporting bureaucracy, which in 2009 absorbed the Homeland Security Council created by President George W. Bush; the Departments of Homeland Security and Justice and their subordinate agencies, especially the Bureau of Customs and Border Protection, FBI, and Drug Enforcement Administration (DEA); specialized subject matter agencies such as the Department of State's Bureau of Consular Affairs, responsible for issuing passports and adjudicating citizenship; various animal and food safety agencies; and the diverse committee structures of Congress discussed in Chapter 7.

The NSC is an interagency body, reporting to the president and composed of cabinet and senior subcabinet officials whose departments or agencies have security-related responsibilities. Its now defunct counterpart, the Homeland Security Council, produced the first *National Strategy for Homeland Security* in July 2002, subsequently revised in 2004 and 2007, along with several presidential directives, a non-regulatory form of policy making.[30] There is little evidence that cross-border issues with Canada are dealt with regularly at this level.

Rather, the principal political links are between the secretary of homeland security and her Canadian counterpart, the minister of public safety. On operational issues, multiple parallel links exist among senior departmental officials, agency executives representing national police (FBI and RCMP), border services (CBP and CBSA), and food safety (APHIS and CFIA) and coast guard agencies, among others; there are also assorted working-level contacts along with departmental officials posted to each country's embassy. The RCMP also have memoranda of understanding with several specialized US law enforcement agencies.[31]

The DHS secretary meets with her Canadian counterpart at least twice a year, though other meetings can take place on the sidelines of other international events. One DHS official interviewed for this study commented in early 2006 that

The personal relationship at all levels is important and makes an appreciable difference if the relationship is strong and favourable. Down from the senior leadership and Canadian counterparts, the relationship is quite solid and very healthy. That is attributed to a fairly stable workforce in the two countries ... The ADM levels and DG levels [in Canada] tend to stay in place so that you develop relationships of long standing. Building trust, that's important for any relationship.[32]

However, this perception is not always shared. Former DHS assistant secretary Paul Rosenzweig suggests that shifts in US counterterrorism policy after 9/11 led to greater American concerns over policy divergence and Canadian reluctance to align its immigration laws and traveller-screening processes with those of the United States.

Canada has much greater openness to the rest of the world than does the U.S. Canadian asylum policies are more liberal; Canada extends the privilege of visa-free travel to the citizens of many more countries. And, more fundamentally, Canada takes a much lighter hand in screening arriving travellers ... What had earlier been very modest divergences in immigration policy now loomed larger as differences in counterterrorism policy. Some Canadians have yet to come to grips with the new reality that Canada can't have it both ways– it can't both exercise its own sovereign authority over its border policies, and expect the United States not to do the same thing.[33]

Rosenzweig also suggests a decline in trust in cross-border relations among senior officials, reflected in a reluctance to share information due to political sensitivities arising from the Maher Arar affair, noted above, and Canadian reluctance to share information on travellers entering Canada.[34] Other officials whom I interviewed suggested considerable resentment of Canadian lobbying of Congress on the WHTI passport requirements, discussed in Chapter 11, though this might have dissipated with turnover among senior officials. It remains to be seen how these issues will be addressed in negotiations intended to formalize broader perimeter security arrangements announced in February 2011. Several of these issues have been addressed in "perimeter security" negotiations in 2011, which are discussed in Chapter 11.

DHS's size and scale and the diverse mandates of its many legacy agencies have created major challenges for its management, including congressional oversight.[35] They also complicate communication between DHS and many societal actors.[36] External analyses often refer to "stovepipe" tendencies and internal competition among different segments of DHS, as well as with other federal agencies, despite efforts to build partnerships with key stakeholder groups.[37]

These tendencies have been reinforced by frequent turnover in the department's senior management, if not of career officials,[38] and by the tendency of congressional barons to protect their political turf; 108 congressional committees and subcommittees claimed jurisdiction over various DHS activities under the 110th Congress (2007-9).[39] This diffusion of responsibility also enables various constituencies to use the multiple access points of the congressional process to challenge DHS policies that fail to respond adequately to their interests or agendas, as discussed in Chapter 7.

DHS's Bureau of Transportation and Border Security oversees three major border security agencies with responsibilities for different aspects of border security. The Bureau of Customs and Border Protection (CBP) is responsible for the operations of border points (ports of entry), security between border points (border patrol), as well as the administration of immigration laws and compliance with customs regulations and other trade laws and agricultural regulations at the border. Immigration and Customs Enforcement (ICE) oversees enforcement issues away from ports of entry. The US Coast Guard has jurisdiction over maritime aspects of homeland security, including port security, enforcing US laws on commercial ships in American waters, and other aspects of maritime law enforcement. The Transportation Security Administration oversees the security of domestic air and rail transportation systems, including screening air passengers and baggage and ensuring airport and air cargo security.[40] DHS and CBP officials routinely acknowledge the importance of operational efficiency for both their agency and the businesses and citizens who use various ports of entry. However, the department's predominant culture is widely seen to be one of law enforcement and command-and-control approaches to regulation – an approach that rarely lends itself to customer or stakeholder responsiveness in any public setting.[41]

These complex institutional structures have two main implications for Canadian governments attempting to influence US policies toward Canada or that affect Canada. The scale and scope of homeland security functions ensure that the politics and interests associated with these policies are largely domestic. As a result, the international aspect of border issues, though significant, is essentially a small subset of DHS's broader international relationships and those of other federal agencies. Canada is seen as an external actor, an "international security partner" whose actions are seen as complementing but essentially supplemental to US domestic security efforts.[42]

In this context, advancing Canadian interests requires a capacity to engage four parallel policy processes simultaneously. Senior Canadian policy makers must manage their own domestic processes as coherently as possible while anticipating or responding to the spillover effects of many American policies. They must also engage the attention and often opaque processes of relevant agencies of the US executive branch while recognizing that Canadian concerns are often peripheral to the political and policy challenges of their American counterparts.

The third set of processes – engaging senior US leaders in high-level diplomacy – involves a series of judgment calls. Major issues for Canadian officials might be relatively routine administrative matters for their US counterparts. "Going political" can involve risks to the personal relationships critical for effective management of cross-border issues. It can also involve yielding control of issue management to other Canadian departments, especially Foreign Affairs and International Trade, whose priorities are often different from those of police or public safety officials. Although strong personal relations between cabinet officers might be able to resolve some of these issues, resorting to high-level diplomacy is generally effective only when both governments perceive significant policy or political issues to be at stake and when administration officials have the latitude to make decisions independently of Congress.

Finally, Canadian diplomats must be able to engage domestic interest groups and elements of Congress that are often independent policy actors capable of inserting their own priorities into the policy mix in ways that can accommodate, help, or harm related Canadian interests. The inherent complexity of this four-level balancing act is not always appreciated either by domestic Canadian interests or by American officials who sometimes wonder "what the Canadians are up to" on particular files.

Varied Threat Perceptions and Paradigms for Homeland Security

> *Being in favour of coordination ... has come to be like being*
> *against sin; everyone lines up on the right side of the question.*

*In fact, coordination has become ... a word which defies precise
definition but sounds good and brings prestige to the user.*

– *Ray Cline, "Is Intelligence Over-Coordinated?" 1957*[43]

Public safety and homeland security policies can be informed by a variety
of professional perspectives – those of law enforcement, military planning,
public administration, risk management, and emergency preparedness (or
management) – as well as those of the citizens and businesses whose lives
and livelihoods might be affected by these policies.[44] Two major approaches
within the US homeland security community can be characterized as the
"security first," "risk avoidance," or "frontier defence" paradigm and a "risk
management–based" or risk-adjusted cost–benefit paradigm.

The first perspective tends to be oriented toward law enforcement and
command-and-control approaches to regulation. It typically privileges security issues over other considerations – whether economic, societal, or
those related to civil liberties. Its primary objective is to reduce the likelihood of selected public risks. The second approach combines the selective
application of prescriptive regulations, intergovernmental cooperation, and
incentives to secure active collaboration from economic actors and societal
groups in reducing risks to broader publics while enabling citizens and
companies to go about their normal business. It is more likely to accommodate the interests of these groups in pursuing security objectives. In the
context of border security, it does so by creating systems to facilitate pre-
screening and related systems engineering that allow officials of relevant
agencies to focus more of the available resources on combatting crime and
screening higher-risk activities. In practice, there is an ongoing dialogue
between proponents of the two perspectives, whether for tactical purposes
or to secure political support by accommodating elements of both perspectives. Other perspectives tend to focus primarily on civil liberties, personal
privacy, and the protection of identifiable social groups against prescriptive
security measures.[45] Counterterrorism approaches used by both US and
Canadian police agencies also include "preventive policing" – investigative
tools used to identify and monitor aspiring terrorists and members of their
support networks before an actual crime is committed, the use of "sting"
operations, the "Al Capone" approach of using charges for offences not related to terrorism to detain terrorist suspects, and active outreach to members of minority communities to develop trust and potential partnerships
in combatting violent radicalization.[46]

Canadian governments deal with similar issues but with somewhat different emphases. Security objectives have been largely integrated with day-to-day law enforcement efforts, with a strong emphasis on risk management perspectives. Canada's much greater economic dependence on export markets, especially the United States, increases the relative importance of integrating economic and security issues while investing in border infrastructure necessary to make these systems work effectively. Civil liberties perspectives, mediated primarily through the courts, provide more significant constraints on the autonomy of government policy makers and of security and law enforcement agencies that implement these policies. Demographic considerations are also significant – particularly given the importance of immigration in offsetting Canada's aging population and the implications of related societal dynamics for the policy choices of governments.

Although the Chrétien government introduced several new pieces of security legislation after 9/11, including an Anti-Terrorism Act, to provide police, intelligence, and immigration agencies with powers to deal with domestic and external terrorist threats, comments by security officials in both Ottawa and Washington have suggested ongoing concerns over Canada's immigration and refugee policies and the ease with which persons suspected of terrorist links could escape detection, detention, or expulsion.[47]

A more challenging issue, for both countries, is the problem of home-grown terrorism – whether arising from small groups of extremists from diasporic communities or alienated loners mobilized through the Internet.[48] Although police and security experts differ[49] on their assessments of the relative importance of or risks posed by such groups compared with international networks such as al Qaeda, these groups have accounted for most of the terrorism-related arrests made in the United States and Canada since 2005. Such individuals and groups pose an ongoing challenge – but one that requires different approaches to counterterrorism while potentially spreading police resources thin enough to allow other attacks to "get through." A 2010 Congressional Research Service report identified forty "homegrown violent jihadist plots or attacks" in the United States between September 2001 and September 2010, with arrests coming in nineteen separate incidents between May 2009 and August 2010.[50]

A key homeland security priority of the two governments since mid-2009 has been to develop a shared approach to threat perception and risk analysis among their respective law enforcement agencies. This effort led to the preparation of a joint threat assessment document released in March 2011, albeit in heavily sanitized form.[51]

Most business groups express support for the layered defence paradigm that is central to DHS strategies, though they usually argue for its interpretation on the basis of risk management principles and stakeholder engagement rather than risk avoidance. However, business groups in both countries have been critical of poorly designed and implemented policies and programs that either fail to deliver promised benefits for businesses cooperating with security measures or do so at costs sufficient to discourage participation by all except the most trade-dependent industries and firms.[52] Such concerns have been acknowledged by both the Bush and the Obama administrations but have tended to be peripheral to congressional policy priorities. However, they are central Canadian priorities in attempting to influence US security and border management policies.

Border Policy 2003-9: Strategic Drift and Operational Segmentation

> *The question we have to answer is how do we make moving from Detroit to Toronto like moving from Detroit to Chicago? ... The answer has to do with national policies on things like immigration and border security. Unless you have symmetrical approaches to national policies, you won't have symmetrical approaches to security.*
>
> *– David Heyman, interview, Washington, 2006*

The Canadian government's initial response to 9/11 was to propose a series of joint initiatives for coordination across a wide range of security and border management operations that would combine high-level political commitment with detailed steps to address commonly perceived risks and to maintain the operational efficiency of borders for low-risk travellers and business activity. Subsequent initiatives have sought to balance cooperation with adaptation to unilateral American actions, often driven by Congress, in ways that preserve varying degrees of policy discretion, together with respect for or accommodation of Canadian legal and constitutional norms inherent in the concept of sovereignty.[53]

The Smart Border Accord of December 2001 was a bilateral agreement that provided for joint action outlined in a thirty-point action plan. This initiative demonstrated the potential for Canadian-initiated action on these issues but also, ultimately, its inherent limits. Bilateral cooperation during this period was anchored by President Bush's homeland security adviser, former Pennsylvania governor Tom Ridge, who became the first secretary of homeland security in January 2003, and Deputy Prime Minister John Manley, who coordinated Canada's response to 9/11. Ambassador Michael Kergin commented that Manley "had a counterpart with whom he just hit it off. He and Ridge were very similar people. That's why it worked. They both had mandates from their bosses and mandates that would help them ride over some of the personal fiefdoms that people had."[54]

This cooperation survived a cooling of high-level relations over the Chrétien government's opposition to the Iraq War and its shift toward a more cautious, incremental approach to bilateral relations, already discussed in Chapters 2 and 4.[55] The Ridge–Manley process was followed by an equally cordial and functional relationship between their successors, Michael Chertoff and Anne McLellan, in 2004-5. However, more restrictive US homeland security policies, shaped by growing congressional engagement in the policy-making process, were not matched by any corresponding process for North American coordination. Facing an early election, the new Martin government in Canada preferred to maintain a below-the-radar approach to bilateral security relations in order to hold together its own shaky alliance of (generally pro-American) business Liberals and Canadian nationalists – many of whom visibly and vocally despised the Bush administration. This tactical combination of private cooperation and public distance became entrenched after Martin lost his parliamentary majority in June 2004.

Senior Canadian officials sought to recover the close working relationship of the immediate post-9/11 period when cobbling together the Security and Prosperity Partnership (SPP) process with Washington and Mexico City in 2005. The SPP provided a regular forum for meetings of US, Canadian, and Mexican cabinet secretaries and ministers based on agendas flowing from the working group processes. However, in practice, security cooperation functioned on the basis of dual bilateralism – with separate Canada–US and US–Mexican processes defined by different problems, agendas, domestic interest groups, and societal environments. These meetings tended to be characterized by incremental policy- or program-based measures intended to provide the impression of ongoing cooperation.

In practice, the SPP appears to have had little impact on the *substance* of policy, though it provided a forum in which to discuss current issues. Its highly diffuse, segmented nature resulted in its being rapidly shunted to the margins of US domestic policy priorities. This trend was reinforced by growing congressional assertiveness on border, port, and immigration

security issues as the Bush administration proved unable to build effective coalitions with either Republican or Democratic leaders in Congress.
Moreover, Canadian officials were reluctant to see Canada–US border
issues addressed in the same context as those of the Mexican border.[56]

Under such circumstances, proposals by some Canadian business leaders to pursue the creation of a North American security perimeter with the
widespread harmonization of security and economic regulations[57] failed to
gain much political traction in either Ottawa or Washington. Indeed, domestic political pressures and concerns over security risks from anti-
American elements within Canada, combined with the principles of layered security, led DHS officials to take a "belt and suspenders" approach
that combined efforts to "push out" national borders within and beyond
North America with intensified border security measures.[58]

Groups in both countries raised concerns over civil liberties related to
post-9/11 security measures. However, though these concerns were reflected in broader political debates, and ultimately in technical changes to
Canadian anti-terrorism laws, their practical effect on security and border
management policies and practices emerged from a series of court rulings
on individual cases.

Officials interviewed following election of the Harper government in
January 2006 suggested that it initially took a "wait and see" approach to
the cross-border security agenda before deciding how to manage the growing number of security files. Rather than a systematic effort to accommodate American security concerns feared by some groups, the Harper
government generally extended and adapted previous Liberal policies during its first five years in office.[59] The one major exception to this pattern,
proposed revisions to Canada's refugee admission and adjudication system,
was negotiated with opposition parties in Parliament.

Initial trends toward incrementalism were reinforced by decentraliz-
ing responsibility for major cross-border files from the Privy Council
Office to individual departments, though the personalities and priorities
of individual ministers were significant for particular issues.[60] The Harper
government's minority status enforced political caution and a limited willingness to take political responsibility for American policies introduced
without prior consultation.[61] It remains to be seen what impact the
"Beyond the Border" process, which produced a thirty-point action plan
in December 2011 outlining a variety of new and extended measures for
border cooperation, will have on this largely incremental approach to border management.

The following section examines four major policy subfields of US homeland security policies and cross-border collaboration – security and law enforcement; external trade, especially container security; border infrastructure; cross-border travel, immigration, and visa policies – and the relative effectiveness of Canadian governments in influencing the application of these policies toward Canada.

Security, Facilitation, and Border Policies

The scale and scope of homeland security and border management policies, some preceding the events of 9/11, others resulting directly from them, have resulted in the proliferation of American policies that affect Canada directly or indirectly by virtue of the two countries' long border and their extensive and diverse economic and societal relations. The rapid growth of Washington's homeland security bureaucracy, the multiple dimensions of homeland security strategies, and the involvement of dozens of congressional committees in policy making and oversight ensure that there is no overarching US homeland security policy toward Canada – any more than in most other policy fields. Most of these policies are either components of broader US domestic policies with collateral effects in Canada or policies toward allies – some aspects of which can be tailored specifically to accommodate the extent and depth of Canada–US relations.

The Beyond-the-Border process initiated in 2011 combines a step toward exceptionalism in bilateral policy relations (in its abandonment of the post-9/11 one-border policy) with several measures that resemble policies toward other US allies.

Cross-Border Security and Law Enforcement

A central focus of cross-border homeland security responses to 9/11 and ongoing threats of terrorist attacks has been an increased emphasis on law enforcement cooperation. This relationship is scarcely new. Even before 9/11, US and Canadian police forces exchanged intelligence information, maintained liaison missions in the neighbouring country, and cooperated in activities targeting organized crime and other law enforcement issues.

Much cross-border security collaboration falls into the category of policies toward allies given US security and police cooperation with other countries. However, the extent of cross-border cooperation through binational groups such as the Cross-Border Crime Forum, and the development of Integrated Border Enforcement Teams in fifteen border regions across the continent, discussed further in Chapter 11, take on aspects of exceptionalism, particularly when contrasted with the often prickly relations between US and Mexican law enforcement officials. The Border Action Plan released in December 2011 includes new forms of cross-border law enforcement cooperation.

North American and External Trade

US policies relating to the management of foreign trade, whether inside or outside North America, display elements of policies toward allies, with some effort to accommodate the integration of production processes and distribution networks with those in Canada. However, though the latter's dependence on US markets for about three-quarters of its exports makes these issues central priorities for Canadian governments, they comprise only one of many concerns facing DHS and congressional oversight committees.

Enhanced screening processes for maritime, truck, and rail freight shipments entering the United States are driven largely by perceived threats that nuclear, biological, or other weapons could be smuggled through American ports of entry – either placing American citizens at risk of terrorist attacks or significantly disrupting transportation networks should a truck or shipping container be detonated at a major port or cross-border bridge.

The Smart Border Accord and subsequent US policies contemplated considerable integration of port, rail, and truck security policies. Canada served as a pilot project for the introduction of the Container Security Initiative (CSI), many of whose elements are now embedded in the policies of the World Customs Organization (WCO) and International Maritime Organization (IMO). As such, CSI is a classic case of policies toward allies, with elements of exceptionalism built into specific secure freight programs such as the Customs–Trade Partnership against Terrorism (C-TPAT) and the Free and Secure Trade (FAST) program used to screen truck shipments and drivers engaged in cross-border trade with Canada.

However, the introduction of subsequent layers of security, often at the insistence of Congress over the objections of DHS officials, might have added to port and freight security at the margins, but in ways that significantly "thicken" borders with Canada (and other countries), thus shifting the security/trade facilitation balance in the direction of risk avoidance and higher non-tariff barriers to cross-border business dealings.[62] The Harper government's decision to engage in discussions on perimeter security as a trade-off for "trade acceleration" measures in the Beyond-the-Border process reflects efforts to reverse these trends. These issues will be explored further in Chapter 11.

Technology and Infrastructure

Interdependence between Canada and the United States contributes to mutual vulnerability – whether related to physical, economic, or other forms of security. Even though trade between the United States and Canada has levelled off since 2000, the renewal and expansion of border infrastructure has not compensated for the effects of greater security measures that have contributed to unpredictable delays and rising costs of border "thickening."[63]

However, the challenge of border security – and of allocating the resources necessary to increase it – has been increased by escalating demands on border agency budgets in both countries despite their growth between 2002 and 2008. For the United States in particular, border security means security *between* ports of entry as much as at formal border crossings. The 2009 US stimulus bill provided extensive capital funding for the modernization of many border points – albeit with extensive earmarking by key border state senators for projects in their states.

The introduction of new and often untested technologies was widely seen as a means of allocating inherently limited staff and financial resources more effectively across competing functions. However, the Obama administration's termination of the SBInet program in January 2011 demonstrated the inherent difficulty of using new technologies to secure the border effectively.[64]

Despite efforts to build shared border facilities in a few locations, there has been relatively little coordination of border infrastructure improvements since 2001. A major exception has been the development of a new Detroit–Windsor bridge to address bottlenecks at the busiest northern border crossing. The Detroit River International Crossing (DRIC) project was rebranded the New International Trade Crossing by Michigan Governor Rick Snyder in 2011. However, as discussed in Chapter 9, competing interests in Michigan have stretched out the complex processes of regulatory approvals in each country for almost a decade. Other parallel or collaborative projects have been carried out at major crossings in British Columbia, Alberta, Quebec, and New Brunswick. However, the December 2011 Border Action Plan proposes that the two governments develop a five-year Border

Infrastructure Investment Plan to outline specific projects at both large and small remote crossings, subject to annual renewal.[65]

Cross-Border Travel, Immigration, and Visa Policies

The conflation of cross-border travel, immigration, and visa policies offers the single biggest example of diverging threat perceptions and competing priorities between US and Canadian authorities since 9/11. American policies have been driven by two dominant concerns: limiting the risks of terrorism from travellers entering the United States, whether as casual visitors or as visa holders, and controlling the flood of illegal immigration from Mexico, Latin America, and other countries, including Canada, at the margins. Initial efforts to design and enforce such policies have complicated entrenched social relations that transcend national borders, triggering societal and political resistance leading to accommodation by Congress and state and federal agencies, including DHS.[66]

American policies toward Canada are heavily shaped by the different regulatory regimes affecting different modes of transportation, interaction with each country's immigration and visa policies, perceived level of security risk, and exposure to the cross-cutting concerns of US interest group politics and domestic constituencies. Policies on air passengers are governed in large measure by international agreements, with US officials – and often their counterparts from the European Community – seeking to negotiate ways to project their national and regional standards into international regulations. As such, US policies toward Canada are often variations of policies toward allies, though US preclearance facilities in Canadian airports and binational trusted traveller programs such as NEXUS, whose application was extended to all land crossings in 2009, might be seen as evidence of exceptionalism.

The regulation of land border crossings and the coordination of visa policies, both reciprocal and those affecting other countries (discussed at greater length in Chapter 11), are complex issues that defy easy categorization given the multiple levels of analysis involved. These issues overlap with the management of cross-border and border region infrastructure – including bridges, highways, and border control complexes. Although traditionally viewed as domestic concerns, the growth of cross-border trade and overlapping binational clusters of interests in border communities have created new channels for "intermestic" policy making and the complex balancing of local, regional, and national interests.

Conclusion

The discussion of security and border facilitation issues overlaps in important ways with discussions of North American integration in Chapters 3 and 4. US and Canadian governments, while recognizing the global, regional, national, and more local dimensions of these issues, tend to approach them from different ends of the proverbial telescope.

US executive branch policies face the daunting challenge of managing "whole of government" issues that overlap with broader national security questions with global dimensions. Relations with Canada, if not peripheral, inhabit a variety of niches within domestic or international policy subsets of homeland security and trade facilitation – at least in the absence of sufficient integration to allow for full reciprocity and mutual recognition of systems.

However, the creation of such arrangements, such as the idea of a binational border agency advocated by some academics and business groups,[67] challenges deeply entrenched institutional interests and national sentiments in each country. Most important among them are congressional prerogatives over domestic legislation, budgetary policies and oversight of the executive branch, and the right of an independent judiciary in each country to interpret and apply national laws – not least constitutional guarantees of due process, civil liberties, and human rights. They also evoke deeply held views of national sovereignty in all three countries of North America, ranging from patriotic devotion to national institutions and the democratic accountability of governments to their citizens to chauvinistic and sometimes conspiracy-driven displays of fear and loathing for cosmopolitan elites whose agendas are seen to threaten these values.[68] The inherent differences in size and power between the United States and its neighbours further increase the challenges of introducing European-style institutions for border security and management into a North American context – even before the substantial differences in security conditions between Canadian and Mexican borders are considered.

Proposals for a North American security perimeter might be feasible if political and societal interests in each country were to approach the issue on the basis of mutual recognition and verification – much as customs inspectors now conduct inspections of export-oriented firms away from national borders while remaining subject to the primacy of host countries' laws. Such measures would leave national governments (or provinces and states) free to adapt their laws and regulations to changing circumstances as long as they do not discriminate against partner countries or their citizens. Governments could negotiate agreements on consultation processes on prospective regulatory changes with the potential to disrupt cross-border interests, much as existing American regulatory processes provide for structured public consultations on numerous regulatory impact criteria.[69]

However, the levels of mutual trust and shared interest required for such measures are hard enough to introduce during periods of relative peace and prosperity – when policy makers can locate the resources necessary to compensate prospective "losers" from such policies in order to secure the broader social and economic benefits that might emerge from them. They are far more difficult, if not impossible, to achieve during periods of pervasive economic insecurity.

The other option available to policy makers and societal interests is to identify shared interests and objectives on a smaller scale in addressing different aspects of the policy elephant of security and facilitation. The next chapter explores these challenges and opportunities in greater detail.

11

Engaging US Security and Border Policies

The pervasiveness of economic, social, and administrative ties between Canada and the United States and their respective governments makes it both necessary and desirable for their respective government officials to engage one another to develop and refine security and border management policies whose effects cut across national borders.

The shift in US border management and security policies after September 2001 from facilitation to an unconditional emphasis on security completely changed the context of bilateral security relations. Canada's efforts to engage White House officials in a comprehensive approach to border management, symbolized by the Smart Border Accord, were initially successful. However, despite close working-level cooperation among police and border agencies, the proliferation of security initiatives and the cross-cutting forces of American domestic politics discussed in Chapter 10 marginalized cross-border relations with Canada for most of the following decade.

Canadian responses to these pressures contributed to a somewhat reactive and defensive approach to engaging US border management policies for much of the period between 2004 and 2008. Divergence between US and Canadian security and economic priorities contributed to a combination of caution and growing mutual mistrust that prevented Security and Prosperity Partnership (SPP) processes from achieving levels of cooperation similar to the more narrowly focused Smart Border process initiated after 9/11. Both executive and congressional politics tended to favour the projection of US policy priorities and administrative responses on allies rather than the negotiation of agreements based on mutual interest and benefit. The "security first" law enforcement orientation of DHS officials coincided nicely with the preferences of Canadian police and intelligence officials but often worked at cross-purposes with the agendas of other government agencies – let alone those of cross-border business interests or the Canadian courts. This pattern did not shift until the middle of the Obama administration's first term in office.

As a result, Ottawa's evolving approach to bilateral relations on border management issues since 2001 has been characterized by three major objectives:

- pursuing reciprocity and mutual recognition of policies and systems as a tacit condition for accommodation of US pressures for greater security coordination;
- avoiding or limiting the politicization of border management issues unless congressional action (as opposed to unilateral DHS initiatives) pre-empts this option; and
- attempting to minimize linkages between US border management practices with Canada and Mexico, except as US–Mexican practices might follow or parallel best practices along northern borders.

During this period, Canadian officials have placed varying degrees of emphasis on three different "tracks" for engaging the American political system – not just the US government. The first, the executive branch track, emphasizes engagement with relevant bureaucratic, legal, and interagency processes as part of ongoing political and working-level dealings on border management and security issues. The second, the congressional track, attempts to cultivate relations with individual members of Congress on border concerns with the support, as needed, of coalitions of US domestic interests, as discussed in Chapter 7. The third, the public diplomacy track, seeks to maintain a positive public and media image of Canada as a US security partner while cultivating potential sources of political influence beyond the beltway. However, the relative importance of each track varies widely across the range of issues introduced in Chapter 10, reflecting the extent to which each country's policy makers and working-level officials share similar policy goals and have sufficient autonomy to work out their differences outside the glare of publicity or challenges from domestic interest groups.

This chapter explores Canadian efforts to engage US security and border management interests and to influence related American policies toward Canada in four of the five policy subfields introduced in Chapter 10: security and law enforcement, trade-related issues of cargo and freight security, cross-border travel, and immigration and visa policies. It also examines three case studies that have reflected the different political and policy contexts of integrating trade, trucking, and travel security and facilitation: the Container Security Initiative, travel document rules under the Western Hemisphere Travel Initiative (WHTI), and ongoing efforts to introduce land preclearance processes for cross-border freight and travel. Finally, the chapter explores medium- and longer-term options for managing border security and facilitation issues.

Security, Law Enforcement, and Counterterrorism

Since 9/11, security and management policies and practices along the Canada–US border have been generally shaped by a much stronger focus on law enforcement and proactive counterterrorism measures, especially in the United States – although there has been a shift towards "all hazards" approaches under the Obama administration. As previously discussed, these measures incorporate multiple overlapping systems and technologies designed, among other things, to improve information on goods shipments entering the United States, to provide more comprehensive screening processes for visitors and migrants and for enforcing related immigration laws, and to enhance border monitoring between ports of entry to deter smuggling and illegal entry. However, a 2010 US government report indicated that DHS only claimed "situational awareness" of unauthorized entries along 25 percent of the border.[1]

Canadian police and intelligence agencies cannot be said to influence US policies – except perhaps at the margins. Rather, they have sought to expand opportunities for cooperation, working within the disciplines imposed by demands for increased security while respecting civil liberties and legal requirements for due process.

Canada followed the United States in strengthening its anti-terrorism legislation after 9/11, though subsequent legal challenges and legislative reviews have resulted in more extensive checks and balances on the monitoring, detention, and prosecution of persons suspected of terrorist association or activity.[2] Canadian policy shifts reflected three major factors. Domestic police and intelligence agencies had long expressed concern over official toleration of or indifference to the presence of branches of foreign terrorist organizations and related societal support groups dating back to the 1985 Air India bombing, which killed more than 300 Canadian citizens. The 2005-6 annual report of the Canadian Security Intelligence Service (CSIS) noted that the agency had identified thirty-six organizations and 152 individuals for investigation in that year, including alleged spies affiliated with foreign embassies, together with six organizations and fifty-five individuals under investigation for trafficking in materials that could be used to make chemical, biological, radiological, and nuclear weapons.[3] Similar concerns – particularly with respect to the weaknesses of Canada's refugee adjudication and enforcement systems and its exploitation by Islamist radicals subsequently arrested in the United States – also predated 9/11, as symbolized by the arrest of "millennium bomber" Ahmed Ressam in 1999.[4] The ongoing effect of the Ressam incident on American policy makers can be seen from the emphasis placed on it by a leading commentator twelve years later in emphasizing the importance of support for security cooperation with and from Canada.[5]

Even so, DFAIT officials noted that US officials refused Canadian requests for help in limiting "asylum shopping" until early 2004 despite these concerns.[6] Perhaps most importantly, the Chrétien government recognized after 9/11 that its perceived indifference to these issues could place Canadian interests in relatively open borders at serious risk.

However, post-9/11 pressures appear to have increased tensions between security (including RCMP) officials and senior government decision makers over the extent that Canada should adapt its security and law enforcement practices to address these concerns.[7] It is probable that this mutual lack of confidence contributed to the back channel information sharing between security services that resulted in Maher Arar's rendition and torture in 2002-3, if not similar treatment of other Canadians travelling abroad. Subsequent reports suggest that it has also led to the use of "disruption tactics" that increase pressure on suspected persons and groups – leading to controversies over the boundaries of legitimate counterterrorism tactics.[8] The most immediate consequence of the Arar affair – a judicial inquiry that sharply criticized the actions and omissions of Canadian officials – was substantially greater caution in information sharing, including stricter enforcement of third-party rules limiting disclosure of shared information to other agencies (including the courts) without the consent of the agency initially providing that information.[9]

However, American officials whom I interviewed noted that levels of cooperation with counterparts in Canada remained exceptionally high on most law enforcement issues. This cooperation was and is facilitated by a shared professional outlook, including shared concerns over the smuggling activities of organized crime, and the development of significant levels of trust through regular meetings and cooperation on operational issues. These relationships help to distinguish Canada–US security relations from those with Mexico and to work past bureaucratic hurdles created by inter-agency processes in both countries.

Open communications – not only between law enforcement agencies but with political decision makers as well – are critical to building and maintaining confidence. Senior law enforcement and Department of Justice officials meet regularly in the Cross-Border Crime Forum, whose activities range from joint assessments and targeting of criminal threats, especially organized crime groups, to public advisories on major issues. The development of fifteen Integrated Border Enforcement Teams (IBETs), which bring together regional DHS, RCMP, and CBSA officials with state, provincial, and local police counterparts, has contributed to increased operational coordination. Other examples include the Shiprider program, involving joint patrols of RCMP and US Coast Guard officials to contain drug and tobacco smuggling in west coast border waters and the St. Lawrence–Great Lakes region. These activities have fostered a culture of partnership based on mutual recognition of national laws, growing tactical flexibility, and the primacy of home country jurisdiction in monitoring and enforcement operations. These principles are expected to frame joint law enforcement activities along land borders under the NextGen initiative announced by US Attorney General Eric Holder in September 2011 and to be included in the subsequent Border Action Plan.[10]

Operational effectiveness is seen by front-line officials as depending on personal relationships, teamwork, and limited bureaucratic interference from officials in Ottawa or Washington. Even so, limited resources often constrain local police participation unless officers can be seconded to pro-vide liaison with national police or border agencies. Police officials note that differences in national laws and judicial processes governing the dis-closure of evidence and criminal sentencing can often play a significant role in determining the conduct of combined operations – particularly which police forces make arrests.[11] Although it is hard to assess with certainty the overall effect of these activities on broader US security policies toward

Canada – or on overall levels of smuggling and other criminal activity along the border – they appear to have strengthened mutual confidence among police and security officials who might otherwise be inclined to apply more stringent border security measures damaging to broader bilateral relations.

Securing and Facilitating Shippers and Cargo

Combining increased security with efficient border management has proven more challenging than streamlining the flow of goods through each country's Pacific coast and Atlantic coast ports despite Ottawa's best efforts to facilitate the inclusion of Canadian exporters and shipping and trucking firms within the American security perimeter.

The Smart Border Accord accelerated this process. Canadian and US security officials worked closely when introducing the Container Security Initiative (CSI), trusted shipper programs such as Free and Secure Trade (FAST), and supply chain security programs, including the US Customs–Trade Partnership against Terrorism (C-TPAT) and Canada's Partners in Protection (PIP). Shortly after 9/11, Canada's four largest "horizontal" business groups[12] organized the Coalition for Secure and Trade Efficient Borders as a coordinating group for Canadian business interests seeking to influence both governments' border management policies. These groups and others, such as the Lewiston, NY, based Can–Am Business Trade Alliance, have mobilized an extensive web of business interests on both sides of the border to lobby for more efficient management of border security and to facilitate the integration of cross-border supply chains into the cargo security programs initiated under the Smart Border process.

The business lobby's arguments for a more risk management–oriented approach to layered security were initially well received by the US Office (later Department) of Homeland Security (DHS). These influences were reflected in the initial design of CSI, intended to screen the rapidly growing stream of shipping containers entering the United States by ship and rail; the FAST program to screen and certify importers, shippers, and truck drivers prior to their arrival at US land borders; requirements to submit advance notice of cargo shipments; and C-TPAT and PIP – supply chain security initiatives for qualifying companies in each country.

Most of these measures were initially voluntary but with clear incentives to encourage participation through more efficient processing of incoming freight. However, partisan competition contributed to growing one-upmanship over security issues, with Congress imposing progressively

TABLE 11.1

Canada–US southbound land border crossings, cars and trucks, 2000-11

	Cars (millions)	2000 = 100	Trucks (millions)	2000 = 100
2000	36.9	*100.0*	7.0	*100.0*
2001	34.3	92.9	6.8	96.2
2004	30.7	83.1	6.9	98.0
2006	30.0	81.4	6.6	94.3
2007	29.8	80.6	6.5	91.9
2008	28.7	77.7	5.9	83.6
2009	26.7	72.3	5.0	71.2
2010	28.9	78.2	5.4	77.2
2011 (January-August)	21.1	83.7	3.7	77.2

SOURCES: US Bureau of Transportation Statistics, http://www.bts.gov/; author's calculations.

more stringent security measures at land and sea ports of entry. In practice, this often meant the reinspection or screening of cargo that had been screened either on departure from major foreign ports participating in CSI or in passing through Canadian ports in transit to the United States. As a result, business groups in both countries complained that, despite heavy investments to qualify for these programs, administrative weaknesses (including staff shortages, failures to improve processing capacities of land borders or seaports, and inconsistencies in regulatory requirements between and among national programs) meant that they were often unable to reap the promised benefits.[13] However, the political effects of these concerns were drowned out by persistent media reports of "broken borders" and periodic security scares such as the 2006 controversy over the proposed takeover of six American container ports by a Dubai-based firm specializing in port management.[14]

The result has been a steady "thickening" of the border until a sharp recession reduced southbound truck shipments by 22.5 percent between 2007 and 2009, reinforcing earlier trends before recovering somewhat in 2010 and 2011 (see Table 11.1). The contrast between the relatively high levels of policy cooperation and administrative coordination in managing overseas container shipments and continuing frustrations in land border management can best be seen by examining Canada's participation in the Container Security Initiative.

The Container Security Initiative

CSI, introduced in December 2002, was one of several programs introduced after 9/11 to secure US ports and transportation systems against the
risks of terrorist attacks, particularly the potential proliferation of nuclear
and biological weapons. It was designed as part of a multilayered system to
"push out" borders, secure international supply chains, protect shipments
in transit, and improve screening of port employees.

Container shipments to the United States, particularly from China and
other Pacific Rim nations, grew rapidly during the 1990s (see Table 11.2).
During this period, Canada's railways made major acquisitions and strategic
alliances in the United States as part of a broader, market-driven integration
of transportation networks, while more and more North American manufacturers sourced components in China, Europe, and Mexico.[15] Growing
congestion on the US west coast encouraged the expansion of Canadian
and Mexican ports, especially Vancouver and Manzanillo, to handle rising
demand. Securing supply chains and container shipments became critical
to maintaining the rising flow of goods while reducing the likelihood that
Canadian transportation firms and producers dependent on overseas components would be penalized due to more stringent border controls.

CSI's implementation had unilateral, bilateral, and multilateral dimensions, suggesting its location in the category of policies toward allies.
Initially, DHS officials approached counterparts in Canada, the European
Union, and Japan to sign bilateral agreements for the implementation of
CSI standards at qualifying ports, including intelligence sharing on high-
risk cargo and the location of US Customs and Border Protection (CBP)
agents in foreign ports to work with local customs officials. All containers
would be prescreened and evaluated in participating ports before shipment
to the United States. High-risk containers would be searched by foreign
customs and CBP agents. New technologies would be developed and eventually mandated to provide electronic container seals to reduce risks of
tampering with cargo. Containers shipped to the United States would have
to pass through CSI-participating ports – a major incentive for cooperation
by other countries.[16]

Canada became the first pilot project for CSI implementation on a reciprocal basis in 2002 – one of the "action points" in the December 2001
Smart Border Accord. Canadian customs officials were located at the ports
of Seattle–Tacoma and Newark, with CBP officers located in Vancouver,
Halifax, and Montreal. Similar agreements followed with the European

TABLE 11.2
North American container port traffic, 20-foot equivalent units

	1990 = 100	1995	2000	2005	2010
North America	100	141.7	199.2	277.4	291.9
Canada	100	115.7	196.2	276.9	318.9
Vancouver	100	135.9	320.9	558.4	656.1
Pacific Coast	100	136.0	321.0	558.6	745.7
Montreal	100	127.9	178.5	220.8	234.4
United States	100	143.0	195.2	269.5	271.5
Pacific Coast	100	139.5	191.4	281.1	271.3
Atlantic Coast	100	148.2	198.7	255.7	237.1
Mexico	100	175.7	405.5	657.7	1,142.0
Pacific Coast	100	186.1	525.2	1,209.6	2,725.9

SOURCE: American Association of Port Authorities, http://www.aapa-ports.org; author's calculations.

Union in 2002-3. By 2006, 90 percent of the goods arriving in the United States were to follow through CSI-certified ports. DHS officials used agreements with Canada, the European Union, and Japan as a basis for internationalizing CSI standards through the World Customs Organization and International Maritime Organization, though the negotiation of these agreements and development of related international soft law standards took several years.[17]

Resource constraints enforced a risk management approach on the screening of cargo, with CBP support. However, Congress mandated a series of stricter standards in the SAFE Ports Act of 2006, including progress toward mandatory screening of incoming containers at ports. These measures paralleled existing rules requiring VACIS screening of truck and rail containers for radiation on land borders,[18] though some groups suggested that these measures involved unnecessary duplication.

CSI suggests the potential benefits of security cooperation based on reciprocal arrangements and consultations with other stakeholders to integrate security measures with regular business practices. Adding new layers of regulation – often in ways that are not effectively integrated with previous measures – has eroded the original risk management approach. The result has been an accumulation of national policy measures whose interaction attracts serious attention only when major bottlenecks threaten to disrupt entire transportation networks.[19]

Perimeter security negotiations launched in 2011 made rationalization of these processes a priority. The December 2011 Border Action Plan introduced several policy changes long advocated by industry groups, including mutual recognition of air cargo security programs for passenger aircraft, measures to create a "common framework" for each country's trusted trader programs, commitments to develop common data requirements for "in bond" (US) and "in transit" shipments passing through either country for implementation by the end of 2013, and plans for the development for an "Integrated Cargo Security Strategy" by the end of 2014.[20] Although there is some evidence of bipartisan support for these measures, it remains to be seen how these initiatives will be affected by the vagaries of American domestic politics.

Securing Travel versus Securing Borders

The most politically sensitive dimension of border management for Canadian governments relates to processes for managing traffic on the Canada–US land border. Land borders accounted for about 79 percent of the estimated 425 million crossings of US borders in 2004, while about 70 percent of cross-border trade is carried by truck.[21] Without expanded infrastructure and staffing at major ports of entry, tightened security results in increased backups, with direct impacts on legitimate trade, and cuts into accustomed social interactions between border communities. Cross-border tourism is more directly affected by fluctuating exchange rates, gas prices, and other economic factors.

American border management policies affecting individual travellers are focused on controlling entry into the United States to achieve two major objectives: controlling illegal migration, which had reached epidemic proportions by 2002-5, mainly along the US–Mexican border, and identifying prospective terrorists who might attempt to sneak across national borders.

In contrast, Canadian policies tend to separate immigration controls from those relating to routine travellers. Since 9/11, these efforts have been aimed primarily at maintaining efficient processing of border travellers to expedite high levels of trade and tourism and expanding the use of "trusted traveller" programs for frequent travellers to the United States. Recognizing US concerns over past Canadian immigration policies, they have also enhanced the screening of new immigrants and refugees before they reach Canada and introduced legal measures to monitor and, where possible, deport non-citizens who have entered Canada under false pretences. Changes to Canadian rules governing refugee claims and adjudication were introduced in 2010 in response to a sharp spike in refugee claims from Mexico.[22]

After 9/11, the US government introduced a series of bilateral, unilateral, and multilateral measures to expand border security. DHS officials persuaded members of the International Civil Aviation Organization, including Canada, to approve an international standard for the inclusion of machine-readable and biometric identifiers on newly issued passports in 2005. By April 2010, 170 countries were issuing machine-readable passports.[23]

A second set of issues is related to visa waiver programs for persons visiting the United States or Canada for up to three months. Each government allows visitors from preapproved countries with limited likelihoods of overstaying visas (or other immigration law violations) to travel without first requiring them to obtain visas. These arrangements are negotiated on a bilateral basis. The US visa waiver program for travellers applies to thirty-six countries. Canada's program applies to an additional eighteen countries, the United States, Hong Kong, and British overseas territories (see Table 11.3). The gap was closed when the United States extended visa waiver status to several eastern and southern European countries and South Korea in late 2008 while requiring all applicants to possess electronic passports and secure an online travel authorization form before leaving for the United States. The rapid growth of asylum claims by visitors from Mexico and the Czech Republic in 2008 and 2009, combined with high levels of rejections of previous applicants, led Canada to reimpose visa requirements on visitors from both countries in July 2009, souring bilateral relations.[24]

Although Canada and the United States exempt one another's citizens from their visa waiver programs, American officials have sought further harmonization, arguing that integrating the programs is necessary to reduce screening requirements on the Canadian border. But Canadian officials have been disinclined to sacrifice discretion over domestic immigration policies.[25] This issue may have been resolved in December 2011 when Canadian officials agreed to phase in two measures to screen visa-exempt travelers similar to those in the United States: Electronic Travel Authorizations and Advance Passenger Information systems that allow for more effective security screening of passengers.[26]

However, visa issues deal with only a fraction of cross-border travel on either the northern or the southern US border. The greatest political challenges have come from policy changes that affect the lives and accustomed

TABLE 11.3
Visa waiver countries, 2011

Both Countries

Andorra	Germany	Lithuania	Singapore
Australia	Greece	Luxembourg	Slovakia
Austria	Hungary	Malta	Slovenia
Belgium	Iceland	Monaco	South Korea
Brunei	Ireland	Netherlands	Spain
Denmark	Italy	New Zealand	Sweden
Estonia	Japan	Norway	Switzerland
Finland	Latvia	Portugal	United Kingdom*†
France	Liechtenstein	San Marino	

Canada

Antigua and	Croatia	Namibia	St. Kitts and Nevis
Barbuda	Cyprus	Papua New Guinea	St. Vincent
Bahamas	Holy See	Poland	Swaziland
Barbados	Hong Kong SAR	San Lucia	Taiwan
Botswana	Israel†	Solomon Islands	United States§

United States only
Czech Republic

* For unrestricted rights of residence in United Kingdom only (US).
† Including British citizens, British overseas citizens readmissible to the United Kingdom, British national passports issued to persons born, naturalized, or registered in Hong Kong, and citizens of British dependent territories (Canada).
‡ National passport holders only.
§ Including US lawful permanent residents (non-citizens) and residents of Western Samoa.

SOURCES: United States, Department of State, "Visa Waiver Program (VWP)," http://travel.state.gov; Canada, Citizenship and Immigration Canada, "Visitor Visa Exemptions" (Ottawa: Citizenship and Immigration Canada, 11 July 2011).

routines of each country's citizens. This is particularly true of legislation emerging from the 9/11 commission report. Only two of the commission's forty recommendations directly addressed border management issues. One called for a comprehensive biometric entry–exit control system to identify all persons entering and leaving the United States. The other recommended the integration of the "U.S. border security system in a larger network of screening points, ... design[ing] a common screening system, ... and extending these standards among other governments" to determine citizenship, combat the use of fraudulent identification, and allow for cross-references with databases of legal immigrants, terrorists, and criminal suspects.[27]

Initial responses to 9/11 sought to expedite trusted or low-risk travellers who had undergone formal background checks through border crossings, thus reducing waiting lines for frequent low-risk travellers. DHS and the Canada Border Services Agency (CBSA) introduced the joint NEXUS program, though lack of a common technology platform prevented integration of the program's land and air components until 2008. The SENTRI program provided a similar service for travellers between Mexico and the United States.[28] In mid-2008, NEXUS card holders accounted for only 9 percent of crossings at northern US border points despite the program's rapid growth in response to pending passport requirements.[29] However, NEXUS membership has grown from less than 200,000 in 2008 to about 600,000 in late 2011, including about 400,000 Canadians.[30] In 2011, DHS also extended access to its Global Entry trusted traveller program to Canadian NEXUS (and Mexican SENTRI) members – allowing for de facto integration of screening programs for travellers in transit through US airports.

Proposals for an automated entry–exit system for tracking foreign visitors to the United States had been legislated in 1996 as part of broader efforts to control illegal immigration since more than half of illegal migrants were found to have entered the United States legally and overstayed their visas. However, intensive lobbying by US border communities and Canadian interests persuaded Congress to delay and eventually neuter the legislation as excessively intrusive for trade and travel.[31]

DHS announced plans to introduce the US-VISIT program in April 2003 to collect digital photographs and fingerprints of foreign nationals holding non-immigrant visas – beginning in January 2004, anticipating the 9/11 commission recommendation. It also attempted to link the visa waiver expansion to the successful introduction of the program's exit component, which remained effectively inoperative along the Canadian and Mexican borders. Although DHS officials asked their Canadian counterparts to assist in implementing US-VISIT's exit measures by providing data on persons entering Canada from the United States, the latter reportedly put off these requests, citing problems with Canadian privacy legislation,[32] though concerns over sovereignty and other domestic political implications undoubtedly were important factors. Draft regulations tabled in 2008 proposed shifting responsibility for the collection of exit data to airlines. However, strong industry resistance to the downloading of regulatory costs led DHS to test other approaches.[33] The level of bilateral information sharing required for cooperative implementation of an entry–exit system only became politically feasible in Canada in 2011 when combined with broader negotiations for perimeter security and trade facilitation.

Canadians and Mexicans were initially exempted from US-VISIT's requirements, except for those requiring visas for business travel or the pursuit of education, limiting the program's application to about 11 percent of persons crossing land borders in 2005. However, the Intelligence Reform and Terrorism Prevention Act passed by Congress in December 2004 contained provisions requiring all persons entering the United States, including American citizens, to provide a passport or other secure identification indicating their citizenship and eligibility for (re-)entry. Together with debates over BSE and softwood lumber, discussed in Chapter 12, the Western Hemisphere Travel Initiative (WHTI) became one of Canada's three principal disputes with the United States over border management – and the only one to extend more than a few months into the life of the Harper government.

Ironically, another piece of security legislation, the REAL-ID Act of May 2005, provided the basis for eventual resolution of the WHTI dispute. REAL-ID required states to establish a wide range of new security measures to verify the identities of applicants for drivers' licences and renewals in order to deal with concerns over identity fraud and the issuance of licences to illegal migrants. These changes, while ostensibly voluntary, made possession of REAL-ID licences a condition for entry into many federal buildings, federally regulated financial institutions, and internal air travel.[34] These issues are addressed further in the case study on WHTI and enhanced drivers' licences.

The application of these two initiatives to Americans removed any basis for Canada's traditional claim to exemption from US border security measures derived from broad cooperation or comparable domestic measures. The result was a prolonged, tactically flexible effort to shift the terms of debate in the United States and encourage the Bush administration and Congress to consider other, more practical, alternatives to WHTI's passport requirements.

WHTI and Enhanced Drivers' Licences

The WHTI debate in the United States was a relatively small subset of a much larger debate over border management and control overlapping ongoing disputes over immigration, national security and counterterrorism, privacy, and civil liberties. Although most Canadians were largely oblivious to this reality, it shaped Canadian efforts to secure changes to WHTI by focusing on the three major dimensions or tracks of bilateral relations noted earlier: dealings with the executive branch, Congress (including support for interest group coalitions), and public diplomacy. A fourth dimension – provincial–state cooperation on cross-border issues – ultimately combined with congressional pressure to persuade DHS to allow the introduction of enhanced drivers' licences (EDLs) as a secure alternative to passports and to recognize comparable licences introduced by Canadian provinces.

As most international business travellers already possessed (or would usually acquire) passports, the WHTI debate focused on the measure's impact on two specific groups: ordinary Americans (and, to a lesser extent, Canadians) who were unlikely to possess passports or obtain them for only occasional use, and the likely effect of increased scrutiny in creating substantially longer lineups and border delays affecting cross-border trade and tourism.[35]

The predominance of security concerns in the broader American debate led to a gradual shift in Canadian tactics from emphasizing WHTI's impact on trade and economic activity under the Martin government to a "management discourse" under the Harper government. This approach, which reflected lessons drawn from earlier Section 110 debates on entry–exit, focused on the administrative and technical details necessary to translate broad policy goals into action to balance potentially competing goals such as security, trade, and travel facilitation more effectively.[36] However, it also demonstrated the practical limits of congressional lobbying as a strategy to influence American policies toward Canada.[37]

During the Section 110 debate, Canada worked closely with US domestic interests and selected members of Congress to defer funding an integrated entry–exit system capable of monitoring the more than 400 million travellers crossing US borders annually.[38] These efforts successfully exploited separate congressional authorization and appropriation processes to delay funding authorization for pilot projects. Interest groups from border communities actively lobbied key members of Congress who secured legislative changes to dilute or defer action in 1997, 1998, and 2000. The provision's original intent – to strengthen immigration enforcement, especially along the US–Mexican border – made it easier for northern border state senators and congressmen to argue that conditions along the two borders were sufficiently different to warrant different approaches despite evidence that a handful of terrorist suspects arrested in the United States had avoided Canadian immigration controls.[39]

The events of 9/11 fundamentally changed this political environment, but it was not until December 2004 that Chair of the House Judiciary Committee James Sensenbrenner (R-WI) was able to mandate WHTI through the Intelligence Reform and Terrorism Prevention Act. The bill provided two years (until December 2006) to implement the measure for international air travel and most commercial marine vessels and three years (until January 2008) along US land borders with Canada and Mexico.

Initial Canadian efforts engaged three separate processes: internal DHS administrative procedures, government-wide regulatory requirements for cost–benefit analyses and consultations on the economic impacts of major regulations, and congressional windows of opportunity – notably those provided by immigration legislation and annual appropriation bills.

WHTI's enabling legislation required both American citizens and non-citizens to provide either a passport or another secure form of identification confirming the bearer's identity and citizenship before entering or re-entering the United States. Since this measure required Americans to carry passports for the first time to travel abroad, Canadian advocacy in 2005 focused on efforts to use WHTI provisions for other secure forms of iden-tification to secure a partial exemption from the passport requirement. At a bureaucratic level, the two governments set up a working group on stan-dards and documents.

However, these processes were complicated by both legislative and bureaucratic politics that made WHTI a moving target, particularly the Department of State's effective defence of its prerogative to issue passports or alternative documents and passage in June 2005 of the REAL-ID Act, discussed above. Moreover, systemic underfunding of the US-VISIT pro-gram by both Congress and the Office of Management and Budget (OMB) limited the resources available for WHTI implementation as DHS's rapidly rising budgets failed to keep up with the ever-expanding demands of its multiple mandates.[40]

REAL-ID's passage prompted a coalition of business groups from US and Canadian border communities to explore the possibility of making drivers' licences a secure alternative under WHTI. This process was complicated by intense state government opposition to REAL-ID as an unfunded mandate whose cost was later estimated at $14 billion for states and $21 billion over-all – dwarfing the costs of WHTI.[41] Washington State and British Columbia, already working together on a joint tourism promotion campaign for the 2010 Vancouver Olympics, agreed to work toward a joint EDL project, with initial technical work to be done by Washington's Department of Licensing.[42]

DHS initially resisted the EDL proposal, championing instead a US passport card to be issued by the Department of State's passport bureau at roughly half the price of an ordinary passport. DHS officials regularly referred to the "more than 8,000" forms of ID issued by US state and county governments (mainly birth certificates), suggesting the need for a more uniform standard. The resources needed to produce and market the passport card and to double the anticipated volume of annual passport production[43] help to explain Department of State officials' coolness to proposals for systems to accommodate information-sharing requests by state motor vehicle departments necessary to allow the use of REAL-ID–conforming drivers' licences for WHTI compliance.[44]

Particularly after resolution of the softwood lumber dispute in April 2006, embassy and consular officials made the WHTI a priority in their diplomacy, subject to the need to respect congressional sensitivities over possible perceptions of Canadian "interference" in domestic politics.[45] Ottawa, though careful to acknowledge both concerns over border security and the US government's sovereign right "to enhance the security of its borders through improved documentation and other requirements," had argued for the need for a continued partnership in managing the border on the model of the 2001 Smart Border Accord. Although assorted studies estimated WHTI's economic impact on the US tourism industry at between $667 million and $996 million,[46] these figures – though substantial by Canadian standards – were dwarfed in the context of DHS's $140 billion annual budget or the $14 trillion American economy.

Ultimately, the only strategy common to all groups was to seek congressional support for delayed implementation – usually framed in terms of "getting it right" or ensuring that DHS had put in place all measures necessary for effective implementation. This approach reflected the shift from a "trade facilitation discourse" to the "management discourse" discussed earlier.

Rather than challenging "the need for secure documentation for entry into the U.S.," the Harper government emphasized the need to ensure administrative effectiveness in WHTI's implementation. Canadian federal officials sought to ensure field testing and evaluation of WHTI-related technologies and administrative systems prior to full-scale implementation, along with increased investments in adequate border infrastructure in their frequent meetings with administration and congressional officials.[47]

This approach paralleled concerns raised by the Government Accountability Office (GAO), responding to requests by border state members of

Congress.[48] When Prime Minister Harper raised these issues in his July 2006 White House visit, President Bush responded diplomatically that the administration would cooperate with Congress in any legislative revisions that it saw fit to make.[49] However, as in previous years, most of the detailed work of developing alternative proposals was carried out by US interest groups with an immediate stake in the process, many from border communities.

Months of intense lobbying of border state senators by a coalition of borderland Chambers of Commerce and other business groups persuaded the Senate to include language in a September 2006 appropriations bill delaying WHTI and imposing conditions on its implementation.[50] Although these provisions enjoyed bipartisan support from senior senators, Democratic gains in the November 2006 congressional elections increased pressure on DHS to accommodate WHTI opponents, including upstate New York's Louise Slaughter (D-NY), the incoming chair of the powerful House Rules Committee. Secretary of Homeland Security Chertoff announced several administrative concessions in February 2007, followed by approval of an EDL pilot project in Washington State in March. However, pressures for further delays on the land border grew dramatically when the US Passport Office failed to anticipate the flood of passport applications following WHTI's implementation for international air travel in January 2007. This resulted in processing delays of more than three months and congressional intervention on behalf of outraged constituents.[51] As a result, the 2007 appropriations bill included language delaying WHTI's implementation until June 2009, after the Bush administration's departure from office.

Faced with growing congressional resistance, Chertoff adopted the EDL option as a political compromise that allowed DHS to continue WHTI implementation while defusing opposition from states on both borders. By September 2007, New York, Vermont, and Arizona had also announced plans to introduce EDLs, followed by Michigan, and subsequently Minnesota.[52] In November 2007, Chertoff announced that EDLs issued by Canadian provinces meeting agreed standards would qualify as "secure alternatives" under WHTI. By mid-2008, British Columbia had initiated its own EDL pilot project. When WHTI was finally implemented on land borders in June 2009, Ontario, Quebec, and Manitoba were rolling out their own EDLs. There was also a sharp spike in the number of NEXUS cards issued in 2008-9, with program enrollment increasing from fewer than 200,000 to an estimated 355,000 in both countries over eighteen months.

Although American officials indicated that they were prepared for full WHTI implementation in June 2009, initial reports suggested considerable flexibility in enforcement, with travellers without passports warned to obtain them and entered into a DHS database for subsequent review.[53]

The often arcane, highly personalized nature of the American legislative process makes it difficult for outsiders to determine the precise conditions that have contributed to the success or failure of any particular measure. However, five major factors appear to have contributed the development of an alternative satisfactory to Canada:

- the issue's relatively low profile in Washington, limiting the number of entrenched interests outside the US federal bureaucracy with a vested interest in WHTI's implementation;
- the successful mobilization of US domestic interests, independent of Canadian governments, with a strong vested interest in a similar policy agenda;
- the development of a bipartisan coalition in Congress, including senior senators of both parties whose constituents had a vested interest in the proposed changes;
- the latter's capacity to leverage their seniority on the Appropriations Committee first to amend the annual bill authorizing core funding for DHS operations and then to withstand a subsequent challenge from counterparts in the House of Representatives;
- the capacity of senior officials in Washington State to design an administratively practical alternative and mobilize political support in Congress to ensure its serious consideration and support from other border states in its implementation.

These developments suggest the highly contingent nature of policy development in Washington and the need for Canadian policy makers and diplomats to take a flexible, pragmatic approach to policy processes that they cannot control. Interviews with both Canadian and US officials suggest that the persistence of Canada's lobbying, though ultimately effective, eroded the personal relationships on which the management of department-level relations normally depend – contributing to greater American reluctance to address other border-related irritants.[54] However, for a Canadian government immersed in the day-to-day political gamesmanship of managing a minority government, this appears to have been a small price to pay in

defusing a substantial political irritant and allowing provincial governments to implement a nominally "Made in Canada" solution – even at the
cost of delaying progress on land preclearance proposals strongly supported by business groups on both sides of the border.

Land Preclearance/Shared Border Management

A key strategy in combining increased security and border facilitation has
been to "push back borders": that is, addressing potential security threats at
some distance from the border in order to reduce disruption for the vast
majority of low-risk trade and travellers. This has been a central objective of
the Container Security Initiative, the expanded use of "migration integrity
officers" by Canada's immigration department in screening prospective immigrants at embassies and consulates abroad, and proposals for land preclearance or shared border management with the United States, initially
proposed in the Smart Border Accord.

Land preclearance is meant to establish joint customs clearance facilities near border points whose physical characteristics, such as river crossings or congested urban areas, do not lend themselves to expansion on each
side of the physical border. (Similar arrangements have been worked out at
several rural ports of entry in which customs posts have been developed as
shared facilities to permit improved mutual support between US and
Canadian officials.) As a result, land preclearance is tied to both improved
security and border infrastructure renewal projects. After extended discussions, two priority locations were selected for land preclearance pilot
projects in December 2004: near the Thousand Islands border crossing between Ontario and upstate New York, and on Ontario's Niagara frontier in
Fort Erie.

Discussions dragged on for sixteen months as officials sought to work
through different administrative processes in each country. Initially, they
included matters such as compatible computer systems, customs protocols,
and different rules on customs personnel carrying firearms. The last problem was resolved when the Harper government accepted a Canadian health
and safety arbitrator's ruling that issuing firearms to CBSA personnel was
a legitimate safety requirement given the risks of armed fugitives fleeing
across the US border.

However, the two countries came to a sticking point over different
legal procedures governing the collection of fingerprints (a requirement
under US VISIT rules), the detention of suspects, the right of individuals

approaching the border to turn around if refused entry to the United States, and information-sharing protocols.[55] US officials cited the precedent of preclearance facilities at airports, which are deemed to be US territory by previous agreements between the two countries. Canadian officials argued that the more appropriate precedent was that of joint law enforcement practices, in which the laws of the host country took precedence and host country law enforcement officials took the lead in enforcing relevant statutes.

Conversations with Canadian officials suggested that domestic court rulings – and the desire to ensure that any procedures could survive a constitutional challenge – were significant factors in their insistence on the latter precedent. In April 2007, Secretary of Homeland Security Chertoff announced the withdrawal of DHS from discussions on land preclearance facilities as a result of the impasse – incurring substantial criticism from interests in US border communities and from some members of Congress. Reportedly facing strong opposition to the measure within DHS, the Obama administration after taking office in 2009 initially refused to reopen negotiations on land preclearance.

Achieving a working model for land preclearance has remained a priority for cross-border business interests – despite its exclusion from the agenda for perimeter security negotiations announced in February 2011. However, strong pressures from business interests in both countries, as well as from US Senator Charles Schumer (D-NY), led to the inclusion of an agreement to "develop a comprehensive approach to pre-clearance and pre-inspection covering all modes of cross-border trade and travel" in the December 2011 Border Action Plan.[56] A key element appears to be the bundling of multiple administrative issues of interest to one or both governments and major cross-border stakeholder groups into a single package – although the December 2012 deadline for the conclusion of the proposed agreement raises questions of the level of political will available to "close" the deal amid the competing priorities of a presidential election year.

Conclusion

Close cooperation on security (or public safety) issues and border management with the United States is fundamental to Canada's national interests. At an operational level, the realities of interdependence require close cooperation among police, border management, and other security agencies. In recent years, bilateral cooperation has grown to include public health issues, emergency response, cyber-security and related measures to protect critical infrastructure, legally suspect financial transactions, and other non-traditional security issues.

At a political level, effective cooperation based on mutual trust is an essential condition of being able to influence American policies that have the capacity to harm, accommodate, or benefit Canadian interests. At the same time, democratic, constitutional, and sovereignty concerns require governments and law enforcement agencies in both countries to be responsive to public opinion – which can either enable or undermine effective security measures – and accountable to their respective legal and political institutions.

The preservation of domestic political and policy discretion by US homeland security officials creates incentives for similar discretion by Canadian governments – if only to protect Canadian interests from the deliberate or inadvertent shifting of costs to "outsiders." This concept applies within countries as much as between them as government agencies compete for limited budgets and attempt to shift adjustment costs to other agencies, governments, the private sector, and ordinary citizens. Under such circumstances, Canada's position is analogous to that of an American airline, trucking firm, border community, or state government, except that it lacks direct recourse to the American political system or to American courts to protect its interests against arbitrary political or legal action – except in collaboration with coalitions of these actors.

Under such circumstances, Canadian governments need to pursue a four-pronged strategy that acknowledges overlapping interests with American governments and societal actors, the differences imposed by different political, economic, and institutional structures, and ongoing requirements for political and legal accountability to Canadians. Elements of this strategy can be seen in the joint "Beyond the Border" policy statement and action plan released by both national leaders in 2011.[57]

First, it is in the interests of Canada and those of most Canadians to be as fully integrated within North American security structures as is consistent with the equal treatment of American and Canadian citizens and businesses under the law, together with respect for each country's similar but distinct constitutional and legal systems. Since the United States cannot be expected to delegate final responsibility for the security of its citizens to a foreign government, this objective is best served by the pursuit of a mixture of joint, cooperative, and parallel security structures that allows for comparable treatment of each country's citizens and businesses but gives governments enough discretion to remain accountable to their own citizens and legal institutions.

The negotiations for a binational security perimeter have identified four potential areas of common ground. Some of these principles suggest a mixture of the "Shared Border" approach of the 1990s, the Smart Border Accord, and the SPP, including a shared commitment to risk management approaches involving "compatible, interoperable and – where possible – joint measures and technology," "greater sharing of information," an "all-hazards" approach to security collaboration, and emergency management that includes relevant societal stakeholders.[58] These commitments all reflect principles and policies outlined in the Martin government's National Security Strategy of 2004 and continued by the Harper government.

Such approaches can take different forms in different sectors but often reflect the principles of mutual recognition subject to external audit in both countries. Greater operational similarities are generally appropriate in the design of secure freight, secure shipper, and secure traveller programs in which overlapping trade and security regulations allow for more efficient integration with the operations of businesses engaged in regular cross-border commercial networks. Collaboration in international agencies such as the International Maritime Organization, the World Customs Organization, and the International Civil Aviation Organization can complement and reinforce these objectives. The commitment of "Beyond the Border" to "work towards developing an integrating cargo security strategy that ensures compatible screening methods for goods and cargo before they depart foreign ports" for North America is consistent with these objectives.[59]

Moreover, the diverse character of Canada–US border regions suggests the benefits of encouraging greater administrative decentralization in both countries due to the different security challenges and societal and economic interactions in each region as a second key element to integrating security concerns with effective border management. The challenges of managing congested, high-traffic crossings in major urban areas such as Buffalo–Niagara or Detroit–Windsor are very different from those of large swaths of the Pacific Northwest, the rural Great Plains and Prairies, or the closely knit border communities of New England and eastern Canada.

The ongoing development of cooperative emergency management, infrastructure, and law enforcement policies and practices also requires different approaches that reflect the more decentralized character of security challenges and operational responses in each field. The IBET system that has evolved since 2001 is an excellent example of decentralized cross-border cooperation. These activities are more closely aligned with all-hazards models of public safety and homeland security – along with more conventional issues of land-use planning and environmental assessment. As such, they involve multiple stakeholders and varying requirements for stakeholder and community consultation and participation to secure necessary levels of public support and to make policies work effectively.

The creation of "bi-national port operations committees" through the Beyond-the-Border process and through commitments to coordinate border infrastructure investment at both major and smaller border crossings are useful first steps in this direction. Ultimately, such an approach might evolve into regional border commissions comparable to port authorities whose activities cut across jurisdictional boundaries in the United States. These agencies could be supported by societal advisory or consultative bodies including representatives from subnational governments and business and community groups to address the priorities of major stakeholders, including border communities.

At an operational level, some observers have suggested that this strategy could be reinforced by including measures for stakeholder engagement in the performance evaluation criteria for port directors in federal border management agencies.[60] The commitment of "Beyond the Border" to engage subnational governments and accommodate societal stakeholders in "community-based and community-driven efforts," particularly those aimed at dealing with "violent extremism," is another useful step in that direction.[61]

However, such approaches are less feasible in policy fields such as immigration, where policy goals and political sensitivities are not as easily aligned across national borders given different institutional structures, policy histories, and societal environments. Under such circumstances, Canadian governments are wise to pursue independent but complementary policies as a third element of their approach to creating a comprehensive policy of border management and "pushing back the border." The presence of both political and policy similarities and differences can facilitate a degree of cooperation on matters such as the "safe third country" procedures for structuring refugee flows as well as "visa waiver" rules applying to visitors from third countries.

At the same time, however, there needs to be clear communication about the legal and political limits on such cooperation, where necessary, to secure vital national interests. The commitment of "Beyond the Border" to "establish coordinated entry and exit systems at the common land borders," so that "a record of entry into one country into one country could be considered as a record of an exit from the other"[62] will be an interesting test of the two governments' capacity to negotiate previous differences on these issues while respecting each country's privacy laws.

Such approaches are likely to require parallel engagements with appropriate committees of Congress and Parliament with different degrees of control over legal requirements and project funding, and sometimes, with state and provincial governments. American policy experts have acknowledged the value of such arrangements within their own country.[63] They do not require a yielding of sovereignty but can provide useful forums for integrating national, regional, and local priorities in each country and across borders.

A fourth useful initiative would be to provide for a wider range of cross-border staff and executive exchanges between different law enforcement, border, and emergency management agencies to strengthen mutual understanding of their respective cultures and institutional environments. There is a long tradition of such arrangements between the two countries' armed forces. Also useful, if more challenging to arrange, would be executive and management interchanges between border and transportation security agencies and the private sector firms whose activities they oversee. Such arrangements would provide better mutual understanding of the cultures and logistics of cross-border trade, hopefully contributing to the evolution of more effective and less economically disruptive security systems.

Maintaining effective security and border management in a dynamic economic, societal, and technological environment does not lend itself to "one-size-fits-all" solutions imposed by central governments and political processes that are often distant from regional and community stakeholders. Rather, effective and adaptable policy responses require ongoing communications between senior government agencies and practitioners inside and outside government who deal with these issues on a regular basis. Although security issues do not lend themselves readily to transparent, participatory styles of government, effective citizen participation in both countries is necessary to achieve the levels of cooperation and political legitimacy needed to make such policies sustainable over the long term. Achieving these objectives will require not just cooperation between governments but also the ability to work constructively with domestic stakeholders so that these policies are seen to work for the mutual benefit of citizens and governments alike.

12

"Just a Trade Dispute"?
Proximity and Distance from
Different Perspectives

Canada and the United States enjoy the world's largest bilateral trading relationship. Dispute resolution processes under NAFTA have been relatively successful in resolving most cross-border trade irritants and in depoliticizing these disputes so that they rarely affect broader cross-border economic or political relationships. However, exceptions to this general rule can create political difficulties, reflecting historical Canadian fears of the unilateral exercise of American power.

The number and seriousness of bilateral trade and related commercial disputes have declined in recent years, though certain chronic irritants remain, as noted in Chapter 3. US trade officials express ongoing concerns over Canadian governments' slowness in introducing and securing passage of legislation to implement international agreements expanding protection of intellectual property rights. However, Canada's dependence on American markets substantially increases sensitivities over unilateral US actions to restrict trade or enforce American policy preferences in international economic relations. These risks often take the form of congressional or regulatory pressures, sometimes reinforced by special interest litigation, to limit access to US markets and disrupt existing supply chains for Canadian manufacturing, resource, or agricultural exports.

The declining number of trade disputes often makes Canadian responses to remaining disruptions seem disproportionate to American policy makers. However, public expectations of generally unhindered market access under CUFTA and NAFTA tend to increase political sensitivities associated with remaining conflicts and their effects on Canadian public attitudes toward North American integration.

This chapter reviews the efforts of Canadian officials and societal interests to engage and influence these policies, assesses their relative success, and presents lessons applicable to future policy discussions – particularly as they relate to the potential broadening and deepening of North American integration.

BSE, Food Safety Rules, and Cross-Border Beef and Cattle Trade

The Problem

Protecting public health and safety is a fundamental role of modern governments that encourages preservation of state sovereignty and related regulatory powers. Article XX of GATT includes health and safety among objectives justifying exceptions to general WTO trade rules.[1] However, the growth of agricultural trade and related public health issues from foodborne pathogens increases the challenges of coordination among businesses, consumers, and agencies responsible for protecting public and animal health. These issues raise three major questions. How should governments and different segments of the agrifood sector collaborate to maintain and, when necessary, increase food and animal safety and health standards? How should national agencies respond when they detect potentially significant threats to public or animal health in their own countries or among major trading partners? How should policy makers respond when particular interests attempt to exploit public concerns over food safety to limit foreign competition in domestic markets?

The discovery in 2003 of bovine spongiform encephalopathy (BSE) – "mad cow disease" – first in Canada, then in the United States, brought these questions starkly into focus. It triggered a series of political and legal battles over conditions for resuming trade in cattle and beef (processed cattle meat) products. This case illustrates the open and fragmented character of US political and regulatory processes, the many opportunities for rent seeking by particular interests, and the challenges facing Canadian interests when drawn into the crossfire of American domestic policy processes.

The Background

US and Canadian food supplies are generally perceived to be among the world's safest. However, during the 1990s, the Centers for Disease Control and Prevention estimated that "foodborne diseases cause[d] approximately 76 million illnesses, 325,000 hospitalizations, and 5,000 deaths each year in the United States."[2] Most of these illnesses are of domestic origin, resulting from private or commercial disregard for public health standards or elementary common sense. However, the growth of efficient North American and global distribution systems can allow the distribution of contaminated food across wide areas, with related challenges for its tracing and recall.

BSE is a neurological disease found in cattle. Its spread is thought to result largely from "feeding infected cattle parts back to cattle."[3] The 1986 British BSE epidemic resulted in the destruction of its cattle herd and contamination of cattle around the world. Canada and the United States subsequently closed their borders to cattle imports from any country in which BSE was detected. BSE, in the form of Creutzfeldt-Jacob disease (CJD), can be transmitted to humans by eating contaminated beef, though no North American cases have yet been reported. As of mid-2011, sixteen cases of BSE had been identified in Canada and three in the United States (one imported from Canada).[4]

Sensitivity to BSE also has major economic implications. Cattle and beef production rank second in US and Canadian farm sales. US cattle exports accounted for about 10 percent of production in 2003 but only 3 percent within North America.[5] But Canadian cattle exports to the United States generated nearly 50 percent of its industry sales that year.[6]

The May 2003 detection of BSE in Alberta prompted the US Department of Agriculture (USDA) to close the border to Canadian cattle and beef imports. The border was reopened to selected imports of Canadian beef in September 2003. Responding to Canadian requests, related measures to tighten food chain safety, and pressures from associated American domestic interests, Ann Veneman, the US agriculture secretary, ordered a regulatory review to establish conditions for resuming trade. USDA released an interim rule (regulation) in November 2003 to take effect in January 2004. However, Washington State's subsequent discovery of BSE in an imported Canadian cow frustrated this process.[7]

Most major US export markets closed their borders to American beef, resulting in an 80 percent drop in exports. The United States tabled a revised rule to reopen the border to beef from Canadian cattle over thirty months of age. However, R-CALF, a Montana-based ranchers' group, successfully challenged the rule in a local court in April 2004.[8] Discussions to reopen trade in younger cattle dragged on for months. Regulatory consultations required by US law drew about 4,000 stakeholder responses. Political jockeying included challenges from opponents of the rule, including R-CALF and most western border-state senators, and endorsements from supporters of the rule, including the National Cattlemen's Beef Association and the American Meat Institute. When a final rule reopening the border was tabled in January 2005, R-CALF again obtained a blocking injunction in March. However, the US Court of Appeal threw out this decision in July, allowing for the border's immediate reopening.[9] Japan and South Korea subsequently reopened their borders to US beef exports aged under thirty months in late 2005 and early 2006 – but only after extracting substantial regulatory concessions.

These incidents had major effects on both industries. US and Canadian industry costs between 2003 and 2005 were estimated at $US 5 billion and $C 6-7 billion, with the latter largely offset by taxpayer-funded adjustment programs.[10] Canadian exports recovered slowly between 2005 and 2008, only to drop sharply in 2009 with implementation of new US Country-of-Origin Labeling (COOL) rules.

Influencing American Policies toward Canada

Canadian governments engage US food safety policy makers at three overlapping levels: technical–scientific, administrative, and political. The first level involves the exchange of technical information and scientific knowledge on the causes and detection of, and the relative effectiveness of responses to, particular health hazards. The second level focuses on specific regulatory and administrative measures to translate these ideas into effective policies. And the third level is explicitly political, involving contacts among cabinet and senior administrative officials.

Technical and Administrative Issues

Outbreaks of animal or plant diseases are a significant test for international public health and trade rules. One USDA official whom I interviewed described it as the challenge of distinguishing among "sound science, political science, and pseudo-science."[11] Technical food safety discussions are carried out mainly by administrators and scientists working for Agriculture and Agri-Food Canada, Health Canada, and USDA. "Surveillance, inspection, and enforcement" are the responsibility of the Canadian Food Inspection Agency (CFIA), USDA's Animal and Plant Health Inspection Services (APHIS) for international inspections, USDA's Food Safety Inspection Service (FSIS) for domestic inspections, and, for processed foods, the US Food and Drug Administration (FDA). Other governments and industry organizations are involved through parallel risk management processes: Hazard Assessment and Critical Control Point (HACCP) systems.[12]

These discussions can take place bilaterally, trilaterally, or through the Organization of International Epizootics (OIE), the global standard-setting body for animal health issues.[13] OIE guidelines are "soft laws" formed by the consensus of animal health scientists and the governments to which they report. Officials interviewed described the OIE process as driven primarily by departmental scientists.[14]

The British BSE epidemic prompted Canada, the United States, and other countries to introduce domestic and trade-based countermeasures. By 1991, both countries had banned cattle imports from affected countries and organized surveillance programs to trace potentially infected animals. In 1997, both countries introduced bans on recycling mammalian proteins into cattle feed – a practice used by ranchers and feedlots to encourage weight gain.[15] NAFTA countries developed standards to impose common restrictions on BSE-affected countries. After Canada invoked these standards in 2000 to ban Brazilian beef imports, the United States and Mexico followed suit.[16]

In August 2003, US, Canadian, and Mexican officials met to begin redesigning relevant animal health rules to "reflect the adequacy of a country's safeguards in addressing whatever level of risk is found through a scientifically valid risk assessment."[17] This process responded to both Canadian concerns over US border closings and the potential for BSE in American herds. All three countries planned to shift from total trade bans to risk management–based policies, even before discovering BSE in an American herd. One industry representative commented that "the one-time event signaled to us that we may have a problem in all of North America. We wanted the US to follow OIE, because the way that the US treats other countries will be the way other countries treat us."[18]

US officials confirmed that Canadian officials were in compliance with existing OIE standards by August 2003. However, complex American regulatory processes, political caution, and aggressive litigation by protectionist cattle interests delayed border reopening for almost two years – to the intense financial distress of Canadian cattle ranchers and feedlots. One observer noted that "you had to unwind the precedents you had created between 1989 and 2003. Then we faced this dilemma of being treated as we had treated other countries."[19]

The bilateral process with Canada, the development of a US domestic rule to allow the resumption of cattle trade, and OIE processes continued in parallel for twenty-one months. The final BSE guidelines provided for a graduated set of rules based on relative risk: "negligible," "controlled," and "unknown."[20] During this period, both countries strengthened internal measures to prevent, detect, and combat the potential spread of BSE and worked closely with OIE officials to build international confidence. In July 2004, the USDA passed a "final rule" (regulation) excluding specified risk materials (SRMs) and other cattle material from human food, dietary supplements, and cosmetics. A similar Canadian ban took effect in July 2006.[21] Officials from both countries "worked very closely together," maintaining relations "on a broad spectrum from the working level, to the senior level, to the political level."[22] However, ongoing litigation delayed implementation of the final rule, not allowing border reopening until mid-July 2005.

Both US and Canadian officials explicitly defended the admission of cattle from Canada as "within the limits permitted under OIE guidelines for trading with a country with some BSE" as part of a broader American trade strategy.[23] However, this process was far more intensely contested in the United States than in Canada.

Engaging the American Political System

The cattle industry, including feedlots, has been the largest US agricultural subsector in recent years.[24] The twenty largest cattle-producing states accounted for 82 percent of cattle production in 2000 (see Table 12.1). The dispersion of the cattle and feedlot sectors provides them with substantial political influence in Washington – reflecting the adage that "all politics is local."

Industry representation is divided among meat-packing firms – particularly the American Meat Institute (AMI) and the National Meat Association (NMA); the National Cattlemen's Beef Association (NCBA), whose members include many export-oriented ranchers; and the Ranchers Cattlemen Action Legal Fund – United Stockgrowers of America (R-CALF USA), which largely represents import-competing ranchers.

AMI, whose membership also includes the owners of Canada's largest meat-processing companies, strongly supported immediate border reopening. The NCBA supported a phased reopening, beginning with cattle aged under thirty months – the approach chosen by USDA. R-CALF pursued a comprehensive lobbying and litigation strategy to limit imports – including

TABLE 12.1

Largest US cattle-producing states, 2002, and 2005 Senate vote on reopening border to Canadian cattle imports

State	Percent	Both senators voted to open border	Both senators voted to keep border closed
Texas	16.6	●	
Missouri	6.3	●	
Oklahoma	6.1		●
South Dakota*	5.1		●
Kansas	4.6	●	
Montana*	4.5		●
Kentucky	3.4	●	
Tennessee	3.3	●	
Iowa	3.0		
Florida	2.9	●	
North Dakota*	2.9		●
Arkansas	2.8	●	
Alabama*	2.3		●
California	2.2		●
Wyoming*	2.2		●
Colorado	2.2		
Virginia	2.0	●	
Georgia	1.0	●	
Mississippi	1.7	●	

* States with more cattle than people in the 2000 census.

SOURCES: United States, Department of Agriculture, *U.S. Census of Agriculture 2002*, Table 11 (Washington, DC: US Department of Agriculture, 2004), 327-35, http://www.agcensus.usda.gov; United States Senate, US Senate Roll Call Votes, 109th Congress, 1st Session, S.J. Res. 4, 3 March 2005, http://www.senate.gov/.

passage of restrictive COOL legislation in the 2002 farm bill and comparable state legislation. Their respective strategies reflected both the US cattle and meat industries' growing dependence on export revenues and pressures on smaller producers to compete with rising imports – measures consistently opposed by NCBA.[25]

The integrated nature of North American cattle and beef industries contributed to close cross-border cooperation among major industry stakeholders. One Canadian official commented that "we had natural allies with a common goal and a common interest who were able to bring pressure on the USDA and on the hill."[26] Ironically, the extent of integration might have delayed border reopening because of the need to treat different segments of the industry symmetrically in each country. One Canadian official noted that,

Because a significant number of our cattle were coming down here for processing ... when the first rule came out, it was originally going to have animals under thirty months plus meat (without specified risk materials) over thirty months being allowed into the United States. That would have given our meat-processing industry a huge advantage over the US domestic industry. So they decided to go one step at a time.[27]

The Canadian Embassy's public diplomacy focused on increasing awareness of the border closing's contribution to economic and job losses beyond the beltway, often working closely with US feedlot owners and meat processors. However, the most critical factor aligning the interests of both governments and their respective industries was the decision of the Japanese and South Korean governments to cut off US (and Canadian) cattle and beef export markets.

Secretary of Agriculture Mike Johanns, the governor of Nebraska, a major cattle-feeding state, before his January 2005 appointment, reportedly provided important political leadership for the administration's border-opening policy.[28] Senators of both parties from northern-border cattle states generally opposed reopening the border to Canadian imports, whereas senators from most southern states generally supported its reopening. Senators from states with smaller cattle sectors tended to vote along party lines, with Republicans supporting administration efforts to reopen the border and Democrats opposing them (see Table 12.1).

Congress can use its powers over legislation, appropriation (spending), and regulatory oversight to micromanage just about any form of government operation from which it is not explicitly excluded by the US Constitution. Under the Small Business Regulatory Enforcement Fairness Act of 1996, "major" regulations "cannot take effect for 60 days from publication in the *Federal Register* or presentation to Congress (whichever is later)" to permit congressional review. A joint resolution can veto the rule within sixty legislative days.[29] In March 2005, the Senate voted 52-46 to support a resolution (S.J. Res. 4) disapproving the USDA rule of 4 January. However, the House leadership, strengthened by President Bush's veto threat, declined to take further action.[30] Table 12.2 summarizes the vote by party, region, and state-level exposure to cattle interests.

Evaluation and Lessons Learned
Despite major economic disruption in Canada, the BSE case definitely reflects the tradition of exceptionalism in American policies toward Canada

TABLE 12.2

Vote on closing the border to Canadian cattle, Senate Joint Resolution 4, March 2005

	Yes (keep border closed)			No (approve border-opening rule)		
	Total	Republicans	Democrats	Total	Republicans	Democrats
Top 20 cattle states	17	8	9	23	20	3
Northern	12	4	8	2	2	0
Southern	5	4	1	21	18	3
Other states	35	5	30	23	22	1
Bordering Canada	11	2	9	7	7	0

SOURCES: See Table 12.1; author's calculations.

– even if qualified by the workings of US interest group politics. NAFTA countries developed agricultural trade and related food safety policies even before BSE was discovered. Within three months of the initial incident, officials from all three countries had met to develop a process for resuming trade with "minimal risk" countries. Canada was the primary beneficiary of that policy even before the OIE guidelines came into effect.

The identification and cultivation of close cross-border working relationships with major interest groups with identical or complementary interests were central to eventual border reopening. Similarly, US food industry groups, supported by the Canadian government, were able to defer COOL funding and implementation for almost six years following its initial approval by Congress – mainly by persuading congressional allies to refuse enabling appropriations – though this issue became a major trade irritant, which is still in litigation at the WTO in early 2012.[31]

Significant challenges remain in coordinating or harmonizing food safety rules between the United States and Canada. Kerr and Hobbs suggest that NAFTA and SPP working groups set up to advance this process have been largely ineffective,[32] although improved coordination and mutual recognition of food safety measures are identified as priorities of both the Beyond-the-Border and Regulatory Cooperation Council processes initiated in 2011.[33] Regulatory differences reflect the complexity of the American regulatory system and extensive interagency and industry–government competition in developing and implementing new rules and systems. If

Canada's BSE lobby can be termed an eventual success, the huge cost of this trade disruption suggests that enhancing cross-border cooperation to develop and monitor food safety policies remains critical to reducing future risks to Canadian farmers and food processors.

Softwood Lumber: Power, Dependence, and Interest Group Politics

The Problem

The United States and Canada have engaged in successive disputes over the regulation of trade in softwood lumber since 1982 (Softwood I-IV). Softwood II, which resulted in the negotiation of a managed trade agreement in 1986, was a major impetus for the negotiation of the 1988 Canada–US Free Trade Agreement, which included a dispute resolution process capable of disciplining applications of US trade remedy laws.[34] This case study addresses the eventual resolution and outcomes of Softwood IV (2002-6), the latest round in the long-standing dispute.

The Canada–US softwood lumber dispute reflects the convergence of four different challenges: a long history of competing interests between each country's primary resource producers; the effects of special interest lobbying and litigation on Canadian security of access to US markets; the difficulties of reconciling different national and subnational policy regimes; and the viability of CUFTA and NAFTA dispute resolution processes challenged by systematic litigation.

These debates – particularly over interpretations of trade remedy laws and NAFTA tribunal powers – are fundamental to dominant perspectives of softwood disputes in each country. Special interest litigation has repeatedly prompted governments to negotiate periodic truces embodied in managed trade· agreements.[35] However, such agreements have encouraged challenges to the credibility and even constitutionality of NAFTA's dispute settlement mechanism, fundamentally threatening the most important institutional discipline on protectionist measures.[36]

The Background

Softwood IV was actually the third such dispute to trigger anti-dumping (AD) and countervailing (CVD) duties under US trade remedy laws since the 1980s. Softwood I was dismissed by a 1983 finding that Canadian commercial and regulatory practices did not violate US trade laws. Softwood II resulted in a preliminary Department of Commerce ruling that provincial stumpage fees constituted an illegal subsidy resulting in "injury" to US industries. When the department imposed a preliminary 15 percent duty, the Mulroney government opted to negotiate the first Softwood Lumber Agreement (SLA I) in December 1986, which imposed a similar export tax, subject to revision should provinces change their forest management policies. Allan Gotlieb described SLA I as "bad [but] the least bad for Canada" among prospective alternatives.[37] By the agreement's expiry in December 1991, export taxes had been largely or completely eliminated in Quebec and British Columbia as a result of internal regulatory changes.

Although Ottawa insisted that CUFTA applied to the sector,[38] softwood exports faced continued litigation. These disputes led the Chrétien government to negotiate another agreement, which took effect in May 1996.[39] SLA II, which expired in 2001, allowed for sizable duty-free exports of Canadian lumber to the United States, with a graduated export tax when Canadian exports exceeded that quota. During this period, Canadian exports came to account for about one-third of the American lumber market.[40]

When SLA II expired in 2001, the US lumber industry immediately resorted to litigation (Softwood IV), alleging damages from Canadian imports based on alleged subsidies inherent in the stumpage fees and other forest management policies of six Canadian provinces. The stakes were increased by the 1999 passage of the Byrd Amendment authorizing the payment of AD/CVD duties directly to US industry plaintiffs. Efforts to head off trade remedy actions through high-level negotiations failed as each government was too strongly committed to its industry's negotiating position to accept an out-of-court settlement.[41]

The Canadian industry, supported by federal and provincial governments, challenged what had, by now, become *pro forma* protectionist rulings from the US Department of Commerce on several fronts, including American courts, Chapter 19 dispute resolution panels under NAFTA, and the WTO.

Influencing American Policies toward Canada: Institutional

The Martin government supported direct and industry litigation on several fronts, including a successful multiparty WTO challenge to the Byrd Amendment. Although Congress finally passed legislation rescinding the offending law in December 2005, it delayed implementation until October 2007 – an example of systematic procedural delays as bargaining tactics. In April 2006, the US Court of International Trade ruled that Byrd Amendment remedies violated US law because the former did not specifically refer to Canada and Mexico as required under the US NAFTA Enabling Act.[42]

Protracted litigation under NAFTA's dispute resolution processes resulted in a series of small technical gains for Canada. However, the Department of Commerce sidestepped these rulings, reflecting an entrenched culture of litigation aimed at extracting trade concessions from foreign countries, the political influence of lumber state senators of both parties, and an initial WTO ruling that found that the stumpage policies of British Columbia and other provinces did indeed constitute a countervailing subsidy. The WTO ruling was subsequently overturned on appeal but not until August 2006 – several months after the signing of a Framework Agreement on Softwood Lumber.[43]

Influencing American Policies toward Canada:
Political and Interest Group Factors
The Martin government made the softwood issue a top priority in its dealings with the Bush administration. Canadian diplomats and business interests in Washington used conventional coalition-building strategies, notably working with the US home-building industry to counter domestic lumber industry influence in Congress. Martin became increasingly outspoken in his criticism of American protectionism and the administration's failures to respond to NAFTA panel rulings, describing them as a "breach of faith."[44] This rhetoric, intended to solidify his minority government's image as a defender of Canadian interests, both stirred and exploited public resentment of American tactics in Canada. US lumber producers were also raising the political stakes by challenging the constitutionality of NAFTA's dispute resolution provisions.

The Canadian lumber industry maintained a relatively united front through most of 2005, reflecting favourable outcomes from litigation. Several large BC-based firms responded to higher tariffs by restructuring and consolidating their operations to increase efficiency. US lumber prices were at record levels in 2004, allowing more efficient firms to reap growing sales and profits. The steady rise in the Canadian dollar's US exchange rate, from 62.5 cents in January 2002 to 86.1 cents and trending upward by December 2005, combined with rising costs of litigation increased many producers' openness to the Bush administration's repeated signals that it was open to negotiating a settlement.

However, major Canadian business groups also deplored the increasingly confrontational tone of bilateral relations for creating unnecessary friction. Manufacturing and energy industry associations strongly criticized proposals from individual federal ministers to link the softwood dispute with restrictions on Canadian energy exports or retaliatory tariffs on other US imports that would just raise their production costs.

Ironically, while Martin raised the rhetorical stakes, Canadian trade officials were quietly exploring a negotiated solution, and Ottawa was discussing regulatory changes with provincial governments that would satisfy US negotiators and avoid future legal challenges. The Canadian ambassador, Frank McKenna, and Martin's chief of staff, Tim Murphy, later "confirmed the two sides were within striking distance of a deal" when an election was called in November 2005.[45]

The Softwood Lumber Agreement of 2006

The January 2006 federal election resulted in a new Conservative government under Stephen Harper pledged to deal with several festering cross-border irritants. The newly appointed ambassador, Michael Wilson, described the softwood file as "my top priority bar none, not only because of the hardship it is causing to many Canadians, but also because it is becoming the barometer by which many Canadians view the state of our relations."[46]

Senior Canadian officials echoed this concern in interviews, noting that the softwood issue was both dominating the public face of bilateral relations and distorting domestic attitudes toward NAFTA in both countries. Indeed, the US lumber industry's constitutional challenge to NAFTA's dispute resolution system, while opposed by both governments, threatened to destroy the treaty framework. As Minister of International Trade (later Industry) David Emerson observed, "if you kill the dispute resolution section of NAFTA, you're essentially killing NAFTA because, without dispute resolution and respect for dispute resolution, you don't really have much of an international treaty to protect Canadians."[47] Some observers also suggested that, if legal action succeeded in ending Softwood IV, the US industry was expected to launch even more trade remedy actions – Softwood V.

For the provinces and much of the Canadian lumber industry, rising exchange rates and the accumulation of duties paid risked diminishing returns from further litigation. Although near-record prices prevailing in early 2005 (see Figure 12.1) allowed larger BC firms to export profitably, many other companies found themselves in growing financial difficulties.

For Harper himself, coming to an agreement meant "tak[ing] the subject off the table, in the sense that the American president and the Canadian prime minister can now talk about other subjects. In recent years, every

TABLE 12.3
The 2006 Softwood Lumber Agreement's export tax options

Price per thousand board feet	Option A Export charge (%)	Option B Export charge plus volume restraint
Over $US 355	0	0
$US 336-55	5	2.5% + regional share of 34% of US consumption
$US 316-55	10	3% + regional share of 32% of US consumption
$US 315 or under	15	5% + regional share of 30% of US consumption

SOURCE: Canada, Foreign Affairs and International Trade Canada, and United States, Office of US Trade Representative, *Softwood Lumber Agreement between the Government of Canada and the Government of the United States of America* (Ottawa and Washington: DFAIT and USTR, 2006), 8.

time they met the conversation was dominated by softwood lumber to the detriment of reaching any other discussion."[48] Consulting closely with the three largest lumber-exporting provinces, British Columbia, Ontario, and Quebec, the government announced the principles for a framework agreement with the United States in April 2006. It provided provinces with the choice between two export tax regimes, one with duty-free trade when US benchmark prices exceeded $355 per 1,000 cubic feet, the other a mixture of lower tax rates and regional quotas to accommodate different economic conditions facing regional industries (see Table 12.3). This figure was comfortably below the cyclical peaks in lumber prices reached in 1997-99 under SLA II and during the more recent cyclical peak of 2004-5 (see Figure 12.1).

Ottawa would expedite reimbursement of more than 80 percent of the $US 5.3 billion in duties previously collected to companies that terminated legal actions against the US government and signed the agreement. The balance – about $US 1 billion – would be split between a mix of "community initiatives" and a controversial $500 million "signing bonus" to the US lumber industry. In return, the agreement offered seven years of relative regulatory (if not market) stability.[49]

The Canadian industry was deeply divided over the proposed agreement. Several large firms supported the deal. Others were sharply critical – either because they had hoped to win legal vindication (and larger financial settlements) in the courts, or because they objected in principle to

FIGURE 12.1
Softwood lumber prices, 1996-2006

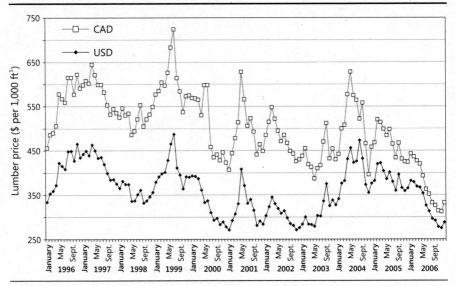

SOURCES: Random Lengths: Information Services for the Forest Industry, http://www.randomlengths.com/; North American Homebuilders Association, http://www.nahb.com/; author's calculations.

FIGURE 12.2
Softwood lumber prices under SLA III, 2007-11

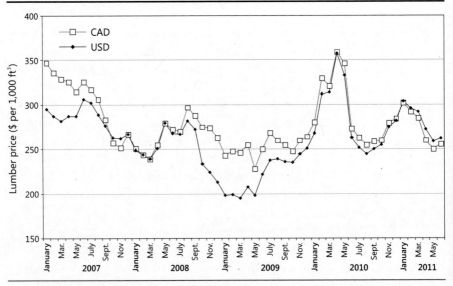

SOURCES: Random Lengths: Information Services for the Forest Industry, http://www.randomlengths.com/; North American Homebuilders Association, http://www.nahb.com/; author's calculations.

another SLA as an unnecessary concession to US protectionism and a substitution of power politics for NAFTA's dispute resolution rules. Others argued that market share restrictions in provinces opting for the lower export tax rate would artificially restrict their growth.

The "final" agreement (SLA III), announced in July 2006, spelled out the complex process for defining and implementing the export tax regime. Although consistent with the framework agreement, it prompted threats of a full-scale retreat by the three largest provinces and much of the Canadian industry. The federal government argued that the deal represented a significant improvement on previous managed trade agreements: (1) ensuring duty-free market access, except for "surge protection" measures, when lumber prices were over $355 – as they had been for twenty-six of the thirty months prior to signing of the "final" agreement; (2) confirming an arm's-length provision for binding arbitration through the London Court of International Arbitration (LCIA), which it argued would provide stronger protection than NAFTA against legal harassment; (3) providing a process for negotiating "policy exits" to limit future trade harassment; (4) recognizing British Columbia's new forest management regime, as requested by the provincial government; and (5) providing relative stability through a seven-year agreement. Implementation of the agreement would require letters of agreement by companies whose claims against the US government totalled 95 percent of the tariffs under dispute.[50]

Ottawa also argued that the agreement, which had involved concessions on both sides, was the best deal that could be negotiated under current circumstances and that the United States was most unlikely to come back to the negotiating table. Minister of International Trade David Emerson also noted that Ottawa would terminate its subsidies for legal actions by Canadian lumber firms in the United States.

Much of the industry criticized perceived defects in the agreement. The opposition parties, especially the federal Liberals and NDP, loudly attacked SLA III as a sellout of Canadian interests. Critics argued that gains from greater regulatory stability didn't compensate for the $1 billion in duties retained by the Americans. However, falling US housing prices signalled a declining demand for Canadian lumber exports – placing many Canadian firms at risk of rising financial losses whether or not SLA III was in place.[51] Thousands of layoffs[52] in Quebec's relatively inefficient forest industry in 2006 reinforced such perceptions, prompting that province's industry to extend reluctant support to the agreement and enabling Bloc Québécois MPs to ensure its passage through a minority Parliament.

Policy Outcomes

SLA III was formally signed in September 2006 and implemented the following month. US trade representative Susan Schwab made a few technical adjustments in response to Canadian requests, enabling the BC government and forest industry to save face in endorsing it.[53] US housing prices, new home construction, and lumber prices dropped sharply during the following year – a slump that became a crisis with the US and global financial panic in 2008-9. Average lumber prices dropped from $US 379 ($C 453) in the twelve months before the framework agreement's signing to $US 240 ($C 268) during the same period in 2008-9 (see Figure 12.2), with prices averaging $US 276 ($C 280) in 2010 and 2011. The overhang of home foreclosures forced many Canadian firms to look for growth in other foreign markets, especially China. Some Canadian firms have also expanded their US holdings, pointing to the potential for greater cross-border integration that has reduced the intensity of trade disputes in other sectors.

In December 2006, the Federal Court of Appeal in Washington threw out the US lumber industry's constitutional challenge to NAFTA's dispute resolution processes as outside its jurisdiction, based on SLA III's effect on cancelling the NAFTA panel rulings that had prompted the industry's challenge.[54] The agreement experienced "teething pains" in 2007, including litigation arising from provincial measures assisting industry restructuring amid changing markets.[55] Four disputes have been referred to the LCIA arbitration panel. A 2008 ruling confirmed British Columbia's and Alberta's exemption from volume-based limits applying to Ontario and Quebec producers. A 2009 ruling confirmed that Ottawa had miscalculated export quotas, triggering a supplementary tax. A ruling in early 2011 held that certain Ontario and Quebec industry assistance programs failed to comply with the agreement, triggering additional 0.1 and 2.6 percent surcharges, respectively.[56] A dispute over British Columbia's program to salvage pine beetle–damaged trees remains in litigation in early 2012.

Evaluation and Lessons Learned

The softwood lumber dispute demonstrates the capacity of a well-organized, well-funded industry with significant congressional support to capture American regulatory processes and to drag out litigation almost indefinitely. In some ways, US treatment of Canada on the softwood issue is comparable to that of other major countries in defending selected import-competing industries: attempting to exploit and prolong trade remedy litigation to force trading partners to agree to terms of market access less favourable than those available under existing trade agreements. (The European Union has used similar practices in failing to implement WTO rulings on some disputes.)[57]

Canada's resort to three separate legal processes – NAFTA's Chapter 19, the US Court of International Trade, and WTO dispute resolution – opened the door to conflicting rulings, given differences in relevant legal standards, though Canada's position was largely vindicated in all three venues. However, authoritative rulings in the latter two cases came after Canada's federal government had already made a clear commitment to negotiate a new managed trade agreement, effectively negating their outcomes.

Under normal circumstances, SLA III (as with most "voluntary export restraint" agreements) would have allowed more efficient Canadian exporters to share in the benefits of higher lumber prices – if at the expense of American consumers. The prolonged collapse of US housing markets has led the industry and the BC government to the diversification of exports to China and other Asian markets, with some success by 2010-11.

Under such circumstances, it is difficult to determine whether SLA III represents a defeat for broader Canadian trade policies or a pragmatic adaptation to strategic litigation and a cyclical decline in Canada's terms of trade in forest products. The agreement has contributed to ongoing industry restructuring, reinforcing changes dictated by prevailing market conditions. Provincial adjustment programs have been constrained to varying degrees, though some environmental groups argue that this might have contributed to more sustainable forest practices.[58]

However, protracted trade litigation involving primary industries with limited firm-level cross-border operations, even under the latest agreement, suggests that Canadian forest sector firms might find it more productive in the long term to acquire and restructure US forest industry assets while expanding overseas markets. Over time, this strategy could help to blunt two major elements in US lumber industry strategy: the pursuit of managed trade agreements to extract a larger share of profits from existing markets,[59] and the capacity to exploit foreign-owned US producers' relatively limited market share to extract protectionist policies from Congress.

Perhaps the greatest test of managed trade in softwood lumber will be the willingness of Canadian provincial governments to renew SLA III upon its expiry in 2015, following its short-term extension by the two governments early in 2012, rather than reverting to the trench warfare of trade litigation. Although media reports suggest the likelihood that both governments will announce a decision to renew the in 2012, current political and economic conditions make such calculations uncertain at best.

Buy American: A Case Study in Reciprocity

The Problem
In February 2009, the US Congress passed stimulus legislation that committed almost $800 billion to spending and tax measures intended to promote recovery from the 2008-9 recession. Section 1605 of the American Recovery and Reinvestment Act of 2009 (ARRA) mandated that all iron, steel, and manufactured goods used in public works projects funded under the act be "produced in the United States."[60] ARRA imposed a 25 percent price differential for foreign goods to be considered in stimulus-funded projects.[61] However, unlike similar measures in 2002, neither Canada nor Mexico received NAFTA exemptions. Although viewed as a relatively minor trade dispute in Washington, Buy American legislation became 2009's biggest controversy in bilateral relations.

Although there is only anecdotal evidence of the economic impact of the Buy American strategy, Canadian businesses and governments perceived its extension as a precedent for future protectionist measures that could disrupt their access to US markets and supply chains. It panicked Canadian business groups already struggling with the recession and the effects of exchange rate shifts on their competitiveness, as more than half of Canadian-produced manufactured goods were being exported to the United States.

American policy analysts, while divided along broader ideological and interest-based perspectives, were more likely to view Buy American in the context of either broader structural problems facing the US economy or gaps in trade agreements that provided foreign-based firms with relatively greater access to US markets than their governments conceded to American firms.

The Background
The Buy American concept was not new for US government procurement: the purchase of goods and services for use by governments. Congress passed a Buy American Act in 1933, though allowing the president to waive its application if deemed in the national interest. The Buy America Act of 1982 mandated domestic preferences for mass-transit–related procurement. Such legislation is more common in state and local politics. Thirty-nine states have some form of domestic procurement preferences.[62]

FIGURE 12.3
American states not subscribing to the WTO Government Procurement
Agreement

Alabama	Nevada	North Carolina	South Carolina
Alaska	New Jersey	North Dakota	Virginia
Georgia	New Mexico	Ohio	West Virginia
Indiana			

Historically, trade treaties such as CUFTA and NAFTA have been designed to address tariff, regulatory, and other national policies that can create artificial barriers to the exchange of goods and services. These agreements established rules governing reciprocal access by businesses based in one country to federal government procurement in the other – subject to certain restrictions related to national security and other specified exemptions. Former trade negotiator Bill Dymond notes that, though NAFTA negotiations addressed the possible elimination of subnational procurement restrictions, American negotiators argued that Canadian provincial procurement markets were not large enough to warrant more than a modest easing of existing restrictions.[63]

The US government has generally been slow to bind the purchasing activities of local governments, preferring to provide fiscal or regulatory incentives on issues of overriding national importance. In Canada, the federal government can negotiate international economic treaties, but its power to implement or enforce them in areas of provincial jurisdiction is limited by past court rulings.

The Uruguay Round of 1995 included a limited procurement agreement signed by the United States, Canada, the European Community, Japan, and eight other countries, subsequently including China. The plurilateral Agreement on Government Procurement (GPA), which took effect in 1996, contained provisions for subnational governments (e.g., states, provinces, and municipalities) to open their markets to foreign vendors of goods and services in return for reciprocal access for businesses based in other signatory countries. These rules applied to contracts valued above specified thresholds with special rules for purchases of construction and other services by entities, including designated public utilities, subnational governments, and/or government business enterprises.[64] Eighty-two Canadian and seventy-nine US government departments and agencies were listed under the agreement, with comparable thresholds for market access. Figure 12.3 lists the thirteen US states that have not ratified the agreement.

Domestic Politics and Interest Group Pressures

The Harper government's response to Buy American was complicated by cross-cutting pressures from domestic interest groups, including municipal governments. The strongest pressures facing Canadian governments to challenge the Buy American provisions came from Canadian manufacturers. Some Canadian firms reported previously sold goods being torn out of stimulus-funded construction projects and other disruptions of existing supply chains.[65] Some groups, including major unions and the Federation of Canadian Municipalities, urged the imposition of similar Buy Canadian measures, with exemptions for countries allowing reciprocal access to government procurement.[66] Others suggested that Ottawa should exercise its constitutional powers over trade and commerce to override provincial procurement preferences – even at the risk of overruling a century of judicial precedents.[67]

Instead, Minister of International Trade Stockwell Day approached provincial governments to seek their support for a reciprocal agreement on subnational procurement involving provincial ratification of the GPA in June 2009. This approach recognized the traditional US bias toward reciprocity and the challenge of securing legislative changes from a protectionist majority in Congress. It also enabled Ottawa to engage provinces in pending trade discussions with the European Union; EU officials were demanding access to provincial markets as a key factor in these talks.[68] Ultimately, all provinces responded favourably, though some demanded sectoral exemptions similar to those of some US states.[69]

Influencing American Policies toward Canada: Political and Interest Group Factors

Organized labour, especially the United Steelworkers, has long been the most vocal proponent of expanded Buy American legislation. Business groups were (and are) divided between those whose interests are primarily domestic and those with broader international or cross-border interests, including the US Chamber of Commerce and the National Association of Manufacturers.[70] The enormous US federal budget deficit – which ultimately reached $1.27 trillion in 2009-10 – and chronic goods trade deficits, which averaged $816 billion annually between 2005 and 2008, reinforced congressional reluctance to borrow heavily to fight the recession without some restrictions on offshore purchases. However, as with most major bilateral issues, Buy American was peripheral to broader US political debates.

President Obama distanced himself, rhetorically at least, from the more strident protectionist voices in Congress. However, his overloaded domestic agenda limited his ability or willingness to invest political capital in issues marginal to the priorities of his party's congressional leadership. These realities structured negotiations with Canada, limiting practical options to those that could be pursued within existing executive powers without reference to Congress.

Although Prime Minister Harper made Buy American a major focus of the NAFTA summit in August 2009 and his subsequent bilateral visit to the White House, President Obama downplayed the issue. Some administration officials suggested that the Canadians were overreacting.[71] However, the president subsequently appointed a special negotiator, Stuart Eisenstat, to meet with Don Stephenson, the Canadian associate deputy minister of trade, to resolve the issue.

The Agreement

Negotiations over the proposed agreement addressed four major issues: (1) Canadian access on a most-favoured-nation basis to subnational procurement contracts under Section 1605(a) of ARRA; (2) ongoing access by US-based firms to Canadian subnational procurement markets under the WTO Government Procurement Agreement; (3) creation of an executive branch process to address future American legislation that might restrict Canadian access to US markets; and (4) alignment of the terms of the proposed agreement with existing Canadian provincial and territorial commitments under Canada's recently expanded Agreement on Internal Trade (AIT).

The two governments announced the draft agreement in February 2010.[72] US trade representative Ron Kirk somewhat hyperbolically characterized the agreement as opening up market access to US firms pursued "for years," while the Harper government emphasized its success in "standing up for Canadian businesses and workers."[73] However, though the agreement addressed each country's short-term agenda by negotiating reciprocal access provisions, its outcomes in other areas were essentially symbolic. The US government was to "take the necessary administrative steps" to exclude "Canadian iron, steel, or manufactured goods in procurement covered by Annex 2 of the 1994 GPA" from ARRA's restrictive Buy American

provisions.[74] Both countries agreed to provide access to construction services purchased by subnational governments under the GPA for a period of
twenty months – the period anticipated for the continued roll-out of such
projects under the 2009 US stimulus bill, subject to extension by mutual
agreement.

Canada committed, on behalf of its provincial and territorial governments, to adhere to Articles I to XXI of the WTO Government Procurement
Agreement of 2007, subject to a specified list of exemptions submitted by
individual governments. Each province agreed to establish domestic arm's-
length dispute resolution mechanisms for disputes with US suppliers, comparable to NAFTA's existing provisions. Agency-specific exclusions
paralleled existing US state-level exemptions from the GPA. Most provinces
exempted their MUSH (municipalities, postsecondary, schools, and hospi-
tals) sectors. In addition, five provinces and two territories claimed "regional
development" exemptions comparable to those in the AIT. These provisions
were paralleled by US exemptions for small business and minority-owned
business set-asides as well as access to government assistance programs.

Both countries agreed to ongoing consultations on disputed interpretations of the agreement and to "enter into discussions to explore an agreement that would expand, on a reciprocal basis, commitments with regard to
market access for government procurement."[75]

Evaluation and Lessons Learned

The Buy American case study demonstrates the continued influence of protectionist interests in the American political system and the challenges of
securing significant changes to legislation after its passage by Congress.
The Canadian government's reaction to the Buy American Act of 2009 ultimately succeeded in securing high-level negotiations from the Obama
administration despite the president's earlier reluctance. The administration's willingness to negotiate in good faith can be seen from the Harper
government's ability to secure an agreement after only five months of negotiations on terms fairly close to Canada's original offer.

Politicians in both countries might have overstated the importance of the
bilateral procurement agreement of February 2010. Most contracts under
the stimulus bill had already been tendered. Ottawa had long promoted the
idea of more open provincial procurement processes in its efforts to liberal-
ize trade policies. Business groups were generally enthusiastic, while union
leaders and nationalists were generally critical, suggesting that Canada had
short-changed local suppliers in return for minimal long-term gains.[76]

The president's decision to include Buy American provisions in a "jobs bill" submitted to Congress in September 2011[77] demonstrated the fragility of the administration's commitment to its agreement with Canada, although most elements of the bill were derailed by partisan and procedural jockeying. It also demonstrated the capacity of the Harper government to avoid responding publicly to what previous governments might have viewed as a provocation while persevering with negotiations toward improved coordination of border management and increased regulatory cooperation.

The longer-term value of the procurement agreement is uncertain at best, whatever its value as an incremental step toward more open trade and the protection of cross-border supply chains. The progress of negotiations on border and regulatory cooperation measures in a pre-election year suggests that cross-border collaboration is possible on issues with limited political visibility and strong stakeholder support in Washington. However, such cooperation remains vulnerable to the willingness of key American interest groups to politicize cross-border issues for domestic political purposes, which was particularly apparent during the Bush administration.

Conclusion

The case studies in this chapter demonstrate the diversity both of American policies toward Canada and of the strategic and tactical responses of Canadian policy makers to influence these evolving policies. Traditional diplomacy – bilateral state-to-state discussions or negotiations carried out by authoritative actors subject to direct high-level political control – remains relevant to the extent that trade disputes become politicized. However, persistent differences in power and the relative importance of each country to the other's economic well-being lend themselves more to managing policy differences based on a mixture of governmental autonomy, reciprocity, and "national treatment" of one another's citizens than to the elusive pursuit of comprehensive political or regulatory solutions. So do the political realities of trade policies as two-level games. Diplomatic strategies to avoid or manage trade disputes under such circumstances tend to be decentralized and situational – or dependent on the circumstances of particular cases, as demonstrated by the case studies in this chapter.

Border restrictions imposed in response to the discovery of BSE in Canada in 2003 were ultimately resolved through cross-border regulatory cooperation. However, the two-year process to reopen the border to

Canadian cattle exports demonstrated both the complexities of the American regulatory system (poorly understood by Canadians) and the risks to Canadian producers from special interest politics and aggressive trade litigation.

The huge costs of border-closing measures to producers, processors, and taxpayers demonstrate the importance of *proactive and cooperative* approaches to food safety. Although subsequent bilateral agreements on managing borders when public health emergencies occur have addressed some of these concerns, ongoing negotiations over a Canada–US security perimeter provide a potential venue for additional cooperation – if one that could benefit from much greater transparency. However, the growth of global food supply chains, each with its related concerns over food and animal health safety, demonstrates the extent to which managing these issues within North America has become interdependent with broader (and more diverse) international approaches to health, safety, related environmental issues, and barriers to trade.

The softwood lumber case reflects both the politics of clientelism in US lumber interests' successful efforts to externalize the costs of structural adjustments to changing markets and cyclical downturns in market prices. It also reflects the proclivity of larger economic powers to engage in strategic trade policy games in responding to declining terms of trade and rising trade deficits. Unlike the European Union, China, or Japan, which are large and insular enough to engage in comparable tactics with relative impunity, Canada's continuing dependence on US export markets makes it necessary to work within institutionalized, rules-based approaches to dispute resolution – even if leading to suboptimal outcomes, as with the current Softwood Lumber Agreement.

Canada's success in negotiating a subnational procurement agreement with the United States also demonstrates the extent to which North American trade issues are increasingly linked with broader trade and investment relationships in which expectations of reciprocity extend beyond North America. Adherence to the WTO's Government Procurement Agreement provided a face-saving way for both US and Canadian negotiators to resolve the 2009-10 Buy American dispute to mutual advantage. It also provided a possible framework in which to address similar issues that have emerged in ongoing trade talks between Canada and the European Union. However, without provisions for congressional ratification, the Canada–US procurement agreement remains essentially a temporary fix that will require further negotiations to avoid similar disputes in the future.

The diverse nature of US policies toward Canada shapes the policy tools used and the strategic approaches taken by Canadian policy makers to influence their development and evolution. Regional and interest group conflicts within the United States create openings for complementary cross-border interests to exercise some degree of influence in Congress. Ideologically based challenges to US national interests are likely to trigger a corresponding American response – one unlikely to be conducive to Canadian interests. The realities of "intermesticity" in both countries suggest that the effectiveness of Canadian efforts to influence American policies toward Canada depends on a combination of engagement and mobilization that reflects the blurring of traditional distinctions between domestic and international economic policy processes.

Depending on the political salience in each country of the policies in question, Canadian initiatives can be strategic, sectoral, and tactical or reactive. The sustained pursuit of strategic approaches depends on governments in both countries perceiving sufficient gains from negotiations to justify investment of the necessary political and bureaucratic resources – and the related management of domestic political trade-offs.

Sectoral initiatives are more likely to depend on the existence of shared or complementary interests on both sides of the border that outweigh the relative influence of import-competing interests. These cross-border coalitions were critical to the resolution of the BSE and Buy American case studies but have not succeeded in overcoming entrenched conflicts between competing primary producers in ongoing disputes over forest industry restructuring and country-of-origin labelling.

Without broad political support for more strategic or comprehensive sectoral strategies in both countries, the tactical or reactive approach that has become the stock-in-trade of Canadian diplomats will remain the default option in managing bilateral trade relations. The openness of the American political process to competing interests and the diverse bilateral or "intermestic" issues that emerge from these processes suggest that there is no substitute for persistent diplomacy and cross-border coalition building when engaging the American political system. Particular issues can be resolved on a piecemeal or sectoral basis; however, as Dyment has argued, the overall economic relationship is viewed more realistically as an evolving series of challenges to be managed, not a problem to which there is a solution.[78]

13

Shared Energy, Shared Energies?

Engaging American Energy Policies

Energy and related environmental policies can be viewed as a proxy for the broader Canada–US relationship. Bilateral energy relationships have been complementary but asymmetrical since the late 1980s. The United States is the world's largest net importer of oil and, until recently, natural gas. Canada is a major energy exporter, reliant on export markets for the development of large-scale projects, but one almost entirely dependent on US export markets, at least until pipeline capacity is expanded to facilitate exports through west coast ports. The two countries' energy markets are interwoven and interdependent, with firms from each country having extensive investments in the other. However, energy markets and trade are highly segmented, with major and growing differences between different energy subsectors – especially oil, natural gas, and electricity generation and transmission.

This segmentation is reinforced by major internal geographic differences in energy endowments – a reality that requires the balancing of regional interests in both countries and that limits the capacity of their central governments to pursue coherent energy and related environmental policies. Last but not least, the environmental effects of energy development and distribution have prompted the growth of domestic and cross-border societal networks that help to shape the context for energy development and trade. These networks both reinforce and provide a counterweight to greater economic integration. As a result, the politics of energy and related environmental issues in the United States are primarily domestic in character, and there is a strong North American influence on Canadian policies mediated by the cross-cutting effects of decentralized federal structures.[1]

These factors ensure that the bilateral politics of energy and related environmental issues consistently engage all three dimensions of the Canada–US relationship. Its political–strategic dimension is largely shaped by American dependence on imports for 49 percent of annual US oil consumption (2010) and 12 percent of natural gas usage (2010)[2] – although both figures have declined significantly in recent years. These realities, which have been reinforced since 2000 by resource nationalism and state-owned or -controlled energy firms' control of more than 80 percent of global oil and natural gas reserves,[3] make Canadian energy imports central to American energy security. Similarly, cross-border interconnections between electricity distribution networks create vulnerabilities to widespread power outages resulting from acts of nature, technical factors, human error, or deliberate sabotage.

The trade–commercial dimension of the energy relationship is enormous. Canada is the largest American supplier of net US crude oil imports (21.5 percent in 2010); more than the next two suppliers, Mexico and Saudi Arabia combined, 88 percent of net US natural gas imports, and uranium.[4] The scale of Canadian oil sands exports – about 50 percent of Canadian oil production – has had the effect of reducing overall US oil prices, creating a growing gap between US and global price benchmarks.[5] Oil, gas, and pipeline firms based in both countries have extensive North America–wide operations, reinforced by broader trends toward joint ventures on major projects that have created a deeply integrated North American industry. The rising trend in global oil prices, driven primarily by continuing supply constraints and growing demand in developing countries, has contributed greatly to chronic US trade deficits, the US dollar's gradual decline against many other currencies (including Canada's), and the erosion of Canadian manufacturers' competitiveness in US export markets. Although these factors might ultimately result in the "peaking" of global oil production, as suggested by some analysts, they are expected to generate significantly higher energy costs in coming years, increasing pressures for the substitution of energy sources. These realities also affect broader patterns of North American trade. Regional interconnections in electricity distribution, though not as pronounced in absolute terms, have contributed to greater interdependence in that dimension of energy policies.

TABLE 13.1
Canada's energy production in the global context, 2009

	Rank	Percentage of world total
Crude oil production	7	3.9
Natural gas	3	5.6
Hydroelectric power	3	11.7
Natural uranium	2	22.0
Crude oil reserves	2*	

* 178 billion barrels.
SOURCE: Canada, House of Commons, "Attention Canada: Towards a Canadian Sustainable Energy Strategy: A Discussion Paper," seventh report of the Standing Senate Committee on Energy, Environment, and Natural Resources (Ottawa: House of Commons, 2010), 4.

The psychological–cultural dimension of energy and related environmental relationships is just as complex and variable. NAFTA's "proportionality" clause, which limits Canada's capacity to restrict energy exports in the event of supply shortages to the proportion of Canadian production previously shipped to the United States, was as much a by-product of the desire of Canada's energy-producing provinces to restrict Ottawa's power to interfere with future export contracts as of US concerns over energy security – whatever the discomfort it might have caused some Canadian nationalists. The restructuring of Canada's energy sector since the 1980s has seen the emergence of several large, internationally competitive Canadian firms, reduced the relative prominence of American firms, and attracted substantial overseas investment – notably from France, China, and Korea.[6] These factors have reduced the centrality of resource nationalism in Canadian policy debates, though some analysts question Canada's current dependence on energy and other resource exports on both political and economic grounds.[7] Canada might not be the energy superpower touted by the Harper government – even if it ranked third and seventh in global gas and oil production, respectively, in 2009 (see Table 13.1). However, the relative dependence of Canadian governments on direct and indirect revenues from energy (and other resource) development has contributed to the substantial realignment of federal interests with those of major energy-producing provinces. The Canadian Energy Research Institute suggests that the oil and gas sector's contribution to Canadian GDP is expected to rise from 11 percent in 2010 to nearly 15 percent in 2020 and generate as many as 540,000 new jobs – about 44 percent of them outside Alberta.[8] As a result, both federal Conservatives and Liberals have favoured the industry's continued growth, supporting domestic energy interests as a major element of Canadian policy advocacy in the United States.[9]

These realities increase the visibility and vulnerability of Canadian interests in the partisan and ideological crossfires of American domestic politics. The distributed nature of American energy and environmental policy making provides multiple opportunities for economic and societal interest groups to influence the design and implementation of federal, state, and local policies. Canadian concerns might be at the margins of American policy debates, but these debates directly affect Canadian policy makers and interest groups, especially given the multiple opportunities for citizen and interest group participation. Conversely, cross-border alliances have emerged in which US environmental interests directly attempt to influence Canadian public opinion and Canadian government policies, using many of the same coalition-building tactics as Canadian economic interests in attempting to protect and advance their interests in Washington and in US regional- or state-level policy making.[10] The extensive (if asymmetrical) and overlapping jurisdictions of state and provincial governments on energy and environmental issues add yet another dimension, reflected in both the institutionalization of cross-border regional networks and the efforts of provincial governments to project their interests and influence in the United States.

This chapter explores the evolution of North American energy integration since the 1990s and the growing interaction of energy and environmental policies. It examines Canadian efforts to influence American policies toward Canada at four main levels: interaction between the executive branches of the two central governments, Canadian engagement with Congress, the networking activities of Canadian energy interests in Washington, and the growing activity of provincial governments in developing their own networks of influence in the United States. Finally, the chapter assesses the major factors that will shape the evolution of bilateral energy and related environmental policy relations in coming years and their implications for Canadian policies and priorities.

Energy Policies: The Scope of Play

> *For many decades now, the United States has been without an energy policy ... The American people continue to demand*

plentiful and cheap energy without sacrifice or inconvenience.
But emerging technologies are not yet commercially viable to
fill shortages and will not be for some time.

– Edward Djerejian and Leslie Gelb, "Foreword," 2001[11]

The energy policy processes of American governments are highly fragmented. This reality reflects the shifting collage of federal departments and agencies that share jurisdiction over various aspects of energy policy – even before environmental issues, the role of Congress, the activities of state and local governments, and the role of the courts in adjudicating disputes are taken into consideration. They are further reinforced by the multiple market and geographical contexts for the extraction, production, refining, and distribution of diverse energy resources that, along with various citizen and interest group pressures, frame the bottom-up dimensions of policy making.

A 2001 Council on Foreign Relations report, quoted above, suggests that the United States has lacked a national energy policy over the long term. This statement, which could also apply to Canada, was and remains true in the sense that there is no overarching strategic US government policy that defines overall objectives or manages internal and external trade-offs. The latter include combining relative security and affordability of supply, adaptation to changing global conditions, and public expectations for the preservation and enhancement of environmental quality.

Other observers suggest that, despite this formal absence, US energy policies since the 1970s have been characterized by five major themes:

increasing and diversifying sources of conventional and non-conventional energy supplies, both at home and abroad; encouraging ... the adoption of improvements in conservation and fuel efficiency; establishing and expanding the Strategic Petroleum Reserve (SPR); ... ensuring that critical infrastructure remain secure and transit routes for international energy shipments remain open; and reliance on Saudi Arabia to balance oil markets and moderate prices.[12]

Arguably, both positions have been broadly true under the Bush and Obama administrations since 2001. The development and distribution of most American energy sources remain largely market-driven, despite extensive subsidies for the development of new energy sources and technologies and ongoing debates over the mix of pricing and regulatory measures appropriate to pursuing assorted environmental policy goals. Policy development remains intensely contested, sometimes within the executive branch, but more consistently within the decentralized committee systems of Congress, since the effects of interest group competition have been magnified by partisan and ideological combat. In some cases, particularly for climate change and other environmental issues, state governments have attempted to fill the resulting gaps in policy development. In others, incremental policy development is punctuated by a mixture of partisan gridlock and trench warfare on strategic policy issues and guerrilla tactics in using legislative and appropriation processes to lay down "markers" for future policy development.

The practical effects of congressional gridlock and incremental regulatory changes within the executive branch are that market-driven factors have substantially outpaced formal policy shifts in driving policy change. Although the United States remains self-sufficient in most forms of energy, growing dependence on oil and, increasingly, natural gas imports made *energy security* a major national issue under the Bush administration. Rapid increases in global energy consumption between 2000 and 2008, especially in developing economies, outpaced the growth of supplies. These trends contributed to the escalation of global oil prices and projections that looming natural gas shortages would require major new infrastructure developments to facilitate large-scale liquid natural gas (LNG) imports. But rising prices and looming shortages also prompted the development of new technologies that enabled large-scale production of shale gas within North America beginning in 2006 – pushing the prospect of significant LNG imports well into the future.

The rapid escalation in imported oil prices from an average $US 22 per barrel in 2001, to $36 in 2004, to $59 in 2006, and to $92 in 2008[13] (peaking above $127 in July 2008) gave a strong impetus to the rapid development of Alberta's oil sands. Combined with the effects of the 2008-9 recession and lingering high unemployment, it has also reinforced resistance to higher energy taxes among American consumers – derailing congressional Democrats' efforts to pass cap-and-trade legislation in 2009-10[14] and precluding the emergence of an international consensus on measures to address climate change issues.

Persistent concerns over energy security, combined with environmental barriers to developing new refinery capacity, have made it easier to adapt Gulf refineries to process Canadian bitumen shipments and to build new pipeline capacity to carry Canadian oil to Oklahoma and the Gulf Coast than to convert existing infrastructure to other energy sources, as suggested by various policy entrepreneurs. Although Congress has expanded alternative energy subsidies, much the same can be said for the continued dependence of many midwestern and southern US states on coal-fired electricity generation rather than increased reliance on nuclear power (or various "renewable" sources), as suggested by many advocacy groups.

Taken together, these trends have resulted in most aspects of Canada–US energy and environmental policy relations becoming subsets of US domestic politics and policies to a greater degree than was previously the case. They include at least four of the five types of bilateral policy relations discussed in previous chapters. US strategic energy policies tend to treat Canada as an allied nation if not one whose energy resources are a de facto extension of US domestic resources. The Department of State's policies for authorizing cross-border pipelines, though implemented on a case-by-case basis, sometimes display characteristics of exceptionalism, as do policies governing reliability standards for domestic and cross-border electrical grids. Selected congressional measures with the potential to affect cross-border energy trade tend to treat Canada as a dependent or satellite nation, as do the political tactics of some American interest groups. Periodically, Canadian diplomats must also scramble to avoid the effects of policy inadvertence since congressional actors forget or ignore the extent of bilateral energy interdependence.

The broad outlines of Canadian policies have continued to follow US policy trends, as with gradual shifts toward the deregulation of markets for natural gas and oil in the 1980s[15] and regulatory changes prompting greater openness to market forces in electricity generation and distribution during the 1990s.[16] Broader trends toward economic integration, which reinforced the integration of energy markets during the 1990s, have encouraged Canadian governments to pursue parallel or complementary energy and environmental policies in many areas.[17]

However, growing US dependence on Canadian imports has also made Canada increasingly vulnerable to American domestic political conflicts over the interaction between environmental and energy policies – as demonstrated by the raucous debate over the Keystone XL pipeline in 2010-11. These debates have very different effects on Canadian engagement with the policy processes of the executive branch, Congress, and state governments – focused as they are on influencing American policies toward Canada.

Engaging the Executive Branch

> *We did discuss the matter you raised ... I think it is clear to anyone who understands this issue that the need of the United States for fossil fuels far in excess of its ability to produce such energy will be the reality for some time to come. And the choice that the United States faces ... is whether to increase its capacity to accept such energy from the most secure, most stable, and friendliest location it can possibly get that energy, which is Canada, or from other places that are not as secure, stable, or friendly to the interests and values of the United States.*
>
> *– Stephen Harper, joint press conference with President Barack Obama, February 2011*[18]

> *He's indicated to me ... that he has an open mind in regards to what the final decision may or may not me. I take that as his answer. And you can appreciate that I would not comment on the domestic politics of this issue or any other issue here in the United States.*
>
> *– Stephen Harper, joint press conference with President Barack Obama, December 2011*[19]

Given its size and scope, the politics of engaging the executive branch varies enormously with the relative salience of particular energy-related issues (in both countries' political contexts), the degree of alignment between the two governments' interests and priorities at various levels of analysis, and the degree to which the executive branch is an independent political actor in particular issues or finds itself constrained by the vagaries of congressional processes.

Energy interdependence, driven largely by market forces but facilitated by government policies, remains the strongest factor contributing to policy cooperation between the two central governments. The direct and indirect contributions of energy exports to Canadian governments (provincial and federal) have steadily reinforced incentives for market integration since the early 1990s. The primacy of provincial jurisdiction in Canadian energy policies and the Chrétien government's decision to coordinate the design and implementation of its environmental policies with the provinces during the 1990s have placed certain limits on the scope for bilateral energy and environmental cooperation since that time.[20] Canadian federal governments can exercise a limited degree of policy leadership but are heavily influenced by the need to reconcile regional interests and accommodate the constitutional jurisdictions of provincial governments.

Depending on public perceptions of the current US administration, Ottawa's policy discretion can also be constrained by nationalist sentiments in Canada – as during much of the latter Bush administration (2001-9). As a result, though Canadian governments have sought to institutionalize relations with the US executive branch on energy and, more recently, environmental policies, the extent of cooperation and coordination is inherently limited to those areas in which both federal governments share effective jurisdiction. However, Gattinger argues that the "Canada–US energy policy relations have been characterized primarily by policy coordination, collaboration, and ... implicit harmonization of broad policy directions, owing to the many shared interests and considerable degree of energy interdependence between the two countries."[21]

As noted in Table 13.2, strategic policy alignment between the two governments has varied substantially depending on economic and market conditions and the relative consistency of their energy and environmental agendas. Strategic alignment was probably closest during the Clinton administration. Falling global energy prices and US electricity deregulation created a community of interests between Canadian producers and American consumers that both governments accommodated and encouraged. Cross-border administrative cooperation between the US Federal Energy Regulatory Commission (FERC) and Canada's National Energy Board (NEB) could be conducted below the political radar to mutual economic advantage – as in the coordination of their regulatory activities to facilitate the expansion of cross-border pipeline and electricity transmission capacity.[22] Both the Clinton administration and the Chrétien government supported the 1998 Kyoto Accord on greenhouse gas emissions, though the US Senate's 97-0 vote making its acceptance subject to conditions beyond the administration's control constrained opportunities for closer policy alignment.

The Bush administration's initial push for greater North American energy cooperation in the interests of US energy security was welcomed by Canada's oil- and gas-producing provinces in 2001-2, even if the Chrétien government responded carefully to avoid arousing nationalist sentiments.

TABLE 13.2
Strategic political and policy alignment of US and Canadian governments
on energy and related environmental policy issues

		Strategic energy	Strategic environmental	Overall
1993-2000	Clinton–Chrétien	Cooperative	Initially aligned	Broadly aligned
2001-3	Bush–Chrétien	Limited*	Limited → declining	Functional alignment
2004-5	Bush–Martin	Limited*	Limited → conflicting	Functional alignment
2006-8	Bush–Harper	Cooperative	Parallelism	Functional alignment
2009-10	Obama–Harper	Cooperative	Cooperative	Broadly aligned

* Distinction between moderate distance in public political relationships and close cooperation in bureaucratic relationships between the two governments.

The three NAFTA countries formed the North American Energy Working Group (NAEWG) to exchange information on energy supplies, projected demands, and potential infrastructure developments among mid-ranking officials. But the Bush administration's rejection of the Kyoto process in the absence of firm commitments by major emerging economies left a legacy-minded Chrétien caught between strong Canadian public support for Kyoto's ratification and the practical difficulties of transition for a private sector economy inextricably integrated within North American markets.

Although energy cooperation was high on the trilateral agenda of the Security and Prosperity Partnership (SPP) after 2005, the Martin government's political relationship with the Bush administration declined sharply as the former exploited domestic anti-American and anti-Bush sentiments in its unsuccessful pursuit of re-election. Even so, generally close cooperation was maintained between mid- and working-level officials, especially in "areas of mutual interest" reinforced by continuing interdependence.[23]

The Harper government has generally sought close relations with the White House and executive branch on both energy and environmental issues. It has consistently addressed the Bush and Obama administration's concerns over energy security, attempting to protect US market access for

Canadian oil sands and other energy production while working closely with American negotiators in broader global climate policy negotiations. Although less enthusiastic about climate change initiatives than the Obama administration, the Harper government has made a virtue of necessity in signalling its commitment to align its broad policy initiatives with those of Washington while maintaining similar degrees of flexibility on sector-specific fiscal and regulatory measures.[24] However, the Obama administration's decision in November 2011 to defer consideration of TransCanada Corporation's proposed Keystone XL pipeline in response to intense lobbying by environmental groups has strongly reinforced Ottawa's commitment to diversify Canada's energy exports outside North America.

At the functional policy level of senior officials and regulators, policy cooperation has been relatively consistent, especially on issues of limited political salience. Mouafo, Dukert, Gattinger, and others have noted a number of institutional arrangements for policy collaboration between the two governments.[25] The Energy Consultative Mechanism (ECM), dating back to conflicts over the Trudeau government's National Energy Program in 1981, provides for semi-annual meetings of senior officials of the two governments. Although Bush administration energy department officials sometimes questioned the ECM's utility or purpose, Canadian officials have been reluctant to abandon a process that provides a formal opportunity to exchange views and identify ongoing opportunities for or concerns between the two governments.[26] In 2010, this interagency forum included representatives from the US Department of the Interior, Environmental Protection Agency (EPA), Federal Energy Regulatory Commission, and Office of the Federal Coordinator for Alaska Natural Gas Transportation Projects.[27] The importance of close intergovernmental working relations increased substantially with growing pressures from elements of the Democratic congressional leadership to restrict Canadian oil sands imports after the Democrats took control of Congress in November 2006.

The information-sharing processes of NAEWG, subsumed in the SPP, might have facilitated medium-term planning of energy infrastructure in both countries, though lack of transparency made it substantially more difficult to evaluate its effectiveness. Even so, observers in both countries suggest that it has been useful in facilitating closer Canada–US energy integration.[28] As noted above, senior officials of FERC and NEB have met regularly since the 1990s to coordinate their approaches to regulating cross-border energy projects, notably pipelines, electricity transmission corridors, and related environmental approvals. The North American Electric Reliability Corporation has institutionalized previous cross-border cooperation among electric utilities to coordinate technical standards to avoid the kinds of power disruptions that blacked out much of the US midwest and northeast, and Canadian provinces from Manitoba to New Brunswick in August 2003. The so-called Clean Energy Dialogue, launched in 2009, has provided a platform for semi-annual meetings of cabinet-level officials and a framework for coordination of a number of bilateral policy initiatives.[29] These activities all support what Verrastro described above as a core goal of US energy policies: increasing and diversifying sources of conventional and non-conventional energy supplies.

Canadian officials have actively supported efforts to encourage greater fuel efficiency under both the Bush and Obama administrations while recognizing that these debates are dominated by competition among US domestic interest groups. However, integration of the two countries' automotive sectors ensures that policy changes in one country will be paralleled by the other, even if differences in technical standards might require equivalent rather than identical measures to facilitate harmonization.

One exception to this pattern has involved Canadian opposition to oil and gas exploration in the Arctic National Wildlife Refuge (ANWR), a cause championed by energy interests, most Republican senators, and the Bush administration during its incumbency. Canadian opposition has hinged primarily on environmental factors, particularly the potential migration of caribou herds across the Alaska–Yukon border and their related effects on the livelihoods of Aboriginal communities in the area. However, the segmented nature of congressional policy processes allows Canadian interests to work with both Republican and Democratic administrations on numerous issues while "agreeing to disagree" on issues of lower political salience.

Embassy officials in both countries provide a critical relay point for political information both on issues of immediate interest to their respective governments and in seeking to influence broader patterns of public and interest group opinion. Maintaining US market access for a wide array of Canadian energy sources has been a central priority for Canadian Embassy officials in Washington during the past decade while providing the impetus for ongoing representation of the Alberta and Manitoba governments in the American capital. US government officials whom I interviewed noted that, while their primary contacts are with Canadian federal officials, they also recognize the political and constitutional roles of provincial governments – usually treading carefully in recognition of Canadian political sensitivities.

However, on most important issues, national policy-making processes remain functionally autonomous from bilateral or trilateral arrangements, however constrained by the practical realities of energy interdependence. Gattinger suggests that FERC's decision-making processes impose de facto harmonization by providing conscious incentives to stakeholders and policy makers to engage in policy emulation.[30] All new cross-border pipeline developments require Department of State approval under US law – rarely withheld but usually subject to regulatory conditions recommended by other executive branch agencies, including the EPA. State and local agencies – or the federal courts – can also function as independent policy actors whose consent for new projects, or the expansion of existing ones, must be negotiated by major stakeholders. Nebraska's strong opposition to the proposed siting of the Keystone XL pipeline across the state's environmentally sensitive Sand Hills was central to the State Department's decision in 2011 to withhold authorization from the project until alternative routes could be explored.[31]

The relative openness of American regulatory process litigation can often result in significant delays or restructuring of cross-border infrastructure and other projects. For example, in 2010-11, the multi-billion-dollar Kearl Lake oil sands project in Alberta was delayed by almost a year by litigation by Idaho residents seeking to block 207 truck shipments of mining equipment along narrow mountain roads on environmental and safety grounds, even after Imperial Oil, Exxon/Mobil's Canadian subsidiary, had negotiated necessary permits and pledged significant infrastructure improvements in Idaho, Montana, and Alberta.[32]

The advocacy of Canadian energy exports and related interests in Washington and beyond the beltway remains central to both Canadian federal and provincial cross-border diplomacy – whether in the day-to-day advocacy of Embassy officials, public statements (and quiet diplomacy) by successive ambassadors, regular visits to Washington and attendance at governors' conferences by senior provincial politicians, or prime ministerial intervention during periodic White House visits.[33] Given the scale and scope of Canadian energy exports and the primacy given to maintaining US market access in Canadian economic diplomacy, it could scarcely be otherwise. However, these activities require a very different type of diplomacy when engaging Congress.

Engaging Congress

> *It's better to be at the table than on the menu.*
>
> – Senator Robert Byrd, cited in Zwick, 2011[34]

Canada's engagement of Congress on energy and related environmental issues is both proactive and reactive. The growing intensity of energy-related debates in Congress, particularly with the increased salience of related climate change policies in 2006-10, requires both Canadian diplomats and provincial governments to identify prospective allies in Congress to protect Canadian interests against the crossfire of special interests on Capitol Hill. The diversity of US domestic regional and sectoral stakeholders on energy issues also requires Canadian energy diplomacy to fashion a series of microstrategies capable of engaging discrete issues. Such efforts can be anticipatory, trying to "get ahead" of congressional action by building relations with well-situated members of Congress, often in cooperation with coalitions of US and Canadian interest groups, or arranging for the tabling of legislation that might subsequently be incorporated into broader omnibus or appropriation bills. They can be reactive, trying to head off or modify legislation with potentially adverse effects on Canadian interests or even to revise such legislation in subsequent sessions of Congress. Such initiatives can also include cooperation with US domestic interests engaged in mobilizing members of Congress to lobby the executive branch on various regulatory initiatives – for example, Department of State decisions on the licensing of cross-border pipelines in the "public interest." However, even successful Canadian diplomats need to avoid being caught in the middle of broader partisan contests – as with the decision of Republican congressional leaders to champion legislation challenging President Obama's decision to defer approval of Keystone XL as part of broader efforts to frame economic policy debates before the 2012 presidential election.[35]

Canadian lobbying can also involve ongoing negotiations over legislative details as part of ongoing congressional log rolling and brokerage, in which interest groups (and foreign governments) must often settle for the accommodation of their interests rather than clear wins or losses. These tactics have already been noted in Chapter 7 in the context of the 2005 US Energy Act.[36] To keep these efforts in perspective, however, it is worth noting that the Canadian Embassy has four full-time staff members who focus primarily on energy and environmental issues, supported as required by its congressional relations staff, the selective engagement of senior Embassy officials, and the parallel, but not necessarily coordinated, activities of provincial representatives.

The incremental, segmented nature of congressional policy making means that different committees and subcommittees of each house can have different perspectives. These perspectives can reflect the interests and agendas of particular committee and sub-committee chairs, particularly to the extent that they have become advocates for particular economic or societal interests. For example, among key decision makers on the sprawling House Energy and Commerce Committee, Joe Barton (R-TX) was a key advocate for his state's energy interests and often supportive of related Canadian interests during his time as chair (2004-7). John Dingell (D-MI), who served as chair from 1981 to 1994, was a strong advocate for his state's automotive industries and unions, often working closely with Rick Boucher (D-VA), who, as chair of its Clean Air Subcommittee, played a major role in obtaining accommodation for his state's and district's coal-mining and power generation interests.

Henry Waxman (D-CA) was a much stronger advocate for greenhouse gas (GHG) reduction as committee chair in 2007-11, reflecting both the views of his Beverly Hills constituents and the interests of west coast power consumers, whose temperate climate reduces their exposure to the costs of implementing proposed climate change measures.[37] Waxman's support of Section 526 of the US Energy Independence and Security Act of December 2007, which restricted US government purchases of oil with higher than average life-cycle GHG emissions, was widely viewed as challenging Canadian oil sands imports. The measure, which prompted extensive lobbying of both the Bush administration and Congress by Canadian diplomats, and efforts by some security-oriented members of Congress to overturn it through legislation under the jurisdiction of other committees, has not significantly restricted Canadian oil exports. However, it expands the potential for policy making through litigation.[38]

Waxman's effort to secure passage of cap-and-trade legislation in 2009 required major concessions not only to coal-state and power-generating interests but also to farm interests championed by Agriculture Committee chair Collin Peterson (D-MN). US ethanol subsidies extracted by farm-state legislators, though widely criticized on both energy efficiency and environmental grounds, have prompted emulation by successive Canadian governments following pressure from their own agricultural lobbies.

Although Republican leaders who assumed control of the House following the 2010 congressional elections favour expanding Canadian energy imports,[39] it remains to be seen what impacts these changes will have on broader policy trends.

Even when the leadership of one house of Congress has priorities that work at cross-purposes to Canadian interests, the nature of the congressional game often leaves multiple openings to exercise countervailing influence, as long as it is done with tact and sensitivity to American domestic interests. Jurisdiction over energy and related environmental policies is typically more fragmented in the Senate than in the House. At least six separate committees, Energy and Natural Resources, Finance, Environment and Public Works, Foreign Relations, Agriculture, and Commerce and Transportation, claimed jurisdiction over different elements of cap-and-trade legislation, which foundered in the Senate in 2009-10. In addition, members of the Armed Services Committee play an active role in energy issues affecting security interests – whether in seeking the repeal of Section 526 or in promoting the contribution of Alberta's oil sands to US energy security.[40] Regional interests and a greater culture of collegiality among ranking committee members tend to balance underlying partisan tendencies in the Senate. Senators from oil-, coal-, and uranium-producing states and their respective staff advisers provide multiple points of contact for Canadian diplomats seeking to ensure that Canadian energy interests receive a hearing on Capitol Hill.

Embassy staff maintain records of the relative dependence of particular states and districts on Canadian oil and gas imports and of major employers who supply Canadian energy firms with everything from the giant dump trucks used for oil sands mining to wind turbines sold to Canadian electric utilities. As noted in Chapter 9, the creation of Alberta's office within the Canadian Embassy directly responded to perceptions that Alberta's energy interests needed the benefit of direct advocacy beyond that provided by traditional federal diplomatic activities. Following the Democrats' victory in the 2006 congressional elections, former Alberta environment minister Gary Mar replaced former energy minister Murray Smith as the province's point man in Washington. Mar faced an uphill battle in responding to environmental groups' efforts to demonize oil sands imports as "dirty oil" and, in more hyperbolic terms, "the dirtiest oil on the planet."[41] Mar has had greater success in persuading less ideologically committed advocacy groups and opinion shapers of Canadian energy imports' contribution to US energy security – particularly that of northern states such as

Minnesota and Michigan.[42] However, the effectiveness of provincial advocacy largely depends on the extent to which it reinforces, rather than conflicts with, broader Canadian diplomatic efforts and trends in American public opinion. It also depends on Canadian policy makers' willingness to recognize and address underlying causes of environmental advocacy in both countries.

Engaging Business and Societal Organizations

Canadian governments' management of bilateral energy and environmental policy relations is an excellent example of Allan Gotlieb's dictum that their advocacy in Washington is usually more effective when focused on matters of interest to Americans. Much of the activity of Canadian governments and business interest groups on these issues involves the cultivation of information and interest group networks to facilitate the projection of Canadian interests.

Energy sector interest groups maintain close connections with their counterparts in Washington and in most border regions. The Canadian Electricity Association has long worked with the Edison Electric Institute to facilitate cross-border electricity trade and coordinate technical standards. The North American Electric Reliability Corporation (NERC) emerged from years of such cooperation among public utilities and regulators. Indeed, Richard Drouin, who served as NERC's chair between 2001 and 2009 and played a leading role in shaping legislation to convert it from a voluntary to a government-mandated organization, was chair of Hydro-Quebec during much of this period.

Similar cooperation is visible among oil and gas and pipeline sector firms and interest groups. The Canadian Association of Petroleum Producers (CAPP), which represents upstream and midstream oil and gas producers, in contrast to the more fragmented structure of US industry associations, maintains close relations with the American Petroleum Institute and other sector groups in Washington. CAPP's hiring of Tom Huffaker, the outgoing US consul general in Calgary, to become its vice-president of policy and environment in 2009,[43] reflects the central role of American political and regulatory processes for Canadian energy interests. Such interests also play a direct role in Canadian public diplomacy. Their activities include contributions to university- and think tank–sponsored conferences, especially those associated with ongoing Canadian studies programs, and financing advocacy advertisements in Washington-area publications as part of ongoing competition for public attention with major environmental interest groups such as the Natural Resources Defense Council and the Sierra Club.

Canadian diplomats play an active if usually low-profile role in this competition, particularly since major environmental groups have targeted Canadian oil sands imports as part of a broader campaign to limit new sources of hydrocarbon supply so that rising prices make alternative fuels more economically viable. This lobby has actively challenged building of the Keystone XL pipeline intended to ship oil sands crude to the major oil hub of Cushing, Oklahoma – within easy reach of US Gulf Coast refineries. Challenges by major environmental groups have made the Keystone XL project the most high-profile issue involving Canada in the United States since long-lived allegations over the origins of the 9/11 terrorists, and have triggered countervailing lobby efforts by energy interests and supporters of energy security.[44]

Although Embassy lobbying becomes publicly visible from time to time, the volume and cost of advocacy advertising in Washington and other major media markets are such that Canadian officials usually view such expenses as relatively inefficient uses of scarce resources. The effectiveness of such activities depends on the extent to which Americans – if they are aware of Canada's status as the largest single source of US energy imports – view these activities as a net source of economic benefit or a net social and environmental cost. Paradoxically, the greater the extent to which Canadian energy interests expand their footprint in the United States, the more the political and legal battles over these issues are likely to take place outside Washington – increasing the relevance of state and local governments to Canadian diplomats and economic interests.

Engaging the States

State governments retain an extensive role in energy and environmental policies, particularly on land-use and transportation policies within their boundaries. Large states, especially California, play an influential role as trend setters for other states – as in its introduction of a Low Carbon Fuel Standard, with implications for refining and marketing petroleum products. Governors of large and medium-sized states might seek to build interstate policy networks to coordinate a variety of energy and environmental policy initiatives – such as the Western Climate Initiative launched by west coast states and the Regional Greenhouse Gas Initiative (RGGI) grouping several northeastern states during the past decade. Regional energy and environmental issues are regularly on the agendas of regional governors' and state legislators' associations, often with the participation of neighbouring Canadian premiers and other senior politicians. As discussed in Chapter 9, they are also central topics of cross-border discussions through PNWER and the Conference of New England Governors and Eastern Canadian Premiers.

Canadian governments engage these processes on multiple levels. Energy issues are frequently on the agendas of federal consulates, whether by identifying state-level initiatives that can affect cross-border energy trade, networking with regionally significant decision makers and societal interests, or cooperating with cross-border initiatives of provincial governments. Consular officials track issues or measures in different regions that might have spillover effects in other elements of cross-border relations. For example, when officials in Montana vigorously objected to proposed plans for natural gas drilling in British Columbia's upper Flathead Valley in 2006-7, federal officials quietly declined to intervene, noting ongoing disputes with North Dakota affecting the Red River basin draining into Canada.[45] The dispute was later settled after direct discussions between the parties. Energy issues were central to the decision to locate a consulate in Anchorage under the Enhanced Representation Initiative in 2005 to monitor developments related to the Alaska Gas Pipeline, ongoing disputes over drilling in the Arctic National Wildlife Refuge, and several other issues.

Energy issues are central to the cross-border policy relations of several provincial governments. Most provincial electric utilities have interconnections with counterparts in neighbouring US states and regions – creating extensive regulatory, marketing, and related political issues for ongoing discussions. Cultivating export markets is critical to the business plans of provincial electric utilities in Quebec, New Brunswick, Manitoba, British Columbia, and, more recently, Newfoundland and Labrador as well as to broadening markets for private sector co-generation facilities created or contemplated as part of the ongoing diversification of domestic energy sources in most parts of Canada. The development of alternative energy sources and the creation of new transmission capacity are frequent topics for discussion at annual PNWER meetings, with extensive participation by private sector interests as well as senior decision makers from provincial and state governments.

However, though cross-border issues can affect state and provincial energy policies, they generally do so primarily at the margins. Hydro-Quebec's proposed takeover of NB Power in 2009 prompted some adverse comments in Maine before the deal collapsed following political backlash in New Brunswick.[46] British Columbia's carbon tax regime was a direct by-product of the Campbell government's engagement in the Western Climate Initiative, though it remains to be seen how BC policies will evolve under his successors. Perhaps more significant in the medium to longer term are challenges surrounding renewal of the Columbia River Treaty, which involves provisions for the sharing of benefits from coordinated flood control measures and related issues of power generation between British Columbia and Washington State. The range of domestic stakeholders in both countries is now far greater than when the treaty was first negotiated in the 1960s. It is too early to anticipate with any certainty the political and interest group trade-offs and outcomes of state and federal policy processes related to the treaty's prospective renewal in 2014. However, informed observers suggest that these complexities are likely to spill over into negotiations, testing the political skills of negotiators in both countries.

Canada–US Relations and the Evolution of Energy Policies within North America

> *As the Middle East and North Africa are in turmoil, and with greater turmoil possible, it behooves us to focus on more diversified energy sources, and especially oil sources, closer to home or at the very least from places that are facing less instability and civil strife. Canada is one of the most stable countries on the planet and will likely be so well into the future ... The Canadians are the most important and most reliable source of imported oil we have.*
>
> *– Paul Sullivan, testimony, 2011*[47]

Policy decisions by Canadian and American governments have facilitated the integration of North American energy markets and infrastructure since the 1980s. Prospects of growing geopolitical risks abroad and declining supplies from other western hemisphere countries have increased US receptiveness to Canadian energy imports despite countervailing domestic pressures from environmental groups. Fears about US energy security and economic competitiveness, reinforced by domestic partisan and ideological conflicts, have largely precluded government-led restructuring of energy industries or coherent political leadership on climate change and related issues.

Under such circumstances, Canada has been – and is likely to remain – a policy taker on most major issues whose domestic policy flexibility will depend in large measure on its capacity to parallel US environmental policies while diversifying markets for its energy exports and accommodating widely varying provincial resource endowments and energy policies.

The Obama administration has been relatively open to working with Canada on shared policy goals in recent years, as demonstrated by the Department of State's general openness to facilitating increased Canadian imports (prior to its deferral of regulatory approval for the Keystone XL pipeline in November 2011) and the Department of Energy's ongoing collaboration in developing new technologies to facilitate the commercialization of alternative fuels and various forms of environmental mitigation. The strategic trade-offs of American energy policies suggest that any future US administration will take a comparable approach, whatever the differences in detail that might emerge from balancing the priorities of different interest groups. The comparable reluctance of most Canadian political parties to take zero-sum approaches to regional interests suggests that ongoing policy cooperation will continue to the extent that it serves the pragmatic interests of Canadian governments.

Similarly, failing major policy or environmental shocks, American energy and environmental policies are likely to be dictated less by executive branch priorities than by "legislative pragmatism"[48] – the log rolling and special interest payoffs necessary for congressional approval of the multidimensional but largely incremental energy bills of recent years. However, as noted above, these processes leave opportunities for Canadian governments to advance their interests – if at the margins of the American political system. They can also be affected by the business decisions of major market participants, such as the potential for major gas producers to respond to the rising gap between the prices of natural gas and diesel fuel either by converting the former into the latter or by creating an infrastructure to retail liquid natural gas to long-distance truckers.[49]

The greater the degree to which industry-specific production and distribution processes are integrated across borders, the greater the likelihood that Canada will adopt (or adapt) American regulatory initiatives – as in the harmonization of fuel economy and emissions standards for the automotive and transportation sectors. However, continued provincial ownership and regulatory control of domestic electricity generation and distribution, combined with ongoing pressures on economic competitiveness from rising electricity prices and other factors, will limit the cross-border harmonization of domestic electricity policies – as opposed to those facilitating cross-border trade.

Continuing regional differences in energy sources and demands in both countries – combined with Mexico's continuing political gridlock and national sensitivities – make it unlikely that a single energy policy will emerge between the United States and Canada, let alone Mexico, whatever the competing aspirations of domestic energy industries and environmental groups.[50] American consumers (and taxpayers) have not shown much willingness to sacrifice either their lifestyles or their living standards to finance the enormous investments in conventional and alternative energy sources necessary to reduce current levels of import dependence. For this reason, bilateral energy policy cooperation is likely to focus on the pursuit of greater energy efficiency through the more effective organization of existing energy infrastructure, including refineries and electricity transmission lines, and the cooperative development of new technologies that can enhance energy efficiency and mitigate GHG emission levels.

The two greatest threats to such cooperation are likely to be the efforts of American interest groups to pursue unilateral policy decisions to restrict Canadian energy imports and the re-emergence of regional divisions within Canada that undercut Ottawa's ability to negotiate with the US government. These challenges suggest that Ottawa and the provinces should develop a three-level strategy to engage their American neighbours effectively while reducing the ability of US domestic interest groups to disrupt bilateral relations.

Internally, Canadian governments need to accommodate diverse provincial resource endowments and related fiscal measures to finance the diversification and renewal of their own energy industries in ways consistent with mitigating climate change. This can be done through explicit carbon taxes (and corresponding reductions in other taxes) as in British Columbia, technology funds in Alberta and Saskatchewan, or regional carbon exchanges in Ontario and Quebec. The Harper government's decision to bridge these measures with a strategy linking federal policies to the costs of industry-specific adjustments in the United States[51] is a practical approach to avoiding the erection of new environmental restrictions on trade. Even so, the government should seek formal American recognition of such arrangements in a bilateral (or, when feasible, trilateral) agreement with the United States (and Mexico). Any such agreement should include a binding, arm's-length dispute resolution process similar to that negotiated under the 2006 Softwood Lumber Agreement.

Overwhelming dependence on a single export market significantly limits Ottawa's negotiating flexibility in any such discussions. To increase its leverage, Canadian governments should continue to encourage non–North American investment in the measured expansion of oil sands production and related infrastructure development – including one or more pipelines to enable exports beyond North America. The capacity to access Asian markets limits American interest groups (and their Canadian counterparts) in restricting Canada's ability to develop its own resources in the interests of its own citizens.[52] Such policies should be accompanied by enhanced environmental standards, appropriate regulatory controls over corporate governance, and increased provisions for resource upgrading in Canada where economically viable.

At the same time, both federal and provincial governments should continue to cooperate with their American counterparts in developing new technologies and alternative energy resources, including an expanded electricity grid that could facilitate the integration of widely dispersed wind and solar generation facilities. Cooperative cross-border regional and economic linkages are the most effective way to mobilize shared interests to counter protectionist measures and encourage the development and renewal of more sustainable energy industries.

Canada–US energy cooperation has been facilitated by the decentralization of political and economic power in both countries during the past three decades and the development of creative business and environmental responses to the challenges of energy development. Given inherent disparities of size and power, adapting such approaches appears to be the most realistic response to the challenges of the foreseeable future that serves the diverse interests of Canadians and Americans.

14 CONCLUSION

Managing Bilateral Relations in
an Evolving North America

On the surface, Canada's position within North America in early 2012 resembles the well-worn trope of the "peaceable kingdom."[1] Its economy is adjusting, with challenges, to massive changes in the terms of trade and the industrial structures of several major economic sectors, especially steel, automotive, forestry, and mining, since 2002.

Fears of rampant American protectionism have subsided, if not disappeared, with the reversion to congressional politics as usual on energy and climate change issues, whatever the ongoing risks from political and ideological polarization, and the sharply declining use of "trade remedy measures" as a means of harassing cross-border trade, even during the 2008-9 recession.[2] However, political and economic trends both inside and outside North America are forcing a significant re-evaluation of both Canadian and American priorities in international economic policy but in significantly different contexts.

Successive Canadian governments' cultivation of interdependence with the United States since the 1980s – within the broader frameworks of North American integration, evolving international markets, and governance structures for trade and capital – has increased Canada's sensitivity to changes in American economic conditions and policy priorities. As a result, the reciprocal, if asymmetrical, character of cross-border economic and political relations requires thoughtful policy makers and policy analysts to consider American perspectives on the relationship if seeking to influence American policies toward Canada.

The progressive shift of economic power to the large emerging economies of China, India, and Brazil creates multiple and unpredictable dynamics for Canada. On the one hand, it provides opportunities for Ottawa to serve as a creative broker in dealings with other large and medium-sized economies through institutions such as the G-20 and the International Monetary Fund – as demonstrated by the Harper government's successful diplomacy in negotiations on the coordination of international financial regulation. On the other, this shift poses a major challenge to US international economic leadership, the priorities of senior American decision makers in a variety of international negotiations, and the relative economic security – or insecurity – of large elements of the American public. The highly polarized character of American domestic politics in recent years, and the stresses likely to result from slow economic growth and prolonged "deleveraging" following the household and government debt binges of recent years, create an unpredictable political climate in Washington for many issues affecting bilateral relations. These trends also increase the challenges for Canadian governments of maintaining domestic policy discretion on "intermestic" issues since Canada remains a relatively small, necessarily open actor among large, self-absorbed economic powers. This challenge is particularly significant in the interaction of energy and environmental issues, the continuation of secure access to US markets by Canadian-based industries, and related issues of border management and security.

This chapter explores strategic options currently debated by Canadian policy makers and policy entrepreneurs for managing Canada–US relations and the ongoing dynamics of North American integration in the evolving context of Canada's broader international economic relations. It concludes by offering an alternative approach that acknowledges the fundamentally contingent character of American policies toward Canada and the conditions for the successful engagement with ongoing processes of North American integration while addressing fundamental Canadian interests in sustaining economic competitiveness and the capacity for maintaining policy choice.

The Canada–US Relationship as It Is

Any realistic assessment of the future of the Canada–US relationship – or that of North America as a whole – must begin not in abstractions or idealized visions of the future but in an assessment of the relationship as it is. Without a clear-headed understanding of the bilateral relationship's place in the broader foreign, security, international economic, and domestic politics of each country, it is unlikely that Canadian governments will be able to pursue the kinds of coherent or relatively consistent policies necessary to meet their central policy objectives while influencing American policies toward Canada in ways that will complement and reinforce them over the next ten to fifteen years.

The bilateral relationship continues to be shaped by its fundamental asymmetries of size, power, and relative importance within and perspectives on the international system. As demonstrated by Charles Doran in the early 1980s and by many other scholars and practitioners since then, these disparities are not inherently disadvantageous to Canada as long as its policies are not seen to be hostile or threatening to central US interests.[3] If not to the same extent as during the Cold War, US foreign policy priorities remain oriented primarily toward broader questions of international security and order, whereas the enduring focus of Canada's foreign policy has been on its bilateral relations with the United States, especially the trade–commercial dimension.

Although the post-1989 primacy of economic factors in bilateral relations has reasserted itself under the Obama administration, continuing concerns over homeland and border security create ongoing incentives to work toward the development of an effective security perimeter as long as such measures do not substantially constrain Canada's capacity to broaden its trade links outside North America or to maintain functional, independent immigration policies. In contrast, American policies toward Canada have generally been subsets of policies toward allies or by-products (intentional or incidental) of US domestic policies and politics. Even if trends toward closer North American economic integration have been offset since 2005 by major shifts in Canada's terms of trade, they are still central to the economic calculations of major Canadian industries, foreign investors, and Canadian governments.

These circumstances have induced the Obama administration to adopt a relatively cautious, status quo approach to trade issues. However, domestic economic instability and political polarization have limited its ability to engage broader economic issues or continental issues. There has been incremental progress on cross-border cooperation with Canada in a few areas, including initial steps toward greater regulatory cooperation under the perimeter security and regulatory cooperation processes launched in

2011.[4] However, there appears to be minimal political will in any of North America's three countries to explore further trilateral economic integration other than through the incremental adaptations of "dual bilateralism": the tendency of Canada and Mexico to engage the United States (and vice versa) separately on their respective policy concerns.

Similarly, the "competitive liberalization" that characterized US and Mexican trade policies during the Bush administration reflected the independent decisions of each government to pursue its own multitrack trade policies, an approach paralleled by the Harper government since 2007. However, rather than facilitating closer economic integration within North America, these strategies have increased the complexities and costs of national rules of origin and other administrative trade measures.[5] The absence of a congressional majority supportive of further trade liberalization since 2006 has limited the ability or willingness of successive administrations to pursue the policies of reciprocal market opening that have been central to US international economic leadership since the 1940s. These factors have contributed to the continuing decentralization of bilateral policy relations since NAFTA's ratification in 1993 – punctuated by brief bursts of political attention from the White House when consistent with broader priorities of the administration.

This tendency has discouraged what Bow describes as "hard linkage" in cross-border policy relations: the formal withholding of cross-border cooperation in one policy field as a negotiating tactic intended to force the other government's cooperation on unrelated issues. Even so, this reality does not preclude "soft linkages" in which progress on one aspect of sectoral policy negotiations can be tacitly linked to satisfying the other country's demands on related policy issues.[6]

In response, Canadian governments have adopted a sectorally segmented approach to cross-border relations, often actively cultivating the support of relevant US domestic interests for sector-specific and microlevel initiatives. These processes reflect the continuing centrality of two-level games – the building of complementary domestic coalitions on both sides of the border. They also reflect the frequent ability of Canadian diplomats and cross-border interests to assemble (or take advantage of pre-existing) "blocking coalitions" capable of constraining or diluting policy measures with potentially adverse effects on cross-border relations.

Canada's bilateral relations with the United States have also been complicated by the growing implications of US policies toward Mexico. Although this reality has been most visible in the American insistence

since 9/11 on parallel or complementary measures on both borders to protect US domestic security as an ongoing condition of access to low-risk
trade and travel, Mexico's protracted narco-insurgency and its shifting
domestic political climate have created more recent opportunities for the
dilution of the US one-border policy regarding homeland security.[7]

The United States, being far larger, more economically diversified, and
less trade-dependent than Canada, neither needs nor is inclined to coordinate its broader economic policies with those of its neighbour.[8] In Stephen
Clarkson's felicitous phrase, North America has become "too big for the
small issues and too small for the big issues."[9] The United States *might*
choose to negotiate reciprocal agreements with Canada, often as part of a
broader agenda to project its policy goals into broader multilateral negotiations. However, American policy makers might be less willing to tip their
hands by committing themselves to prior agreements with Canada (and/or
Mexico) when major trade-offs depend on the outcomes of negotiations
with major regional powers, such as the European Union, China, or Brazil.

Even so, the broader internationalization of policy relations can also allow for the coordination of Canada–US (or North American) positions that
enable each country to advance its specific and overlapping interests in
broader international fora – as with the negotiation of shared approaches to
animal health policies following the BSE outbreak of 2003. Alternatively,
negotiations in a broader international forum can provide a wider context
in which to negotiate arrangements that, though reflecting comparable
policy goals, are capable of accommodating greater policy differentiation
arising from national differences. The recent emergence of the G-20 as a
major forum for brokering the interests of major regional powers has given
Canada the potential for greater manoeuvring room on issues such as climate change and proposals for a global bank tax than would have been
available in other contexts dominated by the United States and European
Union.[10] These factors help to explain both the context for its policy engagement with the United States and the major strategic options pursued by
Canadian governments and major societal interests in recent years.

Strategic Options for the Canada–US Relationship

Ottawa's default approach to bilateral relations since 9/11 has been one of
careful incremental policy management. Hesitant to position themselves
too close to a Bush administration unpopular in Canada, and constrained
between 2004 and 2011 by the dynamics of minority Parliaments, both

Liberal and Conservative governments have sought to position most of their bilateral initiatives below the political radar to maximize the benefits of proximity to the United States while limiting its perceived costs, often calculated in terms of domestic political advantage. Although its majority victory in the 2011 federal election has given the Harper government greater flexibility in pursuing medium-term policy objectives, its initial actions suggest the incremental extension of policy directions introduced since 2006.

This approach reflects the persistent defensiveness of Canadian policies toward the United States. Bow suggests that Canada's embrace of comprehensive free-trade agreements in the 1980s was initially a defensive strategy to offset or avoid the effects of American special interest politics and their tendency to offload adjustment costs from growing trade pressures through the use of contingent protection (trade remedy) measures. Joining NAFTA was a defensive measure to reduce the possibility of a series of preferential ("hub and spoke") trade agreements that could place Canada at a strategic disadvantage, whether in relative access to US markets or as a platform for foreign investment serving North American markets.[11] This concern was later borne out in the Bush administration's pursuit of competitive liberalization through bilateral trade agreements after 2001.

Canada's pursuit of the Smart Border Accord reflected similar concerns over the potential use of border security measures as non-tariff barriers. Although the Harper government subsequently opened the door to formal recognition of a North American security perimeter in return for accommodation of Canadian concerns over other border management issues, there appears to be little willingness to subordinate Canada's relatively functional immigration policies to American preferences. And, apart from Canada's largely symbolic ratification of the Kyoto Accord, its climate change policies have reflected a series of defensive adaptations to American policies that remain mired in international blame shifting and congressional log rolling.[12]

At the same time, senior political and bureaucratic advisers to successive prime ministers have created a variety of processes to persuade their American counterparts to engage Canadian priorities and concerns. They have complemented these initiatives by expanding the resources available for diplomatic advocacy and networking in the United States, both inside and outside the Washington beltway, and by working more closely than ever before with provincial governments in their cross-border dealings with state-level counterparts.

Although some observers have criticized this strategy, it has effectively tranquillized domestic debates over free trade and economic integration, removing most aspects of cross-border relations from the often overheated (and factually challenged) rhetoric of partisan politics. As a result, as even veteran nationalist Clarkson has noted, free trade, symbolized by CUFTA and NAFTA, has become "a politically dead issue" in Canada even if remaining politically controversial in the United States and Mexico.[13] Bilateral negotiations on a shared security perimeter and regulatory coordination were virtually non-issues in the 2011 federal election, which led to the first Conservative majority government since 1988.

Every turn of Canadian and US electoral cycles raises new hopes, fears, and efforts at agenda setting on bilateral and North American issues. The possibility of President Obama's replacement by American voters in November 2012 could well reduce Ottawa's domestic political flexibility in pursuing shared security or regulatory agendas, notwithstanding its current parliamentary majority, by reawakening the ghosts of liberal and social democratic anti-Americanism in an electorate generally favourable to the current president. However, broader trends are forcing Canadian governments to examine their options in the context of ongoing changes in the international economic system.

Incremental Policy Change

Bow suggests three broad strategic options for managing Canada–US relations.[14] The first, "learn to live with it" (i.e., the uncertainties arising from the persistence of special interest politics and its tendency to spill over into cross-border relations) is effectively a continuation of the status quo under the Chrétien, Martin, and Harper governments. This approach to bilateral policy relations is essentially sectoral and largely ad hoc, working with domestic interest networks in the United States to promote the accommodation of Canadian interests and mobilizing cross-border coalitions of interests as required to deal with particular threats. For example, the Regulatory Cooperation Council formed in 2011 to identify opportunities for improved regulatory coordination to reduce transaction costs in cross-border trade appears to be a more focused repackaging of similar efforts under the Security and Prosperity Partnership.

However, cultivating coalitions of complementary and supportive US interests on particular issues is not sufficient to advance a broader economic integration agenda, let alone any form of political integration, a concept with minimal support in either country. Nor, given the fragmentation of

US domestic policy processes and the continuing vulnerability of American taxpayers, workers, and consumers during a period of wrenching economic adjustment, can Canadians count on the forbearance of such interests when redistributive domestic coalitions emerge intent on shifting the burden of adjustment to other Americans and foreigners?

A Canada–US Grand Bargain?

A second medium-term option frequently canvassed by Canadian business interests has been the pursuit of a "grand bargain" with the United States to institutionalize a new installment of the special relationship between the two countries.[15] Derek Burney, Canada's former ambassador in Washington, and John Manley, former Liberal deputy prime minister, now head of the Canadian Council of Chief Executives, have been the strongest proponents of this option in recent years. Its supporters, who emphasize the importance of pursuing closer economic integration and developing binational institutions, tend to view American economic power and Canadian dependence on US markets as defining realities that must be embraced if Canada is to make the most of its location alongside the world's largest economy.

For example, Burney has suggested creating a binational commission empowered to

- streamline customs and entry provisions along our shared border;
- spearhead coherent rationalization of overlapping and needlessly different standards and regulations that hobble the integrated nature of our two economies;
- recommend ... harmonization of immigration and refugee policies;
- examine the merits of a Common External Tariff regime ... to reduce inefficient rules of origin provisions; and
- intensify police collaboration specifically to address security concerns, illicit drug traffic, and the activities of organized crime that straddle our border.[16]

Burney has also recommended the extension of NORAD's mandate from current air and sea coordination to create a shared North American defence perimeter, including shared cyberspace defences by 2017, in the hope of reducing security-related barriers to legal trade and travel along the Canada–US border. He has also proposed the appointment of special envoys to work out "a more coherent approach" to overlapping environmental and energy policies – or, failing the political will to achieve such an objective, that Canada harmonize unilaterally to US standards in recognition of the two countries' deeply intertwined economies. Some, if by no means all, of these proposals are reflected in the careful incrementalism of perimeter security and regulatory cooperation action plans announced in December 2011.

Advocates of the grand bargain strategy suggest that only by taking the initiative in the pursuit of a comprehensive approach to bilateral concerns can Canada hope to secure sufficient political attention in Washington to cut through the habitual log rolling and gridlock of congressional and special interest politics. Neither, Burney argues, does such an approach require Canada to mortgage its freedom of action in foreign or international economic policy relations to US approval.

However, the changing environment for US economic policy making, whether international or domestic, clearly works against revival of the special relationship. American diplomats whom I interviewed noted that several countries think of themselves as having a special relationship with the United States, including Great Britain, Israel, and Australia – though cultivating these relations does not appear to be a major priority for an Obama administration intent on reducing its strategic commitments around the world.[17] Although the Harper government has been careful to cultivate a cooperative relationship with the United States in broader international negotiations, there is little evidence that the administration perceives that a comprehensive bilateral agreement with Canada would advance its central priorities or interests.

First, Canada's mature trade relations with the United States offer relatively few incentives for the latter to invest the political capital and bureaucratic resources necessary to deepen economic integration. Given intense skepticism toward trade liberalization among major Democratic Party constituencies, any movement toward further economic liberalization is contingent on reciprocity – the prospective gains for American exporters and their domestic suppliers from opening up sizable new markets – as with the 2010 agreement on subnational procurement. Although potential efficiency gains can be significant for Canadian firms, they are relatively modest for Americans in the context of a $14 trillion economy. The Washington Declaration of February 2011 simply reflects a broader extension within North America of domestic policy initiatives whose implementation might be reinforced at the margin through cooperation with Canada.

Second, domestic US political considerations make it difficult for administration officials to accommodate a comprehensive integration agreement with Canada without taking Mexico – and the political influence of Mexican Americans – into consideration. However, the sectoral and segmented character of North American policy relations allows both Canada and Mexico to deal separately with the United States on most major issues. Ironically, the collapse of the Department of State's apparent preference for trilateral approaches to broader integration measures can be traced to the continuing gridlock in Congress on the deeply polarizing topic of US immigration reform.

Third, the intense polarization of US domestic and congressional politics offers little short-term hope for the kind of bipartisan consensus among legislators whose constituents might benefit from greater bilateral economic integration. Senior Democratic and Republican leaders might have demonstrated a willingness to accommodate Canadian interests on selected issues. However, the kinds of regulatory and security-related measures that are the focus of the latest round of business proposals for a grand bargain cut deeply into congressional prerogatives. This reality makes it more difficult to attract the kinds of powerful sponsors whose patronage would be necessary to smooth the passage of enabling legislation. Moreover, such proposals go well beyond the trade-related measures that might hope to benefit from the renewal of Trade Promotion Authority (TPA or "fast track") by a new Congress. Given the dynamics of these processes, presidential pursuit of such authority will probably have to await the results of the 2012 (or even 2016) presidential and congressional elections.

As a result, any medium-term progress on further *bilateral* integration, to the extent that it might be saleable to the Canadian public, is contingent on five major factors: strong presidential commitment, the capacity of such arrangements to advance broader US policy initiatives, authoritative bipartisan sponsorship in Congress, an expanded fast-track-style process to allow for passage of the necessary enabling legislation without its being dismantled by special interests, and the capacity to assemble a cross-border coalition of economic and societal interests to support such initiatives. Although it might be possible to cultivate domestic constituencies for such ideas in coming years, they are unlikely to take root until a new generation of leaders emerges capable of overcoming the toxic polarization of US domestic politics. These considerations give rise to a third set of options: a trilateral approach to institutionalizing North American governance.

Greater Institutionalization within North America?

Several proposals have emerged in recent years to develop formal, supranational governance institutions for North America comparable to those from which the European Union eventually emerged. The Fox administration's early 2001 proposal to link formal agreements on migration and economic development, dubbed the "whole enchilada," were echoed by American political scientist Robert Pastor's proposals for a "North American community."[18]

Comparable to Burney's proposal for bilateral special envoys, Pastor has proposed a council of senior envoys from all three governments to propose overarching institutions for trilateral cooperation with a permanent secretariat, a mandate to identify major barriers to further integration, and calibrated responses to them.[19] Pastor identifies the challenge of Mexico's internal disparities and underdevelopment as a key priority that could become the object of an EU-style development fund, financed proportionately by the United States and Canada. A trilateral task force report sponsored by the Council on Foreign Relations (CFR) proposed a diluted version of these proposals, though one skeptical of Mexico's capacity to make effective use of a development fund on the scale initially proposed.[20] Pastor's vision has minimal appeal in Canada, even among major business organizations that have called for closer integration. However, it has reinforced a broader tendency among American and Mexican policy makers and academics to focus on trilateral approaches to further integration – and to linking the liberalization of trade and investment activity under NAFTA with a commitment to a broader development agenda in Mexico.[21] However, even observers sympathetic in principle to formalizing European-style North American governance to encourage more balanced economic development within the region acknowledge that these proposals have minimal political support.[22]

Even before the SPP's quiet demise early in the Obama administration, Mexican political scientist Isabel Studer cogently argued that the history and domestic political culture of each country have created major barriers to the development of shared political institutions. They include what she describes as a "U.S. exceptionalism" deeply rooted in liberal individualism, anti-statism, a major role for domestic politics in shaping international commitments, and resistance to the transfer of American sovereignty to transnational institutions; the breakdown of the cross-partisan consensus on trade liberalization in the United States; and enduring nationalist sentiments in both Canada and Mexico.[23]

If anything, these sentiments have been reinforced by Mexico's persistent narco-insurgency, the ongoing deadlock on US immigration reforms, and related debates over its southern border security. Even during times of greater prosperity, conversations with Canadian government officials suggested that, having mortgaged a disproportionate share of Canada's international aid budget to supporting US efforts in Afghanistan, Ottawa is disinclined to curtail further its policy discretion through a sizable multi-year fiscal commitment to Mexico.[24] If anything, this outlook has been reinforced subsequently by a profound skepticism of the viability of any form of international social engineering and the renewed prospect of domestic fiscal austerity in Canada. These realities have led Mexican commentators such as Jorge Castañeda to recognize that any progress on the migration and development agenda – however unlikely in the deeply polarized US political environment – will require a bilateral US–Mexican initiative.[25]

Canada's economic and political interdependence with the United States, deep mutual insecurities embedded in US–Mexican relations, and the asymmetries of economic and power relationships that characterize the latter's bilateral relations with its North American neighbours have imposed practical limits on Canada's ability to negotiate a grand bargain – bilateral or trilateral – to shape the evolution of North American integration for the foreseeable future.

Managing the Challenges of Contingency

The pursuit of Canada's core interests in North America traditionally has required a capacity to engage the attention of senior American decision makers and to do so in the context of their broader priorities. An outward-looking North America provides a springboard for growth, generating sufficient economic surpluses to offset the economic and social costs of adjusting to an increasingly competitive global economy. A more defensive, inward-looking United States has been more inclined to shift the burdens of economic (and sometimes political) adjustment to its neighbours. An inward-looking Canada is effectively on its own.

However, it is not enough to pursue defensive strategies in bilateral relations to protect and promote Canadian interests within the North American "box," though all Canadian governments have done so during the past decade. It is also vital for Canadian governments to encourage positive US engagement within the broader international economic system, and its specialized governance structures, while pursuing complementary policies that reinforce Canada's capacity for choice inside and outside North

America. Given inherent disparities of power and influence among major industrial nations, and the prospect that the only certainty is likely to be uncertainty, any such approach requires a broad but flexible strategy that enables Canadian governments to manage the contingencies of American policies and broader political and economic events in and beyond North America.

Canada's location in North America will continue to require its engagement of US domestic policies and interest politics to maintain and reinforce the social linkages necessary to ensure that integrated production systems and markets, supported by generally open borders, serve the self-interest of different groups of Americans, not just Canadians. Such approaches have largely insulated Canadians from the protectionism that is almost a reflexive response of American special interest politics to adverse economic trends. Apart from the softwood lumber dispute, Canada has been minimally affected by US trade remedy measures since the 2001-2 recession.[26] Since the negotiation of the latest Softwood Lumber Agreement in 2006, the two countries have taken only three cases to WTO dispute resolution, including two multiparty challenges to American corn subsidies and Country-of-Origin Labeling (COOL) regulations.[27] Resolution of the 2009 Buy American dispute demonstrated substantial goodwill between Washington and Ottawa.

In contrast, challenges facing the United States and other leading economic powers are increasingly global in scope. As such, they often involve negotiating terms of engagement among national (or, in Europe, supranational) governments: the terms on which national governments will cooperate with one another, and the ground rules for competition among their corporate citizens, often reflecting very different models of capitalism and state intervention. These issues include international debates over financial sector regulation, traditionally the jealously guarded prerogative of national governments, the interaction of environmental, energy, and trade policies, and trans-Pacific trade relations. In some cases, Canadian and American policy goals and core interests overlap. In others, there is the potential for cooperation but also for "beggar thy neighbour" approaches to shifting the costs of economic adjustment. In still others, Canada's interests might be closer to those of more solvent "creditor" nations than the deeply indebted Americans.

Canada's capacity for choice in its economic policies – including the capacity to negotiate reciprocal agreements on issues of mutual benefit – thus depends largely on its capacity to engage American power at several levels of analysis: global (including relations among major economic powers), bi- and trilateral, sectoral and subsectoral. Canada's capacity to cultivate influence in Washington is probably greatest on broader economic issues due to its engagement in the G-8, G-20, and other multilateral fora. However, such influence largely depends on the extent to which Canadian interests parallel or coincide with those of the United States, thus enabling Canadian diplomats to broker compromises with major regional powers in ways that acknowledge US interests without necessarily sharing them. The Harper government's cooperation with the Obama administration on international environmental negotiations in 2009-10 reflected the first approach; the former's efforts to negotiate alternatives to the global bank tax advocated by the European Union, with support from Washington, reflected the second. The Harper government's decision in late 2011 to initiate negotiations to join the Trans-Pacific Partnership (along with the United States and Japan) involves a more complex set of calculations.

The growing diversity of national interests and governmental systems is more conducive to consensus-based "soft law" approaches to international cooperation, which allow national governments to tailor their application of general principles to the institutions, economic structures, and political cultures of individual countries[28] rather than pursue a rigid "one size fits all" approach. Such arrangements can often be to Canada's advantage when dealing with regulatory enthusiasms emerging from Washington or Brussels, which often reflect these governments' internal political pressures and special interest trade-offs. The circumstances governing such policy and tactical choices are likely to vary in different contexts. However, they are more likely to facilitate international cooperation and, where necessary, mutual forbearance while leaving more room for both national and regional governance arrangements that often emerge from shared interests or policy responses rooted in the direct engagement of stakeholders and citizens.

The Trade Policy Challenge

A second major governance challenge is likely to emerge from the long-term effects of large-scale, entrenched US trade and fiscal deficits. Combined with the rising costs of providing public services to aging populations facing most industrial countries, these trends could provoke a long, slow decline in American living standards or a fiscal crisis that could trigger the kind of wrenching structural adjustments that Canada experienced during the 1990s.

This prospect, combined with the fluctuation of Canada–US exchange rates around parity and relative terms of trade linked to global commodity prices, suggests the likelihood that Canada will have to continue diversifying its export markets to maintain its economic growth while adapting to incremental trends toward North American economic integration. This paradox can be seen in the coincidence in 2009 between a sharp, recession-induced drop in Canada's US exports – $99 billion or 26.7 percent – and the panicked response of Canadian manufacturers to US Buy American legislation, which ultimately resulted in the reciprocal lowering of barriers to subnational procurement. The medium-term difficulties facing a deeply indebted US economy also point to longer-term challenges for Canada of depending on a single dominant export market as a primary source of its economic growth. Even so, the gravitational pull of its location in North America and the heavily market-driven character of trade and investment relations rooted in similar business and legal cultures, relative physical proximity, and established business relationships demonstrate the challenge of diversifying Canada's trade relations substantially in the short and medium terms.

The instinctive tendency of large countries to externalize their costs of adjustment to others will require Canada to maintain and possibly extend its diplomatic and coalition-building efforts in the United States while finding new resources to continue broadening its international economic diplomacy. The Harper government has recognized that an important precondition for resolving the problems of competitive liberalization and related administrative costs arising from complex rules of origin is to negotiate a series of parallel trade agreements with countries ranging from Colombia to Korea. Such measures might be of limited value in expanding overall Canadian trade – at least in comparison with potential deals with the European Union, India, China, or Mercosur. However, they are a necessary precondition for negotiating a common external tariff with the United States (and possibly Mexico) when their respective domestic political conditions permit, thus making the most of Canada's location as a platform for investment in North America's highly integrated economy. Potentially, the same can be said of Canada's participation (with the United States) in ongoing Trans-Pacific Partnership negotiations, though joining this emerging trade club could require major changes to Canada's entrenched system of agricultural supply management.

The outcome of the 2011 federal election and the prospect of adding twenty-seven new seats in urban Ontario, British Columbia, and Alberta (along with three in Quebec) following the scheduled redistribution of parliamentary representation might have created some of the necessary conditions for such a policy shift. Previous Liberal and Conservative governments depended for their survival on fifteen to twenty seats in rural Ontario and Quebec heavily dependent on supply managed agriculture. The New Democrats' unprecedented gains in Quebec in 2011, the virtual destruction of the Bloc Québécois, and major Conservative gains in urban Ontario have created a domestic political dynamic capable of supporting further trade liberalization in agriculture – at least to the extent that fiscal conditions permit the kind of compensation for long-entrenched public entitlements that has allowed for the diversification of western Canadian agriculture.

A similar process of triangulation applies to energy and environmental relations with the United States. Canadian energy exports remain significant to US energy security, particularly in northern-tier states. However, short-term limits on alternative markets make such exports vulnerable to major political and regulatory shifts – and opportunistic litigation. Canada's capacity to influence the interaction of American environmental and energy policies will depend partly on insulating producers from trade measures based on perceptions that they face lower costs from environmental regulations than their American competitors. Canadian governments' capacity to take a proactive approach to domestic environmental regulation – both place-based and that relating to GHG emissions – is one part of this equation, though policy shifts must recognize deep regional differences within Canada resulting from different resource endowments and their impacts on interregional transfers. Policy discretion will also depend on Canada's capacity to cultivate alternative export markets for its energy resources together with the pipeline and other infrastructure necessary to support them.

As a result, Canada's policy engagement with the United States on these issues will continue to resemble a multilevel game. One level will involve varying degrees of cooperation in international negotiations. Another might require selective harmonization with US microlevel regulations in recognition of integrated production networks and supply chains. Others might involve efforts to coordinate selective sectoral policies in areas of mutual advantage recognized by US interest groups, still others the pursuit of policy parallelism when required by competing interests in Canada or by the effects of American domestic interest group politics in pushing Canadian interests to the margins of debate. Although asymmetry will remain a given, the management of bilateral policy relations will be shaped by the complexities and contingencies of policy environments in both countries.

The extent of economic integration has contributed to the creation of parallel interest networks in both countries in multiple policy fields. These networks offer the potential for cross-border coalition building on selected issues – whether creative in the sense of cultivating shared interests across national borders or defensive in their capacity to modify or prevent US domestic initiatives hostile to significant Canadian interests. (Of course, cross-border coalition-building can cut both aways, as with the efforts of environmental groups to limit further development of Alberta's oil sands or to prevent the construction of pipelines to export their output – whatever the policy preferences of Canadian governments.[29]) However, the diversity of economic and societal interests that has led to the extensive decentralization of policy formation in both countries, usually mediated through Congress in the United States and through provincial and regional policies in Canada, offers limited scope for the politics of grand visions.

Influencing American policies toward Canada will continue to be a vital and inescapable element of the foreign and "intermestic" policies of its governments. However, their capacity to do so effectively will depend not only on the skill of their diplomacy and their cultivation of interest networks in both countries but also on the coherence of their domestic policies. A well-managed Canada that accommodates regional interests, fosters continued economic growth, creates a culture of opportunity for native-born and new Canadians, and does so in a context of economic and environmental sustainability will be in far better shape to adapt to a changing policy environment than a country consumed by its own insecurities, divisions, and zero-sum politics. Thus, influencing American policies toward Canada depends as much on cultivating competence, capacity, and creativity at home and abroad as it does on engaging the American elephant next door. Others can help in that task. However, as with traditional views of charity, Canada's capacity for choice starts at home.

Notes

Chapter 1: Introduction

1 More recently, political scientist Brian Bow likened the two countries' relationship to that of a crocodile and a crocodile bird, mutually useful in ways that never obscure fundamental distinctions in power and the nature of their interdependence. Brian Bow, *The Politics of Linkage: Power, Interdependence, and Ideas in Canada–US Relations* (Vancouver: UBC Press, 2010), 1-2.

2 Livingston T. Merchant, ed., *Neighbours Taken for Granted: Canada and the United States* (New York: Frederick A. Praeger, 1965); Charles F. Doran, *Forgotten Partnership: U.S.–Canada Relations Today* (Baltimore: Johns Hopkins University Press, 1984); Edelgard Mahant and Graeme S. Mount, *Invisible and Inaudible in Washington* (Vancouver: UBC Press; East Lansing: Michigan State University Press, 1999).

3 Richard Gwyn, *The 49th Paradox: Canada in North America* (Toronto: McClelland and Stewart, 1965).

4 See, for example, Paul Cellucci, *Unquiet Diplomacy* (Toronto: Key Porter, 2005); Michael H. Wilson, "Canada and the United States: Common Values, Uncommon Partnership," speaking notes for an address to the Canadian Association of New York, 15 May 2006, Foreign Affairs Canada, http://www.dfait-maeci.gc.ca/.

5 Helen V. Milner, *Interests, Institutions, and Information: Domestic Politics and International Relations* (Princeton, NJ: Princeton University Press, 1997), 9.

6 See, for example, Bertrand Marotte, "Canadians, Americans Agree that Border Should Stay: Polls," *Globe and Mail*, 14 March 2011.

7 At 15.8 percent (2009), the Hispanic American population of the United States (two-thirds of Mexican background) exceeds Canada's total population by about 45

percent. US Census Bureau, *Statistical Abstracts of the United States: 2011,* Table 9 (Washington, DC), 13, http://www.census.gov/, http://www40.statcan.ca/.

8 Bayless Manning, "The Congress, the Executive, and Intermestic Affairs: Three Proposals," *Foreign Affairs* 55, 2 (January 1977): 306-24; Michael Kergin, "Remarks Delivered to the Houston World Affairs Council," 21 March 2001, Foreign Affairs and International Trade Canada, http://www.canadainternational.gc.ca/.

9 Walter Russell Mead, *Power, Terror, Peace, and War* (New York: Alfred A. Knopf, 2005).

10 George Hoberg, ed., *Capacity for Choice: Canada in a New North America* (Toronto: University of Toronto Press, 2002); Brian Bow and A. Patrick Lennox, eds., *An Independent Foreign Policy for Canada?* (Toronto: University of Toronto Press, 2008); Stephen Clarkson, *Uncle Sam and Us: Globalization, Neo-Conservatism, and the Canadian State* (Toronto: University of Toronto Press, 2002); Stephen Clarkson, *Does North America Exist? Governing the Continent after NAFTA and 9/11* (Toronto: University of Toronto Press, 2008).

11 David Dyment, *Doing the Continental: A New Canadian-American Relationship* (Toronto: Dundurn Press, 2010), 31-32.

12 Jeff Heynen and John Higginbotham, *Advancing Canada's Interests in the United States* (Ottawa: Canada School of Public Service, 2004); Dieudonné Mouafo, Nadia Ponce Morales, and Jeff Heynen, *A Compendium of Canada–U.S. Relations* (Ottawa: Canada School of Public Service, 2004); Monica Gattinger and Geoffrey Hale, eds., *Borders and Bridges: Canada's Policy Relations in North America* (Toronto: Oxford University Press, 2010); Greg Anderson and Christopher Sands, eds., *Forgotten Partnership Redux: Canada–U.S. Relations in the 21st Century* (Amherst, NY: Cambria Press, 2011).

13 Gattinger and Hale, *Borders and Bridges,* 3-8.

14 Clarkson, *Does North America Exist?,* 454.

15 Anne Marie Slaughter, *A New World Order* (Princeton, NJ: Princeton University Press, 2004); Gattinger and Hale, *Borders and Bridges.*

16 Doran, *Forgotten Partnership,* 8, 53-66.

17 Confidential interview, US Department of State, 2005.

18 Allan Gotlieb, *The United States in Canadian Foreign Policy,* O.D. Skelton Lecture, 10 December 1991 (Ottawa: Foreign Affairs and International Trade Canada, 1991), 7.

19 Allan Gotlieb, *I'll Be with You in a Minute, Mr. Ambassador* (Toronto: University of Toronto Press, 1991); Bow, *The Politics of Linkage,* 5.

20 See, for example, Eugene Donati, "Opposed Triangles: Policy-Making and Regulation in Canada and the United States," *Policy Options* 23, 3 (April 2001): 44-49.

21 Clarkson, *Does North America Exist?,* 20.

22 Richard Cooper, *The Economics of Interdependence,* published for the Council on Foreign Relations (New York: McGraw-Hill, 1968), 5-30; Doran, *Forgotten Partnership,* 50.

23 Clarkson, *Does North America Exist?,* 31-44; Jorge G. Castañeda, "Towards a Reset in U.S.-Mexican Relations," *Washington Post,* 17 May 2010.

24 Greg Anderson and Christopher Sands, *Negotiating North America: The Security and Prosperity Partnership* (Washington, DC: Hudson Institute, 2007).

25 Christopher Sands, *The Canada Gambit* (Washington, DC: Hudson Institute, 2011).

26 Milner, *Interests, Institutions, and Information*, 11.

27 Heynen and Higginbotham, *Advancing Canada's Interests in the United States;* confidential interviews, Privy Council Office (PCO), Foreign Affairs and International Trade Canada (DFAIT), US Department of State, 2005-9.

28 Bow, *The Politics of Linkage.*

29 Mouafo, Morales, and Heynen, *A Compendium of Canada–U.S. Relations.*

30 James N. Rosenau, *Distant Proximities* (Cambridge, MA: Harvard University Press, 2003); Greg Anderson and Christopher Sands, "Fragmegration, Federalism, and Canada–U.S. Relations," in *Borders and Bridges: Canada's Policy Relations in North America*, edited by Monica Gattinger and Geoffrey Hale (Toronto: Oxford University Press, 2010), 41-58.

31 This is a recurring observation of Canada's ambassadors to Washington, if one still treated as newsworthy by American commentators. See, for example, Gotlieb, *I'll Be with You in a Minute;* Robert Novak, "The Politics of Ports," *Washington Post*, 27 February 2006.

32 Robert Putnam and Nicholas Bayne, *Hanging Together: Co-operation and Conflict in the Seven-Power Summits* (Cambridge, MA: Harvard University Press, 1987); Milner, *Interests, Institutions, and Information.*

33 Slaughter, *A New World Order.*

34 Gattinger and Hale, *Borders and Bridges*, 13.

35 Geoffrey Hale and Monica Gattinger, "Variable Geometry and Traffic Circles: Navigating Canada's Policy Relations in North America," in *Borders and Bridges: Canada's Policy Relations in North America*, edited by Monica Gattinger and Geoffrey Hale (Toronto: Oxford University Press, 2010), 372-73.

36 Heynen and Higginbotham, *Advancing Canada's Interests in the United States*, 18; see also Mahant and Mount, *Invisible and Inaudible in Washington.*

37 Confidential interviews, DFAIT, US Department of State, 2005-9; see also Doran, *Forgotten Partnership;* Allan Gotlieb, *The Washington Diaries: 1983-1991* (Toronto: McClelland and Stewart, 2006); Reginald Stuart, *Dispersed Relations: Americans and Canadians in Upper North America* (Washington, DC: Woodrow Wilson Center Press; Baltimore: Johns Hopkins University Press, 2008).

38 Mahant and Mount, *Invisible and Inaudible in Washington*, 14.

39 Hart suggests that the "special relationship" was "based on a mutual understanding that broad geopolitical interests should, when necessary, overrule narrow commercial policy concerns." Michael Hart, *Canada: A Trading Nation* (Vancouver: UBC Press, 2002), 282.

40 See, for example, Christopher Sands, "How Canada Policy Is Made in the United States," in *Vanishing Borders: Canada among Nations, 2000*, edited by Maureen Appel Molot and Fen Osler Hampson (Toronto: Oxford University Press, 2000), 47-72; Andrew Cohen, *While Canada Slept? How We Lost Our Place in the World* (Toronto: McClelland and Stewart, 2003); Allan Gotlieb, *Romanticism and Realism in Canada's Foreign Policy*, Benefactors Lecture, 3 November 2004 (Toronto: C.D. Howe Institute, 2004).

41 Allan Gotlieb, "The Future of Canada–US Relations: Bring Back the Special Relationship," in *American Myths: What Canadians Think They Know about the United States*, edited by Rudyard Griffiths (Toronto: Key Porter, 2009), 78.

42 Hart, *Canada: A Trading Nation*, 214-17; Joseph Jockel, *Canada in NORAD, 1957-2007: A History* (Montreal: McGill-Queen's University Press, 2007).

43 Hart, *Canada: A Trading Nation*, 288; Alan Freeman, "Former US President 'Got Us in' G8," *Globe and Mail*, 3 January 2007.

44 Gotlieb, *The Washington Diaries*, 102-3, 113-14.

45 Geoffrey Hale, "People, Politics, and Passports: Contesting Security, Trade, and Travel on the US–Canadian Border," *Geopolitics* 16, 1 (2011): 27-69; see also Chapter 11 of this volume.

46 See, for example, Slaughter, *A New World Order*; John J. Kirton and Michael J. Trebilcock, "Introduction: Hard Choices and Soft Law in Sustainable Global Governance," in *Hard Choices, Soft Law: Voluntary Standards in Global Trade, Environment, and Social Governance*, edited by John J. Kirton and Michael J. Trebilcock (Burlington, VT: Ashgate, 2004), 3-13.

47 See, for example, Steven W. Hook, *U.S. Foreign Policy: The Paradox of World Power* (Washington, DC: CQ Press, 2005), 336-37; Peter J. Katzenstein, *A World of Regions: Asia and Europe in the American Imperium* (Ithaca, NY: Cornell University Press, 2005), 231.

48 Daowei Zhang, *The Softwood Lumber War* (Washington, DC: RFF Press, 2007).

49 Stuart, *Dispersed Relations*.

50 Milner, *Interests, Institutions, and Information*, 8-9.

51 Putnam and Bayne, *Hanging Together*, 260; Milner, *Interests, Institutions, and Information*, 9.

52 Geoffrey Hale, "Canada–US Relations in the Obama Era: Warming or Greening?," in *How Ottawa Spends: 2010-2011*, edited by G. Bruce Doern and Christopher Stoney (Montreal: McGill-Queen's University Press, 2010), 50-51.

53 Ibid.; Hale and Gattinger, "Variable Geometry and Traffic Circles," 373.

54 See, for example, Stephen Clarkson, ed., *An Independent Foreign Policy for Canada?* (Toronto: McClelland and Stewart, 1968); Anderson and Sands, *Negotiating North America*; Stephanie R. Golob, "The Return of the Quiet Canadian: Canada's Approach to Regional Integration after 9/11," in *An Independent Foreign Policy for Canada?*, edited by Brian Bow and A. Patrick Lennox (Toronto: University of Toronto Press, 2008), 83-99.

55 Doran, *Forgotten Partnership*, 37.

Chapter 2: Guns, Globes, and Gardening

1 Cited in James Travers, "PM's Turn to Cut a Rug with U.S.," *Toronto Star*, 14 February 2009; confidential interviews, US Department of State, 2006-9.

2 Carl Ek, *Canada–U.S. Relations*, CRS Report 96-397 (Washington, DC: Congressional Research Service, 1 May 2006), 7; Bill Clinton, "Remarks to International Conference on Federalism," Forum of Federations, Mont Tremblant, Quebec, 1999.

3 Christopher Sands, "The Rising Importance of Third Country Issues in Canada's Relations with the United States," in *Canada among Nations 2006: Minorities and Priorities,* edited by Andrew F. Cooper and Dane Rowlands (Montreal: McGill-Queen's University Press, 2006), 134.

4 Elinor Sloan, *Security and Defence in the Terrorist Era* (Montreal: McGill-Queen's University Press, 2005).

5 Stuart, *Dispersed Relations,* 215.

6 David T. Jones and David Kilgour, *Uneasy Neighbo(u)rs: Canada, the USA, and the Dynamics of State, Industry, and Culture* (Toronto: John Wiley and Sons Canada, 2007), 210-11.

7 Confidential interviews, US Department of State, 2006, 2009.

8 See, for example, Ek, *Canada–U.S. Relations: 2006,* 7-21; Carl Ek, *Canada–U.S. Relations,* Report 96-397 (Washington, DC: Congressional Research Service, 12 May 2009), 10-22.

9 David J. Bercuson and Denis Stairs, eds., *In the Canadian Interest? Assessing Canada's International Policy Statement* (Calgary: Canadian Defence and Foreign Affairs Institute, 2005); Bow and Lennox, *An Independent Foreign Policy for Canada?;* Stephen Clarkson, "The Choice to Be Made," in *Readings in Canadian Foreign Policy: Classic Debates and New Ideas,* edited by Duane Bratt and Christopher Kukucha (Toronto: Oxford University Press, 2006), 46-61; Gotlieb, *Romanticism and Realism in Canada's Foreign Policy.*

10 Charles Doran, "Canada–U.S. Relations: Personality, Pattern, and Domestic Politics," in *Handbook on Canadian Foreign Policy,* edited by Patrick James, Marc O'Reilly, and Nelson Michaud (Lanham, MD: Lexington, 2006), 396-400.

11 Ibid.

12 Lloyd Axworthy, "Choices and Consequences in a Liberal Foreign Policy," in *Searching for the New Liberalism: Perspectives, Policies, Prospects,* edited by Howard Aster and Thomas S. Axworthy (Oakville, ON: Mosaic Press, 2003), 63-79; Michael Byers, *Intent for a Nation* (Vancouver: Douglas and McIntyre, 2007); Thomas S. Mowle, *Allies at Odds? The United States and the European Union* (New York: Palgrave Macmillan, 2004), 12, 46-50.

13 Derek Burney, "Foreign Policy: More Coherence, Less Pretence" (Ottawa: Centre for Trade Policy and Law, 14 March 2005), 14.

14 Ibid.

15 Thomas A. Axworthy, "On Being an Ally: Why Virtue Is Not Reward Enough" (Ottawa: Institute for Research on Public Policy, 2004); Norman Hillmer, Fen Hampson, and David Carment, "Smart Power in Canadian Foreign Policy," in *Canada among Nations 2005,* edited by Norman Hillmer, Fen Hampson, and David Carment (Montreal: McGill-Queen's University Press, 2006), 3-17.

16 David J. Bercuson and Denis Stairs, "Introduction," in *In the Canadian Interest? Assessing Canada's International Policy Statement,* edited by David J. Bercuson and Denis Stairs (Calgary: Canadian Defence and Foreign Affairs Institute, 2005), 1-5.

17 Stuart, *Dispersed Relations,* 283-84.

18   Bow, *The Politics of Linkage.*

19   Confidential interviews, US Department of State, 2006, 2007; Cellucci, *Unquiet Diplomacy,* 38.

20   Dwight N. Mason, "Canadian Defense Priorities: What Might the United States Like to See?," in *Policy Papers on the Americas,* vol. 15, study 1 (Washington, DC: Center for Strategic and International Studies, 2004), 1.

21   Gotlieb, *The Washington Diaries,* 535.

22   Jockel, *Canada in NORAD;* Janice Stein and Eugene Lang, *The Unexpected War: Canada in Kandahar* (Toronto: Viking Canada, 2007).

23   Confidential interviews, Canadian Department of Foreign Affairs, US Departments of State and Homeland Security (DHS), 2006-9.

24   Doran, "Canada–U.S. Relations"; Gotlieb, *The Washington Diaries.*

25   Heynen and Higginbotham, *Advancing Canada's Interests in the United States;* Mason, "Canadian Defense Priorities"; Doran, "Canada–U.S. Relations"; Ek, *Canada–U.S. Relations, 2009;* confidential interviews, Privy Council Office, DFAIT, 2006-8, US Department of State, 2005-9.

26   Sands, "How Canada Policy Is Made in the United States," 65-69.

27   Mason, "Canadian Defense Priorities," 3; Cellucci, *Unquiet Diplomacy,* 75-76.

28   Ek, *Canada–U.S. Relations,* 6.

29   See, for example, Norman Spector, "Nix the Toys for the Boys," *Globe and Mail,* 10 October 2002.

30   Mason, "Canadian Defense Priorities," 3; Cellucci, *Unquiet Diplomacy,* 75-76; Jones and Kilgour, *Uneasy Neighbo(u)rs;* J.L. Granatstein, "Sometimes Peace Means Making War," in *American Myths: What Canadians Think They Know about the United States,* edited by Rudyard Griffiths (Toronto: Key Porter, 2009), 24.

31   Confidential interview, former White House adviser, 2006.

32   Harvey Sapolsky, "Canada: Crossing the Line," *Breakthroughs* 14, 1 (2004): 31-37; Sara A. Carter, "NATO Seen Cool to Hot Spots in Afghanistan," *Washington Times,* 17 January 2008.

33   Sands, "The Rising Importance of Third Country Issues," 127; Julianne Smith and Michael Williams, "What Lies Beneath: The Future of NATO through the ISAF Prism" (Washington, DC: Center for Strategic and International Studies, 2008); Jeffrey J. Schott, ed., *Free Trade Agreements: US Strategies and Priorities* (Washington, DC: Institute for International Economics, 2004).

34   Stein and Lang, *The Unexpected War,* 78-90.

35   Ibid., 62-72, 91-108.

36   Cited in ibid., 65.

37   Sands, "The Rising Importance of Third Country Issues," 126; Douglas Bland, "Pursuing Our Hemispheric Interests," *Globe and Mail,* 4 September 2009.

38   Canada, DFAIT, *The Americas: Priorities and Progress* (Ottawa: DFAIT, 2009); Bland, "Pursuing Our Hemispheric Interests."

39   Stephen Harper, "Reviving Canadian Leadership in the World," speech to Woodrow Wilson International Center for Scholars, Calgary, 5 October 2006.

40   Gotlieb, *The Washington Diaries,* 399.

41 Campbell Clark, "PM Plans 'Inside the Wire' Afghan Role while U.S. Presses for Riskier One," *Globe and Mail*, 11 November 2010; Campbell Clark, "Extension Was Result of Rare Bipartisan Effort," *Globe and Mail*, 18 November 2010.

42 David Rothkopf, *Running the World: The Inside Story of the National Security Council and the Architects of American Power* (New York: Public Affairs, 2006).

43 United States, Commission on National Security in the 21st Century, *New World Coming: Phase I Report on the Emerging Security Environment in the First Quarter of the Twenty-First Century*, the Hart-Rudman Report (Washington, DC: 1999), 109.

44 Confidential interview, US Department of State, 2006.

45 Dwight N. Mason, "Time to Expand NORAD," in *Security and Sovereignty: Renewing NORAD – One Nation, Two Voices*, edited by Marcia R. Seitz-Ehler (Washington, DC: Woodrow Wilson International Center for Scholars, 2005), 2-7.

46 Jockel, *Canada in NORAD*; Joseph T. Jockel and Joel J. Sokolsky, "Renewing NORAD – Now if Not Forever," *Policy Options* (July-August 2006): 53-58.

47 I am indebted to Bernard Brister for this useful distinction.

48 Victor E. Renuart, "Statement to Senate Armed Services Committee" (Washington, DC: US Northern Command News, 6 March 2008), 12.

49 Ek, *Canada–U.S. Relations*, 9-10. "Canada's proposed purchase of 65 F-35s to replace its aging CF-18 fighters has been called into question due to project delays, substantial cost-overruns, and alleged abuses of procurement processes by National Defence officials." John Ivison, "Tories to Reopen F-35 Debate," *National Post*, 3 April 2012, A1.

50 Mason, "Canadian Defense Priorities."

51 See, for example, David Pugliese, "Air Force Needs $520M to Keep Flying," *Ottawa Citizen*, 17 April 2008; David Pugliese, "Navy at Risk of Running Aground," *Ottawa Citizen*, 18 April 2008.

52 Gotlieb, *The Washington Diaries*, 130, 400, 535.

53 Confidential interview, DFAIT, 2006.

54 Confidential interview, DFAIT, 2008.

55 Canada, Department of National Defence, *Canada First Defence Strategy* (Ottawa: DND, 2008); Bland, "Pursuing Our Hemispheric Interests."

56 Canada, DFAIT, *Smart Border Accord* (Ottawa: DFAIT, 2001); Cellucci, *Unquiet Diplomacy*, 95-99; Sloan, *Security and Defence in the Terrorist Era*, 62-65.

57 Confidential interview, PCO, 2005.

58 Anderson and Sands, *Negotiating North America*; Jerome R. Corsi, *The Late, Great USA: The Coming Merger with Mexico and Canada* (Los Angeles: World Ahead Media, 2007).

59 Janet Napolitano, "Transcript of Remarks to 'Towards a Better Border: The United States and Canada'" (Washington, DC: Brookings Institution, 25 March 2009); Sands, *The Canada Gambit*.

60 Louis Belanger, "An Unsustainable Institutional Design: Incompleteness and Delegation Deficit in NAFTA," in *Governing the Americas: Assessing Multilateral Institutions*, edited by Gordon Mace and Paul Haslam (Boulder, CO: Lynne Rienner Publishers, 2007), 195-212; Isabel Studer, "Obstacles to Integration: NAFTA's Institutional Weakness," in *Requiem or Revival? The Promise of North American*

Integration, edited by Isabel Studer and Carol Wise (Washington, DC: Brookings Institution Press, 2007), 53-76.

61 Jeffrey Davidow, *The US and Mexico: The Bear and the Porcupine* (Princeton, NJ: Marcus Weiner Publishing, 2005), 15-18; George W. Grayson, *Mexico: Narco-Violence and a Failed State?* (New Brunswick, NJ: Transaction, 2010), 231-40.

62 Bernard J. Brister, "The Same Yet Different: The Evolution of the Post-9/11 Canada–United States Security Relationship," in *Borders and Bridges: Navigating Canada's International Policy Relations*, edited by Monica Gattinger and Geoffrey Hale (Toronto: Oxford University Press, 2010), 82-99; confidential interviews, DFAIT, 2005-8.

63 Colin Freeze and Marina Jimenez, "Mexico's Drug War Becomes Canadian Security Issue," *Globe and Mail*, 5 March 2009.

64 See, for example, Bow, *The Politics of Linkage*, 75-101.

65 Douglas C. Nord, "The North in Canadian-American Relations: Searching for Collaboration in Melting Seas," in *Borders and Bridges: Navigating Canada's Policy Relations in North America*, edited by Monica Gattinger and Geoffrey Hale (Toronto: Oxford University Press, 2010), 120-37.

66 Drew Fagan, address to the biennial conference of the Association for Canadian Studies in the United States, Toronto, 15 November 2007.

67 Jessa Gamble, "Drawing Lines on the Sea: Nations Stake Claims on Arctic Ocean Riches," *Scientific American*, 10 November 2008, http://www.scientificamerican.com/; Juliet Eilperin, "U.S., Canada Map Edges of Continent on Seafloor," *Washington Post*, 11 September 2008.

68 Lassi Heinenen and Heather Nicol, "A New Northern Security Agenda," in *Borderlands: Comparing Border Security in North America and Europe*, edited by Emmanuel Brunet-Jailly (Ottawa: University of Ottawa Press, 2007), 117-63; confidential interview, DFAIT, 2008.

69 United States, White House, "Arctic Region Policy," National Security Presidential Directive 66 and Homeland Security Presidential Directive 25 (Washington, DC: 9 January 2009); Sheldon Alberts, "Ratifying Treaty Best Way to Resolve Arctic Claims," *Ottawa Citizen*, 7 April 2009; Randy Boswell and Juliet O'Neill, "Clinton Blasts Canada for Exclusive Arctic Talks," *Ottawa Citizen*, 30 March 2010.

70 Michael Byers, "A Thaw in Relations," *Ottawa Citizen*, 6 March 2008.

71 Mowle, *Allies at Odds?*, 41.

72 Confidential interview, US Department of State, 2006.

73 "A Defeat for Anti-Americanism," Editorial, *Washington Post*, 20 January 2006.

74 Clarkson, *Uncle Sam and Us*.

75 Bow, *The Politics of Linkage*.

76 Thomas A. Axworthy, "A Strong Canada in a Strong Continent," *Toronto Star*, 30 December 2007.

Chapter 3: Multilevel Games

1 Confidential interview, DFAIT, 2006.

2 Gotlieb, *I'll Be with You in a Minute, Mr. Ambassador*, 32-33.

3 Geoffrey Hale and Stephen Blank, "North American Economic Integration and Comparative Responses to Globalization – Overview," in *Borders and Bridges: Navigating Canada's Policy Relations in North America,* edited by Monica Gattinger and Geoffrey Hale (Toronto: Oxford University Press, 2010), 21-40.

4 World Trade Organization, *International Trade Statistics: 2010* (Geneva: WTO, 2011), 4, 12, 17; United States, *2011 Trade Policy Agenda and 2010 Annual Report of the President of the United States on the Trade Agreements Program* (Washington, DC: Office of the United States Trade Representative, 2010), Annex 1.

5 Guy Stanley, "Borders and Bridges: Free Trade, Supply Chains, and the Creation of a Joint Trading Platform: Canada–US Industrial Development since 1980," in *Borders and Bridges: Canada's Policy Relations in North America,* edited by Monica Gattinger and Geoffrey Hale (Toronto: Oxford University Press, 2010), 306-23; Canada, Policy Research Institute, *The Emergence of Cross-Border Regions between Canada and the United States: Reaping the Promise and Public Value of Cross-Border Regional Relationships – Final Report* (Ottawa: Industry Canada, 2008), 6.

6 Hart, *Canada: A Trading Nation.*

7 Brian W. Tomlin, Norman Hillmer, and Fen Osler Hampson, *Canada's International Policies: Agendas, Alternatives, and Policies* (Toronto: Oxford University Press, 2008), 92-95.

8 Schott, *Free Trade Agreements.*

9 Alan Freeman, "Latin America Visit by Harper to Focus on Foreign Policy," *Globe and Mail,* 12 July 2007.

10 Aaron Sydor, "The Rise of Global Value Chains," in *Seventh Annual Report on Canada's State of Trade,* edited by Jean-Bosco Sabuyhoro and Aaron Sydor (Ottawa: DFAIT, 2007), 57-58.

11 Cited in Bill Dymond and Michael Hart, "Navigating New Trade Routes: The Rise of Value Chains, and the Challenges for Canadian Trade Policy," Commentary 259 (Toronto: C.D. Howe Institute, 2008).

12 Geoffrey Hale, "The Dog that Hasn't Barked: The Political Economy of Contemporary Debates on Canadian Foreign Investment Policies," *Canadian Journal of Political Science* 41, 3 (2008): 719-47; Canada, Competition Policy Review Panel, *Compete to Win: Final Report* (Ottawa: Industry Canada, 2008).

13 Paul Frazer, correspondence with author, 2011.

14 Tip O'Neill and Gary Hymel, *All Politics Is Local: And Other Rules of the Game* (Holbrook, MA: Bob Adams, 1994); Christopher J. Kukucha, "Sub-Federal Trade and the Politics of North American Economic Integration: Evaluating the Cross-Border Exports of American States," in *Borders and Bridges: Canada's Policy Relations in North America,* edited by Monica Gattinger and Geoffrey Hale (Toronto: Oxford University Press, 2010), 270-88.

15 Confidential interview, DFAIT, 2008.

16 Heynen and Higginbotham, *Advancing Canada's Interests in the United States,* 18.

17 Belanger, "An Unsustainable Institutional Design."

18 Alexander Moens, *Mad Cow: A Case Study in Canadian–American Relations* (Vancouver: Fraser Institute, 2006); confidential interviews, former US government official, industry association officials, 2006.

19 United States, White House, and Canada, Privy Council Office, "Beyond the Border: A Shared Vision for Economic Security and Economic Competitiveness," Washington, DC, and Ottawa, 7 December 2011.

20 Andrea Mandel-Campbell, *Why Mexicans Don't Drink Molson: Rescuing Canadian Business from the Suds of Global Obscurity* (Vancouver: Douglas and McIntyre, 2007).

21 Geoffrey Hale, "Getting Down to Business: Rebuilding Canada–US Relations," in *How Ottawa Spends: 2007-2008,* edited by G. Bruce Doern (Montreal: McGill-Queen's University Press, 2007), 65-86.

22 Daniel Leblanc, "Ottawa Aims to Soften U.S. Arms-Contract Rules," *Globe and Mail,* 15 January 2007; Daniel Leblanc, "U.S. Rules Slowing Delivery of Helicopters, Other Equipment," *Globe and Mail,* 26 March 2007.

23 Gotlieb, *I'll Be with You in a Minute, Mr. Ambassador;* Judith Goldstein, "International Forces and Domestic Politics: Trade Policy and Institution Building in the United States," in *Shaped by War and Trade: International Influences on American Political Development,* edited by Ira Katznelson and Martin Shefter (Princeton, NJ: Princeton University Press, 2002), 211-35; I.M. Destler, *American Trade Politics,* 4th ed. (Washington, DC: Institute for International Economics, 2005).

24 Gotlieb, *I'll Be with You in a Minute, Mr. Ambassador,* 35.

25 His comment was in response to the announcement of a strategic alliance between WestJet and Southwest Airlines. Cited in Virginia Galt, "Westjet Tackles US Market," *Globe and Mail,* 9 July 2008.

26 Gautam Sen, "The United States and the GATT/WTO System," in *US Hegemony and International Organizations,* edited by Rosemary Foot, S. Neil MacFarlane, and Michael Mastanduno (New York: Oxford University Press, 2003), 116; Destler, *American Trade Politics,* 16.

27 Gotlieb, *I'll Be with You in a Minute, Mr. Ambassador,* 27-28.

28 Sands, *The Canada Gambit,* 20, 25.

29 Gotlieb, *"I'll Be with You in a Minute, Mr. Ambassador,* 28.

30 Cited in Milner, *Interests, Institutions, and Information,* 4; Novak, "The Politics of Ports."

31 Goldstein, "International Forces and Domestic Politics," 213.

32 Jeanne J. Grimmett, "Why Certain Trade Agreements Are Approved as Congressional-Executive Agreements Rather than as Treaties," CRS Report 97-896 (Washington, DC: Congressional Research Service, Library of Congress, 28 July 2004).

33 Destler, *American Trade Politics,* 346-47; Derek H. Burney, *Getting It Done* (Montreal: McGill-Queen's University Press, 2005), 210-20.

34 Destler, *American Trade Politics,* 331-42.

35 Confidential interview, US Department of Commerce, 2006.

36 Ibid.

37 Moens, *Mad Cow;* Stanley Tromp, "Canada Lobbied U.S. over Pipeline," *Financial Post,* 24 January 2011; Tom Zeller Jr., "Oil Sands Effort Turns on a Fight over a Road," *New York Times,* 22 October 2010.

38 Bernard M. Hoekman and Michel M. Kostecki, *The Political Economy of the World Trading System*, 2nd ed. (Toronto: Oxford University Press, 2001); Gary Clyde Hufbauer and Jeffrey J. Schott, *NAFTA Revisited* (Washington, DC: Institute for International Economics, 2005).

39 Heynen and Higginbotham, *Advancing Canada's Interests in the United States.*

40 US Census Bureau, "Income Statistics," Table H-3, http://www.census.gov/.

41 Jacqueline Thorpe, "Sweet Deal for the Sugar Industry," *Financial Post*, 2 June 2008; Mary R. Brooks, *The Jones Act under NAFTA and Its Effects on the Canadian Shipbuilding Industry* (Halifax: Atlantic Institute for Market Studies, 2006).

42 Paul Frazer, interview, Washington, DC, 2006.

43 Carl Meyer, "More than Shades of SPP in Perimeter Deal," *Embassy*, 4 February 2011, 1; Steven Chase, "Canada Concerned at Including Mexico in Talks with U.S.: Wikileaks Release," *Globe and Mail*, 3 March 2011.

44 Confidential interviews, DFAIT, 2006-8, members of "Canada policy community" in Washington.

45 For example, Wendy Dobson, "Shaping the Future of the North American Economic Space: A Framework for Action," Commentary 162 (Toronto: C.D. Howe Institute, 2002); John P. Manley, Pedro Aspe, and William Weld, *Building a North American Community: Report of an Independent Task Force* (New York: Council on Foreign Relations, 2005); Derek Burney, "Canada–US Relations at 150," paper presented at the Canada @ 150: Rising to the Challenge Conference, Calgary, 28 March 2010.

46 Conversations with senior business stakeholders and Canadian government officials, 2011.

47 United States, White House, *Improving Regulation and Regulatory Review: Executive Order* (Washington, DC: Office of the Press Secretary, 2011).

48 Schott, *Free Trade Agreements*; Hufbauer and Schott, *NAFTA Revisited.*

49 Edward Alden, *The Closing of the American Border* (New York: Harper, 2008); Geoffrey Hale and Christina Marcotte, "Border Security, Trade, and Travel Facilitation," in *Borders and Bridges: Navigating Canada's Policy Relations in North America*, edited by Monica Gattinger and Geoffrey Hale (Toronto: Oxford University Press, 2010), 100-19.

50 Meyer, "More than Shades of SPP in Perimeter Deal"; Sands, *The Canada Gambit.*

51 Hale and Gattinger, "Variable Geometry and Traffic Circles," 367.

52 Canada, DFAIT, "Negotiations and Agreements," http://www.international.gc.ca/; John Ibbitson, "Trade Key to PM's Idea of Success," *Globe and Mail*, 26 December 2011.

53 Hale and Blank, "North American Economic Integration."

54 Gattinger and Hale, *Borders and Bridges*, 1-18.

55 Sands, *The Canada Gambit.*

56 Gotlieb, "The Future of Canada–US Relations"; Burney, "Canada–US Relations at 150."

Chapter 4: Neighbo(u)rs, Friends, and Strangers

1 Dyment, *Doing the Continental*, 33-34.

2 Adopted from Doran, *Forgotten Partnership*, 85-86.

3 Robert Fulford, "Bred in the Bone," in *American Myths: What Canadians Think They Know about the United States*, edited by Rudyard Griffiths (Toronto: Key Porter, 2009), 63-74; Andrew Cohen, "Our Mythology of Values," in *American Myths: What Canadians Think They Know about the United States*, edited by Rudyard Griffiths (Toronto: Key Porter, 2009), 137-50.

4 Gattinger and Hale, *Bridges and Borders*.

5 Dyment, *Doing the Continental*, 138.

6 See, for example, Ekos Research Associates, "Bushwhacking and Other Ingredients of Canadian Outlook on the USA," *Time Magazine* Poll, 25 October 2004, http://www.ekos.ca/; Fulford, "Bred in the Bone"; Cohen, "Our Mythology of Values."

7 Doran, "Canada–U.S. Relations."

8 Gotlieb, *Romanticism and Realism in Canada's Foreign Policy*, 1.

9 Pierangelo Isernia, "Anti-Americanism in Europe during the Cold War," in *Anti-Americanisms in World Politics*, edited by Peter J. Katzenstein and Robert O. Keohane (Ithaca, NY: Cornell University Press, 2007), 59; Peter J. Katzenstein and Robert O. Keohane, "Varieties of Anti-Americanism: A Framework for Analysis," in *Anti-Americanisms in World Politics*, edited by Peter J. Katzenstein and Robert O. Keohane (Ithaca, NY: Cornell University Press, 2007), 27-33.

10 Mark Milke, "Limits on Deliberative Democracy in Canada: A Study of Political Culture and How Attitudes towards the United States Shape Canadian Policy Debates" (PhD diss., University of Calgary, 2008); Stuart, *Dispersed Relations*.

11 For distinctions between "autonomy" and "independence," see Gattinger and Hale, *Borders and Bridges*; Geoffrey Hale, "Maintaining Policy Discretion: Cross-Border Policy-Making and North American Integration," in *An Independent Foreign Policy for Canada?*, edited by Brian Bow and R. Patrick Lennox (Toronto: University of Toronto Press, 2008), 137-62.

12 See, for example, Jeffrey M. Ayres, "Political Economy, Civil Society, and the Deep Integration Debate in Canada," *American Review of Canadian Studies* 34, 4 (2004): 621-47.

13 Dan Dunsky, "Why We Bash America," *National Post*, 21 December 2005; Sheldon Alberts, "McKenna Blasts His Own Party's Anti-U.S. Rhetoric," *Ottawa Citizen*, 2 March 2006; Milke, "Limits on Deliberative Democracy in Canada."

14 Milke, "Limits on Deliberative Democracy in Canada"; Gordon Hoekstra, "EthicalOil.org Slams Environmental Groups for Taking U.S. money," *Vancouver Sun*, 4 January 2012.

15 Janice Tibbetts, "One in Five Believes in Conspiracy," *National Post*, 11 September 2006; Nik Nanos, "Free Trade at 20: SES/Policy Options Exclusive Poll: Canadians, Americans Agree Both Better off with Free Trade," *Policy Options* 28, 9 (October 2007): 1-8; Marcus Gee, "Poll Highlights Unease over U.S. Foreign Policy," *Globe and Mail*, 13 December 2007; Robert O. Keohane and Peter J. Katzenstein, "Political Consequences of Anti-Americanism," in *Anti-Americanisms in World Politics*, edited by Peter J. Katzenstein and Robert O. Keohane (Ithaca, NY: Cornell University Press, 2007), 296.

16 John P. Manley, "Creating a North American Community: Chairman's Statement from an Independent Task Force on the Future of North America," interview transcript (New York: Council on Foreign Relations, 14 March 2005); Paul Frazer,

remarks to the US–Canada Relations Seminar, Duke University, 27 January 2006.

17 Milke, "Limits on Deliberative Democracy in Canada"; Amanda Carpenter, "Hot Button: Canada and U.S.," *Washington Times*, 1 June 2009.

18 Dan Dunsky, "Canada's Three Solitudes," *National Interest* 82 (2005-6): 94-99; Michael Adams, *Fire and Ice: The United States, Canada, and the Myth of Converging Values* (Toronto: Penguin, 2003).

19 David N. Biette and Douglas Goold, *Renewing the U.S.–Canada Relationship: The 105th American Assembly* (Toronto: Canadian Institute for International Affairs; Washington, DC: Woodrow Wilson International Center for Scholars, 2005), 7.

20 The Strategic Counsel, "A Tale of Two Nations: State of Canadian/American Public Opinion: A Report to the *Globe and Mail* and CTV," 2008.

21 Cameron D. Anderson and Laura B. Stephenson, "Moving Closer or Drifting Apart? Assessing the State of Public Opinion on the U.S.–Canadian Relationship" (London, ON: Canada–US Institute, University of Western Ontario, 2010), 5-7.

22 Matthew Mendelsohn, Robert Wolfe, and Andrew Parkin, "Globalization, Trade Policy, and the Permissive Consensus in Canada," *Canadian Public Policy* 28, 3 (2002): 351-71; Nanos, "Free Trade at 20"; Gloria Galloway, "Canadians Share Americans' Anxiety," *Globe and Mail*, 28 June 2008; Norval Scott, "Our Views of the U.S.," *Globe and Mail*, 8 December 2008.

23 Christopher Sands, "Canada as Minor Ally: Operational Considerations for Relations with the United States," notes for a presentation to the 2003 Canadian Crude Oil Conference, Kananaskis, AB, 5 September 2003 (Washington, DC: Center for Strategic and International Studies), 8.

24 David G. Haglund, "French Connection? Quebec and Anti-Americanism in the Transatlantic Community," paper presented to the biennial meeting of the Association of Canadian Studies in the United States, 18 November 2007.

25 Anne McLellan, comments in the roundtable New Leadership in U.S.–Canada Relations, 27 June 2006 (Washington, DC: Center for Strategic and International Studies); Paul Frazer, conversations with the author, 2007; Keohane and Katzenstein, "Political Consequences of Anti-Americanism," 294; Strategic Counsel, "Views on Canadian Foreign Policy and the Mulroney-Schreiber Saga" (Toronto: Strategic Counsel, 10 December 2007).

26 Hale, "Getting Down to Business"; Beth Gorham, "Harper Can Disagree with U.S., MP," *Ottawa Citizen*, 28 January 2006.

27 Ekos Research Associates, *Results of Ekos/CBC News Survey* (Toronto: Ekos Research Associates, 19 January 2009), 9-10.

28 Milke, "Limits on Deliberative Democracy in Canada."

29 Canada, Prime Minister's Office, and United States, White House, "Beyond the Border: A Shared Vision for Perimeter Security and Economic Competitiveness," Ottawa and Washington, DC, 4 February 2011; Tim Harper, "The Canada–U.S. Relationship: Out of Sight, Out of Mind," *Toronto Star*, 22 April 2011.

30 Rheal Seguin, "Harper's Rebuke Catches U.S. Envoy Off Guard," *Globe and Mail*, 28 January 2006.

31 Confidential interviews, DFAIT, US Department of State, 2005-9; see also "A Defeat for Anti-Americanism," *Washington Post*.

32 Jeffrey Jones, "Iran, North Korea Still Americans' Least Favorite Countries" (Princeton, NJ: Gallup, 11 February 2011); Bertrand Marotte, "Canadians, Americans Agree Border Should Stay: Polls," *Globe and* Mail, 14 March 2011.

33 See, for example, the annual review of Canada–US relations published by the non-partisan Congressional Research Service.

34 Geoffrey Hale and Jamie Huckabay, "Canadian Public Diplomacy in the United States: Which Public? How Diplomatic?," paper presented at the conference of the Association for Canadian Studies in the United States, Toronto, 15 November 2007.

35 Gotlieb, *The Washington Diaries*, 165.

36 Commission on National Security in the 21st Century, *New World Coming*, 115.

37 Ekos Research Associates, *Ekos/PPF Symposium: Rethinking North American Integration – Part II; Economic Dimensions* (Toronto: Ekos Research Associates, 18 June 2002), 9-10.

38 Pew Research Center, "Foreign Policy Attitudes Now Driven by 9/11 and Iraq" (Washington, DC: Pew Research Center, 18 August 2004), 17.

39 For a cross-section of public opinion polls on attitudes toward trade and trade policies, see http://www.pollingreport.com/.

40 Pew Research Center, "Foreign Policy Attitudes Now Driven by 9/11 and Iraq."

41 Pew Research Center, "Support for Free Trade Recovers Despite Recession" (Washington, DC: Pew Research Center, 28 April 2009); Jeffrey M. Jones, "Americans More Negative than Positive about Foreign Trade" (Princeton, NJ: Gallup, 18 February 2009).

42 Paul Frazer, remarks to the US–Canada Relations Seminar, Duke University, 27 January 2006.

43 Cellucci, *Unquiet Diplomacy*, 115.

44 Heynen and Higginbotham, *Advancing Canada's Interests in the United States.*

45 Mouafo, Morales, and Heynen, *A Compendium of Canada–U.S. Relations.*

46 Heynen and Higginbotham, *Advancing Canada's Interests in the United States,* 7-8, 21.

47 Paul Frazer, conversations with the author, 2006, 2007.

48 Confidential interview, DFAIT, 2005.

49 Confidential interview, US Department of State, 2005.

50 Confidential interview, senior US government official, 2009; see also Jones and Kilgour, *Uneasy Neighbo(u)rs,* 12.

51 Confidential interview, senior US government official, 2009.

52 Sands, *The Canada Gambit.*

53 Sands, "Canada as Minor Ally," 8.

54 Axworthy, "On Being an Ally," 4.

Chapter 5: Governing from the Centre?

1 John W. Kingdon, *Agendas, Alternatives, and Public Policies,* 2nd ed. (New York: Longmans, 1995).

2 Confidential interviews, PCO, 2005; Burney, "Canada–US Relations at 150"; Colin Robertson, "CDA_USA 2.0: Intermesticity, Hidden Wiring, and Public Diplomacy," in *Canada among Nations, 2007: What Room for Manoeuvre?,* edited by

Jean Daudelin and Daniel Schwanen (Montreal: McGill-Queen's University Press, 2008), 269.

3 Geoffrey Hale, "The Buy-American Controversy: A Case Study in Canada–U.S. Trade Relations" (Waterloo, ON: Portal for North America, Centre for International Governance Innovation, University of Waterloo, 2010), http://www.portalfornorth america.org/.

4 Bow, *The Politics of Linkage*, 176ff.

5 Christopher Waddell, "The Auto Industry Bailout: Industrial Policy or Job-Saving Social Policy?," in *How Ottawa Spends: 2010-2011*, edited by G. Bruce Doern and Christopher Stoney (Montreal: McGill-Queen's University Press, 2010), 150-67; Hale, "The Buy-American Controversy."

6 John Kirton and Jenilee Guebert, "Soft Law, Regulatory Coordination, and Convergence," in *Borders and Bridges: Canada's Policy Relations in North America*, edited by Monica Gattinger and Geoffrey Hale (Toronto: Oxford University Press, 2010), 59-76.

7 Hale and Gattinger, "Variable Geometry and Traffic Circles."

8 Heynen and Higginbotham, *Advancing Canada's Interests in the United States;* Mouafo, Morales, and Heynen, *A Compendium of Canada–U.S. Relations;* John Higginbotham and Jeff Heynen, "Managing through Networks: The State of Canada–U.S. Relations," in *Canada among Nations 2004: Setting Priorities Straight*, edited by David Carment, Fen Osler Hampson, and Norman Hillmer (Montreal: McGill-Queen's University Press, 2005), 123-40; confidential interviews, DFAIT, 2005-7.

9 Geoffrey Hale, "The Unfinished Legacy: Liberal Policy on North America," in *How Ottawa Spends: 2003-2004*, edited by G. Bruce Doern (Toronto: Oxford University Press, 2003), 25-43; Geoffrey Hale, "Cross-Border Relations: Moving beyond the Politics of Uncertainty?," in *How Ottawa Spends: 2005-2006*, edited by G. Bruce Doern (Montreal: McGill-Queen's University Press, 2005), 121-42; Hale, "Getting Down to Business"; Hale, "Canada–US Relations in the Obama Era."

10 Donald Savoie, *Governing from the Centre: The Concentration of Power in Canadian Politics* (Toronto: University of Toronto Press, 1999); Donald Savoie, *Power: Where Is It?* (Montreal: McGill-Queen's University Press, 2010), 129-35.

11 Savoie, *Governing from the Centre*, 313.

12 Confidential interviews, DFAIT, 2006-9; PCO, 2006.

13 Gotlieb, *The Washington Diaries;* Jockel, *Canada in NORAD;* Bow, *The Politics of Linkage;* James G. Fergusson, *Canada and Ballistic Missile Defence: 1954-2009* (Vancouver: UBC Press, 2010).

14 Hale, "Cross-Border Relations"; confidential interviews, DFAIT, US Department of State, 2005-7; "A Defeat for Anti-Americanism," *Washington Post;* Allan Gotlieb, "Martin's Bush-League Diplomacy," *Globe and Mail*, 26 January 2006.

15 Juliet Eilperin, "Administration Delays Decision on Oil Pipeline," *Washington Post*, 11 November 2011; United States, White House, "Statements by President Barack Obama and Prime Minister of Canada," transcript (Washington, DC: Office of the Press Secretary, 7 December 2011).

16 Gotlieb, *The Washington Diaries;* Burney, *Getting It Done.*

17 Burney's leadership of Canada's delegation in last-minute negotiations to conclude the FTA, together with Minister of Finance Michael Wilson, is one prominent example of this phenomenon. I observed another in an informal ambassadorial dinner given for Clerk of the Privy Council Kevin Lynch and Prime Ministerial Chief of Staff Ian Brodie in Washington in mid-2006.

18 Jockel, *Canada in NORAD;* Stein and Lang, *The Unexpected War;* Fergusson, *Canada and Ballistic Missile Defence,* 3-5; Brister, "The Same yet Different."

19 Mouafo, Morales, and Heynen, *A Compendium of Canada–U.S. Relations;* Higginbotham and Heynen, "Managing through Networks."

20 Confidential interviews, DFAIT, 2006; Eddie Goldenberg, *The Way It Works: Inside Ottawa* (Toronto: McClelland and Stewart, 2006), 291-98.

21 Hale, "Cross-Border Relations"; confidential interviews, PCO, DFAIT, 2005-6.

22 Canada, *Securing an Open Society: Canada's National Security Policy* (Ottawa: PCO, 2004); Reg Whitaker, "Made in Canada: The New Public Safety Paradigm," in *How Ottawa Spends: 2005-2006 – Managing the Minority,* edited by G. Bruce Doern (Montreal: McGill-Queen's University Press, 2005), 77-95; Bercuson and Stairs, *In the Canadian Interest?*

23 Confidential interviews, PCO, 2006.

24 Confidential interview, DFAIT, 2006. These comments were echoed by numerous federal civil servants interviewed at the time. Hale, "Getting Down to Business," 67.

25 Hale, "Getting Down to Business," 69-70.

26 Confidential interviews, DFAIT, 2006-9; Hale, "Canada–US Relations in the Obama Era."

27 Christopher J. Kukucha, *The Provinces and Canadian Foreign Trade Policy* (Vancouver: UBC Press, 2008).

28 Confidential interview, DFAIT, 2005.

29 Ontario signed an MOU with DFAIT in 2010 to establish an office within the Washington Embassy but had not appointed a formal representative by mid-2011.

30 Confidential interview, DFAIT, 2006-7.

31 Goldenberg, *The Way It Works,* 271-85.

32 Confidential interviews, PCO, 2005-6.

33 Confidential interviews, DFAIT, 2006-8.

34 Gotlieb, *The Washington Diaries,* 102-3, 353; confidential interviews, DFAIT, PCO, 2006-8.

35 Gotlieb, *The Washington Diaries.*

36 Alberts, "McKenna Blasts His Own Party's Anti-U.S. Rhetoric"; confidential interviews, DFAIT, 2005-7; US Department of State, 2005-7; and Washington press corps, 2006.

37 Angelo Persichilli, "With Softwood Past Them, Harper and Bush Will Talk Trade and Security," *Embassy* 106 (2006): 1 [edited interview transcript].

38 Brian Milner, "Mexico Sides with Canada to Oppose Global Bank Tax," *Globe and Mail,* 29 May 2010.

39 Cited in Alan K. Henrikson, "Niche Diplomacy in the World Public Arena: The Global 'Corners' of Canada and Norway," in *The New Public Diplomacy: Soft Power in International Relations,* edited by Jan Melissen (Basingstoke, UK: Palgrave Macmillan, 2005), 76.

40 Hale and Huckabay, "Canadian Public Diplomacy in the United States."

41 Brian Hocking, "Rethinking the 'New' Public Diplomacy," in *The New Public Diplomacy: Soft Power in International Relations*, edited by Jan Melissen (Basingstoke, UK: Palgrave Macmillan, 2005), 35; Paul Sharp, "Revolutionary States, Outlaw Regimes, and the Techniques of Public Diplomacy," in *The New Public Diplomacy: Soft Power in International Relations*, edited by Jan Melissen (Basingstoke, UK: Palgrave Macmillan, 2005), 106.

42 Terry Colli, "Public Diplomacy as a Global Phenomenon," remarks to the Mershon Center, Ohio State University, 28 April 2006.

43 Confidential interviews, DFAIT, 2006-7; US Department of State, US DHS, 2005-9.

44 Confidential interviews, DFAIT, 2006-8.

45 Alexander Panetta, "NAFTAgate Began with Off-Hand Remark from Harper's Chief of Staff," *The Standard* (St. Catharines, ON), 5 March 2008; L. Ian MacDonald, "Harper Plays the Oil Card with Skill," *Gazette* [Montreal], 23 April 2008; James Travers, "No Open Tory Arms for McCain," *Toronto Star*, 14 June 2008.

46 Colli, "Public Diplomacy as a Global Phenomenon," 2.

47 Sheldon Alberts, "PMO Hires Two Former White House Strategists," *National Post*, 16 April 2009; Mary Anastasia O'Grady, "Stephen Harper: A Resolute Ally in the War on Terror," *Wall Street Journal*, 27 February 2009; Jake Tapper, "Interview with Canadian PM Stephen Harper," ABC News, 10 August 2009, http://blogs.abcnews.com/; Jane Taber, "Stephen Harper Shoots and Scores on NBC," *Globe and Mail*, 16 February 2010.

48 Douglas Macdonald and Debora L. VanNijnatten, "Canadian Climate Change Policy and the North American Influence," in *Borders and Bridges: Canada's Policy Relations in North America*, edited by Monica Gattinger and Geoffrey Hale (Toronto: Oxford University Press, 2010), 177-93; Hale, "Canada–US Relations in the Obama Era."

49 Hale, "Canada–US Relations in the Obama Era."

Chapter 6: Network Diplomacy

1 Gotlieb, *I'll Be with You in a Minute, Mr. Ambassador*, viii, 28.

2 Paul Frazer, remarks to US–Canada Relations seminar, Duke University, January 2006.

3 Ibid.; confidential interviews, US Department of State, 2007; US DHS, 2009; DFAIT, 2008-9.

4 I recall a conversation with an eminent and respected Canadian political scientist who viewed such activities as an intolerable invasion of national sovereignty, especially if similar activities were to be conducted by foreign government officials stationed in Canada.

5 Milner, *Interests, Institutions, and Information*, 9; Putnam and Bayne, *Hanging Together*, 260.

6 Confidential interviews, DFAIT, 2007-10; Anne McLellan, comments in the roundtable New Leadership in U.S.–Canada Relations, 27 June 2006 (Washington, DC: Center for Strategic and International Studies).

7 Rothkopf, *Running the World;* Gotlieb, *The Washington Diaries.*
8 Bow, *The Politics of Linkage.*
9 Susan Delacourt, "PM Issues Warning to NAFTA Foes," *Toronto Star,* 23 April 2008.
10 Gotlieb, *I'll Be with You in a Minute, Mr. Ambassador;* Gotlieb, *The Washington Diaries.*
11 Confidential interviews, DFAIT, 2006, 2008.
12 Gotlieb, *The Washington Diaries,* 399; Gotlieb, *I'll Be with You in a Minute, Mr. Ambassador,* 33-35.
13 Interview with Michael Kergin, 2008.
14 Confidential interview, DFAIT, 2010.
15 Gotlieb, *The Washington Diaries.*
16 Confidential interview, senior US government official, 2009.
17 Confidential interview, DFAIT, 2006; Kate Dunsmore, "Connecting Canada and Terrorism: The Year after 9/11 in the *New York Times,*" paper presented at the Western Social Science Association conference, Calgary, 14 April 2007.
18 Interview with Paul Frazer, 2007.
19 Confidential interviews, DFAIT, Ottawa and Washington, DC, 2005-10; confidential interviews, provincial representatives in Washington, DC, 2006-9.
20 Gotlieb, *I'll Be with You in a Minute, Mr. Ambassador,* 36.
21 Anderson and Sands, *Negotiating North America.*
22 Sands, *The Canada Gambit.*
23 Mouafo, Morales, and Heynen, *A Compendium of Canada–U.S. Relations.*
24 Gotlieb, *I'll Be with You in a Minute, Mr. Ambassador,* 140-41.
25 Ibid., 142-43.
26 Gattinger and Hale, *Borders and Bridges,* 13; confidential interview, DFAIT, 2006.
27 Confidential interviews, DFAIT, 2006-9, US Department of Agriculture, 2006.
28 Gotlieb, *I'll Be with You in a Minute, Mr. Ambassador,* 53.
29 Paul Frazer, correspondence with author, September 2011.
30 Panetta, "Harper Aide Triggered NAFTA-Gate; Leslie Campbell, "Time to Start Doing American-Style Politics," *Embassy,* 4 June 2008, 7.
31 Gotlieb, *I'll Be with You in a Minute, Mr. Ambassador,* 35; confidential interviews, DFAIT, 2006-9.
32 Anupama Narayanswamy, Luke Rosiak, and Jennifer LaFleur, "Adding It Up: The Top Players in Foreign Agent Lobbying" (Washington, DC: Sunlight Foundation and ProPublica, 2009); United States, Department of Justice, "Quick Search by Foreign Principal: Canada," *Foreign Agents Registration Act* (Washington, DC: US Department of Justice, 2010), http://www.justice.gov/.
33 Confidential interview, DFAIT, 2009.
34 Interview with Paul Frazer, 2007.
35 Confidential interviews, US Department of State, 2006-9.
36 Bow, *The Politics of Linkage,* 75-76, 87-89.
37 Paul Rosenzweig, "Why the U.S. Doesn't Trust Canada," *Maclean's,* 5 October 2009, http://www.macleans.ca/; confidential interviews, US Department of State, DFAIT, 2007-9.

38 Confidential interview, US DHS, 2009.
39 Gotlieb, *I'll Be with You in a Minute, Mr. Ambassador*, 43-44.

Chapter 7: Canada and Congress

1 Charles F. Doran and Joel J. Sokolsky, *Canada and Congress: Lobbying in Washington* (Halifax: Centre for Foreign Policy Studies, Dalhousie University, 1985), 47.
2 Gotlieb, *I'll Be with You in a Minute, Mr. Ambassador*, 33-35, 43ff.
3 Ibid., 44.
4 Bow, *The Politics of Linkage*, 172.
5 Confidential interview, DFAIT, 2006.
6 Ibid.
7 Ibid.
8 Confidential interview, DFAIT, 2008.
9 Rey Koslowski, "Immigration Reforms and Border Security Technologies" (New York: Social Science Research Council, 2006).
10 Christopher Sands, "Fading Power or Rising Power: 11 September and Lessons from the Section 110 Experience," in *Readings in Canadian Foreign Policy*, edited by Duane Bratt and Christopher J. Kukucha (Toronto: Oxford University Press, 2007), 249-64.
11 Fred Sissine, *Energy Independence and Security Act of 2007: A Summary of Major Provisions*, CRS Report 34294 (Washington, DC: Congressional Research Service, 2007), 3-4, http://energy.senate.gov/.
12 Martin Mittelstaedt, "Alberta Crude May Be Too Dirty, U.S. Law Says," *Globe and Mail*, 15 January 2008; Sheila McNulty, "Canada Warns US over Oil Sands," *Financial Times* [London, UK], 9 March 2008; confidential interviews, DFAIT, 2008; Keith Gerein, "U.S. Senators Propose Bill to Open Flow of Oilsands," *Calgary Herald*, 2 October 2010.
13 Robertson, "CDA_USA 2.0," 278.
14 Confidential interview, DFAIT, 2008.
15 Interview with Paul Frazer, 2006.
16 Geoffrey Hale, "Signalling across the Fence: Canada–US Relations and the Politics of Intermesticity," paper presented at the Annual Meeting of the Western Social Science Association, Calgary, 12 April 2007; confidential interviews, DFAIT, 2006.
17 Confidential interview, DFAIT, 2007.
18 Confidential interview, DFAIT, 2006.
19 Mancur Olsen, *The Logic of Collective Action: Public Goods and the Theory of Groups* (Cambridge, MA: Harvard University Press, 1965).
20 Hale, "People, Politics, and Passports."
21 Canada, DFAIT, "State Trade Fact Sheets: 2009" (Ottawa: DFAIT, 2009).
22 Confidential interviews, DFAIT, 2006-9.
23 Narayanswamy, Rosiak, and LaFleur, "Adding It Up."
24 Confidential interview, DFAIT, 2007.
25 Interview with Paul Frazer, 2007.
26 Interview with Michael Kergin, 2008.

27 Doran and Sokolsky, *Canada and Congress*, 25-26.
28 Ibid., 26-28.
29 Robertson, "CDA_USA 2.0," 274.
30 Gotlieb, *I'll Be with You in a Minute, Mr. Ambassador*, 72; confidential interviews, DFAIT, 2006-10.
31 Beth Gorham, "Canada Lobbies U.S. Legislators on Security," *Toronto Star*, 16 June 2006; Sheldon Alberts, "Canada Is 'Secure,' CSIS Boss Tells U.S.," *National Post*, 16 June 2006.
32 Confidential interviews, DFAIT, 2006.
33 Doran and Sokolsky, *Canada and Congress*, 29.
34 Ibid., 22-23; Gotlieb, *I'll Be with You in a Minute, Mr. Ambassador*, 47.
35 Confidential interview, DFAIT, 2006.
36 See page 61; Goldstein, "International Forces and Domestic Politics," 213.
37 Confidential interview with Washington government relations professional, 2009.
38 Interview with Paul Frazer, 2006.
39 Hale, "People, Politics, and Passports."
40 Confidential interview, DFAIT, 2006.
41 Confidential interview, DFAIT, 2010.
42 See, for example, Robertson, "CDA_USA 2.0," 274.
43 Confidential interview, Washington government relations professional, 2009.
44 "The Keystone Ultimatum," *Wall Street Journal*, 16 December 2011.
45 Golob, "The Return of the Quiet Canadian."
46 Confidential interview, senior US government official, 2009.
47 Paul Frazer, remarks to the US–Canada Relations Seminar, Duke University, 27 January 2006.
48 Confidential interview, DFAIT, 2006.
49 Ibid.
50 Confidential interview, US Department of State, 2007.
51 Beth Gorham, "Bush Flexible on Border ID," *Winnipeg Free Press*, 7 July 2006.
52 Tonda MacCharles, "PM Urges U.S. Restraint on Border," *Toronto Star*, 21 September 2006.
53 Rosenzweig, "Why the U.S. Doesn't Trust Canada"; confidential interviews, US Department of State, US DHS, 2007-9.
54 Confidential interview, US DHS, 2009.
55 Confidential interview, US Department of State, 2007.
56 Gotlieb, *The Washington Diaries*, 165, 220, 372, 376-82, 445-46.
57 Interview with Paul Frazer, 2006.
58 Frazer, remarks to the US–Canada Relations Seminar, Duke University, 27 January 2006; confidential interview, DFAIT, 2007.
59 Gotlieb, *The Washington Diaries*, 399.

Chapter 8: Canadian Public Diplomacy in the United States

1 Robert B. Reilly, "The Battle for Hearts and Minds," remarks to the annual meeting of the Philadelphia Society, Philadelphia, 1 April 2006.

2 Doran and Sokolsky, *Canada and Congress*, 13.
3 Paul Sharp, "Revolutionary States, Outlaw Regimes, and the Techniques of Public Diplomacy," in *The New Public Diplomacy: Soft Power in International Relations*, edited by Jan Melissen (Basingstoke, UK: Palgrave Macmillan, 2005), 106.
4 Terry Colli, "Public Diplomacy as a Global Phenomenon," remarks to the Mershon Center, Ohio State University, 28 April 2006.
5 Colli, "Public Diplomacy as a Global Phenomenon."
6 Brian Hocking, "Rethinking the 'New' Public Diplomacy," in *The New Public Diplomacy: Soft Power in International Relations*, edited by Jan Melissen (Basingstoke, UK: Palgrave Macmillan, 2005), 35.
7 Colli, "Public Diplomacy as a Global Phenomenon."
8 Dunsmore, "Connecting Canada and Terrorism." Former Embassy public affairs minister Paul Frazer suggested in a May 2007 interview that this problem went back even further to the Chrétien government's failure to respond effectively to the arrest of "millennium bomber" Ahmed Ressam, a failed Canadian refugee claimant, in late 1999 before he could follow through on a planned bombing of Los Angeles International Airport.
9 Jan Melissen, "The New Public Diplomacy: Between Theory and Practice," in *The New Public Diplomacy: Soft Power in International Relations*, edited by Jan Melissen (Basingstoke, UK: Palgrave Macmillan, 2005), 21.
10 Interview with Paul Frazer, 2006.
11 Henrikson, "Niche Diplomacy in the World Public Arena."
12 Doran and Sokolsky, "Canada and Congress," 17.
13 Sands, "How Canada Policy Is Made in the United States"; Sands, "The Rising Importance of Third Country Issues in Canada's Relations with the United States."
14 Gotlieb, *The Washington Diaries;* Stephen F. Knott, ed., *Interview with Frank Carlucci*, Ronald Reagan Oral History Project (Charlottesville, VA: Miller Center for Public Affairs, University of Virginia, 2001); Stephen F. Knott, ed., *Interview with George Schulz*, Ronald Reagan Oral History Project (Charlottesville, VA: Miller Center for Public Affairs, University of Virginia, 2002).
15 Confidential interviews, DFAIT, 2005, 2006; Dunsmore, "Connecting Canada and Terrorism."
16 Gotlieb, *I'll Be with You in a Minute, Mr. Ambassador,* 117-31; Robertson, "CDA_ USA 2.0."
17 Robertson, "CDA_USA 2.0," 268-69, 272ff.
18 Gotlieb, *I'll Be with You in a Minute, Mr. Ambassador,* 32.
19 Center for Responsive Politics, "Lobbying Database," http://www.opensecrets. org/.
20 Narayanswamy, Rosiak, and LaFleur, "Adding It Up"; US Department of Justice, "Quick Search by Foreign Principal."
21 Confidential interview, Washington government relations professional, 2006.
22 Manley, Aspe, and Weld, *Building a North American Community.*
23 Tamara Kay, *NAFTA and the Politics of Labor Transnationalism* (New York: Cambridge University Press, 2011).

24 Confidential interview, Washington government relations professional, 2007; US Department of Justice, "Quick Search by Foreign Principal," http://www.fara.gov/.

25 Gotlieb, *The Washington Diaries*, 300-1, 376-86.

26 Confidential interviews, DFAIT, 2007-9; Canada policy community in Washington, 2011.

27 Confidential interviews, DFAIT, 2006-9.

28 United States, White House, "Remarks by President Obama and Prime Minister Stephen Harper of Canada in Joint Press Availability," 4 February 2011.

29 Confidential interviews, DFAIT, 2006-7; Washington press gallery, 2006.

30 Lee Anne Goodman, "U.S. Border Deal Not about Sovereignty, Harper Says after Obama Meeting," *Okotoks Western Wheel*, 4 February 2011.

31 Confidential interviews, DFAIT, 2006, 2008, 2010.

32 See http://www.connect2canada.com/.

33 Natural Resources Defense Council, "Strip Mining for Oil in Endangered Forests" (Washington, DC: June 2006), http://www.nrdc.org/.

34 Government of Alberta, "A good neighbor lends you a cup of sugar. A great neighbor supplies you with 1.4 million barrels of oil per day" [advertisement], *Washington Post*, 2 July 2010; "A Reminder of U.S. Self-Interest" [editorial], *Globe and Mail*, 3 July 2010.

35 Hale, "Getting Down to Business."

36 Paul Wells, "He's Unbelievable!," *Maclean's*, 14 December 2005, http://www.macleans.ca/; Don Butler, "The Politics of Bush-Bashing," *Ottawa Citizen*, 17 December 2005.

37 Confidential interview, DFAIT, 2006.

38 Fred Barnes, "How Spending Cuts, Not Higher Taxes, Saved Canada," *Wall Street Journal*, 21 July 2011.

39 Corsi, *The Late, Great USA*; Kelly Patterson, "'Treasonous' Integration Plan Sparks U.S. Storm," *Calgary Herald*, 17 February 2007.

40 See, for example, Sally C. Pipes, "Canadian Patients Face Long Waits for Low-Tech Healthcare," *Washington Examiner*, 9 June 2009; David Gratzer, "Canada's ObamaCare Precedent," *Wall Street Journal*, 9 June 2009.

41 Dunsmore, "Connecting Canada and Terrorism"; Sheldon Alberts, "Napolitano Chided for Linking Canada to 9/11," *Ottawa Citizen*, 22 April 2009.

42 Sands, "Fading Power or Rising Power"; James Bissett, "Americans Are Right to Worry," *Ottawa Citizen*, 27 April 2009.

43 Manley, Aspe, and Weld, *Building a North American Community*; North American Competitiveness Council (NACC), "Meeting the Global Challenge: Private Sector Priorities for the Security and Prosperity Partnership of North America – 2008 Report to Leaders" (Ottawa, Washington, Mexico City: NACC, 2008).

44 Daniel Schwanen, "Deeper, Broader: A Roadmap for a Treaty of North America," in *The Art of the State: Thinking North America*, Folio 4, edited by Thomas J. Courchene, Donald Savoie, and Daniel Schwanen (Montreal: Institute for Research in Public Policy, 2004), 39-50; Gary C. Hufbauer and Claire Brunel, "Economic Integration in North America," in *Free Trade in Free Fall? Canada–U.S. Non-Tariff*

Barriers, edited by Stephanie McLuhan, One Issue, Two Voices 8 (Washington, DC: Canada Institute, Woodrow Wilson Institute for Scholars, 2008), 2-7; Alexander Moens, with Michael Cust, "Saving the North American Security and Prosperity Partnership: The Case for a North American Standards and Regulatory Area" (Vancouver: Fraser Institute, 2008); United States, White House, and Canada, Privy Council Office, "United States–Canada Regulatory Cooperation Council: Joint Action Plan," Washington, DC, and Ottawa, 7 December 2011.

45 Confidential interview, Washington government relations professional, 2009.

46 Confidential interviews, US and Canadian business association representatives, 2006-7.

47 BESTT: Business for Economic Security, Tourism and Trade.

48 William A. Kerr and Jill E. Hobbs, "Agricultural Trade and Food Safety," in *Borders and Bridges: Navigating Canada's International Policy Relations in North America,* edited by Monica Gattinger and Geoffrey Hale (Toronto: Oxford University Press, 2010), 344-60.

49 United States, White House, and Canada, Privy Council Office, "United States-Canada Regulatory Cooperation Council: Joint Action Plan," 18.

50 See, for example, Kay, *NAFTA and the Politics of Labor Transnationalism.*

51 See, for example, Robert A. Pastor, *Toward a North American Community: Lessons from the Old World for the New* (Washington, DC: Institute for International Economics, 2001); Robert A. Pastor, "A North American Community," *Norteamérica* 1, 1 (2006): 209-19; Manley, Aspe, and Weld, *Building a North American Community.*

52 Higginbotham and Heynen, "Managing through Networks," 123-40; Studer, "Obstacles to Integration."

53 Sands, *The Canada Gambit;* Meyer, "More than Shades of SPP in Perimeter Deal."

54 Anderson and Sands, *Negotiating North America;* Hale and Gattinger, "Variable Geometry and Traffic Circles."

Chapter 9: Beyond the Beltway

1 Rosenau, *Distant Proximities;* Anderson and Sands, "Fragmegration, Federalism, and Canada–U.S. Relations."

2 Hale and Gattinger, "Variable Geometry and Traffic Circles."

3 Richard Simeon, "Important? Yes. Transformative? No. North American Integration and Canadian Federalism," in *The Impact of Global and Regional Integration on Federal Systems,* edited by Harvey Lazar, Hamish Telford, and Ronald Watts (Montreal: McGill-Queen's University Press, 2003), 126ff.; Roger Gibbins, "Regional Integration and National Contexts: Constraints and Opportunities," in *Regionalism in a Global Society,* edited by Stephen G. Tomblin and Charles S. Colgin (Peterborough, ON: Broadview Press, 2004), 37-56.

4 Simeon, "Important? Yes. Transformative? No," 128-29.

5 Stephen G. Tomblin, "Conceptualizing and Exploring the Struggle over Regional Integration," in *Regionalism in a Global Society,* edited by Stephen G. Tomblin and Charles S. Colgin (Peterborough, ON: Broadview Press, 2004), 79-80.

6 Simeon, "Important? Yes. Transformative? No," 145.

7   Belanger, "An Unsustainable Institutional Design"; Clarkson, *Does North America Exist?*

8   This trend continued through 2010 for seven provinces, with Nova Scotia exporting more to other provinces than other countries in 2009-10.

9   Kukucha, "Sub-Federal Trade and the Politics of North American Economic Integration."

10 Canada, Department of Finance, *Fiscal Reference Tables* (Ottawa: Department of Finance, 2011), Tables 33, 36, 39; federal and provincial spending, including transfers to other governments, totalled 39.4 and 54.9 percent, respectively.

11 *Canada (A-G) v. Ontario (A-G),* [1937] A.C. 326 at 347 (P.C.) [*Labour Conventions*].

12 Donald R. Smiley and Ronald L. Watts, *Intrastate Federalism in Canada,* Vol. 39, Research Report, Royal Commission on the Economic Union and Development Prospects for Canada (Toronto: University of Toronto Press, 1985).

13 See http://www.usgovernmentspending.com/, http://www.usgovernmentrevenue. com/.

14 Gattinger and Hale, *Borders and Bridges.*

15 G. Bruce Doern and Monica Gattinger, *Power Switch: Energy Regulatory Governance in the Twenty-First Century* (Toronto: University of Toronto Press, 2003), 71-91.

16 Zhang, *The Softwood Lumber War.*

17 Allan Olson, "Hydro-Diplomacy," speech to the Association for Canadian Studies in the United States, San Diego, 21 November 2009.

18 Michelle Morris, "Talking Turkey about a Knotty Question: International and Domestic Pressures on the Governance of the St. Mary and Milk Rivers" (Honours undergraduate thesis, University of Lethbridge, 2009).

19 Stanley, "Borders and Bridges," 316.

20 Carrie Tait, "Imperial Oil Project Meets Heavy Traffic," *Globe and Mail,* 24 March 2011.

21 Christopher Sands, "Towards a New Frontier: Improving the U.S.–Canadian Border" (Washington, DC: Brookings Institution, 2009).

22 Geoffrey Hale, *In Search of Border Management* (Toronto: Canadian International Council, 2009).

23 Sands, "Towards a New Frontier," 16-17.

24 Bill Shea, "Blanchard: Canada Loan Offer for New Detroit River Bridge Was MDOT's Idea," *Crain's Detroit Business,* 3 May 2010; Jeff T. Wattrick, "Roy Norton Interview: Politics at the United States' and Canada's Busiest Border Crossing," www.MLive.com, 3 August 2011.

25 Andrea Billups, "New Bridge Linking U.S., Canada on Hold," *Washington Times,* 20 October 2011.

26 Robertson, "CDA_USA 2.0," 268

27 Betsy Guzman, "The Hispanic Population: Census 2000 Brief," C2KBR/01-3 (Washington, DC: US Census Bureau, 2001), http://www.census.gov/; Karen R. Humes, Nicholas A. Jones, and Roberto R. Ramirez, "Overview of Race and Hispanic Origin: 2010," C2010BR-02 (Washington, DC: US Census Bureau 2011), http://www.census.gov/.

28 Sands, "Fading Power or Rising Power."

29 This section reflects extended conversations with officials of DFAIT over several years.

30 Confidential interview, DFAIT, 2006.

31 Michaud and Boucher note that Quebec established its first foreign office as early as 1872. Nelson Michaud and Marc T. Boucher, "Les relations internationales du Québec comparées" (Québec: Ministère des relations internationales, gouvernement du Québec, 2006), 19. See also Christopher J. Kukucha, "Dismembering Canada? Stephen Harper and the Foreign Relations of Canadian Provinces," *Review of Constitutional Studies* 14, 1 (2009): 28-35.

32 Kukucha, *The Provinces and Canadian Foreign Trade Policy*, 43-58.

33 Christopher Sands, "Big in Detroit City: The Politics of the 2009 North American Auto Industry Bailouts," paper presented at the Annual Meeting of the American Political Science Association, Washington, DC, 3 September 2010.

34 G. Bruce Doern and Brian W. Tomlin, *Faith and Fear: The Free Trade Story* (Toronto: Stoddart, 1991), 258-61; Kukucha, "Dismembering Canada?," 49.

35 Zhang, *The Softwood Lumber War.*

36 Kukucha, "Dismembering Canada?," 41-44.

37 Paul Gérin-Lajoie, speech to Montreal consular corps, 12 April 1965, cited in Michaud and Boucher, "Les relations internationales du Québec comparées," 4; my translation.

38 Confidential interviews, DFAIT, 2005.

39 Kukucha, *The Provinces and Canadian Foreign Trade Policy*, 61-97; Emma S. Norman and Karen Bakker, "Governing Water across the Canada–US Borderland," in *Borders and Bridges: Canada's Policy Relations in North America*, edited by Monica Gattinger and Geoffrey Hale (Toronto: University of Toronto Press, 2010), 194-212.

40 Provincial relations are generally characterized by "informality," with meetings taking place "outside the context of legal agreements." Mouafo, Morales, and Heynen, *A Compendium of Canada–U.S. Relations*, 6-7.

41 Michaud and Boucher, "Les relations internationales du Québec comparées," 14.

42 Kukucha, "Dismembering Canada?," 43.

43 Kukucha, "Dismembering Canada?," 42; Mouafo, Morales, and Heynen, *A Compendium of Canada–U.S. Relations*, 6-7.

44 Council of Great Lakes Governors, "Great Lakes–St. Lawrence River Basin Water Resources Compact Implementation," updated 3 November 2009.

45 See above, page 204.

46 Jane Taber, "Canada's Carbon Diplomat," *Globe and Mail*, 21 October 2009.

47 Canada, Transport Canada, and Government of Manitoba, "The Government of Canada and Manitoba Announce New Measures to Attract Investment and Boost Trade," press release, 8 October 2009.

48 Emmanuel Brunet-Jailly, "Cross-Border Relations in Detroit, Niagara, and Vancouver," *Journal of Borderland Studies* 21, 2 (2007): 10-13.

49 Hale and Marcotte, "Border Security, Trade, and Travel Facilitation."

50 Canada, Policy Research Institute, *The Emergence of Cross-Border Regions between Canada and the United States*, iv.

51 Ibid., 10-11.

52 Ibid., 6.

53 Dieudonné Mouafo, "Regional Dynamics in Canada–United States Relations," paper presented at the Annual Meeting of the Canadian Political Science Association, Winnipeg, 3 June 2004.

54 Gordon Campbell, Ed Stelmach, and Brad Wall, "A Novel Partnership to Build the New West," *Calgary Herald*, 15 March 2009; Geoffrey Hale, "Canadian Federalism and North American Integration: Managing Multi-Level Games," in *The State in Transition: Challenges for Canadian Federalism*, edited by Michael Behiels and François Rocher (Ottawa: Invenire Books, 2011), 237-67.

55 Mouafo, Morales, and Heynen, *A Compendium of Canada–U.S. Relations;* Gotlieb, *The Washington Diaries;* Hale, "People, Politics, and Passports."

56 Five states: Alaska, Idaho, Montana, Oregon, and Washington; three provinces: Alberta, British Columbia, and Saskatchewan; and two Canadian territories: Northwest Territories and Yukon.

57 Hale, "Canadian Federalism and North American Integration."

58 Confidential interviews, government of Alberta, government of Quebec, 2006-8.

59 Confidential interviews, government of Manitoba, 2006, 2009.

60 Confidential interview, provincial government representative in Washington, 2006.

61 Confidential interview, Canadian policy community in Washington, 2006.

62 Hale, "The Buy-American Controversy."

63 Michael D. Cohen, James G. March, and Johan P. Olsen, "A Garbage Can Model of Organizational Choice," *Administrative Science Quarterly* 17, 1 (1972): 1-25.

Chapter 10: Smart Borders or Thicker Borders?

1 Frank P. Harvey, "Canada's Addiction to American Security: The Illusion of Choice in the War on Terrorism," *American Review of Canadian Studies* 35, 2 (2005): 265-94; Richard J. Kilroy, "Perimeter Defense and Regional Security Cooperation in North America: United States, Canada, and Mexico," *Homeland Security Affairs*, Proceedings of the Workshop on Preparing for and Responding to Disasters in North America (2007), http://www.hsaj.org/.

2 Doran, *Forgotten Partnership*, 53.

3 Stephen E. Flynn, "The False Conundrum: Continental Integration vs. Homeland Security," in *The Rebordering of North America*, edited by Peter Andreas and Thomas Bierstecker (New York: Routledge, 2003), 112.

4 Confidential interview, US Department of State, 2005.

5 Cellucci, *Unquiet Diplomacy*, 15, 131-46.

6 Christopher Bellavita, "Changing Homeland Security: What Is Homeland Security?" *Homeland Security Affairs* 4, 2 (2008): 1.

7 Ibid.

8 United States, Department of Homeland Security, "Mission Statement" (Washington, DC: DHS, 2003).

9 United States, Department of Homeland Security, *One Team, One Mission, Securing Our Homeland: U.S. Department of Homeland Security Strategic Plan, Fiscal Years 2008-2013* (Washington, DC: DHS, 2008), 2.

10 See, for example, Alden, *The Closing of the American Border.*

11 United States, Department of Homeland Security, *Quadrennial Homeland Security Review: A Strategic Framework for a Secure Homeland* (Washington, DC: DHS, 2010), 14.

12 Flynn, "The False Conundrum"; Daniel Prieto, "The Limits and Prospects of Military Analogies for Homeland Security," in *Threats at Our Threshold: Homeland Defense and Homeland Security in the New Century*, edited by Bert B. Tussing (Washington, DC: Center for Strategic and International Studies, 2006), 85-110.

13 DHS, *Quadrennial Homeland Security Review*, 11.

14 See Michael Levi, *On Nuclear Terrorism* (Cambridge, MA: Harvard University Press, 2007); Ian Macleod, "Obstacle Course," *Ottawa Citizen*, 17 November 2007.

15 Canada, Prime Minister's Office, and United States, White House, "Beyond the Border."

16 Canada, *Securing an Open Society*; Patrick J. Smith, "Anti-Terrorism in North America: Is There Convergence or Divergence in Canadian and US Legislative Responses to 9/11 and the US–Canada Border?," in *Borderlands: Comparing Border Security in North America and Europe*, edited by Emmanuel Brunet-Jailly (Ottawa: University of Ottawa Press, 2007), 282.

17 United States, National Commission on Terrorist Attacks on the United States, *The 9/11 Commission Report* (Washington, DC: National Commission on Terrorist Attacks on the United States, 2004), 387-89.

18 Jeffrey Passel and D'Vera Cohn, "U.S. Unauthorized Immigration Flows Are Down Sharply since Mid-Decade" (Washington, DC: Pew Hispanic Center, 1 September 2010), 4-6.

19 Confidential interview, US DHS, 2005.

20 Sands, *The Canada Gambit*, 5.

21 US-VISIT: United States Visitor and Immigrant Status Indicator Technology.

22 See, for example, Graham Allison, *Nuclear Terrorism: The Ultimate Preventable Catastrophe* (New York: Henry Holt, 2004); Levi, *Nuclear Terrorism*; David Ignatius, "Portents of a Nuclear al-Qaeda," *Washington Post*, 11 October 2007.

23 Smith, "Anti-Terrorism in North America."

24 Confidential interviews, US DHS, 2005; Public Safety and Emergency Preparedness Canada, 2005, 2006.

25 Canada, Commission of Inquiry into the Actions of Canadian Officials in Relation to Maher Arar, *Report of the Events Relating to Maher Arar: Analysis and Recommendations* (Ottawa: PCO, 2006); Andrew Duffy, "The Secret Trial," *Ottawa Citizen*, 22 June 2008; Colin Freeze, "Are Security Certificates Obsolete?," *Globe and Mail*, 25 September 2009.

26 Hale, "People, Politics, and Passports"; confidential interviews, DFAIT, US DHS, 2008.

27 See, for example, Doug Struck, "Terrorist Allegations Detailed in Canada," *Washington Post*, 7 June 2006; Joshua Kurlantzick, "Canada's Terrorism Problem," *New Republic*, 7 June 2006, http://www.tnr.com/; Brigitte McCann, "Bienvenue à Montréalistan," *Le Journal de Montreal*, 16 March 2007; Ian Macleod, "The Warning Lights Are All Blinking Red," *Ottawa Citizen*, 23 February 2008; Graeme

Hamilton, "Terror Plotter Undone by Online Activities," *National Post*, 2 October 2009.

28 Colin Freeze, "Pakistani-Canadian Guilty of Terrorism," *Globe and Mail*, 10 June 2011.

29 Christine E. Wormuth, "Is a Goldwater-Nichols Act Needed for Homeland Security?" in *Threats at Our Threshold: Homeland Defense and Homeland Security in the New Century*, edited by Bert B. Tussing (Washington, DC: Center for Strategic and International Studies, 2006), 84.

30 United States, Office of Homeland Security, *National Strategy for Homeland Security* (Washington, DC: White House, 2002); United States, Homeland Security Council, *National Strategy for Homeland Security* (Washington, DC: White House, 2007); United States, Department of Homeland Security, *Homeland Security Presidential Directives* (Washington, DC, 4 June 2008); http://www.dhs.gov/.

31 Mouafo, Morales, and Heynen, *A Compendium of Canada–U.S. Relations*.

32 Confidential interview, US DHS, 2006.

33 Rosenzweig, "Why the U.S. Doesn't Trust Canada."

34 Ibid.

35 See, for example, Spencer S. Hsu, "DHS Strains as Goals, Mandates Go Unmet," *Washington Post*, 6 March 2008; Ellen Nakashima, "Reports Cite Lack of Uniform Policy for Terrorist Watch List," *Washington Post*, 18 March 2008.

36 See, for example, United States, Department of State and Department of Homeland Security, *Preserving Our Welcome to the World in an Age of Terrorism: Report of the Secure Borders and Open Doors Advisory Committee* (Washington, DC: Department of State and Department of Homeland Security, 2008).

37 Susan B. Glasser and Michael Grunwald, "Prelude to Disaster: The Making of DHS," *Washington Post*, 22 December 2005; Prieto, "The Limits and Prospects of Military Analogies for Homeland Security"; Paul N. Stockton and Patrick S. Roberts, "Findings from the Forum on Homeland Security after the Bush Administration: Next Steps in Building Unity of Effort," *Homeland Security Affairs* 4, 2 (2008): 1.

38 Spencer S. Hsu, "DHS Plagued by Turnover in Top Positions," *Washington Post*, 16 July 2007; confidential interview, US DHS, 2006.

39 David Heyman and James Jay Carafano, *DHS 2.0: Rethinking the Department of Homeland Security* (Washington, DC: Center for Strategic and International Studies and Heritage Foundation, 2004); Arnaud de Borchgrave, "Global Fatigue and Trust Deficit," *Washington Times*, 25 January 2010.

40 Blas Nuñez-Neto, "Border Security: Key Agencies and Their Missions," RS 21899 (Washington, DC: Congressional Research Service, 13 May 2008). A recent exception is the introduction in 2011 of "ready lanes" at seventeen border crossings, four on the US-Canada border, for travellers with RFID-enabled and WHTI-compliant forms of identification. http://www.getyouhome.gov/.

41 Confidential interviews, US DHS, DFAIT, 2006-8.

42 United States, Government Accountability Office, "Border Security: Enhanced DHS Oversight and Assessment of Interagency Coordination Is Needed for the Northern Border," GAO-11-97 (Washington, DC: GAO, 2010).

43 Ray S. Cline, "Is Intelligence Over-Coordinated?," *Studies in Intelligence* 1, 4 (1957): 11-18, cited in Prieto, "The Limits and Prospects of Military Analogies for Homeland Security," 85.

44 Bellavita, "Changing Homeland Security."

45 Ibid.; Hale, "People, Politics, and Passports."

46 Jerome P. Bjelopera and Mark A. Randol, "American Jihadist Terrorism: Combating a Complex Threat," Report 41416 (Washington, DC: Congressional Research Service, 20 September 2010), 3-4.

47 Smith, "Anti-Terrorism in North America"; Martin Collacutt, "Canada's Inadequate Response to Terrorism: The Need for Immigration Reform" (Vancouver: Fraser Institute, 2006); Colin Freeze, "Get Tougher on Terrorism, FBI Director Tells Canada," *Globe and Mail*, 19 July 2006; Jeff Sallot, "CSIS Kept Tabs on 274 Terror Suspects Last Year," *Globe and Mail*, 27 October 2006; Rosenzweig, "Why the U.S. Doesn't Trust Canada"; Sands, *The Canada Gambit*, 10.

48 Michelle Shephard, "Made in Canada Threat Worries CSIS," *Toronto Star*, 11 February 2006; Stewart Bell and Adrian Humphreys, "Terrorism's 'New Guard,'" *National Post*, 4 May 2006; Mitchell D. Silber and Arvin Bhatt, "Radicalization in the West: The Homegrown Threat" (New York: NYPD Intelligence Division, 2007); Macleod, "The Warning Lights Are All Blinking Red"; Marc Sageman, "The Next Generation of Terror," *Foreign Policy* 165 (2008): 36-42; Stewart Bell, "Solo Terrorists Pose New Threat: Report," *National Post*, 10 June 2008.

49 For a contrary perspective, see Bruce Hoffman, "The Myth of Grass-Roots Terrorism," *Foreign Affairs* 87, 3 (2008): 133-38.

50 Bjelopera and Randol, "American Jihadist Terrorism," 1, 65-123.

51 US Bureau of Customs and Border Protection, Canada Border Services Agency, and Royal Canadian Mounted Police, "United States–Canada Joint Border Threat and Risk Assessment" (Washington, DC: CBP; Ottawa: CBSA, RCMP, 2010).

52 Danielle Goldfarb, *Is Just-in-Case Replacing Just-in-Time? How Cross-Border Trading Behaviour Has Changed Since 9/11* (Ottawa: Conference Board of Canada, 2007); North American Competitiveness Council, *Building a Secure and Competitive North America: 2007 Report to Leaders* (Washington, DC: North American Competitiveness Council, 2007); United States, Departments of State and Homeland Security, *Preserving Our Welcome to the World;* Canadian Chamber of Commerce and United States Chamber of Commerce, *Finding the Balance: Reducing Border Costs while Strengthening Security* (Ottawa: Canadian Chamber of Commerce; Washington, DC: United States Chamber of Commerce, 2008); United States Chamber of Commerce and Canadian Chamber of Commerce, *Finding the Balance: Shared Border of the Future* (Washington, DC: United States Chamber of Commerce; Ottawa: Canadian Chamber of Commerce, 2009).

53 Hale, "Maintaining Policy Discretion."

54 Interview with Michael Kergin, 2008.

55 Hale, "Cross-Border Relations."

56 Ibid.; Geoffrey Hale, "Sharing a Continent: Security, Insecurity, and the Politics of 'Intermesticity,'" *Canadian Foreign Policy* 12, 3 (2005-6): 31-43; McLellan, "New Leadership in U.S.–Canada Relations"; confidential interviews, PCO, 2005.

57 See, for example, Dobson, "Shaping the Future of the North American Economic Space"; George Haynal, "The Next Plateau in North America: What's the Big Idea?," *Policy Options* 25, 6 (2004): 35-39; Manley, Aspe, and Weld, *Building a North American Community.*

58 Joel J. Sokolsky and Philippe Lagassé, "Suspenders and a Belt: Perimeter and Border Security in Canada–U.S. Relations," *Canadian Foreign Policy* 12, 3 (2005-6): 15-29.

59 Hale, "Getting Down to Business."

60 Confidential interviews, PCO, DFAIT, Public Safety Canada, 2006-10.

61 Confidential interview, Prime Minister's Office, 2006.

62 Geoffrey Hale, *In Search of Effective Border Management* (Toronto: Canadian International Council, 2009).

63 See, for example, Anne Goodchild, Steven Globerman, and Susan Albrecht, "Service Time Variability at the Blaine, Washington, International Border Crossing and the Impact on Regional Supply Chains," Research Report 3 (Bellingham, WA: Border Policy Research Institute, 2007); Canadian and US Chambers of Commerce, *Finding the Balance.*

64 Chuck Neubauer, "'Virtual Fence' Got Late Review of Costs, Benefits," *Washington Times*, 1 February 2011.

65 United States, White House, and Canada, Privy Council Office, "Beyond the Border," 17.

66 Emmanuel Brunet-Jailly, "Borders, Borderlands, and Security: European and North American Lessons and Policy Suggestions," in *Borderlands: Comparing Border Security in North America and Europe,* edited by Emmanuel Brunet-Jailly (Ottawa: University of Ottawa Press, 2007), 351-57; Hale, "People, Politics, and Passports."

67 Michael Kergin and Birgit Mathiessen, *Border Issues Report: A New Bridge for Old Allies* (Toronto: Canadian International Council, 2008).

68 See, for example, Corsi, *The Late, Great USA.*

69 See, for example, Schwanen, "Deeper, Broader."

Chapter 11: Engaging US Security and Border Policies

1 United States, Government Accountability Office, "Border Security: Enhanced DHS Oversight and Assessment of Interagency Coordination Is Needed for the Northern Border," GAO-11-97 (Washington, DC: GAO, 2010).

2 Smith, "Anti-Terrorism in North America"; Colin Freeze, "Divisive Terror Law Losing Traction," *Globe and Mail*, 21 September 2009.

3 Sallot, "CSIS Kept Tabs on 274 Terror Suspects Last Year."

4 Sands, "Fading Power or Rising Power."

5 James Carafano, "Obama Administration Gets One Border's Security Right," *Washington Examiner*, 19 December 2011, http://www.washingtonexaminer.com/.

6 Confidential interview, DFAIT, 2006.

7 Jeff Sallot, "McLellan Contradicts CSIS on Torture Policy," *Globe and Mail*, 16 September 2005; James Bissett, "We Need Security Certificates," *National Post*, 20 April 2006; confidential interviews, Public Safety Canada, DFAIT, 2005-6.

8 Andrew Duffy, "Ottawa Author Attacks RCMP for Terror-Fighting Strategy," *Ottawa Citizen*, 26 August 2008; Colin Freeze, "Torture Report Urges Ottawa to Better Protect Rights," *Globe and Mail*, 22 October 2008; Ian Macleod, "Suspected Terrorist Activities Foiled," *National Post*, 10 November 2009.
9 Confidential interviews, Department of Homeland Security and Public Safety Canada, 2005-6.
10 Eric Holder, "Speech to Northern Border Summit, Lake Placid, NY" (Washington, DC: Department of Justice, 14 September 2011), http://www.justice.gov/.
11 Superintendent Bill Ard, RCMP, presentation to the Border Regions in Transition conference, Victoria, BC, 13 January 2008; Jonathan Kent, "Canada–US Border Management between the Ports-of-Entry: The Other 6,397 Kilometres," paper presented at the Border Regions in Transition conference, Bellingham, WA, 14 January 2008; confidential interview, Public Safety Canada, 2008.
12 Canadian Chamber of Commerce, Canadian Manufacturers and Exporters, Canadian Council of Chief Executives, and Canadian Federation of Independent Business.
13 See, for example, Canadian and US Chambers of Commerce, *Finding the Balance*; North American Competitiveness Council, "Meeting the Global Challenge"; United States, Departments of State and Homeland Security, *Preserving Our Welcome to the World*.
14 Novak, "The Politics of Ports."
15 Stephen Blank, Graham Parsons, and Juan Carlos Villa, "Freight Transportation Infrastructure Policies in Canada, Mexico, and the US: An Overview and Analysis," Working Paper 5 (Washington, DC: North American Transportation Competitiveness Research Council, 2008).
16 United States, Bureau of Customs and Border Protection, "Fact Sheet" (Washington, DC: CBP, 2005).
17 Robert C. Bonner, "Diplomacy and Security: CSI and the Effort to Make the Global Green Lane Vision a Reality," remarks to the conference The Quest for the Global Green Lane: Improving Cargo Security from Concept to Reality, Center for Strategic and International Studies, Washington, DC, 8 February 2006; Michael Schmitz, remarks to the conference The Quest for the Global Green Lane: Improving Cargo Security from Concept to Reality, Center for Strategic and International Studies, Washington, DC, 8 February 2006.
18 VACIS: Vehicle and Cargo Inspection System (stationary gamma-ray scanning system used to examine dense freight shipments to detect contraband, weapons, and other potentially dangerous goods).
19 Blank, Parsons, and Villa, "Freight Transportation Infrastructure Policies in Canada, Mexico, and the US."
20 United States, White House, and Canada, Privy Council Office, "Beyond the Border," 5-7, 11-12.
21 Richard M. Stana, "Border Security: US VISIT Program Faces Strategic, Operational, and Technological Challenges at Land Ports of Entry" (Washington, DC: Government Accountability Office, 2007), 10.

22 Gloria Galloway, "Kenney Proposes a Two-Stream Approach to Refugee Reform," *Globe and Mail*, 30 March 2010.

23 International Civil Aviation Organization, *ICAO MRTD Report 1:1* (Montreal: ICAO, 2006), 8; International Civil Aviation Organization, *ICAO MRTD Report 5:2* (Montreal: ICAO, 2010), 3.

24 Michelle Collins, "Cabinet Pulls the Plug on Mexican and Czech Visa-Free Travel," *Embassy*, 15 July 2009, 1.

25 Confidential interviews, DFAIT, US think tank, Washington, DC, 2006; Jan Sliva, "EU Tells Canada to Extend Visa-Fee Rules," *Toronto Star*, 17 September 2007; Canadian Press, "Ottawa Lifts Visa Rules for Czech and Latvian Visitors," *The Record* (Kitchener, ON), 1 November 2007; Reuters, "EU Threatens Visa Requirement for US Diplomats," *Der Spiegel* (international online edition), 23 July 2008, http://www.spiegel.de/.

26 United States, White House, and Canada, Privy Council Office, "Beyond the Border," 8.

27 United States, National Commission on Terrorist Attacks on the United States, *The 9/11 Commission Report*, 387-89.

28 SENTRI: Secure Electronic Network for Travelers Rapid Inspection.

29 Brenna Neinast and Michele James, "Northern Border Security," statement to the US Senate Committee on Homeland Security and Governmental Affairs, Havre, MT, 2 July 2008, 8.

30 Michael Den Tandt, "A Welcome Thinning of the Border," *National Post*, 7 December 2011.

31 Sands, "Fading Power or Rising Power"; Koslowski, "Immigration Reforms and Border Security Technologies."

32 Confidential interview, DFAIT, 2006.

33 Spencer S. Hsu, "U.S. Readies Plan to ID Departing Visitors," *Washington Post*, 8 November 2009.

34 Koslowski, "Immigration Reforms and Border Security Technologies." DHS finally issued the Final Rule implementing the REAL-ID Act on 7 March 2011, with an implementation date for participating states of 15 January 2013. United States, Department of Homeland Security, "REAL ID Final Rule" (Washington, DC: September 2011).

35 About 23 percent of Americans possessed passports in 2006, compared with about 40 percent of Canadians; these figures had increased to 35 percent and 64 percent, respectively, by 2011. Passport Canada, *Annual Report: Fiscal Year 2010-2011* (Ottawa: Passport Canada, 2011), 6; United States, Department of State, "Passport Statistics" (Washington, DC: Bureau of Consular Affairs, 2011), http://travel.state.gov/.

36 Hale, "Politics, People, and Passports."

37 Sands, "Fading Power or Rising Power"; interviews with Paul Frazer, 2006-7; confidential interviews, Canadian Embassy, Washington, DC, 2006-9.

38 Koslowski, "Immigration Reforms and Border Security Technologies," 4.

39 Sands, "Fading Power or Rising Power," 254-57.

40 Confidential interview, US Department of Homeland Security, 2006.

41 Business for Economic Security, Tourism and Trade (BESTT), "Proposed Solution to WHTI and REAL-ID" (Bellingham, WA: BESTT, 2006); United States, Department of Homeland Security, "Minimum Standards for Driver's Licenses and Identification Cards Acceptable by Federal Agencies for Official Purposes: Proposed Rule," *Federal Register,* 9 March 2007, 10819-58.

42 Jake Ellison, "State, B.C. Join Forces to Fight Passport Proposal," *Seattle Post-Intelligencer,* 12 November 2006; Liz Luce, "Washington State's Enhanced Driver License and Identification Card Initiative," presentation to the annual summit of Pacific Northwest Economic Region, Anchorage, AK (Olympia, WA: Washington State Department of Licensing, 24 July 2007); confidential interviews, governments of Ontario, British Columbia, and Washington State, 2006-9.

43 The Bureau of Consular Affairs reports that 1.54 million passport cards were issued in fiscal year 2009, a figure that has declined to 1.17 million in fiscal year 2011.

44 REAL-ID does not require the provision of citizenship data on drivers' licences, only confirmation of legal residence in the United States. Proposed DHS regulations require only a bar code identification system for REAL-ID compliance, and WHTI regulations mandated the use of RFID (radio frequency identification) technology on passports and US passport cards.

45 Confidential interviews, DFAIT, 2006-9.

46 United States, Department of Homeland Security and Department of State, "Documents Required for Travelers Arriving in the United States at Air and Sea Ports of Entry: Notice of Proposed Rulemaking, *Federal Register,* 11 August 2006, 46166.

47 Internal Canadian government documents; confidential interviews, DFAIT, 2006-9.

48 Richard A. Stana, "Observations on Efforts to Implement the Western Hemisphere Travel Initiative on the U.S. Border with Canada," letter to Loretta Sanchez, Louise M. Slaughter, and John M. McHugh (Washington, DC: GAO, 25 May 2006).

49 Gorham, "Bush Flexible on Border ID."

50 BESTT, "Proposed Solution to WHTI and REAL-ID"; Patrick Leahy, "House Leaders Drop 11th Hour Bid to Kill Leahy Amendment that Mandates Improvements in New Border-Crossing System" (Washington, DC: Office of Senator Leahy, 29 September 2006).

51 Jen Haberkorn, "Passport Backlog Prompts a Waiver," *Washington Times,* 9 June 2007; Jen Haberkorn, "Passport Seekers Inundate Office," *Washington Times,* 20 June 2007.

52 "Enhanced Drivers License Bill Passes Legislature," *International Falls Daily Journal,* 12 May 2010. Minnesota EDLs will be available in 2013.

53 Richard Barth and Thomas Winkowski, "Joint Statement to Subcommittee on Border, Maritime, and Global Counterterrorism, House Committee on Homeland Security" (Washington, DC: CBP, 7 May 2009).

54 Confidential interviews, DFAIT, US DHS, 2008.

55 Richard M. Stana, "Various Issues Led to the Termination of the United States–Canada Shared Management Pilot Project," GAO-08-1038R (Washington, DC: GAO, 4 September 2008).

56 Jerry Zremski, "Deal in Works to Inspect Trucks Headed to U.S. in Canada," *Buffalo News*, 9 October; United States, White House, and Canada, Privy Council Office, "Beyond the Border," 14.

57 Canada, Prime Minister's Office, and United States, White House, "Beyond the Border"; United States, White House, and Canada, Privy Council Office, "Beyond the Border."

58 Ibid.

59 Canada, Prime Minister's Office, and United States, White House, "Beyond the Border," 4.

60 Sands, "Towards a New Frontier."

61 United States, White House, and Canada, Privy Council Office, "Beyond the Border," 4.

62 Ibid., 10.

63 See, for example, Joel Bagnal, "Goldwater–Nichols for the Executive Branch: Achieving Unity of Effort," in *Threats at Our Threshold: Homeland Security in the New Century*, edited by Bert J. Pilling (Washington, DC: Center for Strategic and International Studies, 2006), 45-54; Prieto, "The Limits and Prospects of Military Analogies for Homeland Security"; Sands, *The Canada Gambit*.

Chapter 12: "Just a Trade Dispute"?

1 Hoekman and Kostecki, *The Political Economy of the World Trading System*, 197-201, 339.

2 Donna U. Vogt, "Food Safety Issues in the 109th Congress," CRS Report RL-31853 (Washington, DC: Congressional Research Service, 16 June 2005), 2.

3 Geoffrey S. Becker, "BSE ('Mad Cow Disease'): A Brief Overview," CRS Report RS-22345 (Washington, DC: Congressional Research Service, 19 December 2006), 1.

4 Extension Disaster Education Network, "Agricultural Disasters: Confirmed BSE Cases" (Baton Rouge: Louisiana State University, 2011).

5 Becker, "BSE ('Mad Cow Disease')," 3-4; Ek, *Canada–U.S. Relations*, 46.

6 Danny G. LeRoy and K.K. Klein, "Mad Cow Chaos in Canada: Was It Just Bad Luck or Did Government Policies Play a Role?," *Canadian Public Policy* 31, 4 (2005): 387-88.

7 CBC News, "In Depth: Mad Cow," http://www.cbc.ca/; Moens, *Mad Cow*, 27-29.

8 Moens, *Mad Cow*, 30-33.

9 Ibid., 34-41.

10 Ibid., 46, 48; Kurt Klein and Danny G. LeRoy, "BSE in Canada: Were Economic Losses to the Beef Industry Covered by Government Compensation?," *Canadian Public Policy* 36, 2 (2010): 221-40.

11 Confidential interview, former USDA official, 2006. See also Kerr and Hobbs, "Agricultural Trade and Food Safety," 344-60.

12 Grace Skogstad, "Multilateral Regulatory Governance of Food Safety: A Work in Progress," in *Rules, Rules, Rules, Rules: Multilevel Regulatory Governance*, edited by G. Bruce Doern and Robert Johnson (Toronto: University of Toronto Press, 2006), 160-61, 166.

13 Ibid., 168.
14 Confidential interview, former USDA official, 2006.
15 Sarah A. Lister and Geoffrey S. Becker, "Bovine Spongiform Encephalopathy (BSE or 'Mad Cow Disease'): Current and Proposed Safeguards," CRS Report RL-32199 (Washington, DC: Congressional Research Service, 20 September 2006), 7, 18-30.
16 Confidential interview, DFAIT, 2006.
17 Lister and Becker, "Bovine Spongiform Encephalopathy," 9.
18 Confidential interview, US agribusiness organization, 2006.
19 Ibid.
20 Lister and Becker, "Bovine Spongiform Encephalopathy," 10.
21 Geoffrey Becker, "Bovine Spongiform Encephalopathy (BSE or 'Mad Cow Disease') in North America: A Chronology of Selected Events," CRS Report RL-32932 (Washington, DC: Congressional Research Service, 27 July 2006), 16-30.
22 Confidential interviews, former USDA official, DFAIT official, US agribusiness association, 2006.
23 Becker, "Bovine Spongiform Encephalopathy," 28.
24 United States, Census Bureau, *Statistical Abstract of the United States: 2011*, Table 818 (Washington, DC: US Census Bureau, 2011), 533.
25 National Cattlemen's Beef Association, "Statement from NCBA Vice President of Government Affairs Colin Woodall Regarding WTO Ruling on US Country of Origin Labeling," press release (Washington, DC: 18 November 2011), http://www.beefusa.org/.
26 Confidential interview, DFAIT, 2006.
27 Ibid.
28 Confidential interviews, DFAIT, former USDA officials, 2006.
29 Becker, "Bovine Spongiform Encephalopathy," 21.
30 Ibid., 23.
31 Confidential interview, DFAIT, 2006, 2007; Geoffrey S. Becker, "Country-of-Origin Labeling for Foods," CRS Report 97-508 (Washington, DC: Congressional Research Service, 20 March 2006), 1.
32 Kerr and Hobbs, "Agricultural Trade and Food Safety," 349-54.
33 United States, White House, and Canada, Privy Council Office, "Beyond the Border," 7, 14; United States, White House, and Canada, Privy Council Office, "United States-Canada Regulatory Cooperation Council: Joint Action Plan," 7-8.
34 Burney, *Getting It Done*, 112-21; Gotlieb, *The Washington Diaries*, 484-93.
35 See, for example, Burney, *Getting It Done*, 155-56; Gotlieb, *The Washington Diaries*, 412-15.
36 See, for example, Coalition for Fair Lumber Imports, *Lumber Alert 4* (Washington, DC: 3 March 2006).
37 Gotlieb, *The Washington Diaries*, 414-15.
38 Burney, *Getting It Done*, 155-56.
39 Foreign Affairs and International Trade Canada, "Canada–U.S. Softwood Lumber Trade Relations (1982-2006)" (Ottawa: DFAIT, 2006).
40 Janaki R.R. Alavalapati and Shiv Mehrotra, "Political Economy of the Canada–U.S. Softwood Lumber Trade Dispute," in *International Agricultural Trade Disputes:*

Case Studies in North America, edited by Andrew Schmitz et al. (Calgary: University of Calgary Press, 2005), 139-47.

41 Jeanne J. Grimmett and Vivian C. Jones, "The Continued Dumping and Subsidy Offset Act ('Byrd Amendment')," CRS Report RL 33045 (Washington, DC: Congressional Research Service, August 2005); Goldenberg, *The Way It Works,* 303-5.

42 Grimmett and Jones, "The Continued Dumping and Subsidy Offset Act."

43 Warren Giles, "U.S. Tariffs Violated Trade Deal, WTO Says," *Financial Post,* 16 August 2006.

44 Shawn McCarthy, "PM Links Softwood Dispute to Energy," *Globe and Mail,* 7 October 2005.

45 Alberts, "McKenna Blasts His Own Party's Anti-U.S. Rhetoric"; Tim Murphy, "Canada Calling: When It Comes to U.S. Relations, the Harper Government Should Keep Blandishments to a Minimum and Its Priorities Straight," *Globe and Mail,* 15 March 2006.

46 Wilson, "Canada and the United States," 14.

47 Confidential interviews, DFAIT, 2006; Jane Taber, "Lumber a Domestic Issue," *Globe and Mail,* 17 October 2005.

48 Persichilli, "With Softwood Past Them, Harper and Bush Will Talk Trade and Security."

49 Canada, *Framework Agreement on Softwood Lumber* (Ottawa: DFAIT, 2006).

50 Canada, DFAIT, and Office of United States Trade Representative, *Softwood Lumber Agreement between the Government of Canada and the Government of the United States of America* (Ottawa: DFAIT; Washington, DC: USTR, 1 July 2006).

51 Stephen Atkinson, "The Softwood Lumber Agreement" (Montreal: BMO Capital Markets, 11 July 2006); Peter Kennedy, "Forest Industry Shudders at Housing Forecast," *Globe and Mail,* 12 July 2006.

52 Bertrand Marotte, "Forest Industry Layoffs Top 6,000," *Globe and Mail,* 16 August 2006.

53 Peter Morton, "U.S. Issues 'Comfort Note' on Softwood," *Financial Post,* 19 August 2006.

54 *Coalition for Fair Lumber Imports, Executive Committee v. United States of America et al.,* US Court of Appeals, District of Columbia Circuit, 05-1366 (12 December 2006).

55 Steve Mertl, "Canada–U.S. Softwood Deal Has Teething Problems," *Globe and Mail,* 17 February 2007.

56 Steven Chase, "Canada Ekes Out Victory in Softwood Fight," *Globe and Mail,* 5 March 2008; Canadian Press, "U.S. Claims Victory in Latest Softwood Lumber Fight over 2006 Deal," *Truro Daily News,* 27 February 2009; Foreign Affairs and International Trade Canada, "Arbitration over Ontario and Quebec Programs: London Court of International Arbitration Ruling on Softwood Lumber" (Ottawa: DFAIT, 21 January 2011).

57 Hoekman and Kostecki, *The Political Economy of the World Trading System,* 80-84; Grimmett and Jones, "The Continued Dumping and Subsidy Offset Act."

58 Mark D. Froese, *Canada at the WTO: Trade Litigation and the Future of Public Policy* (Toronto: University of Toronto Press, 2010), 53.

59 James A. Brander, "Rationales for Strategic Trade Policy and Industrial Policy," in *Strategic Trade Policy and the New International Economics,* edited by Paul Krugman (Cambridge, MA: MIT Press, 1986), 23-46.

60 Mitch Potter and Les Whittington, "'Buy American' Wording Finalized," *Toronto Star,* 13 February 2009.

61 Tonda MacCharles and Les Whittington, "Obama's 'Buy American' Plan Blasted," *Toronto Star,* 30 January 2009.

62 Department of Foreign Affairs and International Trade Canada, "The Buy American and Buy America Acts" (Ottawa: DFAIT, 22 May 2009); Dana Frank, *Buy American: The Untold Story of Economic Nationalism* (Boston: Beacon Press, 1999).

63 Bill Dymond, "The Facts on the FTA," *Financial Post,* 12 June 2009.

64 World Trade Organization, "The Plurilateral Agreement on Government Procurement (GPA)" (Geneva: WTO, n.d.).

65 John Ivison, "U.S. Stimulus Stifling Canada," *National Post,* 30 April 2009; Paul Vieira, "Manufacturers Seek Buy U.S. Exemption," *Financial Post,* 5 June, 2009.

66 Ken Lewenza, "It's Time to Start Buying Canadian," *Financial Post,* 3 February 2009; "How to Tackle 'Buy America'" [editorial], *Toronto Star,* 5 June 2009; William Robson et al., "What to Do about Buy America?," *Globe and Mail,* 15 June 2009.

67 Lawrence Herman, "Ourselves to Blame," *Financial Post,* 9 June 2009; Dymond, "The Facts on the FTA."

68 Brian Laghi et al., "Premiers Rally behind Harper in Fight against Buy American," *Globe and Mail,* 5 June 2009.

69 Brian Laghi, "Premiers Look for Reciprocal Deal with U.S. on Access to Markets," *Globe and Mail,* 8 August 2009.

70 Sheldon Alberts and Mike Blanchfield, "Obama Urges Congress to Soften Protectionist Trade Message," *National Post,* 3 February 2009.

71 Brian Montopoli, "Obama: 'Buy American' Provision Hasn't Hurt Trade," CBS News, 10 August 2009; Steven Chase, Josh Wingrove, and Campbell Clark, "Obama Underplays Buy American Policy," *Globe and Mail,* 11 August 2009; Jeffrey Simpson, "Obama on Buy American: Please Stay Calm Canada," *Globe and Mail,* 17 September 2009.

72 Canada, DFAIT, and Office of the United States Trade Representative (USTR), *Agreement between the Government of Canada and the Government of the United States of America on Government Procurement* (Ottawa: DFAIT; Washington, DC: USTR, 11 February 2010).

73 United States, Office of the US Trade Representative, "Kirk Comments on US-Canada Procurement Agreement" (Washington, DC: Office of the US Trade Representative, 5 February 2010); Foreign Affairs and International Trade Canada, "Canada and United States Reach Agreement on Buy American," Press Release 56 (Ottawa: DFAIT, 5 February 2010).

74 Canada, DFAIT, and USTR, *Agreement,* 6.

75 Canada, DFAIT, and USTR, *Agreement,* 7.

76 "Not yet Decisive Victory" [editorial], *Globe and Mail,* 6 February 2010; John Ivison, "Give Harper Some Credit for Getting It Done," *National Post,* 6 February

2010; Lawrence Herman, "We Need Only One Voice at the Table," *Globe and Mail*, 9 February 2010; "Buy America Deal Requires Scrutiny" [editorial], *Toronto Star*, 21 February 2010.

77 Laura Dawson and Paul Frazer, "A 'Buy America' Wake Up Call for Canada," *Toronto Star*, 25 September 2011.

78 Dyment, *Doing the Continental*, 32.

Chapter 13: Shared Energy, Shared Energies?

1 Monica Gattinger, "Canada's Energy Policy Relations in North America: Towards Harmonization and Supranational Approaches?," in *Borders and Bridges: Canada's Policy Relations in North America*, edited by Monica Gattinger and Geoffrey Hale (Toronto: Oxford University Press, 2010), 139-57; Joseph M. Dukert, "North America," in *Energy Cooperation in the Western Hemisphere*, edited by Sidney Weintraub with Annette Hester and Veronica R. Prado (Washington, DC: Center for Strategic and International Studies), 133, 140; Macdonald and VanNijnatten, "Canadian Climate Change Policy and the North American Influence."

2 Calculated on "net import" basis. United States, Energy Information Administration, "Petroleum Statistics" (Washington, DC: EIA, 2011); United States, Energy Information Administration, "Natural Gas Statistics" (Washington, DC: EIA, 2011), http://www.eia.gov/.

3 James A. Baker III Institute for Public Policy of Rice University, "The Changing Role of National Oil Companies in International Energy Policy," Policy Report 35 (Houston: Baker Institute, 2007), 1.

4 US Energy Information Administration, "U.S. Natural Gas Imports by Country" (Washington, DC: EIA, 2011); US Energy Information Administration, "U.S. Imports by Country of Origin: Total Crude Oil and Products" (Washington, DC: EIA, 2011).

5 Shawn McCarthy and Nathan Vanderklippe, "Surge of Alberta Oil Tames Rise in Prices," *Globe and Mail*, 20 January 2011.

6 Geoffrey Hale, "'In the Pipeline' or 'Over a Barrel'? Managing Canada–U.S. Energy Interdependence," *Canadian–American Public Policy* 76 (2011).

7 Dyment, *Doing the Continental*, 76-86; Diane Francis, "Canada's Case of Dutch Disease," *Financial Post*, 14 April 2011.

8 Barrie McKenna, "A Country Built on Crude," *Globe and Mail*, 7 February 2011.

9 See, for example, Stanley Tromp, "Canada Lobbied U.S. over Pipeline," *Financial Post*, 24 January 2011; confidential interviews, DFAIT, 2006-10.

10 David N. Biette, ed., *Moving toward Dialogue: Challenges in Canada–US Energy Trade*, One Issue, Two Voices 2 (Washington, DC: Canada Institute, Woodrow Wilson Center for International Scholars, 2004); Vivian Krause, "U.S. Cash vs. Oil Sands," *Financial Post*, 15 October 2010; Trish Audette, "PM Worried 'Foreign' Money Could 'Hijack' Gateway Pipeline," *Calgary Herald*, 7 January 2012.

11 Edward Djerejian and Leslie H. Gelb, "Foreword," in *Strategic Energy Policy: Challenges for the 21st Century: Report of an Independent Task Force Co-Sponsored*

by the James A. Baker III Institute of Public Policy at Rice University and the Council on Foreign Relations, chaired by Edward L. Morse (New York: Council on Foreign Relations, 2001), v-vi.

12 Frank Verrastro, "The United States," in *Energy Cooperation in the Western Hemisphere*, edited by Sidney Weintraub with Annette Hester and Veronica R. Prado (Washington, DC: Center for Strategic and International Studies, 2007), 41.

13 United States, Energy Information Administration, "EIA Short-Term Energy Outlook: Annual Average Imported Crude Oil Price" (Washington, DC: EIA, 2011). Average import prices in 2010 and 2011 were $75.87 and $102.29, respectively.

14 Ryan Lizza, "As the World Burns," *New Yorker*, 11 October 2010. http://www.newyorker.com/.

15 André Plourde, "The Changing Nature of National and Continental Energy Markets," in *Canadian Energy Policy and the Struggle for Sustainable Development*, edited by G. Bruce Doern (Toronto: University of Toronto Press, 2005), 51-82.

16 Doern and Gattinger, *Power Switch*.

17 Gattinger, "Canada's Energy Policy Relations in North America"; Macdonald and VanNijnatten, "Canadian Climate Change Policy and the North American Influence."

18 United States, White House, "Remarks by President Obama and Prime Minister Stephen Harper of Canada in Joint Press Availability" [transcript] (Washington, DC: Office of the Press Secretary, 4 February 2011).

19 United States, White House, "Statements by President Barack Obama and Prime Minister Stephen Harper of Canada," 7 December 2011.

20 Mark Winfield and Douglas Macdonald, "The Harmonization Accord and Climate Change Policy: Two Case Studies in Federal-Provincial Environmental Policy," in *Canadian Federalism: Performance, Effectiveness, and Legitimacy*, 2nd ed., edited by Herman Bakvis and Grace Skogstad (Toronto: Oxford University Press), 266-88.

21 Monica Gattinger, "Canada–US Energy Relations: From Domestic to North American Energy Policies?," in *Policy: From Ideas to Implementation*, edited by Glen Toner, Leslie A. Pal, and Michael J. Prince (Montreal: McGill-Queen's University Press, 2010), 214-15.

22 Paul Ziff, "Cross-Border Energy Regulatory Collaboration in Its Context: Energy Balances and Energy Policy," in *Moving toward Dialogue: Challenges in Canada–U.S. Energy Trade*, edited by David N. Biette, One Issue, Two Voices 2 (Washington, DC: Canada Institute, Woodrow Wilson International Center for Scholars, 2004), 2-15.

23 Confidential interviews, DFAIT, US Department of Energy, 2005-8; Gattinger, "Canada–US Energy Relations," 215-16.

24 Hale, "Canada–US Relations in the Obama Era"; Gattinger, "Canada's Energy Policy Relations in North America"; Gattinger, "Canada–US Energy Relations."

25 Mouafo, Morales, and Heynen, *A Compendium of Canada–U.S. Relations*; Dukert, "North America"; Gattinger, "Canada–US Energy Relations."

26 Confidential interview, US Department of Energy, 2009.

27 US Department of State, "U.S.–Canada Energy Consultative Mechanism Meets" (Washington, DC: Office of the Spokesman, 6 December 2010).

28 NAEWG has not met since the fall of 2007, although energy officials of the three countries met periodically in other settings. Dukert, "North America," 134-35; Gattinger, "Canada–US Energy Relations," 217.

29 United States, Department of Energy, and Environment Canada, "U.S. Clean Energy Dialogue: Backgrounder" (Washington, DC: Department of Energy; Ottawa: Environment Canada, 16 September 2009).

30 Gattinger, "Canada–US Energy Relations," 218.

31 Eilperin, "Administration Delays Decision on Oil Pipeline."

32 Joel Millman, "Kearl Project Hits Roadblock – in Idaho," *Globe and Mail*, 22 October 2010; Tom Zeller Jr., "Oil Sands Effort Turns on a Fight over a Road," *New York Times*, 22 October 2010.

33 See, for example, Tromp, "Canada Lobbied U.S. over Pipeline"; Matthew Daly, "Canada PM Urges US to Approve Oil Pipeline," *Seattle Times*, 4 February 2011.

34 Robert Byrd, cited in Jesse Zwick, "Old Senator, New Tricks," *New Republic Online*, 25 January 2011, http://www.tnr.com/.

35 Juliet Eilperin and Steven Mufson, "Republicans Turn Keystone XL into Election Issue," *Washington Post*, 15 December 2011.

36 Hale, "'In the Pipeline' or 'Over a Barrel'?"

37 See, for example, Michael Sivak, "Where to Live in the United States: Combined Energy Demand for Heating, Cooling in the 50 Largest Metropolitan Areas," *International Journal of Urban Policy and Planning* 25 (2008): 396-98; Jonathan Rockwell and Mark Muro, "Cap and Trade Costs: Place Matters," *New Republic Online*, 3 November 2009, http://www.tnr.com/.

38 Barrie McKenna and David Parkinson, "U.S. Law Puts Chill on Oil Sands," *Globe and Mail*, 24 June 2008; John Partridge, "Oil Sands Safe from U.S. Law, Advocates Say," *Globe and Mail*, 1 October 2008.

39 Sheldon Alberts, "Mideast Crisis Boon for Oilsands," *Calgary Herald*, 25 February 2011.

40 Partridge, "Oil Sands Safe from U.S. Law, Advocates Say"; Lizza, "As the World Burns"; Mary-Jo Laforest, "U.S. Senator Calls Oilsands 'Very Impressive' after Tour with Alberta Premier," *Lethbridge Herald*, 18 September 2010; Gerein, "U.S. Senators Propose Bill to Open Flow of Oilsands."

41 Kenny Bruno et al., *Tar Sands Invasion: How Dirty and Expensive Oil from Canada Threatens America's New Energy Economy* (San Francisco: Corporate Ethics International, 2010), 9, 29. This label has also been applied to US oil shale production, which allegedly generates four times the GHG emissions of Canadian oil sands production. Jay Mouawad, "Oil Shale: Viable Domestic Energy, or 'Dirtiest Fuel on the Planet,'" *New York Times Online*, 30 September 2008, http://www.nytimes.com/.

42 See, for example, Shantel Beach, "The U.S. Targets Canada's Oil Sands" (Washington, DC: Council on Hemispheric Affairs, 15 December 2009); "Say Yes to This Pipeline" [editorial], *Washington Post*, 6 February 2011; Alberts, "Mideast Crisis Boon for Oilsands."

43 Deborah Yedlin, "New CAPP Boss Brings Insight into U.S.," *Calgary Herald*, 30 March 2009.

44 Trish Audette, "Premier Defends Oil Sands to U.S.," *Calgary Herald*, 2 July 2010; Government of Alberta, "A Good Neighbor Lends You a Cup of Sugar"; "Muck and Brass," *The Economist*, 20 January 2011, http://www.theeconomist.com/; Michael Levi, "A Shortsighted Victory in Delaying the Keystone Pipeline," *New York Times*, 10 November 2011.
45 Confidential interview, DFAIT, 2007.
46 Gordon S. Weil, "An Analysis of the NB Power/Hydro Quebec MOU" (Halifax: Atlantic Institute for Market Studies, 3 December 2009); Canadian Press, "Maine Governor Voices Concerns with Charest over Power Deal," *The Telegraph-Journal* (Saint John, NB), 31 December 2009; Gordon S. Weil, "The Modified New Brunswick/Quebec Memorandum of Understanding on NB Power: An Updated Analysis" (Halifax: Atlantic Institute for Market Studies, 26 January 2010); Marianne White, "N.B., Quebec Scrap Deal," *Financial Post*, 25 March 2010.
47 Paul Sullivan, "Written Testimony in Support of Oral Testimony of Professor Paul Sullivan ... for the Western Hemisphere Subcommittee of the Foreign Affairs Committee, U.S. House of Representatives" (Washington, DC: House Committee on Foreign Affairs, 31 March 2011).
48 David Brooks, "Vince Lombardi Politics," *New York Times*, 30 June 2009.
49 See, for example, Nathan Vanderklippe, "Turning Natural Gas into Diesel: A Big Bet on an Old Alchemy," *Globe and Mail*, 19 March 2011.
50 Dukert, "North America," 151.
51 Jim Prentice, "Speaking Points: Council for Clean and Renewable Energy" (Ottawa: Environment Canada, 25 October 2009).
52 For example, see Audette, "PM Worried 'Foreign' Money Could 'Hijack' Gateway Pipeline"; Joe Oliver, "Radicals Threaten Resource Development," *Financial Post*, 10 January 2012; Jeffrey Simpson, "'Foreign Money' Is a Hypocritical Diversion," *Globe and Mail*, 11 January 2012.

Chapter 14: Conclusion

1 See, for example, William Kilbourn, *Canada: A Guide to the Peaceable Kingdom* (New York: St. Martin's Press, 1971); David A. Charters, "The (Un)Peaceable Kingdom: Canada and Terrorism before 9/11," *Choices* 9, 4 (2008).
2 Michael Hart and Bill Dymond, "Free Trade and Dispute Settlement: Time to Declare Victory," *Policy Options* 28, 9 (October 2007): 45-51; Hale and Gattinger, "Variable Geometry and Traffic Circles," 367.
3 See, more recently, Bow, *The Politics of Linkage*; Dyment, *Doing the Continental*; Anderson and Sands, *Forgotten Partnership Redux*.
4 Hale, "The Buy-American Controversy"; Sands, *The Canada Gambit*.
5 Belanger, "An Unsustainable Institutional Design"; Jeffrey J. Schott, "Trade Negotiations among NAFTA Partners: The Future of North American Economic Integration," in *Requiem or Revival? The Promise of North American Integration*, edited by Isabel Studer and Carol Wise (Washington, DC: Brookings Institution, 2007), 76-88.

6 Bow, *The Politics of Linkage*, 4-6.
7 Sands, *The Canada Gambit*, 5, 19.
8 Gattinger and Hale, *Borders and Bridges*, 8.
9 Stephen Clarkson, remarks to the conference of the Association for Canadian Studies in the United States (ACSUS), San Diego, 14-17 November 2009.
10 Hale, "Canada–US Relations in the Obama Era."
11 Bow, *The Politics of Linkage*, 166.
12 Hale, "Canada–US Relations in the Obama Era."
13 Clarkson, *Does North America Exist?*, 453.
14 Bow, *The Politics of Linkage*, 177-80.
15 Dobson, "Shaping the Future of the North American Economic Space."
16 Burney, "Canada–US Relations at 150," 3.
17 Walter Russell Mead, "The Carter Syndrome," *Foreign Policy* 177 (January-February 2010): 58-64. A possible exception to this strategic retrenchment may be Obama's embrace, in 2011, of the Trans-Pacific Partnership and related security commitments. Walter Russell Mead, "America's Play for Pacific Prosperity," *Wall Street Journal*, 30 December 2011.
18 Pastor, *Toward a North American Community.*
19 For an updated version, see Robert A. Pastor, *The North American Idea: Vision of a Continental Future* (New York: Oxford University Press, 2011), 167-202.
20 Manley, Aspe, and Weld, *Building a North American Community.*
21 Studer, "Obstacles to Integration"; Golob, "The Return of the Quiet Canadian."
22 Clarkson, *Does North America Exist?*, 37-43.
23 Studer, "Obstacles to Integration," 58-68.
24 Confidential interview, Prime Minister's Office, 2006.
25 Jorge G. Castañeda, "Towards a Reset in U.S.–Mexican Relations," *Washington Post*, 17 May 2010.
26 Hale and Gattinger, "Variable Geometry and Traffic Circles," 367.
27 World Trade Organization, "Dispute Settlement: Cases in Chronological Order" (Geneva: WTO, n.d.).
28 Slaughter, *A New World Order.*
29 Gordon Hoekstra, "Environmental Groups Line Up Star Power against Project," *Vancouver Sun*, 4 January 2012.

Bibliography

Adams, Michael. *Fire and Ice: The United States, Canada, and the Myth of Converging Values.* Toronto: Penguin, 2003.

Alavalapati, Janaki R.R., and Shiv Mehrotra. "Political Economy of the Canada–U.S. Softwood Lumber Trade Dispute." In *International Agricultural Trade Disputes: Case Studies in North America,* edited by Andrew Schmitz, Charles Moss, Troy Schmitz, and Won Koo, 139-47. Calgary: University of Calgary Press, 2005.

Alberts, Sheldon. "Canada Is 'Secure,' CSIS Boss Tells U.S." *National Post,* 16 June 2006.

–. "McKenna Blasts His Own Party's Anti-U.S. Rhetoric." *Ottawa Citizen,* 2 March 2006.

–. "Mideast Crisis Boon for Oilsands." *Calgary Herald,* 25 February 2011.

–. "Napolitano Chided for Linking Canada to 9/11." *Ottawa Citizen,* 22 April 2009.

–. "PMO Hires Two Former White House Strategists." *National Post,* 16 April 2009.

–. "Ratifying Treaty Best Way to Resolve Arctic Claims." *Ottawa Citizen,* 7 April 2009.

Alberts, Sheldon, and Mike Blanchfield. "Obama Urges Congress to Soften Protectionist Trade Message." *National Post,* 3 February 2009.

Alden, Edward. *The Closing of the American Border: Terrorism, Immigration, and Security since 9/11.* New York: Harper, 2008.

Allison, Graham. *Nuclear Terrorism: The Ultimate Preventable Catastrophe.* New York: Henry Holt, 2004.

Anderson, Cameron D., and Laura B. Stephenson. *Moving Closer or Drifting Apart? Assessing the State of Public Opinion on the U.S.–Canadian Relationship.* London, ON: Canada–U.S. Institute, University of Western Ontario, 2010.

Anderson, Greg, and Christopher Sands. "Fragmegration, Federalism, and Canada–U.S. Relations." In *Borders and Bridges: Canada's Policy Relations in North America*, edited by Monica Gattinger and Geoffrey Hale, 41-58. Toronto: Oxford University Press, 2010.

–. *Negotiating North America: The Security and Prosperity Partnership.* Washington, DC: Hudson Institute, 2007.

–, eds. *Forgotten Partnership Redux: Canada–U.S. Relations in the 21st Century.* Amherst, NY: Cambria Press, 2011.

Atkinson, Stephen. "The Softwood Lumber Agreement." Montreal: BMO Capital Markets, 11 July 2006.

Audette, Trish. "Premier Defends Oil Sands to U.S." *Calgary Herald,* 2 July 2010.

–. "PM Worried 'Foreign' Money Could 'Hijack' Gateway Pipeline." *Calgary Herald,* 7 January 2012.

Axworthy, Lloyd. "Choices and Consequences in a Liberal Foreign Policy." In *Searching for the New Liberalism: Perspectives, Policies, Prospects,* edited by Howard Aster and Thomas S. Axworthy, 63-79. Oakville, ON: Mosaic Press, 2003.

Axworthy, Thomas A. "On Being an Ally: Why Virtue Is Not Reward Enough." Ottawa: Institute for Research on Public Policy, 2004.

–. "A Strong Canada in a Strong Continent." *Toronto Star,* 30 December 2007.

Ayres, Jeffrey M. "Political Economy, Civil Society, and the Deep Integration Debate in Canada." *American Review of Canadian Studies* 34, 4 (2004): 621-47.

Bagnal, Joel. "Goldwater–Nichols for the Executive Branch: Achieving Unity of Effort." In *Threats at Our Threshold: Homeland Security in the New Century,* edited by Bert J. Pilling, 45-54. Washington, DC: Center for Strategic and International Studies, 2006.

Barnes, Fred. "How Spending Cuts, Not Higher Taxes, Saved Canada." *Wall Street Journal,* 21 July 2011.

Beach, Shantel. "The U.S. Targets Canada's Oil Sands." Washington, DC: Council on Hemispheric Affairs, 15 December 2009.

Becker, Geoffrey S. "Bovine Spongiform Encephalopathy (BSE or 'Mad Cow Disease') in North America: A Chronology of Selected Events." CRS Report RL-32932. Washington, DC: Congressional Research Service, 27 July 2006.

–. "BSE ('Mad Cow Disease'): A Brief Overview." CRS Report RS-22345. Washington, DC: Congressional Research Service, 19 December 2006.

–. "Country-of-Origin Labeling for Foods." CRS Report 97-508. Washington, DC: Congressional Research Service, 20 March 2006.

Belanger, Louis. "An Unsustainable Institutional Design: Incompleteness and Delegation Deficit in NAFTA." In *Governing the Americas: Assessing Multilateral Institutions,* edited by Gordon Mace and Paul Haslam, 195-212. Boulder, CO: Lynne Rienner Publishers, 2007.

Bell, Stewart. "Solo Terrorists Pose New Threat: Report." *National Post,* 10 June 2008.

Bell, Stewart, and Adrian Humphreys. "Terrorism's 'New Guard.'" *National* Post, 4 May 2006.

Bellavita, Christopher. "Changing Homeland Security: What Is Homeland Security?" *Homeland Security Affairs* 4, 2 (2008). http://www.hsaj.org/.

Bercuson, David J., and Denis Stairs, eds. *In the Canadian Interest? Assessing Canada's International Policy Statement.* Calgary: Canadian Defence and Foreign Affairs Institute, 2005.

Biette, David N. *Moving toward Dialogue: Challenges in Canada–U.S. Energy Trade.* One Issue, Two Voices. Issue 2. Washington, DC: Canada Institute, Woodrow Wilson International Center for Scholars, 2004. http://www.wilsoncenter.org/.

Biette, David N., and Douglas Goold. *Renewing the U.S.–Canada Relationship: The 105th American Assembly.* Toronto: Canadian Institute for International Affairs; Washington, DC: Woodrow Wilson International Center for Scholars, 2005.

Billups, Andrea. "New Bridge Linking U.S., Canada on Hold." *Washington Times,* 20 October 2011.

Bissett, James. "Americans Are Right to Worry." *Ottawa Citizen,* 27 April 2009.

–. "We Need Security Certificates." *National Post,* 20 April 2006.

Bjelopera, Jerome P., and Mark A. Randol. "American Jihadist Terrorism: Combating a Complex Threat." Report 41416. Washington, DC: Congressional Research Service, 20 September 2010.

Bland, Douglas. "Pursuing Our Hemispheric Interests." *Globe and Mail,* 4 September 2009.

Blank, Stephen, Graham Parsons, and Juan Carlos Villa. "Freight Transportation Infrastructure Policies in Canada, Mexico, and the US: An Overview and Analysis." Working Paper 5. Washington, DC: North American Transportation Competitiveness Research Council, 2008.

Boswell, Randy, and Juliet O'Neill. "Clinton Blasts Canada for Exclusive Arctic Talks." *Ottawa Citizen,* 30 March 2010.

Boucher, Christian. "Toward North American or Regional Cross-Border Communities: A Look at Economic Integration and Socio-Cultural Values in Canada and the United States." Working paper. Ottawa: Policy Research Initiative, 2005.

Bow, Brian. *The Politics of Linkage: Power, Interdependence, and Ideas in Canada–U.S. Relations.* Vancouver: UBC Press, 2010.

Bow, Brian A., and Patrick Lennox, eds. *An Independent Foreign Policy for Canada?* Toronto: University of Toronto Press, 2008.

Brander, James A. "Rationales for Strategic Trade Policy and Industrial Policy." In *Strategic Trade Policy and the New International Economics,* edited by Paul Krugman, 23-46. Cambridge, MA: MIT Press, 1986.

Brister, Bernard J. "The Same yet Different: The Evolution of the Post-9/11 Canada–United States Security Relationship." In *Borders and Bridges: Canada's Policy Relations in North America,* edited by Monica Gattinger and Geoffrey Hale, 82-99. Toronto: Oxford University Press, 2010.

Brooks, David. "Vince Lombardi Politics." *New York Times,* 30 June 2009.

Brooks, Mary R. *The Jones Act under NAFTA and Its Effects on the Canadian Shipbuilding Industry.* Halifax: Atlantic Institute for Market Studies, 2006.

Brunet-Jailly, Emmanuel. "Borders, Borderlands, and Security: European and North American Lessons and Policy Suggestions." In *Borderlands: Comparing Border Security in North America and Europe*, edited by Emmanuel Brunet-Jailly, 351-57. Ottawa: University of Ottawa Press, 2007.

–. "Cross-Border Relations in Detroit, Niagara, and Vancouver." *Journal of Borderland Studies* 21, 2 (2006): 1-19.

Bruno, Kenny, Bruce Baizel, Susan Casey-Lefkowitz, Elizabeth Shope, and Kate Colarulli. *Tar Sands Invasion: How Dirty and Expensive Oil from Canada Threatens America's New Energy Economy.* San Francisco: Corporate Ethics International, 2010.

Burney, Derek H. "Foreign Policy: More Coherence, Less Pretence." Ottawa: Centre for Trade Policy and Law, 14 March 2005.

–. *Getting It Done.* Montreal: McGill-Queen's University Press, 2005.

Butler, Don. "The Politics of Bush-Bashing." *Ottawa Citizen*, 17 December 2005.

Byers, Michael. *Intent for a Nation.* Vancouver: Douglas and McIntyre, 2007.

–. "A Thaw in Relations." *Ottawa Citizen*, 6 March 2008.

Campbell, Leslie. "Time to Start Doing American-Style Politics." *Embassy*, 4 June 2008, 7.

Canada. *Securing an Open Society: Canada's National Security Policy.* Ottawa: Privy Council Office, 2004.

–. Commission of Inquiry into the Actions of Canadian Officials in Relation to Maher Arar. *Report of the Events Relating to Maher Arar: Analysis and Recommendations.* Ottawa: Privy Council Office, 2006. http://www.pch.gc.ca/.

–. Competition Policy Review Panel. *Compete to Win: Final Report.* Ottawa: Industry Canada, 2008.

–. Department of Foreign Affairs and International Trade Canada. *The Americas: Priorities and Progress.* Ottawa: DFAIT, 11 August 2009.

–. –. "Arbitration over Ontario and Quebec Programs: London Court of International Arbitration Ruling on Softwood Lumber." Ottawa: DFAIT, 21 January 2011. http://www.international.gc.ca/.

–. –. "The Buy American and Buy America Acts." Ottawa: DFAIT, 22 May 2009. http://www.canadainternational.gc.ca/.

–. –. "Canada–U.S. Softwood Lumber Trade Relations (1982-2006)." Ottawa: DFAIT, 2006.

–. –. "Negotiations and Agreements." Ottawa: DFAIT. http://www.international. gc.ca/.

–. Department of National Defence. *Canada First Defence Strategy.* Ottawa: DND, 18 June 2008.

–. Policy Research Institute. *The Emergence of Cross-Border Regions between Canada and the United States: Reaping the Promise and Public Value of Cross-Border Regional Relationships – Final Report.* Ottawa: Industry Canada, 2008. http://www.policyresearch.gc.ca/.

Canada, Passport Office. *Annual Report: 2010-2011*. Ottawa: Passport Canada, 2011. http://www.ppt.gc.ca/.

Canada, Prime Minister's Office, and United States, White House. "Beyond the Border: A Shared Vision for Perimeter Security and Economic Competitiveness." Ottawa: PMO; Washington, DC: White House, 4 February 2011. http://www.pm.gc.ca/.

Canadian Chamber of Commerce and United States Chamber of Commerce. *Finding the Balance: Reducing Border Costs while Strengthening Security.* Ottawa: Canadian Chamber of Commerce; Washington, DC: US Chamber of Commerce, 2008.

Canadian Press. "Ottawa Lifts Visa Requirements for Czech and Latvian Visitors." *The Record* (Kitchener, ON), 1 November 2007.

Carafano, James. "Obama Administration Gets One Border's Security Right." *Washington Examiner*, 19 December 2011. http://www.washingtonexaminer.com/.

Carpenter, Amanda. "Hot Button: Canada and U.S." *Washington Times*, 1 June 2009.

Carter, Sara A. "NATO Seen Cool to Hot Spots in Afghanistan." *Washington Times*, 17 January 2008.

Castañeda, Jorge G. "Towards a Reset in U.S.–Mexican Relations." *Washington Post*, 17 May 2010.

Cellucci, Paul. *Unquiet Diplomacy.* Toronto: Key Porter, 2005.

Charters, David. "The (Un)Peaceable Kingdom: Canada and Terrorism before 9/11." *Choices* 9, 4 (2008). http://www.irpp.org/.

Chase, Steven. "Canada Concerned at Including Mexico in Talks with U.S.: Wikileaks Release," *Globe and Mail*, 3 March 2011.

–. "Canada Ekes Out Victory in Softwood Fight." *Globe and Mail*, 5 March 2008.

Chase, Steven, Josh Wingrove, and Campbell Clark. "Obama Underplays Buy American Policy." *Globe and Mail*, 11 August 2009.

Clark, Campbell. "Extension Was Result of Rare Bipartisan Effort." *Globe and Mail*, 18 November 2010.

–. "PM Plans 'Inside the Wire' Afghan Role while U.S. Presses for Riskier One." *Globe and Mail*, 11 November 2010.

Clarkson, Stephen. "The Choice to Be Made." In *Readings in Canadian Foreign Policy: Classic Debates and New Ideas*, edited by Duane Bratt and Christopher Kukucha, 46-61. Toronto: Oxford University Press, 2006.

–. *Does North America Exist? Governing the Continent after NAFTA and 9/11.* Toronto: University of Toronto Press, 2008.

–. *Uncle Sam and Us: Globalization, Neo-Conservatism, and the Canadian State.* Toronto: University of Toronto Press, 2002.

–, ed. *An Independent Foreign Policy for Canada?* Toronto: McClelland and Stewart, 1968.

Cohen, Andrew. "Our Mythology of Values." In *American Myths: What Canadians Think They Know about the United States*, edited by Rudyard Griffiths, 137-50. Toronto: Key Porter, 2009.

–. *While Canada Slept? How We Lost Our Place in the World.* Toronto: McClelland and Stewart, 2003.

Cohen, Michael D., James G. March, and Johan P. Olsen. "A Garbage Can Model of Organizational Choice." *Administrative Science Quarterly* 17, 1 (1972): 1-25.

Collacutt, Martin. "Canada's Inadequate Response to Terrorism: The Need for Immigration Reform." Vancouver: Fraser Institute, 2006.

Collins, Michelle. "Cabinet Pulls the Plug on Mexican and Czech Visa-Free Travel." *Embassy*, 15 July 2009, 1.

Cooper, Richard. *The Economics of Interdependence*. Published for the Council on Foreign Relations. New York: McGraw-Hill, 1968.

Corsi, Jerome R. *The Late, Great USA: The Coming Merger with Mexico and Canada*. Los Angeles: World Ahead Media, 2007.

Daly, Matthew. "Canada PM Urges US to Approve Oil Pipeline." *Seattle Times*, 4 February 2011.

Davidow, Jeffrey. *The US and Mexico: The Bear and the Porcupine*. Princeton, NJ: Marcus Weiner Publishing, 2005.

Dawson, Laura, and Paul Frazer. "A 'Buy America' Wake Up Call for Canada." *Toronto Star*, 25 September 2011.

De Borchgrave, Arnaud. "Global Fatigue and Trust Deficit." *Washington Times*, 25 January 2010.

Delacourt, Susan. "PM Issues Warning to NAFTA Foes." *Toronto Star*, 23 April 2008.

Den Tandt, Michael. "A Welcome Thinning of the Border." *National Post*, 7 December 2011.

Destler, I.M. *American Trade Politics*. 4th ed. Washington, DC: Institute for International Economics, 2005.

Djerejian, Edward, and Leslie H. Gelb. "Foreword." In *Strategic Energy Policy: Challenges for the 21st Century: Report of an Independent Task Force Co-Sponsored by the James A. Baker III Institute of Public Policy at Rice University and the Council on Foreign Relations*, chaired by Edward L. Morse, v-vii. New York: Council on Foreign Relations, 2001.

Dobson, Wendy. "Shaping the Future of the North American Economic Space: A Framework for Action." Commentary 162. Toronto: C.D. Howe Institute, 2002.

Doern, G. Bruce, and Monica Gattinger. *Power Switch: Energy Regulatory Governance in the Twenty-First Century*. Toronto: University of Toronto Press, 2003.

Doern, G. Bruce, and Brian W. Tomlin. *Faith and Fear: The Free Trade Story*. Toronto: Stoddart, 1991.

Donati, Eugene. "Opposed Triangles: Policy-Making and Regulation in Canada and the United States." *Policy Options* 23, 3 (2001): 44-49.

Doran, Charles F. "Canada–U.S. Relations: Personality, Pattern, and Domestic Politics." In *Handbook on Canadian Foreign Policy*, edited by Patrick James, Marc O'Reilly, and Nelson Michaud, 391-410. Lanham, MD: Lexington, 2006.

–. *Forgotten Partnership: U.S.–Canada Relations Today*. Baltimore: Johns Hopkins University Press, 1984.

Doran, Charles F., and Joel J. Sokolsky. *Canada and Congress: Lobbying in Washington*. Halifax: Centre for Foreign Policy Studies, Dalhousie University, 1985.

Duffy, Andrew. "Ottawa Author Attacks RCMP for Terror-Fighting Strategy." *Ottawa Citizen*, 26 August 2008.

–. "The Secret Trial." *Ottawa Citizen*, 22 June 2008.

Dukert, Joseph M. "North America." In *Energy Cooperation in the Western Hemisphere*, edited by Sidney Weintraub with Annette Hester and Veronica R. Prado, 132-65. Washington, DC: Center for Strategic and International Studies, 2007.

Dunsky, Dan. "Canada's Three Solitudes." *National Interest* 82 (2005-6): 94-99.

–. "Why We Bash America." *National Post*, 21 December 2005.

Dunsmore, Kate. "Connecting Canada and Terrorism: The Year after 9/11 in the *New York Times*." Paper presented at the Western Social Science Association conference, Calgary, 14 April 2007.

Dyment, David. *Doing the Continental: A New Canadian–American Relationship*. Toronto: Dundurn Press, 2010.

Dymond, Bill. "The Facts on the FTA." *Financial Post*, 12 June 2009.

Dymond, Bill, and Michael Hart. "Navigating New Trade Routes: The Rise of Value Chains and the Challenges for Canadian Trade Policy." Commentary 259. Toronto: C.D. Howe Institute, 2008.

Eilperin, Juliet. "U.S., Canada Map Edges of Continent on Seafloor." *Washington Post*, 11 September 2008.

–. "Administration Delays Decision on Oil Pipeline." *Washington Post*, 11 November 2011.

–, and Steven Mufson. "Republicans Turn Keystone XL into Election Issue." *Washington Post*, 15 December 2011.

Ek, Carl. "Canada–U.S. Relations." CRS Report 96-397. Washington, DC: Congressional Research Service, 1 May 2006.

Ekos Research Associates. "Bushwhacking and Other Ingredients of Canadian Outlook on the USA." *Time Magazine* Poll. Toronto: Ekos Research Associates, 25 October 2004. http://www.ekos.ca/.

–. "Ekos/PPF Symposium: Rethinking North American Integration – Part II: Economic Dimensions." Toronto: Ekos Research Associates, 18 June 2002. http://www.ekos.ca/.

–. "Results of Ekos/CBC News Survey." Toronto: Ekos Research Associates, 19 January 2009. http://www.ekos.ca/.

Ellison, Jake. "State, B.C. Join Forces to Fight Passport Proposal." *Seattle Post-Intelligencer*, 12 November 2006.

Extension Disaster Education Network. "Agricultural Disasters: Confirmed BSE Cases." Baton Rouge: Louisiana State University, 2010. http://eden.lus.edu/.

Fergusson, James G. *Canada and Ballistic Missile Defence, 1954-2009*. Vancouver: UBC Press, 2010.

Flynn, Stephen E. "The False Conundrum: Continental Integration vs. Homeland Security." In *The Rebordering of North America*, edited by Peter Andreas and Thomas Bierstecker, 110-27. New York: Routledge, 2003.

Francis, Diane. "Canada's Case of Dutch Disease." *Financial Post*, 14 April 2011.

Frank, Dana. *Buy American: The Untold Story of Economic Nationalism.* Boston: Beacon Press, 1999.

Freeman, Alan. "Former US President 'Got Us in' G8." *Globe and Mail,* 3 January 2007.

—. "Latin America Visit by Harper to Focus on Foreign Policy." *Globe and Mail,* 12 July 2007.

Freeze, Colin. "Are Security Certificates Obsolete?" *Globe and Mail,* 25 September 2009.

—. "Divisive Terror Law Losing Traction." *Globe and Mail,* 21 September 2009.

—. "Get Tougher on Terrorism, FBI Director Tells Canada." *Globe and Mail,* 19 July 2006.

—. "Pakistani–Canadian Guilty of Terrorism." *Globe and Mail,* 10 June 2011.

—. "Torture Report Urges Ottawa to Better Protect Rights." *Globe and Mail,* 22 October 2008.

Freeze, Colin, and Marina Jimenez. "Mexico's Drug War Becomes Canadian Security Issue." *Globe and Mail,* 5 March 2009.

Froese, Marc D. *Canada at the WTO: Trade Litigation and the Future of Public Policy.* Toronto: University of Toronto Press, 2010.

Fulford, Robert. "Bred in the Bone." In *American Myths: What Canadians Think They Know about the United States,* edited by Rudyard Griffiths, 63-74. Toronto: Key Porter, 2009.

Galloway, Gloria. "Canadians Share Americans' Anxiety." *Globe and Mail,* 28 June 2008.

—. "Kenney Proposes a Two-Stream Approach to Refugee Reform." *Globe and Mail,* 30 March 2010.

Galt, Virginia. "Westjet Tackles US Market." *Globe and Mail,* 9 July 2008.

Gamble, Jessa. "Drawing Lines on the Sea: Nations Stake Claims on Arctic Ocean Riches." *Scientific American,* 10 November 2008.

Gattinger, Monica. "Canada's Energy Policy Relations in North America: Towards Harmonization and Supranational Approaches?" In *Borders and Bridges: Canada's Policy Relations in North America,* edited by Monica Gattinger and Geoffrey Hale, 139-57. Toronto: Oxford University Press, 2010.

—. "Canada–US Energy Relations: From Domestic to North American Energy Policies?" In *Policy: From Ideas to Implementation,* edited by Glen Toner, Leslie A. Pal, and Michael J. Prince, 207-31. Montreal: McGill-Queen's University Press, 2010.

Gattinger, Monica, and Geoffrey Hale, eds. *Borders and Bridges: Canada's Policy Relations in North America.* Toronto: Oxford University Press, 2010.

Gee, Marcus. "Poll Highlights Unease over U.S. Foreign Policy." *Globe and Mail,* 13 December 2007.

Gerein, Keith. "U.S. Senators Propose Bill to Open Flow of Oilsands." *Calgary Herald,* 2 October 2010.

Gibbins, Roger. "Regional Integration and National Contexts: Constraints and Opportunities." In *Regionalism in a Global Society,* edited by Stephen G.

Tomblin and Charles S. Colgin, 37-56. Peterborough, ON: Broadview Press, 2004.

Giles, Warren. "U.S. Tariffs Violated Trade Deal, WTO Says." *Financial Post,* 16 August 2006.

Glasser, Susan B., and Michael Grunwald. "Prelude to Disaster: The Making of DHS." *Washington* Post, 22 December 2005.

Goldenberg, Eddie. *The Way It Works: Inside Ottawa.* Toronto: McClelland and Stewart, 2006.

Goldfarb, Danielle. *Is Just-in-Case Replacing Just-in-Time? How Cross-Border Trading Behaviour Has Changed since 9/11.* Ottawa: Conference Board of Canada, 2007.

Goldstein, Judith. "International Forces and Domestic Politics: Trade Policy and Institution Building in the United States." In *Shaped by War and Trade: International Influences on American Political Development,* edited by Ira Katznelson and Martin Shefter, 211-35. Princeton, NJ: Princeton University Press, 2002.

Golob, Stephanie R. "The Return of the Quiet Canadian: Canada's Approach to Regional Integration after 9/11." In *An Independent Foreign Policy for Canada?,* edited by Brian Bow and A. Patrick Lennox, 83-99. Toronto: University of Toronto Press, 2008.

Goodchild, Anne, Steven Globerman, and Susan Albrecht. "Service Time Variability at the Blaine, Washington, International Border Crossing and the Impact on Regional Supply Chains." Research Report 3. Bellingham, WA: Border Policy Research Institute, 2007.

Goodman, Lee Anne. "U.S. Border Deal Not about Sovereignty, Harper Says after Obama Meeting." *Okotoks Western Wheel,* 4 February 2011.

Gorham, Beth. "Bush Flexible on Border ID." *Winnipeg Free Press,* 7 July 2006.

–. "Canada Lobbies U.S. Legislators on Security." *Toronto Star,* 16 June 2006.

–. "Harper Can Disagree with U.S., MP." *Ottawa Citizen,* 28 January 2006.

Gotlieb, Allan. "The Future of Canada–US Relations: Bring Back the Special Relationship." In *American Myths: What Canadians Think They Know about the United States,* edited by Rudyard Griffiths, 75-90. Toronto: Key Porter, 2009.

–. *I'll Be with You in a Minute, Mr. Ambassador.* Toronto: University of Toronto Press, 1991.

–. "Martin's Bush-League Diplomacy." *Globe and Mail,* 26 January 2006.

–. *Romanticism and Realism in Canada's Foreign Policy.* Benefactors Lecture, 3 November 2004. Toronto: C.D. Howe Institute, 2004.

–. *The United States in Canadian Foreign Policy.* O.D. Skelton Lecture, 10 December 1991. Ottawa: DFAIT, 1991.

–. *The Washington Diaries: 1983-1991.* Toronto: McClelland and Stewart, 2006.

Granatstein, J.L. "Sometimes Making Peace Means Making War." In *American Myths: What Canadians Think They Know about the United States,* edited by Rudyard Griffiths, 17-27. Toronto: Key Porter, 2009.

Gratzer, David. "Canada's ObamaCare Precedent." *Wall Street Journal,* 9 June 2009.

Grayson, George W. *Mexico: Narco-Violence and a Failed State?* New Brunswick, NJ: Transaction, 2010.

Grimmett, Jeanne J. "Why Certain Trade Agreements Are Approved as Congressional–Executive Agreements Rather than as Treaties." CRS Report 97-896. Washington, DC: Congressional Research Service, 28 July 2004.

Grimmett, Jeanne J., and Vivian C. Jones. "The Continued Dumping and Subsidy Offset Act ('Byrd Amendment')." CRS Report RL-33045. Washington, DC: Congressional Research Service, 22 August 2005.

Guzman, Betsy. The Hispanic Population: Census 2000 Brief. C2KBR/01-3. Washington, DC: US Census Bureau, 2001. http://www.census.gov/.

Gwyn, Richard. *The 49th Paradox: Canada in North America.* Toronto: McClelland and Stewart, 1965.

Haberkorn, Jen. "Passport Backlog Prompts a Waiver." *Washington Times,* 9 June 2007.

–. "Passport Seekers Inundate Office." *Washington Times,* 20 June 2007.

Hale, Geoffrey. "The Buy-American Controversy: A Case Study in Canada–U.S. Trade Relations." Waterloo, ON: Portal for North America, Centre for International Governance Innovation, University of Waterloo, 2010. http://www.portalfornorthamerica.org/.

–. "Canada–US Relations in the Obama Era: Warming or Greening?" In *How Ottawa Spends: 2010-2011 – Recession, Realignment and the New Deficit Era,* edited by G. Bruce Doern and Christopher Stoney, 48-67. Montreal: McGill-Queen's University Press, 2010.

–. "Canadian Federalism and North American Integration: Managing Multi-Level Games." In *The State in Transition: Challenges for Canadian Federalism,* edited by Michael Behiels and François Rocher, 237-67. Ottawa: Invenire Books, 2011.

–. "Cross-Border Relations: Moving beyond the Politics of Uncertainty?" In *How Ottawa Spends: 2005-2006,* edited by G. Bruce Doern, 121-42. Montreal: McGill-Queen's University Press, 2005.

–. "The Dog that Hasn't Barked: The Political Economy of Contemporary Debates on Canadian Foreign Investment Policies." *Canadian Journal of Political Science* 41, 3 (2008): 719-47.

–. "Getting Down to Business: Rebuilding Canada–US Relations." In *How Ottawa Spends: 2007-2008,* edited by G. Bruce Doern, 65-86. Montreal: McGill-Queen's University Press, 2007.

–. "'In the Pipeline' or 'Over a Barrel'? Managing Canada–U.S. Energy Interdependence." *Canadian American Public Policy* 76 (2011).

–. *In Search of Effective Border Management.* Toronto: Canadian International Council, 2009.

–. "Maintaining Policy Discretion: Cross-Border Policy-Making and North American Integration." In *An Independent Foreign Policy for Canada?,* edited by Brian Bow and R. Peter Lennox, 137-62. Toronto: University of Toronto Press, 2008.

—. "People, Politics, and Passports: Contesting Security, Trade, and Travel on the US–Canadian Border." *Geopolitics* 16, 1 (2011): 27-69.

—. "Sharing a Continent: Security, Insecurity, and the Politics of 'Intermesticity.'" *Canadian Foreign Policy* 12, 3 (2005-6): 31-43.

—. "Signalling across the Fence: Canada–US Relations and the Politics of Intermesticity." Paper presented at the Annual Meeting of the Western Social Science Association, Calgary, 12 April 2007.

—. "The Unfinished Legacy: Liberal Policy on North America." In *How Ottawa Spends: 2003-2004*, edited by G. Bruce Doern, 25-43. Toronto: Oxford University Press, 2003.

Hale, Geoffrey, and Stephen Blank. "North American Economic Integration and Comparative Responses to Globalization: Overview." In *Borders and Bridges: Canada's Policy Relations in North America*, edited by Monica Gattinger and Geoffrey Hale, 21-40. Toronto: Oxford University Press, 2010.

Hale, Geoffrey, and Monica Gattinger. "Variable Geometry and Traffic Circles: Navigating Canada's Policy Relations in North America." In *Borders and Bridges: Navigating Canada's Policy Relations in North America*, edited by Monica Gattinger and Geoffrey Hale, 361-81. Toronto: Oxford University Press, 2010.

Hale, Geoffrey, and Jamie Huckabay. "Canadian Public Diplomacy in the United States: Which Public, How Diplomatic?" Paper presented at the Annual Meeting of the Association for Canadian Studies in the United States, Toronto, 15 November 2007.

Hale, Geoffrey, and Christina Marcotte. "Border Security, Trade, and Travel Facilitation." In *Borders and Bridges: Navigating Canada's Policy Relations in North America*, edited by Monica Gattinger and Geoffrey Hale, 100-19. Toronto: Oxford University Press, 2010.

Hamilton, Graeme. "Terror Plotter Undone by Online Activities." *National Post*, 2 October 2009.

Harper, Stephen. "Reviving Canadian Leadership in the World." Calgary: Woodrow Wilson International Center for Scholars, 5 October 2006.

Harper, Tim. "The Canada–U.S. Relationship: Out of Sight, Out of Mind." *Toronto Star*, 22 April 2011.

Hart, Michael. *Canada: A Trading Nation*. Vancouver: UBC Press, 2002.

Hart, Michael, and Bill Dymond. "Free Trade and Dispute Settlement: Time to Declare Victory." *Policy Options* 28, 9 (2007): 45-51.

Harvey, Frank P. "Canada's Addiction to American Security: The Illusion of Choice in the War on Terrorism." *American Review of Canadian Studies* 35, 2 (2005): 265-94.

Haynal, George. "The Next Plateau in North America: What's the Big Idea?" *Policy Options* 25, 6 (2004): 35-39.

Heinenen, Lassi, and Heather Nicol. "A New Northern Security Agenda." In *Borderlands: Comparing Border Security in North America and Europe*, edited by Emmanuel Brunet-Jailly, 117-63. Ottawa: University of Ottawa Press, 2007.

Henrikson, Alan K. "Niche Diplomacy in the World Public Arena: The Global 'Corners' of Canada and Norway." In *The New Public Diplomacy: Soft Power in International Relations,* edited by Jan Melissen, 67-87. Basingstoke, UK: Palgrave Macmillan, 2005.

Herman, Lawrence. "Ourselves to Blame." *Financial Post,* 9 June 2009.

–. "We Need Only One Voice at the Table." *Globe and Mail,* 9 February 2010.

Heyman, David, and James Jay Carafano. *DHS 2.0: Rethinking the Department of Homeland Security.* Washington, DC: Centre for Strategic and International Studies and Heritage Foundation, 2004. http://www.csis.org/.

Heynen, Jeff, and John Higginbotham. *Advancing Canada's Interests in the United States.* Ottawa: Canada School of Public Service, 2004.

Higginbotham, John, and Jeff Heynen. "Managing through Networks: The State of Canada–U.S. Relations." In *Canada among Nations, 2004: Setting Priorities Straight,* edited by David Carment, Fen Osler Hampson, and Norman Hillmer, 123-40. Montreal: McGill-Queen's University Press, 2005.

Hillmer, Norman, Fen Hampson, and David Carment. "Smart Power in Canadian Foreign Policy." In *Canada among Nations, 2004: Setting Priorities Straight,* edited by Norman Hillmer, Fen Hampson, and David Carment, 3-17. Montreal: McGill-Queen's University Press, 2005.

Hoberg, George, ed. *Capacity for Choice: Canada in a New North America.* Toronto: University of Toronto Press, 2002.

Hocking, Brian. "Rethinking the 'New' Public Diplomacy." In *The New Public Diplomacy: Soft Power in International Relations,* edited by Jan Melissen, 28-43. Basingstoke, UK: Palgrave Macmillan, 2005.

Hoekman, Bernard M., and Michel M. Kostecki. *The Political Economy of the World Trading System.* 2nd ed. Toronto: Oxford University Press, 2001.

Hoekstra, Gordon. "Environmental Groups Line Up Star Power against Project." *Vancouver Sun,* 4 January 2012.

–. "EthicalOil.org Slams Environmental Groups for Taking U.S. Money." *Vancouver Sun,* 4 January 2012.

Hoffman, Bruce. "The Myth of Grass-Roots Terrorism." *Foreign Affairs* 87, 3 (March-April 2008): 133-38.

Holder, Eric. "Speech to Northern Border Summit, Lake Placid, NY." Washington, DC: Department of Justice, 14 September 2011. http://www.justice.gov/.

Hook, Steven W. *U.S. Foreign Policy: The Paradox of World Power.* Washington, DC: CQ Press, 2005.

Hsu, Spencer S. "DHS Plagued by Turnover in Top Positions." *Washington Post,* 16 July 2007.

–. "DHS Strains as Goals, Mandates Go Unmet." *Washington Post,* 6 March 2008.

–. "U.S. Readies Plan to ID Departing Visitors." *Washington Post,* 8 November 2009.

Hufbauer, Gary C., and Claire Brunel. "Economic Integration in North America." In *Free Trade in Free Fall? Canada–U.S. Non-Tariff Barriers,* edited by Stephanie McLuhan, 2-7. One Issue, Two Voices 8. Washington, DC: Canada Institute, Woodrow Wilson International Center for Scholars, 2008.

Hufbauer, Gary Clyde, and Jeffrey J. Schott. *NAFTA Revisited: Achievements and Challenges.* Washington, DC: Institute for International Economics, 2005.

Humes, Karen R., Nicholas A. Jones, and Roberto R. Ramirez. "Overview of Race and Hispanic Origin: 2010." C2010BR-02. Washington, DC: US Census Bureau, 2011. http://www.census.gov/.

Ibbitson, John. "Trade Key to PM's Idea of Success." *Globe and Mail,* 26 December 2011.

Ignatius, David. "Homeland Security's Struggle." *Washington Post,* 6 March 2008.

–. "Portents of a Nuclear al-Qaeda." *Washington Post,* 11 October 2007.

International Falls [MN] *Daily Journal,* "Enhanced Drivers License Bill Passes Legislature," 12 May 2010.

Isernia, Pierangelo. "Anti-Americanism in Europe during the Cold War." In *Anti-Americanisms in World Politics,* edited by Peter J. Katzenstein and Robert O. Keohane, 57-92. Ithaca, NY: Cornell University Press, 2007.

Ivison, John. "Give Harper Some Credit for Getting It Done." *National Post,* 6 February 2010.

–. "Tories to Re-open F-35 Debate." *National Post,* 3 April 2012.

–. "U.S. Stimulus Stifling Canada." *National Post,* 30 April 2009.

James A. Baker III Institute for Public Policy of Rice University. "The Changing Role of National Oil Companies in International Energy Policy." Policy Report 35. Houston: Baker Institute for Public Policy, 2007. http://www.rice.edu/.

Jockel, Joseph. *Canada in NORAD, 1957-2007: A History.* Montreal: McGill-Queen's University Press, 2007.

Jockel, Joseph T., and Joel J. Sokolsky. "Renewing NORAD: Now if Not Forever." *Policy Options* 27, 6 (2006): 53-58.

Jones, David T., and David Kilgour. *Uneasy Neighbo(u)rs: Canada, the USA, and the Dynamics of State, Industry, and Culture.* Toronto: John Wiley and Sons, 2007.

Jones, Jeffrey M. "Americans More Negative than Positive about Foreign Trade." Princeton, NJ: Gallup, 18 February 2009. http://www.gallup.com/.

–. "Iran, North Korea Still Americans' Least Favorite Countries." Princeton, NJ: Gallup, 11 February 2011. http://www. gallup.com/.

Katzenstein, Peter J. *A World of Regions: Asia and Europe in the American Imperium.* Ithaca, NY: Cornell University Press, 2005.

Katzenstein, Peter J., and Robert O. Keohane. "Varieties of Anti-Americanism: A Framework for Analysis." In *Anti-Americanisms in World Politics,* ed. Peter J. Katzenstein and Robert O. Keohane, 9-38. Ithaca, NY: Cornell University Press, 2007.

Kay, Tamara. *NAFTA and the Politics of Labor Transnationalism.* New York: Cambridge University Press, 2011.

Kennedy, Peter. "Forest Industry Shudders at Housing Forecast." *Globe and Mail,* 12 July 2006.

Kent, Jonathan. "Canada–US Border Management between the Ports-of-Entry: The Other 6,397 Kilometers." Paper presented at the Border Regions in Transition conference, Bellingham, WA, 14 January 2008.

Keohane, Robert O., and Peter J. Katzenstein. "Political Consequences of Anti-Americanism." In *Anti-Americanisms in World Politics*, edited by Peter J. Katzenstein and Robert O. Keohane, 273-305. Ithaca, NY: Cornell University Press, 2007.

Kergin, Michael, and Birgit Mathiessen. *Border Issues Report: A New Bridge for Old Allies*. Toronto: Canadian International Council, 2008.

Kerr, William A., and Jill E. Hobbs. "Agricultural Trade and Food Safety." In *Borders and Bridges: Canada's Policy Relations in North America*, edited by Monica Gattinger and Geoffrey Hale, 344-60. Toronto: Oxford University Press, 2010.

Kilbourn, William. *Canada: A Guide to the Peaceable Kingdom*. New York: St. Martin's Press, 1971.

Kilroy, Richard J. "Perimeter Defense and Regional Security Cooperation in North America: United States, Canada, and Mexico." *Homeland Security Affairs*, Supplement 1 (December 2007).

Kingdon, John W. *Agendas, Alternatives, and Public Policies*. 2nd ed. New York: Longmans, 1995.

Kirton, John, and Jenilee Guebert. "Soft Law, Regulatory Coordination, and Convergence." In *Borders and Bridges: Canada's Policy Relations in North America*, edited by Monica Gattinger and Geoffrey Hale, 59-76. Toronto: Oxford University Press, 2010.

Kirton, John J., and Michael J. Trebilcock. "Introduction: Hard Choices and Soft Law in Sustainable Global Governance." In *Hard Choices, Soft Law: Voluntary Standards in Global Trade, Environment, and Social Governance*, edited by John J. Kirton and Michael J. Trebilcock, 3-13. Burlington, VT: Ashgate, 2004.

Klein, Kurt, and Danny G. LeRoy. "BSE in Canada: Were Economic Losses to the Beef Industry Covered by Government Compensation?" *Canadian Public Policy* 36, 2 (2010): 221-40.

Koslowski, Rey. "Immigration Reforms and Border Security Technologies." New York: Social Science Research Council, 2006. http:// borderbattles.ssrc.org/.

Krause, Vivian. "U.S. Cash vs. Oil Sands." *Financial Post*, 15 October 2010.

Kukucha, Christopher J. "Dismembering Canada? Stephen Harper and the Foreign Relations of Canadian Provinces." *Review of Constitutional Studies* 14, 1 (2009): 21-52.

–. *The Provinces and Canadian Foreign Trade Policy*. Vancouver: UBC Press, 2008.

–. "Sub-Federal Trade and the Politics of North American Economic Integration: Evaluating the Cross-Border Exports of American States." In *Borders and Bridges: Canada's Policy Relations in North America*, edited by Monica Gattinger and Geoffrey Hale, 270-88. Toronto: Oxford University Press, 2010.

Kurlantzick, Joshua. "Canada's Terrorism Problem." *New Republic*, 7 June 2006. http://www.tnr.com/.

Laforest, Mary-Jo. "U.S. Senator Calls Oilsands 'Very Impressive' after Tour with Alberta Premier." *Lethbridge Herald*, 18 September 2010.

Laghi, Brian. "Premiers Look for Reciprocal Deal with U.S. on Access to Markets." *Globe and Mail*, 8 August 2009.

Laghi, Brian, Campbell Clark, Steven Chase, and Barrie McKenna. "Premiers Rally behind Harper in Fight against Buy American." *Globe and Mail*, 5 June 2009.

Leahy, Patrick. "House Leaders Drop 11th Hour Bid to Kill Leahy Amendment that Mandates Improvements in New Border-Crossing System." Washington, DC: Office of Senator Leahy, 29 September 2006. http:// leahy.senate.gov/.

Leblanc, Daniel. "Ottawa Aims to Soften U.S. Arms-Contract Rules." *Globe and Mail*, 15 January 2007.

–. "U.S. Rules Slowing Delivery of Helicopters, Other Equipment." *Globe and Mail*, 26 March 2007.

LeRoy, Danny G., and K.K. Klein. "Mad Cow Chaos in Canada: Was It Just Bad Luck or Did Government Policies Play a Role?" *Canadian Public Policy* 31, 4 (2005): 381-99.

Levi, Michael. *On Nuclear Terrorism*. Cambridge, MA: Harvard University Press, 2007.

–. "A Shortsighted Victory in Delaying the Keystone Pipeline." *New York Times*, 10 November 2011.

Lewenza, Ken. "It's Time to Start Buying Canadian." *Financial Post*, 3 February 2009.

Lister, Sarah A., and Geoffrey S. Becker. "Bovine Spongiform Encephalopathy (BSE or 'Mad Cow Disease'): Current and Proposed Safeguards." CRS Report RL-32199. Washington, DC: Congressional Research Service, 20 September 2006.

Lizza, Ryan. "As the World Burns." *New Yorker*, 11 October 2010. http://www.newyorker.com/.

MacCharles, Tonda. "PM Urges U.S. Restraint on Border." *Toronto Star*, 21 September 2006.

MacCharles, Tonda, and Les Whittington. "Obama's 'Buy American' Plan Blasted." *Toronto Star*, 30 January 2009.

Macdonald, Douglas, and Debora L. VanNijnatten. "Canadian Climate Change Policy and the North American Influence." In *Borders and Bridges: Canada's Policy Relations in North America*, edited by Monica Gattinger and Geoffrey Hale, 177-93. Toronto: Oxford University Press, 2010.

MacDonald, L. Ian. "Harper Plays the Oil Card with Skill." *Gazette* [Montreal], 23 April 2008.

Macleod, Ian. "Obstacle Course." *Ottawa Citizen*, 17 November 2007.

–. "Suspected Terrorist Activities Foiled." *National Post*, 10 November 2009.

–. "The Warning Lights Are All Blinking Red." *Ottawa Citizen*, 23 February 2008.

Mahant, Edelgard, and Graeme S. Mount. *Invisible and Inaudible in Washington*. Vancouver: UBC Press; East Lansing: Michigan State University Press, 1999.

Mandel-Campbell, Andrea. *Why Mexicans Don't Drink Molson: Rescuing Canadian Business from the Suds of Global Obscurity*. Vancouver: Douglas and McIntyre, 2007.

Manley, John P. "Creating a North American Community: Chairman's Statement from an Independent Task Force on the Future of North America." Interview transcript. New York: Council on Foreign Relations, 14 March 2005. http://www.cfr.org/.

Manley, John P., Pedro Aspe, and William Weld. *Building a North American Community: Report of an Independent Task Force.* New York: Council on Foreign Relations, 2005.

Manning, Bayless. "The Congress, the Executive, and Intermestic Affairs: Three Proposals." *Foreign Affairs* 55, 2 (1977): 306-24.

Marotte, Bertrand. "Canadians, Americans Agree that Border Should Stay: Polls." *Globe and Mail,* 14 March 2011.

–. "Forest Industry Layoffs Top 6,000." *Globe and Mail,* 16 August 2006.

Mason, Dwight N. "Canadian Defense Priorities: What Might the United States Like to See?" Policy Papers on the Americas 15, Study 1. Washington, DC: Center for Strategic and International Studies, 2004.

–. "Time to Expand NORAD." In *Security and Sovereignty: Renewing NORAD – One Nation, Two Voices,* edited by Marcia R. Seitz-Ehler, 2-7. Washington, DC: Woodrow Wilson International Center for Scholars, 2005.

McCann, Brigitte. "Bienvenue à Montréalistan." *Journal de Montréal,* 16 March 2007.

McCarthy, Shawn. "PM Links Softwood Dispute to Energy." *Globe and Mail,* 7 October 2005.

McCarthy, Shawn, and Nathan Vanderklippe. "Surge of Alberta Oil Tames Rise in Prices." *Globe and Mail,* 20 January 2011.

McKenna, Barrie. "A Country Built on Crude." *Globe and Mail,* 7 February 2011.

McKenna, Barrie, and David Parkinson. "U.S. Law Puts Chill on Oil Sands." *Globe and Mail,* 24 June 2008.

McNulty, Sheila. "Canada Warns US over Oil Sands." *Financial Times* [London, UK], 9 March 2008.

Mead, Walter Russell. "America's Play for Pacific Prosperity." *Wall Street Journal,* 30 December 2011.

–. "The Carter Syndrome." *Foreign Policy* 177 (January-February 2010): 58-64.

–. *Power, Terror, Peace, and War.* New York: Alfred A. Knopf, 2005.

Melissen, Jan. "The New Public Diplomacy: Between Theory and Practice." In *The New Public Diplomacy: Soft Power in International Relations,* edited by Jan Melissen, 3-27. Basingstoke, UK: Palgrave Macmillan, 2005.

Mendelsohn, Matthew, Robert Wolfe, and Andrew Parkin. "Globalization, Trade Policy, and the Permissive Consensus in Canada." *Canadian Public Policy* 28, 3 (2002): 351-71.

Merchant, Livingston T., ed. *Neighbours Taken for Granted: Canada and the United States.* New York: Frederick A. Praeger, 1965.

Mertl, Steve. "Canada–U.S. Softwood Deal Has Teething Problems." *Globe and Mail,* 17 February 2007.

Meyer, Carl. "More than Shades of SPP in Perimeter Deal." *Embassy,* 4 February 2011, 1.

Michaud, Nelson, and Marc T. Boucher. "Les relations internationales du Québec comparées." Québec: Ministère des relations internationales, gouvernement du Québec, 2006.

Millman, Joel. "Kearl Project Hits Roadblock – in Idaho." *Globe and Mail,* 22 October 2010.

Milner, Brian. "Mexico Sides with Canada to Oppose Global Bank Tax." *Globe and Mail,* 29 May 2010.

Milner, Helen V. *Interests, Institutions, and Information: Domestic Politics and International Relations.* Princeton, NJ: Princeton University Press, 1997.

Mittelstaedt, Martin. "Alberta Crude May Be Too Dirty, U.S. Law Says." *Globe and Mail,* 15 January 2008.

Moens, Alexander. *Mad Cow: A Case Study in Canadian–American Relations.* Vancouver: Fraser Institute, 2006.

Moens, Alexander, with Michael Cust. "Saving the North American Security and Prosperity Partnership: The Case for a North American Standards and Regulatory Area." Vancouver: Fraser Institute, 2008.

Morris, Michelle. "Talking Turkey about a Knotty Question: International and Domestic Pressures on the Governance of the St. Mary and Milk Rivers." Honours undergraduate thesis, University of Lethbridge, 2009.

Morton, Peter. "U.S. Issues 'Comfort Note' on Softwood." *Financial Post,* 19 August 2006.

Mouafo, Dieudonné. "Regional Dynamics in Canada–United States Relations." Paper presented at the Annual Meeting of the Canadian Political Science Association, University of Manitoba, Winnipeg, 3 June 2004.

Mouafo, Dieudonné, Nadia Ponce Morales, and Jeff Heynen. *A Compendium of Canada–U.S. Relations.* Ottawa: Canada School of Public Service, 2004.

Mouawad, Jay. "Oil Shale: Viable Domestic Energy, or 'Dirtiest Fuel on the Planet'?" *New York Times Online,* 30 September 2008. http:// greeninc.blogs.nytimes.com/.

Mowle, Thomas S. *Allies at Odds? The United States and the European Union.* New York: Palgrave Macmillan, 2004.

Murphy, Tim. "Canada Calling: When It Comes to U.S. Relations, the Harper Government Should Keep Blandishments to a Minimum and Its Priorities Straight." *Globe and Mail,* 15 March 2006.

Nakashima, Ellen. "Reports Cite Lack of Uniform Policy for Terrorist Watch List." *Washington Post,* 18 March 2008.

Nanos, Nik. "Free Trade at 20: SES/Policy Options Exclusive Poll: Canadians, Americans Agree Both Better Off with Free Trade." *Policy Options* 28, 9 (2007): 1-8.

Narayanswamy, Anupama, Luke Rosiak, and Jennifer LaFleur. "Adding It Up: The Top Players in Foreign Agent Lobbying." Washington, DC: Sunlight Foundation and ProPublica, revised 23 October 2009. http://www.propublica.org/.

Natural Resources Defense Council. "Strip Mining for Oil in Endangered Forests." Washington, DC, June 2006. http://www.nrdo.org/.

Neinast, Brenna, and Michele James. "Northern Border Security." Statement to US Senate Committee on Homeland Security and Governmental Affairs, Havre, MT, 2 July 2008. http:// hsgac.senate.gov/.

Neubauer, Chuck. "'Virtual Fence' Got Late Review of Costs, Benefits." *Washington Times,* 1 February 2011.

Nord, Douglas C. "The North in Canadian–American Relations: Searching for Collaboration in Melting Seas." In *Borders and Bridges: Canada's Policy Relations in North America*, edited by Monica Gattinger and Geoffrey Hale, 120-37. Toronto: Oxford University Press, 2010.

Norman, Emma S., and Karen Bakker. "Governing Water across the Canada–US Borderland." In *Borders and Bridges: Canada's Policy Relations in North America*, edited by Monica Gattinger and Geoffrey Hale, 194-212. Toronto: Oxford University Press, 2010.

Novak, Robert. "The Politics of Ports." *Washington Post*, 27 February 2006.

Nuñez-Neto, Blas. "Border Security: Key Agencies and Their Missions." CRS Report RS-21899. Washington, DC: Congressional Research Service, 13 May 2008.

O'Grady, Mary Anastasia. "Stephen Harper: A Resolute Ally in the War on Terror." *Wall Street Journal*, 27 February 2009.

Oliver, Joe. "Radicals Threaten Resource Development." *Financial Post*, 10 January 2012

Olson, Mancur. *The Logic of Collective Action: Public Goods and the Theory of Groups*. Cambridge, MA: Harvard University Press, 1965.

O'Neill, Tip, and Gary Hymel. *All Politics Is Local: And Other Rules of the Game*. Holbrook, MA: Bob Adams, 1994.

Panetta, Alexander. "NAFTAgate Began with Off-hand Remark from Harper's Chief of Staff." *The Standard* (St. Catharines, ON), 5 March 2008.

Partridge, John. "Oil Sands Safe from U.S. Law, Advocates Say." *Globe and Mail*, 1 October 2008.

Passel, Jeffrey, and D'Vera Cohn. "U.S. Unauthorized Immigration Flows Are Down Sharply since Mid-Decade." Washington, DC: Pew Hispanic Center, 1 September 2010.

Pastor, Robert A. "A North American Community." *Norteamérica* 1, 1 (2006): 209-19.

–. *The North American Idea: Vision of a Continental Future*. New York: Oxford University Press, 2011.

–. *Toward a North American Community: Lessons from the Old World for the New*. Washington, DC: Institute for International Economics, 2001.

Patterson, Kelly. "'Treasonous' Integration Plan Sparks U.S. Storm." *Calgary Herald*, 17 February 2007.

Persichilli, Angelo. "With Softwood Past Them, Harper and Bush Will Talk Trade and Security." *Embassy*, 14 June 2006, 1.

Pew Research Center for People and the Press. "Foreign Policy Attitudes Now Driven by 9/11 and Iraq." Washington, DC: Pew Research Center, 18 August 2004.

–. "Support for Free Trade Recovers Despite Recession." Washington, DC: Pew Research Center, 28 April 2009. http://people-press.org/.

Pipes, Sally C. "Canadian Patients Face Long Waits for Low-Tech Healthcare." *Washington Examiner*, 9 June 2009.

Plourde, André. "The Changing Nature of National and Continental Energy Markets." In *Canadian Energy Policy and the Struggle for Sustainable*

Development, edited by G. Bruce Doern, 51-82. Toronto: University of Toronto Press, 2005.

Potter, Mitch, and Les Whittington. "'Buy American' Wording Finalized." *Toronto Star*, 13 February 2009.

Prieto, Daniel. "The Limits and Prospects of Military Analogies for Homeland Security." In *Threats at Our Threshold: Homeland Defense and Homeland Security in the New Century*, edited by Bert B. Tussing, 85-110. Washington, DC: Center for Strategic and International Studies, 2006.

Pugliese, David. "Air Force Needs $520M to Keep Flying." *Ottawa Citizen*, 17 April 2008.

–. "Navy at Risk of Running Aground." *Ottawa Citizen*, 18 April 2008.

Putnam, Robert, and Nicholas Bayne. *Hanging Together: Co-operation and Conflict in the Seven-Power Summits*. Cambridge, MA: Harvard University Press, 1987.

Renuart, Victor E. "Statement to Senate Armed Services Committee." Washington, DC: US Northern Command News, 6 March 2008. http://www.northcom. mil/.

Reuters. "EU Threatens Visa Requirement for US Diplomats." *Der Spiegel*, 23 July 2008. http://www.spiegel.de/.

Robertson, Colin. "CDA_USA 2.0: Intermesticity, Hidden Wiring, and Public Diplomacy." In *Canada among Nations, 2007: What Room for Manoeuvre?*, edited by Jean Daudelin and Daniel Schwanen, 268-85. Montreal: McGill-Queen's University Press, 2008.

Robson, William, et al. "What to Do about Buy America?" *Globe and Mail*, 15 June 2009.

Rockwell, Jonathan, and Mark Muro. "Cap and Trade Costs: Place Matters." *New Republic Online*, 3 November 2009. http://www.tnr.com/.

Rosenau, James N. *Distant Proximities: Globalization among Nations*. Cambridge, MA: Harvard University Press, 2003.

Rosenzweig, Paul. "Why the U.S. Doesn't Trust Canada." *Maclean's*, 5 October 2009. http://www.macleans.ca/.

Rothkopf, David. *Running the World: The Inside Story of the National Security Council and the Architects of American Power*. New York: Public Affairs, 2006.

Sageman, Marc. "The Next Generation of Terror." *Foreign Policy* 165 (2008): 36-42.

Sallot, Jeff. "CSIS Kept Tabs on 274 Terror Suspects Last Year." *Globe and Mail*, 27 October 2006.

–. "McLellan Contradicts CSIS on Torture Policy." *Globe and Mail*, 16 September 2005.

Sands, Christopher. "Big in Detroit City: The Politics of the 2009 North American Auto Industry Bailouts." Paper presented at the Annual Meeting of the American Political Science Association, Washington, DC, 3 September 2010.

–. *The Canada Gambit: Will It Revive North America?* Washington, DC: Hudson Institute, 2011.

–. "Canada as Minor Ally: Operational Considerations for Relations with the United States." Notes for a presentation to the 2003 Canadian Crude Oil Conference, Kananaskis, AB, 5 September 2003.

–. "Fading Power or Rising Power: 11 September and Lessons from the Section 110 Experience." In *Readings in Canadian Foreign Policy*, edited by Duane Bratt and Christopher J. Kukucha, 249-64. Toronto: Oxford University Press, 2007.

–. "How Canada Policy Is Made in the United States." In *Vanishing Borders: Canada among Nations, 2000*, edited by Maureen Appel Molot and Fen Osler Hampson, 47-72. Toronto: Oxford University Press, 2000.

–. "The Rising Importance of Third Country Issues in Canada's Relations with the United States." In *Canada among Nations, 2006: Minorities and Priorities*, edited by Andrew F. Cooper and Dane Rowlands, 125-44. Montreal: McGill-Queen's University Press, 2007.

–. "Towards a New Frontier: Improving the U.S.–Canadian Border." Washington, DC: Brookings Institution, 13 July 2009.

Sapolsky, Harvey. "Canada: Crossing the Line." *Breakthroughs* 14, 1 (2004): 31-37.

Savoie, Donald. *Governing from the Centre: The Concentration of Power in Canadian Politics*. Toronto: University of Toronto Press, 1999.

–. *Power: Where Is It?* Montreal: McGill-Queen's University Press, 2010.

Schott, Jeffrey J. "Trade Negotiations among NAFTA Partners: The Future of North American Economic Integration." In *Requiem or Revival? The Promise of North American Integration*, edited by Isabel Studer and Carol Wise, 76-88. Washington, DC: Brookings Institution, 2007.

–, ed. *Free Trade Agreements: US Strategies and Priorities*. Washington, DC: Institute for International Economics, 2004.

Schwanen, Daniel. "Deeper, Broader: A Roadmap for a Treaty of North America." In *The Art of the State: Thinking North America*, edited by Thomas J. Courchene, Donald Savoie, and Daniel Schwanen. Montreal: Institute for Research in Public Policy, 2004. http://www.irpp.org/.

Scott, Norval. "Our Views of the U.S." *Globe and Mail*, 8 December 2008.

Sen, Gautam. "The United States and the GATT/WTO System." In *US Hegemony and International Organizations*, edited by Rosemary Foot, S. Neil MacFarlane, and Michael Mastanduno, 115-38. New York: Oxford University Press, 2003.

Sharp, Paul. "Revolutionary States, Outlaw Regimes, and the Techniques of Public Diplomacy." In *The New Public Diplomacy: Soft Power in International Relations*, edited by Jan Melissen, 106-23. Basingstoke, UK: Palgrave Macmillan, 2005.

Shea, Bill. "Blanchard: Canada Loan Offer for New Detroit River Bridge Was MDOT's Idea." *Crain's Detroit Business*, 3 May 2010.

Shephard, Michelle. "Made in Canada Threat Worries CSIS." *Toronto Star*, 11 February 2006.

Silber, Mitchell D., and Arvin Bhatt. "Radicalization in the West: The Homegrown Threat." New York: NYPD Intelligence Division, 2007. http://www. nypdshield.org/.

Simeon, Richard. "Important? Yes. Transformative? No. North American Integration and Canadian Federalism." In *The Impact of Global and Regional Integration on Federal Systems*, edited by Harvey Lazar, Hamish Telford, and Ronald Watts, 123-73. Montreal: McGill-Queen's University Press, 2003.

Simpson, Jeffrey. "Obama on Buy American: Please Stay Calm Canada." *Globe and Mail*, 17 September 2009.

—. "'Foreign Money' Is a Hypocritical Diversion." *Globe and Mail*, 11 January 2012.

Sissine, Fred. "Energy Independence and Security Act of 2007: A Summary of Major Provisions." CRS Report 34294. Washington, DC: Congressional Research Service, 21 December 2007. http://energy.senate.gov/.

Sivak, Martin. "Where to Live in the United States: Combined Energy Demand for Heating, Cooling in the 50 Largest Metropolitan Areas." *International Journal of Urban Policy and Planning* 25 (2008): 396-98.

Skogstad, Grace. "Multilateral Regulatory Governance of Food Safety: A Work in Progress." In *Rules, Rules, Rules, Rules: Multilevel Regulatory Governance*, edited by G. Bruce Doern and Robert Johnson, 157-79. Toronto: University of Toronto Press, 2006.

Slaughter, Anne-Marie. *A New World Order*. Princeton, NJ: Princeton University Press, 2004.

Sliva, Jan. "EU Tells Canada to Extend Visa-Free Rules." *Toronto Star*, 17 September 2007.

Sloan, Elinor. *Security and Defence in the Terrorist Era*. Montreal: McGill-Queen's University Press, 2005.

Smiley, Donald R., and Ronald L. Watts. *Intrastate Federalism in Canada*. Vol. 39 of *Research Reports of the Royal Commission on the Economic Union and Development Prospects for Canada*. Toronto: University of Toronto Press, 1985.

Smith, Patrick J. "Anti-Terrorism in North America: Is There Convergence or Divergence in Canadian and US Legislative Responses to 9/11 and the US–Canada Border?" In *Borderlands: Comparing Border Security in North America and Europe*, edited by Emmanuel Brunet-Jailly, 277-310. Ottawa: University of Ottawa Press, 2007.

Smith, Julianne, and Michael Williams. "What Lies Beneath: The Future of NATO through the ISAF Prism." Washington, DC: Center for Strategic and International Studies, 31 March 2008.

Sokolsky, Joel J., and Philippe Lagassé. "Suspenders and a Belt: Perimeter and Border Security in Canada–U.S. Relations." *Canadian Foreign Policy* 12, 3 (2005-6): 15-29.

Spector, Norman. "Nix the Toys for the Boys." *Globe and Mail*, 10 October 2002.

Stana, Richard M. "Border Security: US VISIT Program Faces Strategic, Operational, and Technological Challenges at Land Ports of Entry." Washington, DC: Government Accountability Office, December 2007. http://www.gao.gov/.

—. "Observations on Efforts to Implement the Western Hemisphere Travel Initiative on the U.S. Border with Canada." Letter to Loretta Sanchez, Louise M.

Slaughter, and John M. McHugh. Washington, DC: Government Account-ability Office, 25 May 2006. http://www.gao.gov/.

–. "Various Issues Led to the Termination of the United States–Canada Shared Management Pilot Project." GAO-08-1038R. Washington, DC: Government Accountability Office, 4 September 2008.http://www.gao.gov/.

Stanley, Guy. "Borders and Bridges: Free Trade, Supply Chains, and the Creation of a Joint Trading Platform: Canada–US Industrial Development since 1980." In *Borders and Bridges: Canada's Policy Relations in North America*, edited by Monica Gattinger and Geoffrey Hale, 307-24. Toronto: Oxford University Press, 2010.

Stein, Janice, and Eugene Lang. *The Unexpected War: Canada in Kandahar.* Toronto: Viking Canada, 2007.

Stockton, Paul N., and Patrick S. Roberts. "Findings from the Forum on *Homeland Security after the Bush Administration: Next Steps in Building Unity of Effort.*" *Homeland Security Affairs* 4, 2 (2008). http://www.hsaj.org/.

The Strategic Counsel. "A Tale of Two Nations: State of Canadian/American Public Opinion: A Report to the *Globe and Mail* and CTV." Toronto: Strategic Counsel, June 2008. http://www.thestrategiccounsel.com/.

–. "Views on Canadian Foreign Policy and the Mulroney–Schreiber Saga." Toronto: Strategic Counsel, 10 December 2007. http://www.thestrategiccounsel.com/.

Struck, Doug. "Terrorist Allegations Detailed in Canada." *Washington Post,* 7 June 2006.

Stuart, Reginald. *Dispersed Relations: Americans and Canadians in Upper North America.* Washington, DC: Woodrow Wilson Center Press; Baltimore: Johns Hopkins University Press, 2008.

Studer, Isabel. "Obstacles to Integration: NAFTA's Institutional Weakness." In *Requiem or Revival? The Promise of North American Integration,* edited by Isabel Studer and Carol Wise, 53-76. Washington, DC: Brookings Institution Press, 2007.

Sullivan, Paul. "Written Testimony in Support of Oral Testimony of Professor Paul Sullivan ... for the Western Hemisphere Subcommittee of the Foreign Affairs Committee, U.S. House of Representatives." Washington, DC: House Com-mittee on Foreign Affairs, 31 March 2011. http://www.internationalrelations. house.gov/.

Sydor, Aaron. "The Rise of Global Value Chains." In *Seventh Annual Report on Can-ada's State of Trade,* edited by Jean-Bosco Sabuyhoro and Aaron Sydor, 47-70. Ottawa: DFAIT, 2007.

Taber, Jane. "Canada's Carbon Diplomat." *Globe and Mail,* 1 October 2009.

–. "Lumber a Domestic Issue." *Globe and Mail,* 17 October 2005.

–. "Stephen Harper Shoots and Scores on NBC." *Globe and Mail,* 16 February 2010.

Tait, Carrie. "Imperial Oil Project Meets Heavy Traffic." *Globe and Mail,* 24 March 2011.

Thorpe, Jacqueline. "Sweet Deal for the Sugar Industry." *Financial Post,* 2 June 2008.

Tibbetts, Janice. "One in Five Believes in Conspiracy." *National Post,* 11 September 2006.

Tomblin, Stephen G. "Conceptualizing and Exploring the Struggle over Regional Integration." In *Regionalism in a Global Society,* edited by Stephen G. Tomblin and Charles S. Colgin, 79-105. Peterborough, ON: Broadview Press, 2004.

Tomlin, Brian W., Norman Hillmer, and Fen Osler Hampson. *Canada's International Policies: Agendas, Alternatives, and Policies.* Toronto: Oxford University Press, 2008.

Travers, James. "No Open Tory Arms for McCain." *Toronto Star,* 14 June 2008.

–. "PM's Turn to Cut a Rug with U.S." *Toronto Star,* 14 February 2009.

Tromp, Stanley. "Canada Lobbied U.S. over Pipeline." *Financial Post,* 24 January 2011.

United States. Commission on National Security in the 21st Century. *New World Coming – Phase I: Report on the Emerging Security Environment in the First Quarter of the Twenty-First Century.* Washington, DC: Commission on National Security in the 21st Century, 15 September 1999.

–. Department of Homeland Security. *Homeland Security Presidential Directives.* Washington, DC: DHS, last modified 4 June 2008. http:/www.dhs.gov. xabout/.

–. –. "Minimum Standards for Driver's Licenses and Identification Cards Acceptable by Federal Agencies for Official Purposes: Proposed Rule." *Federal Register,* 9 March 2007, 10819-58.

–. –. "Mission Statement." Washington, DC: DHS, 2003.

–. –. *One Team, One Mission, Securing Our Homeland: U.S. Department of Homeland Security Strategic Plan, Fiscal Years 2008-2013.* Washington, DC: DHS, 16 September 2008. http://www.dhs.gov/.

–. –. *Quadrennial Homeland Security Review: A Strategic Framework for a Secure Homeland.* Washington, DC: DHS, 1 February 2010. http://www.dhs.gov/.

–. –. "REAL ID Final Rule." Washington, DC: DHS, 14 September 2011.

–. Department of Homeland Security and Department of State. "Documents Required for Travelers Arriving in the United States at Air and Sea Ports of Entry – Notice of Proposed Rulemaking." *Federal Register,* 11 August 2006.

–. Department of State. "U.S.–Canada Energy Consultative Mechanism Meets." Washington, DC: Office of the Spokesman, 6 December 2010. http://www. state.gov/.

–. –. "Visa Waiver Program (VWP)." Washington, DC: Department of State, 2011. http:// travel.state.gov/.

–. Department of State and Department of Homeland Security. "EIA Short-Term Energy Outlook: Annual Average Imported Crude Oil Price." Washington, DC: EIA, 2011. http://www.eia.doe.gov/.

–. –. "Natural Gas Statistics." Washington, DC: EIA, 2011.

–. –. *Preserving Our Welcome to the World in an Age of Terrorism: Report of the Secure Borders and Open Doors Advisory Committee.* Washington, DC: Department of State and DHS, January 2008.

–. –. "Petroleum Statistics." Washington, DC: EIA, 2011.

–. –. "U.S. Imports by Country of Origin: Crude Oil and Products." Washington, DC: EIA, 2011.

–. –. "U.S. Natural Gas Imports by Country." Washington, DC: EIA, 2011.

–. Government Accountability Office. "Border Security: Enhanced DHS Oversight and Assessment of Interagency Coordination Is Needed for the Northern Border." GAO-11-97. Washington, DC: GAO, 2010. http://www.gao.gov/.

–. Homeland Security Council. *National Strategy for Homeland Security.* Washington, DC: White House, 2007. http://www.dhs.gov/.

–. National Commission on Terrorist Attacks on the United States. *The 9/11 Commission Report.* Washington, DC: National Commission on Terrorist Attacks on the United States, 2004.

–. Office of Homeland Security. *National Strategy for Homeland Security.* Washington, DC: White House, 2002. http://www.whitehouse.gov/.

–. Office of the US Trade Representative. "Kirk Comments on US–Canada Procurement Agreement." Washington, DC: Office of the US Trade Representative, 5 February 2010.

–. –. *2010 Trade Policy Agenda and 2009 Annual Report of the President of the United States on the Trade Agreements Program.* Washington, DC: Office of the US Trade Representative, 2010.

–. White House. "Arctic Region Policy." National Security Presidential Directive 66 and Homeland Security Presidential Directive 25. Washington, DC: White House, 9 January 2009.

–. –. *Improving Regulation and Regulatory Review – Executive Order.* Washington, DC: Office of the Press Secretary, 18 January 2011.

–. –. "Remarks by President Obama and Prime Minister Stephen Harper of Canada in Joint Press Availability." Transcript. Washington, DC: Office of the Press Secretary, 4 February 2011.

–. –. "Statements by President Barack Obama and Prime Minister Stephen Harper of Canada." Transcript. Washington, DC: Office of the Press Secretary, 7 December 2011.

–. –. "Statements by President Barack Obama and Prime Minister of Canada Stephen Harper of Canada." Transcript. Washington, DC: Office of the Press Secretary, 7 December 2011.

–. –, and Canada, Privy Council Office. "Beyond the Border: A Shared Vision for Economic Security and Economic Competitiveness." Washington, DC, and Ottawa, 7 December 2011.

–. –, and Canada, Privy Council Office. "United States–Canada Regulatory Cooperation Council: Joint Action Plan." Washington, DC, and Ottawa, 7 December 2011.

United States, Bureau of Customs and Border Protection, and Canada, Border Services Agency and Royal Canadian Mounted Police. "United States–Canada Joint Border Threat and Risk Assessment." Washington, DC: US Department of Homeland Security; Ottawa: Public Safety Canada, 2010. http://www.publicsafety.gc.ca/.

United States, Department of Energy, and Canada, Environment Canada. "U.S. Clean Energy Dialogue: Backgrounder." Washington, DC: Department of Energy; Ottawa: Environment Canada, 16 September 2009.

United States Chamber of Commerce and Canadian Chamber of Commerce. *Finding the Balance: Shared Border of the Future.* Washington: US Chamber of Commerce; Ottawa: Canadian Chamber of Commerce, 21 July 2009.

Vanderklippe, Nathan. "Turning Natural Gas into Diesel: A Big Bet on an Old Alchemy." *Globe and Mail,* 19 March 2011.

Verrastro, Frank. "The United States." In *Energy Cooperation in the Western Hemisphere,* edited by Sidney Weintraub with Annette Hester and Veronica R. Prado, 41-69. Washington, DC: Center for Strategic and International Studies, 2007.

Vieira, Paul. "Manufacturers Seek Buy U.S. Exemption." *Financial Post,* 5 June 2009.

Vogt, Donna U. "Food Safety Issues in the 109th Congress." CRS Report RL-31853. Washington, DC: Congressional Research Service, 16 June 2005.

Waddell, Christopher. "The Auto Industry Bailout: Industrial Policy or Job-Saving Social Policy?" In *How Ottawa Spends: 2010-2011 – Recession, Realignment and the New Deficit Era,* edited by G. Bruce Doern and Christopher Stoney, 150-67. Montreal: McGill-Queen's University Press, 2010.

Wall Street Journal. "The Keystone Ultimatum," 16 December 2011.

Wattrick, Jeff T. "Roy Norton Interview: Politics at the United States' and Canada's Busiest Border Crossing." http://www.MLive.com/, 3 August 2011.

Weil, Gordon S. "An Analysis of the NB Power/Hydro Quebec MOU." Halifax: Atlantic Institute for Market Studies, 3 December 2009. http://www.aims.ca/.

–. "The Modified New Brunswick/Quebec Memorandum of Understanding on NB Power: An Updated Analysis." Halifax: Atlantic Institute for Market Studies, 26 January 2010. http://www.aims.ca/.

Wells, Paul. "He's Unbelievable!" *Maclean's,* 14 December 2005, http://www.macleans.ca/.

Whitaker, Reg. "Made in Canada: The New Public Safety Paradigm." In *How Ottawa Spends, 2005-2006: Managing the Minority,* edited by G. Bruce Doern, 77-95. Montreal: McGill-Queen's University Press, 2005.

White, Marianne. "N.B., Quebec Scrap Deal." *Financial Post,* 25 March 2010.

Winfield, Mark, and Douglas Macdonald. "The Harmonization Accord and Climate Change Policy: Two Case Studies in Federal–Provincial Environmental Policy." In *Canadian Federalism: Performance, Effectiveness, and Legitimacy,* 2nd ed., edited by Herman Bakvis and Grace Skogstad, 266-88. Toronto: Oxford University Press, 2008.

Wormuth, Christine E. "Is a Goldwater–Nichols Act Needed for Homeland Security?" In *Threats at Our Threshold: Homeland Defense and Homeland Security in the New Century,* edited by Bert B. Tussing, 71-84. Washington, DC: Center for Strategic and International Studies, 2006.

Yedlin, Deborah. "New CAPP Boss Brings Insight into U.S." *Calgary Herald,* 30 March 2009.

Zeller, Tom, Jr. "Oil Sands Effort Turns on a Fight over a Road." *New York Times*, 22 October 2010.

Zhang, Daowei. *The Softwood Lumber War.* Washington, DC: RFF Press, 2007.

Ziff, Paul. "Cross-Border Energy Regulatory Collaboration in Its Context: Energy Balances and Energy Policy." In *Moving toward Dialogue: Challenges in Canada–U.S. Energy Trade*, edited by David N. Biette, 2-15. One Issue, Two Voices 2. Washington, DC: Canada Institute, Wilson International Center for Scholars, 2004.

Zremski, Jerry. "Deal in Works to Inspect Trucks Headed to U.S. in Canada." *Buffalo News*, 9 October 2011.

Zwick, Jesse. "Old Senator, New Tricks." *New Republic Online*, 25 January 2011, http://www.tnr.com/.

Index

Printed and bound in Canada by Friesens

Set in Segoe and Warnock by Artegraphica Design Co. Ltd.

Text design: Irma Rodriguez

Copy editor: Dallas Harrison

Proofreader: Frank Chow